D1121811

Donated to

Cottage Grove Public Library

by

D. Hugh Peniston

Cottage Grove Public Library
700 E [illegible] Ave
Cottage Grove, OR 97424

BLOOD ON THE MOON

A. LINCOLN,
Died
April 15th 1865.

BLOOD ON THE MOON

THE ASSASSINATION OF ABRAHAM LINCOLN

EDWARD STEERS Jr.

THE UNIVERSITY PRESS OF KENTUCKY

Cottage Grove Public Librai

Publication of this volume was made possible in part by a grant from the National Endowment for the Humanities.

Copyright © 2001 by The University Press of Kentucky

Scholarly publisher for the Commonwealth,
serving Bellarmine University, Berea College, Centre
College of Kentucky, Eastern Kentucky University,
The Filson Historical Society, Georgetown College,
Kentucky Historical Society, Kentucky State University,
Morehead State University, Murray State University,
Northern Kentucky University, Transylvania University,
University of Kentucky, University of Louisville,
and Western Kentucky University.

All rights reserved.

Editorial and Sales Offices: The University Press of Kentucky
663 South Limestone Street, Lexington, Kentucky 40508–4008

02 03 04 05 5 4 3

Frontispiece: The Apotheosis of Lincoln. D.T. Wiest, *In Memory of Abraham Lincoln: The Reward of the Just*, published by William Smith of Philadelphia, 1865. (Lincoln Museum, Fort Wayne, Ind., no. 4377.)

Library of Congress Cataloging-in-Publication Data

Steers, Edward.
Blood on the moon : the assassination of Abraham Lincoln /
Edward Steers Jr.
p. cm.
Includes bibliographical references and index.
ISBN 0-8131-2217-1 (cloth : alk. paper)
1. Lincoln, Abraham, 1809-1865—Assassination.
2. Booth, John Wilkes,
1838-1865. I. Title.
E457.5 .S788 2001
973.7'092—dc21 2001003413

This book is printed on acid-free recycled paper meeting
the requirements of the American National Standard
for Permanence of Paper for Printed Library Materials.

Manufactured in the United States of America

To
Edward Steers Sr. (1910–90),
whose love of history rubbed off,

to
Patricia Aire Steers,
whose love of me made this book possible,
and

to
Molly,
in whose absence this book would have been
finished one year sooner.

And I will shew wonders in the heavens and in the earth, blood, and fire, and pillars of smoke.

The sun shall be turned into darkness, and the moon into blood, before the terrible day of the Lord cometh.

Joel 2:31–32

CONTENTS

PREFACE

In 1997 the Surratt Society, in Clinton, Maryland, published the *Abraham Lincoln Assassination Bibliography* by Blaine V. Houmes. The bibliography was the first of its kind devoted exclusively to Lincoln's assassination. Listed are approximately 3,000 entries representing 2,900 journal, magazine, newspaper, and newsletter articles and 100 monographs. This number represents roughly 20 percent of the general bibliography (16,000 entries) devoted to Abraham Lincoln. The majority of the 3,000 "assassination" entries are the product of nonacademic or avocational historians who drew most of their material from secondary sources and anecdotal reminiscences that are questionable or can be shown to be incorrect. Many of the assassination books that have included primary sources have relied heavily on secondary sources in their interpretation of the events associated with Lincoln's death.

In *Blood on the Moon* I have relied principally on primary sources and sought independent corroboration of the recollections of those persons who figured prominently in the story. The principal primary sources that form the core of documents concerned with Lincoln's assassination are found in Record Group (RG) 153, Records of the Office of the Judge Advocate General, and Record Group 94, Records of the Adjutant General's Office, located in the National Archives Record Administration (NARA). These records are published as microfilm copies (M-599 and M-619 respectively) and are available from the National Archives as well as several libraries and research facilities throughout the country.

The principal file, M-599, is known as Investigation and Trial Papers Relating to the Assassination of President Lincoln or the "Lincoln Assassination Suspects" (LAS) file. These papers contain a wide range of materials gathered mostly between April 15 and July 3, 1865. The records consist of pretrial interrogations, letters offering information, and the verbatim transcript of the trial proceedings taken down by court reporters skilled in the use of phonography, a form of shorthand writing.

Colonel Henry L. Burnett was called from his post as judge advocate of the Northern Department (Cincinnati, Ohio) and assigned to the office of Joseph Holt, chief of the Bureau of Military Justice. Burnett and his staff gathered evidence from a variety of sources that was used in both the pretrial investigation and the subsequent court trial (court martial case file MM 2251) of those charged with Lincoln's assassination. The combined records, published as microcopy M-599, appear on sixteen microfilm reels numbered 1 through 16.

Record Group 94 contains the records that deal with the claims for reward offered to those persons instrumental in the apprehension of those charged with Lincoln's assassination. In an effort to insure fairness and accuracy in paying the reward money, a special commission, known as the Commission on Rewards for Apprehension of Lincoln Assassins and Others, was established by the adjutant general to receive and adjudicate all claims. These claims and associated documents are published as microcopy M-619, reels 455 through 458.

Shortly after the trial ended, three separate hardback versions of the testimony were published. Petersen and Brothers of Philadelphia published the first manuscript (Petersen version); Ben: Perley Poore, a Boston newspaper journalist, was the second to publish (Poore version); and Ben Pitman, the originator of the trial transcript, was the last to publish (Pitman version). The three versions were published between July 1865 and November 1865.

The versions differ in important ways. The first two versions, Petersen's and Poore's, were copied from the daily newspaper accounts. While the Poore version was edited for typographical errors, the Peterson version lacks editing of any kind. The two versions also lack the closing arguments of the prosecution and defense counsels. Most important, they lack indexing, which makes it difficult to locate testimony by specific witnesses without familiarizing oneself with the entire transcript. Witnesses testifying on the same subject did not always appear chronologically, but were occasionally called out of sequence, making it difficult to read the testimony as it relates to a particular defendant unless one is thoroughly familiar with the contents of the three volumes.

The Pitman version suffers no such deficiency. Pitman gathered the evidence from throughout the transcript as it related to one defendant regardless of chronology and combined it under a single heading. His editing, however, eliminated the questions and frequently summarized the answers. Where the testimony is unclear or in controversy, Pitman does give the testimony verbatim. Most important, the Pitman version contains a chronological index within major headings.

The strengths of Pitman's version are outweighed by its weaknesses. Pitman often merges the witnesses' response to multiple questions by the prosecutors and defense attorneys, summarizing them into a single response. While the Pitman version makes finding particular testimony easier, it can be quite misleading since relevant testimony about one individual may actually appear in different places and times throughout the trial record and relevant testimony may be missed if one does not read the trial record in toto. An example is found among the testimony relating to defendant Samuel A. Mudd. In providing testimony for the prosecution of Samuel Arnold, Federal Detective Eaton G. Horner, who arrested Arnold, stated that Arnold had told him during interrogation that John Wilkes Booth carried a letter of introduction to Samuel Mudd at the time of Booth's first visit to Charles County, Maryland. Patrick

Martin, a Confederate agent working out of Montreal, Canada, gave the letter to Booth. This important piece of evidence showing that Booth's meeting with Samuel Mudd in November 1864 was preplanned on Booth's end ties Mudd into the Confederate underground operating in southern Maryland. Yet none of the biographies written about Samuel Mudd include this important piece of evidence, presumably because the authors of these works did not read the entire trial transcript, or if they did, missed Horner's important testimony. When one reads the Poore text in its entirety, Horner's crucial statement concerning Mudd becomes obvious even though it does not appear under the heading "Samuel A. Mudd" in the Pitman version.

A second example involves the controversy concerning one of the trial exhibits, "Exhibit No. 1," a photograph identified as John Wilkes Booth. The photograph currently found in the envelope marked "Exhibit No. 1" located in the National Archives is a photograph of Edwin Booth, John Wilkes Booth's brother. This finding has led those who believe there was a government conspiracy designed to frame innocent people to claim that the government deliberately used the wrong photograph to mislead witnesses. And yet, a careful reading of the summation of Samuel Mudd's own defense attorney, Thomas Ewing, proves that the photograph introduced as "Exhibit No. 1" was a photograph of John Wilkes Booth. This suggests that those who claim a photograph of Edwin Booth was used in place of an image of John Wilkes Booth at the time of the manhunt for Booth and later during the trial did not read the entire trial transcript or did so carelessly. The testimony pertaining to these two pieces of evidence along with several others are found in M-599 and discussed more fully in this book.

I have relied on the Poore version as the primary source of information, using the Pitman version for chronology and as a cross-reference, consulting its index where necessary. The summations of the prosecution and defense attorneys are also found in Pitman as well as M-599. Most of the quotations used in the present study are taken from the Poore transcript and the letters and statements that appear in M-599 and M-619.

In addition to these two primary sources, there are two other sources that are rich in documentary material that figure prominently in this current book. The first is the *Surratt Courier*, the newsletter of the Surratt Society (Clinton, Maryland). This newsletter has served as an outlet for the findings of several skilled researchers in the Lincoln assassination field. The second is the private file of James O. Hall. Hall has spent over fifty years asking and answering all manner of questions concerned with Lincoln's assassination. During that time he has accumulated an extensive archive of materials from every source imaginable. This archive includes all of the standard documentation located in numerous libraries and archives as well as letters, diaries, memoirs, photographs, interviews, and miscellaneous papers from the families of many of the people associated with the events surrounding Lincoln's death. No study of Lincoln's assassination can be judged complete without utilizing this rich resource.

Sir Isaac Newton, the English physicist and mathematician, when asked what lay behind his genius, said that if it seemed he was able to see further than most people it was because he stood on the shoulders of others. Having spent most of my adult life in basic research, I learned early in my career the truth of Newton's statement. At every step I had the opportunity to stand on the shoulders of others. In this current undertaking, James O. Hall provided the broadest shoulders of all. Recognized by everyone in the field of assassination research as the premier researcher, Hall is also among the most generous. For fifty years he has doggedly burrowed through every archive both public and private leaving no piece of paper unturned. In the process he has amassed an extensive archive that is unique. His willingness to share his files and knowledge has contributed enormously to our current understanding of this important event in American history. Like so many others, I am indebted to James O. Hall for his generous help and counsel.

There are others who have willingly offered their help along the way. Principal among these is William Hanchett, professor emeritus of history at San Diego State University, who provided me with his considerable insight and knowledge and made many suggestions concerning this manuscript. I am also indebted to Terry Alford, professor of history at Northern Virginia Community College, for his helpful comments and critical evaluations, especially in matters concerning John Wilkes Booth. These two historians rescued me on many occasions.

In reviewing my files I find numerous instances of material generously provided by the many friends who have helped me in my research over the years. Among these are Sarah Barley, John C. Brennan (deceased), Robert Borrell, Lynn Conway, Robert Cook, Robert Emmett Curran, Gordon Damann, Paul DeHann, David W. Gaddy, Joseph E. Garrera, Richard and Kellie Gutman, Vicki Heilig, Harold Holzer, Blaine Houmes, Jim Hoyt, Roger D. Hunt, Lance Ingmire, Michael W. Kauffman, Father Robert Keesler, George H. Landes Jr. (deceased), James E.T. Lange, Carolyn Leporini, Kieran McAuliffe, Michael Maione, Horace Mewborn, Steven Miller, Richard D. Mudd, Michael P. Musick, Betty Ownsbey, Roger Norton, Margery Patten, Floyd E. Risvold, Susan Schoelwer, Thomas F. Schwartz, Jane Singer, Richard Sloan, Larry Springer, Wayne Temple, William Tidwell (deceased), Thomas R. Turner, Laurie Verge, Wayne Wesolowski, Rob Wick, Budge Weidman, and Frank J. Williams.

Special thanks are due Maureen Mylander, Joseph and Kathleen Nichols, and Joan Chaconas, who read through numerous versions of the text and made many thoughtful suggestions regarding both content and style. As close friends, they did not hesitate to offer their candid criticism at various stages of the manuscript, for which I am grateful.

I would also like to acknowledge the special help I received from copy editor Noel Kinnamon and from Kieran McAuliffe, who designed the dust jacket and prepared the maps that appear in the book.

Last is my wife, Patricia Aire Steers, who continues to cheerfully share her house and her life with Abraham Lincoln. Without her, this work would have remained only a dream.

The traditional story of Abraham Lincoln's assassination is fraught with errors. There are accidental errors and there are willful errors. No doubt this current work will also contain errors, but none that are willful. Hopefully those that do occur are not substantive and at the very worst prove interesting. The errors that do exist are mine alone and in no way reflect on those who generously shared their wisdom with me.

INTRODUCTION

Abraham Lincoln has become the subject of more writings than any other person in American history. At last estimate, there were approximately 16,000 entries in a bibliography of works on him that Frank J. Williams is compiling.[1] To be sure, a majority of these entries appear as pamphlets or journal articles, but the total number of monographs still ranks Lincoln among the top four individuals in history.[2] The greater number of books written about Lincoln are concerned with his period as a war president and commander in chief while the topics least written about are concerned with his religion and his assassination.

Unlike Lincoln's life, which has been a favorite subject of academic historians, his death has been left almost entirely to the avocational or nonprofessionally trained historians. The first book on Lincoln's assassination written by a professionally trained historian did not appear until 1982, 117 years after his death. A second book appeared one year later in 1983, and a third, in 1999. These three books remain the only books written by academic historians on this important subject to date.[3]

This paucity of writing by academicians remains unexplained. One Lincoln scholar suggested that professional historians allowed the assassination to fall between the two major fields of study, the Civil War and the period of Reconstruction immediately following it.[4] That Lincoln's death did not somehow fit into either category suggests it has little importance to either one. Nothing could be further from the truth. Lincoln's murder was a logical consequence, given the reasons for the Civil War and his pivotal role in it. His death forever changed the course of American history that followed. Yet professional historians mark Lincoln's passing as an end point rather than a continuation.

Contrary to most professional historians' interest, Lincoln's assassination has captivated the general public from a conspiratorial point of view, which may explain why many academicians have shied away from writing about it. William Hanchett, a professionally trained historian whose excellent book on Lincoln's assassination was published in 1983, wrote that Lincoln's death was something that the great body of professional historians thought of as a matter that should be described rather than explained.[5] To these historians, the story of Abraham Lincoln ended with his death. Having been left to nonprofessionally trained historians to explain, much of the telling of Lincoln's murder has fallen short of the quality of research and insightful writing normally found in other academic studies. This has led to a series of publications that espoused bizarre conspiracy theories of his murder. In these studies, Lincoln's secretary of war, Edwin Stanton, is portrayed as an archangel of death orchestrating the murder of his president.[6] Unable to engineer such a monstrous crime alone, Stanton received help from a cadre of the rich and powerful among his northern compatriots. Such theory is based on flawed and even fabricated evidence, all designed to titillate the reader and create a type of shock history that, although financially rewarding to the author, misleads.

In other accounts, authors have focused only on the simplest parts of the story, drawing on secondary sources and ignoring the rich source of primary documents housed in various archives.[7] Once told, this simple story of Lincoln's murder has been retold again and again by replowing the same furrows. Errors of one author soon become incorporated into the works of subsequent authors until repeated so many times they become an integral part of the story. This method of replowing has resulted more in historical fiction than truthful history and left us with many misconceptions. Thus John Wilkes Booth was a madman who acted as a puppet for others; the man cornered in the Virginia barn and killed by army pursuers was not Booth but an innocent bystander who was substituted for Lincoln's killer; Mary Surratt, the keeper of a boarding house frequented by Booth and his cohorts, was an innocent victim of a vengeful government; the military trial that tried Lincoln's killers was an illegal tribunal that sought vengeance, not justice; Booth and his co-conspirators were simply a gang of semi-intelligent miscreants who are described as "the gang that couldn't shoot straight."[8] The most widely held and egregious myth is that Dr. Samuel Alexander Mudd, the Charles County physician who set Booth's broken leg, was an innocent man persecuted for simply following his Hippocratic Oath. None of these commonly held beliefs are true.

Booth was fully rational, and while he received important help from powerful interests, he was no puppet. He died in a tobacco barn twelve days into his attempted escape. Both Dr. Mudd and Mary Surratt were complicit in Booth's conspiracy and were tried before a legally constituted court whose jurisdiction was later upheld by two Federal courts. Mudd was, in fact, the key connection that resulted in Booth's being able to assemble an important group of co-conspirators. Whatever shortcomings Booth and his cohorts had, they could shoot straight enough to murder the president of the United States, nearly murder the secretary of state, and throw the country, if only for a short period, into chaos.

The most persistent of all of the many myths associated with Lincoln's assassination is the myth first promulgated by Otto Eisenschiml, an organic chemist turned avocational historian. In 1937 Eisenschiml published an account of Lincoln's assassination that was the first to put forward the theory that Stanton was behind Lincoln's murder.[9] By carefully manipulating the data and using titillating innuendo, Eisenschiml caught the imagination of a conspiracy-prone public. For the next sixty years Eisenschiml's false theories remained a prominent part of the Lincoln story. Today they form the major basis for the television industry's "documentary" reports on Lincoln's death.

Even those who reject Eisenschiml's silly theories of government complicity in Lincoln's murder still believe in a government conspiracy to falsely try and convict certain individuals who they believe had no part in the crime. Principal among these wrongly convicted individuals is Samuel Mudd. As recently as 1997, a United States congressman delivered a speech on the floor of the House of Representatives declaring that "there is absolutely no evidence to suggest that [Dr. Samuel Alexander] Mudd was either a coconspirator in the assassination of President Lincoln or even aware of the events which had occurred earlier that evening on Friday, April 14, 1865." The congressman concluded his misinformed remarks by urging all of his colleagues to join him "in ensuring that history is recorded accurately."[10] As this book will show, the evidence that Dr. Mudd was a co-conspirator of John Wilkes Booth both before and after Booth's murder of Lincoln is substantial and convincing. Only by adhering to the facts contained in the documentary record will the congressman and others ensure "that history is recorded accurately."

That a subject can be so widely written about and so misrepresented is in itself an interesting phenomenon. Left to nonprofessional historians (and politicians) the story of Lincoln's murder has failed to receive the critical attention usually associated with the research of professional historians. As with all such generalizations, however, this one has its exception. Among the most important research into Lincoln's assassination in this century is that of three nonprofessional historians, William A. Tidwell, James O. Hall, and David W. Gaddy. In 1988 these authors published the results of their careful research into the Confederate Secret Service and its association with Booth in a book titled *Come Retribution: The Confederate Secret Service and the Assassination of Abraham Lincoln.*[11] No account of Lincoln's murder is complete without considering their work. Using many previously untapped primary records, these authors conducted extensive research into the subject of the Confederate Secret Service, and came to the conclusion that high-ranking Confederate officials supported John Wilkes Booth in a conspiracy aimed at capturing Lincoln, a conspiracy that evolved into a plan to create chaos by assassinating President Lincoln, Vice President Andrew Johnson, and Secretary of State William H. Seward.

In *Come Retribution*, Tidwell and his coauthors attempt to show that Jefferson Davis and other members of his cabinet had targeted Lincoln in retaliation for a Union military action aimed at Davis and certain cabinet officials. This military action, which has come to be known as the Kilpatrick-Dahlgren raid, ended in failure, achieving none of its objectives. Nevertheless, the fact that it happened at all was a major break in the code of conduct between the two warring nations.

In early 1864 Lincoln had received distressing reports about the deplorable conditions of Union prisoners and was anxious for their liberation. Lincoln also learned that the Confederate government was planning to remove the prisoners to Andersonville in Georgia. If action were not undertaken soon these prisoners would be beyond the reach of any Union army and all hope for their safe return would pass. A military raid was proposed that had three objectives: to free the Union prisoners, to destroy public buildings and various military facilities including arsenals and railroad equipage, and "to capture some of the leaders of the rebellion" and carry them to Washington.

On February 6, 1864, Brigadier General Isaac Wistar led a large body of Union cavalry on a special raid aimed at the lightly defended capital of Richmond. The Confederate military received advance word of Wistar's raid, and he was stopped before he could breech the outer defenses of Richmond. The raid had to be aborted. Lincoln was clearly disappointed at Wistar's failure.

Three weeks later, a second raid was mounted by Brigadier General Judson Kilpatrick commanding the Third Division, Cavalry Corps, of the Army of the Potomac. This operation was to consist of two parts: Kilpatrick with 3,500 troopers would attack Richmond from the north entering the city while Colonel Ulric Dahlgren, son of Rear Admiral John Dahlgren, would lead a select group of 500 troopers around Richmond entering from the south. Dahlgren and his men would liberate the Union prisoners held in the Confederate prison camp on Belle Isle in the James River and escort them into Richmond. But something new had been added. Dahlgren carried papers that read, "The men must keep together and well in hand, and once in the city it must be destroyed and Jeff Davis and Cabinet killed."

Kilpatrick's attack was quickly blunted and repelled. Dahlgren, unable to reach Belle Isle and cross the rain-swollen James River, abandoned his plan to enter the city from the south. Dahlgren tried to escape with his small band of men eastward to the safety of General Butler's army on the Peninsula. Ambushed by Confederate cavalry, Dahlgren was killed, and the papers on his body calling for the burning of the city and killing of Davis were discovered.

On hearing the content of the Dahlgren orders, Davis believed that Lincoln had authorized the raid and its objectives, including Davis's assassination. In his memoirs, Davis pointedly wrote about Dahlgren and his failed raid: "The enormity of his offenses was not forgotten."[12] The Confederate leaders felt that Lincoln had violated the civilized laws of war and in doing so had lost whatever protection he had under those laws. If Jefferson Davis was fair game, then Abraham Lincoln was fair game. The effect of the raid removed whatever restraints had existed on "black flag warfare."[13]

According to the authors of *Come Retribution*, the Confederacy retaliated with its own plan. Initially, the plan was to capture Lincoln and bring him to Richmond where he would serve as the ultimate bargaining chip in negotiations over prisoner exchange and a cessation of hostilities. In his confession made at the Arsenal prison on May 1, George A. Atzerodt, one of Booth's cohorts, told of an alternative "project" to blow up the White House and kill Lincoln.[14] The origins and details of this scheme are murky, but a team from the Torpedo Bureau in Richmond was sent to join John S. Mosby's cavalry a few days before Richmond fell on April 3. The team carried supplies described as "ordnance" and was headed by an explosives expert, Thomas F. Harney. The plan fell apart when Harney and his assistants were captured on April 10 in a cavalry skirmish in Fairfax County, Virginia, about fifteen miles from Washington.[15]

The book immediately became controversial and was criticized by some members of the historical fraternity as lacking documentary proof. These historians felt the authors of *Come Retribution* had overreached in their effort to link officials of the Confederacy to Booth's plans and actions. Prominent among their views was the belief that an assassination effort by either side was unthinkable under the moral constraints of the period.[16] The perception at the time, and still prevalent today, was of a war fought by gentlemen guided by the highest moral standards and civility. Premeditated violence directed against the civilian leaders of a nation was simply not in the American character.

The authors of *Come Retribution* acknowledge their evidence is largely circumstantial, but point out that clandestine operations leave few paper trails for future historians to follow. Their research explained a Confederate Secret Service not previously appreciated or understood. By carefully pulling together many small pieces of information the authors tell their story. Like so many seemingly random dots in a child's puzzle, pieces of unconnected information lay scattered across the landscape of Lincoln's murder. By connecting all of the dots with one continuous line, the authors were able to come up with a pattern they believed pointed directly to Confederate Secret Service agents who were operating out of Canada and southern Maryland. These authors believe the Kilpatrick-Dahlgren raid gave Jefferson Davis and his advisors ample motivation to retaliate against Lincoln for his perceived offenses.

But Jefferson Davis did not fire the fatal bullet that killed Abraham Lincoln. John Wilkes Booth did. If Jefferson Davis and those around him had targeted the removal of Lincoln as their only hope of success, what motivation did John Wilkes Booth and those instrumental in his plot have? What passion caused Booth to risk so much and to eventually give his life? That is one of the central questions that this book addresses. It is a question previous authors have misinterpreted in attempting to describe the underlying events associated with Lincoln's murder.

Previous studies have isolated Lincoln's murder from the historical events leading up to it. History, however, does not exist as a series of isolated events like so many sound bites in a newscast. It is a continuum of seemingly unrelated and distant events that every so often come together in one momentous collision in time. Like a great asteroid colliding with earth, the small leaden bullet that crashed into Lincoln's brain gave rise to an ominous cloud that spread across the American landscape leaving its fallout on subsequent generations.

The underpinning of the plot to assassinate Lincoln was the institution of slavery. Opposition to slavery had formed the Republican Party. In 1860 that party made Abraham Lincoln its candidate for president of the United States. Secession was the direct result of his election. The Southern States seceded from the Union because of Lincoln's stand against slavery with the hope that they would be allowed to go their own way. That hope failed to materialize, and when Lincoln issued his Emancipation Proclamation in 1863 the Confederacy found itself isolated from any hope of European support, all because of Lincoln and his policies. Southern independence would not happen because of Lincoln's unwavering determination to reunite the country and wipe out the national curse of slavery in the process. Lincoln's resolute stance caused some in the South to conclude that the only answer lay in removing him from his "throne of power"—if not by the ballot, then by the bullet.

The murder of Abraham Lincoln was a cataclysmic event in American history. It had its origins early in the seventeenth century when the first African was brought ashore in bondage. The shift from indentured servitude to slavery in the 1600s started America on a dangerous course from which it did not know how to recover. It grew slowly at first, and then more rapidly until all of the fury and rage surrounding the peculiar institution exploded from the muzzle of a two-inch barrel and smashed into the brain of the man who brought it to an end.

The assassination of Abraham Lincoln is an oft-told story. But it is a story, as historian William Hanchett has written, that "has been described rather than explained."[17] And when explained, it is usually from the perspective of a deranged actor who struck from some mythical concept of revenge. This is not only too simple an explanation, it is flat-out wrong. Booth was neither mad nor alone in his act of murder. Alone he might never have accomplished his deed. Booth received important help from several people not the least of whom was Dr. Samuel Alexander Mudd, the Charles County physician who history has come to believe was the innocent victim of a vengeful government. Mudd's role was as a member of the Confederate clandestine apparatus that operated so successfully in southern Maryland. This is yet another instance where historians have failed to examine the primary record carefully. Had they done so they would have concluded that Dr. Mudd was not only a co-conspirator of Booth, but a pivotal figure in helping Booth assemble his team of cohorts. Booth's ability to elude the authorities during his escape and to get as far as the Garrett farm can also be laid directly at Mudd's feet. Booth benefited more from the help Dr. Mudd gave to him than from any other person connected with Lincoln's murder.

Booth also benefited greatly from the Confederate leadership in Richmond. Whether he was an agent of that leadership or simply a beneficiary can be debated. But in putting together his plans to strike at Lincoln, Booth was aided by key members of the Confederate underground at every step. After capture turned to assassination, that same Confederate apparatus used all of its resources to help Booth in his attempt to escape. If it had not been for key members of the Confederate underground, Booth would never have made his way as far as he did or for as long as he did.

The underlying motive that caused the Southern leadership and men like John Wilkes Booth to risk all in their effort to "get" Lincoln was a common belief that slavery was an essential part of the cultural and economic success of the United States. Booth was a White supremacist. Those who joined with him in his plot to remove Lincoln were also White supremacists whose greatest fear was the emancipation of the Black man. Abraham Lincoln was the architect of those emancipation policies.

While historians have recognized that Booth was a racist who hated Lincoln, they have never connected his racism, or that of his associates, directly to Booth's conspiracy to remove Lincoln as president. In Booth's logic, Julius Caesar and Abraham Lincoln were despots of a feather. Caesar was murdered for taking away the civil liberties of his fellow citizens, while Abraham Lincoln was murdered for trying to extend civil liberties to his fellow citizens. In Booth's mind, there was no difference. Both were tyrants who deserved killing.

When Booth entered the presidential box at Ford's Theatre on the night of April 14, 1865, he held a small derringer in his hand. While it was Booth's hand that held the gun, there were many fingers on the trigger. This book is an effort to explain who those people were and why they were so willing to help pull the trigger that changed the course of American history, and in telling this story, to correct the many misconceptions and false theories that have found their way into one of the most important events in the nation's history.

Part One

A Divided House

Let my enemies prove to the country that the destruction of slavery is not necessary to the restoration of the Union.

Abraham Lincoln, 1864

This country was formed for the white not for the black man.

John Wilkes Booth, 1864

CHAPTER ONE

The Apotheosis

Now he belongs to the ages.

Edwin McMasters Stanton

The voice came over the loudspeaker announcing that the next talk on the assassination of Abraham Lincoln would begin in two minutes. Like ants drawn to sugar, the crowd of tourists began streaming toward the orchestra section of the theater from many directions. Some had been looking at the special box where the president sat that fateful night. Others were downstairs in the exhibit area, viewing the various artifacts that explained the who and why of his death. Still others had been browsing the small gift shop that carried books and memorabilia about the sixteenth president.

As the crowd made its way into the orchestra area it began filling up the rows of seats closest to the stage. Standing at center stage, a man dressed in the green and grey uniform of a park ranger patiently waited for the people to settle down. Like a fussy schoolteacher standing before his class, the ranger stood motionless waiting for his chatty students to give him their undivided attention. After a few minutes a hush fell over the crowd. The ranger continued to wait, allowing the anticipation to slowly build as he surveyed the faces spread out before him. Satisfied that his audience was properly attentive, the ranger spoke: "Good afternoon, ladies and gentlemen, and welcome to Ford's Theatre. This afternoon I want to tell you what happened in this special place on the night of April 14, 1865."

Turning slightly to his left, he motioned to a point twelve feet above the stage to the special box reserved for the president on his visits to the theater. A pair of white lacy curtains elegantly framed two large openings in the box. A pair of American flags were draped over the balustrade as if they had been hurriedly placed with little attention to symmetry. A large engraving of George Washington separated the flags. Over the engraving a blue flag hung loosely from a pole fastened to the column just above the picture. Not visible to the audience, but tucked behind one of the lace curtains, was the red upholstered rocking chair that Lincoln sat in the night of his murder. In reality, the rocker was a reproduction of the original rocker that was on display in the Henry Ford Museum in Dearborn, Michigan. In fact, the presidential box and all of the theater, except for its outer skin of bricks, was a reproduction, or as the Park Service would say, an authentic restoration.

Looking back at his audience, the ranger continued, "At approximately twenty minutes past ten o'clock on that fateful night of April 14, 1865, the famous actor John Wilkes Booth entered the box above you and fired a bullet from a small derringer pistol into the brain of Abraham Lincoln."[1]

The ranger paused and looked down into the faces that were staring up at the box where the president had been seated. For twelve years he had stood on this stage, and for twelve years he had delivered his little speech. And for twelve years he listened patiently to their questions. They were always the same: "Why was Booth allowed in the box?" "Why wasn't Lincoln guarded that night?" "Was it true that Secretary of War Edwin Stanton was behind Lincoln's murder?" "Why did the telegraph mysteriously go dead minutes after Lincoln was shot?" "Didn't Booth really escape and live for many years afterward?"

America's fascination with conspiracy has remained unquenchable. No amount of facts could persuade the multitude that the bodyguard didn't abandon his post, or that Edwin Stanton loved Abraham Lincoln and would never act to harm him, or that Booth was really killed in a barn located on a small Virginia farm twelve days after shooting Lincoln, or that the military telegraph never went dead at any time during the night.

The ranger, sensing he had captured his audience's undivided attention, continued his story. He described how several soldiers cradled the dying president in their arms as they carried him from the box across the rear of the balcony and down the steps to the lobby. Emerging onto the sidewalk in front of the theater, the men were not sure what to do. Suddenly they were beckoned by a flickering light from across the street. The ranger raised his arm high over his head as if he were holding a candle. The audience's eyes looked up at the ranger's hand. "'Bring him in here,' a voice called out from across the street."[2] The ranger repeated the command: "Bring him in here." The audience listened spellbound as the ranger conjured up the image of the mortally wounded president being gently borne to the house of a simple tailor. Staring into the faces below, the ranger slowly repeated the words heard that sorrowful night, "Bring him in here."

Across the street from the theater a young man stood on the steps of the house where he rented a small room on the second floor. Henry Safford was exhausted from several nights of celebrating Robert E. Lee's surrender. He decided to stay in his room this night and rest. Hearing the commotion in the street, he picked up a candle and walked out onto the stoop. In the street below he saw several soldiers carrying the body of an injured man. "Bring him in here," he instinctively called out to the men. "Bring him in here."

A light rain had fallen throughout most of the night. Outside the tailor's house a crowd stood in silent vigil indifferent to their personal discomfort. They had gathered soon after word spread that the president had been shot and taken to the house opposite the theater. Inside, twelve men gathered around a small bed staring at the long figure that lay diagonally across its surface seemingly deep in sleep. The soft sizzle of a gas jet mingled with the rasping sounds of the man's breathing. Among those keeping vigil at the bedside was Secretary of the Navy Gideon Welles, the man Abraham Lincoln affectionately called his "Father Neptune."

Welles had hurried to the president's side as soon as he had heard the tragic news. The message that the president had been attacked and Secretary of State William Seward had been assassinated reached Welles just as he was preparing to retire for the night. Welles had gone up to his room and was in the process of undressing when a messenger arrived with the shocking news. Hurrying on foot the few blocks to Seward's house, Welles met Secretary of War Edwin Stanton who had just arrived in a carriage. The two men rushed up the stairs and into the bedroom where Seward lay still wrapped in bloody sheets. There seemed to be blood everywhere. The scene appeared more horrific than it actually was. Reassured that Seward would live, the two men next hurried to the house where the president had been taken.[3] They arrived a few minutes past eleven o'clock. At the same time, a few miles to the east, a lone rider spurred his horse as he raced up a long incline making his way between two military forts. Passing the forts, the rider turned south and headed into Maryland.

For the next seven hours Welles maintained a bedside vigil while Stanton, who sat in an adjoining room, assumed control of the government. Throughout the night the war secretary, with Chief Justice David Kellogg Cartter of the Supreme Court of the District of Columbia at his side, began issuing directives and taking testimony from those who had information to give. Stanton assumed absolute control, and although well down the line of succession or authority in the civil government, he functioned as if the attack on the president had been a military action.[4] It was a moment of grave national danger, not a time for indecision or faint-hearted action. Stanton was up to the challenge. He would maintain this position for the next three months.

For seven hours the men had kept their vigil, helpless to do anything except wait. Time slipped slowly past, each tick of the clock measured against the failing pulse of the president. A sense of grief weighed heavily on all who were present. The emotional wailing of Mary Lincoln was distressing to even the most hardened heart. Finally, Stanton could stand no more and told an aide to take her from the room and see that she remained in the front parlor. The close atmosphere of the small room had become heavy with the odor of mustard balm and camphor. Welles began to feel light-headed and nauseous. He needed to escape the dreary room if only for a few moments.

Shortly before dawn he slipped out the front door of the house and took a short walk. As he walked past the large groups of people gathered outside he was asked what news there was of the president. "Tell us of Father Abraham, of Massa Linkum. Is there any hope, any at all?" Welles simply shook his head, too emotionally drained to speak. The crowds seemed overwhelmed with grief, especially the Black mourners who seemed to outnumber the White.

Returning to the house, Welles resumed his place near the president. It was a little past seven o'clock, and Lincoln's breathing had slowed considerably. The deathwatch was drawing to an end. Sitting at the president's side was Assistant Army Surgeon Charles Leale, the doctor who had arrived first at the box in Ford's Theatre and had taken charge of the president. Leale now held the comatose president's hand with a firm grip to "let him know that he was in touch with humanity and had a friend."[5] The hand was cold and stiff. There was no movement, not even the slightest twitch to say, "I hear, I feel, I know."

At twenty-two minutes past seven o'clock the end came. Placing a finger against the president's neck, Surgeon General Joseph K. Barnes felt for some sign of a pulse. There was none. Carefully folding the president's arms across his breast the surgeon general declared in a voice choked with emotion, "He is gone."[6] A somber silence ensued as each person in the room seemed transfixed by the awful moment. It cannot be true. He cannot be gone. After what seemed to Welles to be several minutes Stanton broke the silence by asking Lincoln's pastor, Dr. Phineas Gurley, if he would say a prayer. Gurley, minister of the New York Avenue Presbyterian Church, knelt by the bedside and waited as each man in the room sank to his knees. Gurley prayed for the nation, beseeching God to heal the wounds and restore a united country. He asked that God accept his humble servant Abraham Lincoln into His glorious Kingdom. When he finished, the men rose to their feet with a fervent and spontaneous "Amen." Then Stanton, with tears streaming down his cheeks, uttered his immortal words, "Now he belongs to the ages."[7]

Lincoln's death was followed by an outpouring of grief not seen before or since in the nation's history. Easter Sunday heard hundreds of sermons preached in America's churches. Bells rang and cannons boomed in a continuous toll underscoring the great sadness of the time. Stanton's tears were soon mingled with those of millions of mourners who openly wept at the death of their great and good leader. In Boston's Shawmut Congregational Church, Edwin B. Webb spoke to his stricken congregation in solemn words: "The sun is less bright than before, the very atmosphere seems to hold in it for the tearful eye a strange ethereal element of gloom. It is manly to weep today."[8] The majority of Northern preachers compared Lincoln to Moses. Henry Ward Beecher, the country's most famous preacher, likened Lincoln to the biblical leader who after leading his people to the Promised Land was denied entry for himself. Beecher pointed out that the terrible tragedy would fall most heavily on the Black people: "There will be a wailing in places which no ministers shall be able to reach."[9] Others compared Lincoln to George Washington. Together, "they were both equally the vessels of Omnipotence; God chose them to do an unequalled work, not only for this land, but for all mankind."[10] The deification of the man who had once been reviled as "the original gorilla" and "Abraham Africanus the First" was being proclaimed from church pulpits all across the land. The great apotheosis had begun.

CHAPTER TWO

You Are in Danger

> I regret that you do not appreciate what I repeatedly said to you in regard to . . . your own personal safety. You are in danger.
>
> *Ward Hill Lamon*

The sadness over Lincoln's death, like his election in 1860, was sectional. Not everyone agreed with Beecher's and his fellow ministers' pious view of the dead president. To many in the South, Lincoln's death was nothing more than tyrannicide. "Hurrah! Old Abe Lincoln has been assassinated!" a South Carolina girl wrote in her diary on hearing the news.[1] The editor of the *Texas Republican* echoed the views of his readers when he wrote: "It is certainly a matter of congratulations that Lincoln is dead because the world is rid of a monster that disgraced the form of humanity."[2] The *Galveston Daily News* saw the hand of God differently from those in the North: "God Almighty ordered this event or it could never have taken place."[3]

Abraham Lincoln's death was an increasingly popular want during the war years. While assassination was thought to be contrary to the American character, Lincoln's election in 1860 would put it there. After his nomination at Chicago, Lincoln began receiving death threats in various forms. These threats continued after the election. On January 26, 1861, after visiting Lincoln in his temporary office set up in the Illinois state capitol building in Springfield, a man by the name of Joshua Allen wrote his mother: "He has got stacks of preserved fruit and all sorts of such trash which he is daily receiving from various parts of the South, sent him as presents. He had several packages opened and examined by medical men who found them all to be poisoned."[4]

Earlier that same week Lincoln had received a letter warning him of an assassination plot: "I have heard several persons in this place say that if you ever did take the President Chair that they would go to Washington City expressly to kill you."[5] Not all of the letters Lincoln received were from concerned citizens who wanted to forewarn him. Many were from deranged people who simply despised him and wanted to vent their hatred: "God damn your god damned old Hellfire god damned soul to hell god damn you and your god damned family's god damned hellfired god damned soul to hell."[6] Although lacking grammatical skill, the writer got his point across.

Death threats to Lincoln continued unabated throughout his presidency. According to his young secretary, John Hay, Lincoln kept a select group of threatening letters in a "bulging folder in a special pigeonhole" in his White House desk.[7] What was in these letters and why Lincoln chose to keep them is not known. As numerous as these threats were, Lincoln apparently treated them lightly. After all, anyone who seriously contemplated murdering the president wouldn't be foolish enough to write a letter forewarning of his plan. Elizabeth Keckley, Mary Lincoln's seamstress and close friend, wrote in her postwar memoir that Lincoln rarely gave such threatening letters a second thought.[8] While Lincoln downplayed anonymous threats to his life, there were serious forces at work plotting his assassination.

These forces were organized and deadly serious about their mission. Among the earliest of the organized plots to assassinate Lincoln was one that occurred in Baltimore, Maryland, in February 1861. The Baltimore Plot, as it came to be known in later years, was important because of its potential for success. If it had remained undiscovered, Lincoln might never have been inaugurated. The threat came while he was en route to Washington for his inauguration scheduled for March 4, 1861. It involved a plot by members of a group known as the National Volunteers, a secretive paramilitary organization whose core leadership was also affiliated with the anti-Lincoln Knights of the Golden Circle. These two organizations had the overthrow of the government by violent force at the heart of their objectives.

The National Volunteers had been organized by William Byrne, a Baltimore businessman, in the summer of 1860, and was originally designed to aid the presidential candidacy of John C. Breckinridge. After Lincoln's election victory, it shifted its focus to preventing his inauguration by violent means.[9] Members of the National Volunteers had developed a plan to intercept Lincoln in Baltimore and kill him. Baltimore, the last of thirteen stops before Lincoln reached Washington, was a hotbed of secession activity, making it an ideal place to carry out an assassination attempt.

One of the principal meeting places for the anti-Lincoln forces in Baltimore was the bar of Barnum's City Hotel. Members of the local organization met at Barnum's where they fueled their hatred for Lincoln with whiskey and talk of assassination. One of the principal anti-Lincoln people to join the assassination plot was the head barber at Barnum's Hotel, a Corsican immigrant named Cipriano Ferrandini. Ferrandini was a "captain" in the Knights of the Golden Circle and a staunch Confederate sympathizer. He was an advocate of assassination as a principle means to further political aims. When Ferrandini learned that Lincoln would stop over in Baltimore for a luncheon before changing trains, he and others of like mind hatched a plot to kill the president-elect as he passed by carriage through the streets of Baltimore.

Lincoln's train from Harrisburg, Pennsylvania, was scheduled to arrive at the Calvert Street Station in Baltimore shortly after noon on February 23.

Lincoln would then travel by carriage to a luncheon appointment in the city before boarding another train that would take him on to Washington. Ferrandini and his band of assassins planned to start a disturbance and shoot Lincoln from the melee while en route to his luncheon engagement. The plan was reasonable and had a good chance of success. There was only one problem. When Lincoln's train pulled into the Calvert Street station on the morning of the twenty-third, Lincoln was not on it. He was already at the Willard Hotel in Washington safely having thwarted his would-be killers.

Lincoln's safe passage through Baltimore came about as the result of a brilliant detective effort. Working independently, teams of detectives from both the New York police force and Allan Pinkerton's Chicago detective agency had infiltrated the core of the conspiracy. The plot had been discovered and Lincoln warned in advance of its execution. Once convinced that the plot to assassinate him was real, Lincoln secretly changed his travel plans and passed through Baltimore nine hours ahead of schedule.

One cannot read the reports of Allan Pinkerton and his detectives or the accounts of the New York detectives assigned to Baltimore without concluding there was a real threat to Lincoln's life if he kept to his planned schedule through Baltimore. But did the plotters have the nerve to carry out the assassination? Some historians have expressed doubt on this point. So did Lincoln in an 1864 interview with historian Benjamin J. Lossing. Lincoln repeated this doubt to his friend Isaac N. Arnold, then added, "But I thought it wise to run no risk where no risk was necessary."[10] By choosing caution, Lincoln may have averted his assassination.

In January Samuel Felton, president of the Philadelphia, Wilmington, and Baltimore Rail Road, had received credible information that the pro-Confederate apparatus in Maryland planned to sabotage his rail lines and bridges north of Baltimore. Alarmed, Felton moved quickly to protect his property. He hired the famous Chicago detective Allan Pinkerton to investigate those plotting against his railroad. By February 3, Pinkerton, using the alias John H. Hutchinson, was in Baltimore with five of his best agents, including two women, Hattie Lawton and Kate Warne. Within days they discovered a well-developed plan to assassinate Lincoln when he came through Baltimore on February 23 en route to the capital.

With Felton's permission Pinkerton turned his focus to the plot to assassinate Lincoln. In a few days he had enough information to send Kate Warne to Lincoln advisor Norman B. Judd, who was with Lincoln as he traveled to Washington. On February 21, Lincoln and his party arrived in Philadelphia and checked into the Continental Hotel. Judd, after hearing the details of the plot from Mrs. Warne, arranged a conference between Lincoln and Pinkerton in Judd's room. Pinkerton repeated to Lincoln what he had previously told Judd, and recommended that Lincoln change his travel schedule. Lincoln asked many probing questions, but flatly refused to leave

Philadelphia for Washington that night. He had promised to raise the flag at Independence Hall the next morning and to address the Pennsylvania legislature at Harrisburg in the afternoon. He was unwilling to break these promises. Lincoln did agree to think over Pinkerton's suggestion to alter his schedule but only after keeping his commitments in Philadelphia and Harrisburg.

But Pinkerton and his detectives were not the only ones investigating a plot in Baltimore. At the request of Lincoln friends in Washington, the superintendent of New York City police, John A. Kennedy, had sent three of his own detectives to Baltimore. Kennedy's detectives were instructed to report secretly to Colonel Charles P. Stone, an aide to General Winfield Scott.

On the way back to his room, Lincoln bumped into Ward Hill Lamon. Lamon and Lincoln had ridden the Illinois Eighth Judicial Circuit together as lawyers and had become close friends. Lamon had worked hard in Lincoln's senatorial and presidential campaigns and was asked by Lincoln to accompany him on his inaugural trip to Washington. Lamon informed Lincoln that Frederick Seward had just arrived from Washington with an urgent message from Seward's father, Senator William H. Seward. Lincoln agreed to meet with Frederick Seward. After the usual courtesies, Seward handed Lincoln a letter from his father that read:

> Washington Feb. 21st
>
> My dear Sir.
>
> My son goes express to you— He will show you a report made by our detective to General Scott—and by him communicated to me this morning. I deem it so important as to dispatch my son to meet with you wherever he may find you—I concur with Genl Scott in thinking it best for you to reconsider your arrangements. No one here but Genl Scott, myself & the bearer is aware of this communication.
>
> I should have gone with it myself but for the peculiar sensitiveness about my attendance in the Senate at this crisis.
>
> Very truly yours
>
> William H. Seward
>
> The Honorable
> Abraham Lincoln[11]

Lincoln then read the report Seward sent with his letter:

> Feb. 21st/61
>
> A New York detective officer who has been on duty in Baltimore for three weeks past reports this morning that there is seri-

> ous danger of violence to and the assassination of Mr. Lincoln in his passage through that city should the time of that passage be known— He states that there are banded rowdies holding secret meetings, and that he has heard threats of mobbing and violence, and has himself heard men declare that if Mr. Lincoln was to be assassinated they would like to be the men— He states further that it is only within the past few days that he has considered there was any danger, but he now deems it imminent— He deems the danger one which the authorities & people in Balt— cannot guard against— All risk might be easily avoided by a change in the traveling arrangements which would bring Mr. Lincoln & a portion of his party through Baltimore by a night train without previous notice—[12]

With his usual logic, Lincoln went straight to the heart of the problem. Were Pinkerton and Seward referring to the same investigation in Baltimore, or were there two separate investigations? After questioning Seward, Lincoln became convinced that Pinkerton's investigation and that of the New York detectives were completely independent. Lincoln explained the situation in an 1864 interview with historian Benjamin J. Lossing: "He [Frederick Seward] told me that he had been sent at the insistence of his father and General Scott to inform me that their detectives in Baltimore had discovered a plot there to assassinate me. They knew nothing of Pinkerton's movements. *I now believed such a plot to be in existence*" (emphasis added).[13]

Lincoln closed the conference by telling Seward that he would sleep on it and let him know his decision in the morning. The next morning he told Seward that he would change his travel plans as Pinkerton had advised. Frederick Seward immediately informed his father of Lincoln's decision. Pinkerton was now free to revise Lincoln's schedule and provide the necessary security to take him to Washington safely.

Reluctantly, Lincoln changed his travel plans so as to pass through Baltimore several hours ahead of schedule. The original plan had Lincoln leaving Harrisburg at 9 A.M. and traveling directly to Baltimore, arriving at 12:30 P.M. Following the special luncheon in his honor, Lincoln was scheduled to leave Baltimore at 3:00 P.M., arriving in Washington at 4:30 P.M. Instead, Lincoln left Harrisburg fifteen hours ahead of schedule and returned to Philadelphia on a special train provided by the Pennsylvania Railroad. In Philadelphia he transferred to the Philadelphia, Wilmington & Baltimore Rail Road and arrived in Baltimore at 3:30 A.M. Lincoln then transferred to the Baltimore & Ohio train, arriving in Washington at 6:00 A.M., a full nine hours ahead of schedule. Lincoln was met in Washington by Illinois congressman Elihu B. Washburne, who had been tipped off to the schedule change by Senator Seward. The two men took a carriage up to the Willard Hotel where a special suite had been set aside for the president elect and his family.

Later that morning, Pinkerton wired a cryptic message to his chief clerk back at his Chicago headquarters: "Plums [Pinkerton] has Nuts [Lincoln] — arri'd at Barley [Washington] — all right."[14]

Thanks to Pinkerton, Lincoln was safely ensconced in Washington, but it was not without cost. The Baltimore newspapers portrayed a cowardly president elect sneaking into the capital afraid for his life. The *Baltimore Sun* dubbed Lincoln's trip through the city "The 'Underground Railroad' Journey."[15] The *Baltimore American* was more brutal in its criticism: "The whole nation is humiliated, degraded by this wretched and cowardly conduct of the President-elect. Had General [Andrew] Jackson been told that he was threatened by conspirators, he would have crushed the conspiracy by meeting it like a man."[16]

An inventive *New York Times* reporter, Joseph Howard Jr., filed a story describing Lincoln as having skulked into the capital in disguise wearing "a Scotch plaid cap and very long military cloak."[17] The derisive description was repeated so often that it soon became a part of history. The fact is that Lincoln wore neither a Scotch plaid cap nor a long military cloak. Howard simply made this up to embellish his account. Elihu Washburne described Lincoln's appearance this way: "He had on a soft, low-crowned hat, a muffler around his neck, and a short bob-tailed overcoat."[18]

In his 1864 interview with Lossing, Lincoln explained what happened: "In New York some friend had given me a new beaver hat in a box, and in it had placed a soft wool hat. I had never worn one of the latter in my life. I had this box in my room. Having informed a very few friends of the secret of my new movements, and the cause, I put on an old overcoat that I had with me, and putting the soft hat in my pocket, I walked out of the house at a back door, bareheaded, without exciting any special curiosity. Then I put on the soft hat and joined my friends without being recognized by strangers, for I was not the same man."[19]

The damage had been done, however. Lincoln's enemies depicted him as a coward, sneaking into Washington in the dead of night, fearful of nonexistent dangers. The cartoonists had a field day. In a famous cartoon by Baltimorean Adalbert Volck, Lincoln is portrayed as arriving in Washington in a boxcar marked "freight bones." He is shown wearing the Scotch plaid cap and long military cloak referred to in Howard's newspaper article, peering out of a partly opened boxcar door in astonishment at an outraged tomcat.[20]

Certainly Lincoln was sensitive to the criticism and often responded in a defensive manner. One can only speculate on how much this criticism contributed to his well-known aversion to the trappings of a bodyguard—or to the lack of attention to security details at Ford's Theatre on the night of April 14, 1865.

Although threats to Lincoln's life continued to be received after the

Cottage Grove Public Librai

inauguration, he still resisted the appointment of a bodyguard, much to the concern of his old friend Ward Hill Lamon, whom Lincoln appointed United States marshal for the District of Columbia. Convinced that the Baltimore plot was real, Lamon rode in Lincoln's coach and the sleeping car on the night trip to Washington. He remembered the playful words of his friends back in Springfield: "We intrust the sacred life of Mr. Lincoln to your keeping; and if you don't protect it, never return to Illinois, for we will murder you on the spot."[21] The words seemed less playful after the harrowing threat in Baltimore.

Lamon had been concerned for Lincoln's safety from the outset of his presidency. He constantly urged Lincoln to accept some form of official protection. Seven years after Lincoln's death Lamon wrote: "In the spring and early summer of 1862 I persistently urged upon Mr. Lincoln the necessity of a military escort to accompany him to and from his residence and place of business, and he as persistently opposed my proposition, always saying, when the subject was referred to, that there was not the slightest occasion for such precaution."[22]

Despite Lincoln's negative attitude toward protection, Company K of the 150th Pennsylvania Volunteer Infantry was assigned to the White House as "bodyguard" in the fall of 1862. Despite its designation as bodyguard, this unit appears to have functioned as little more than providing guard duty over the grounds of the White House and the president's summer retreat at Soldiers' Home. It did not appear to provide personal protection to the president as he moved about the area. Included among their unofficial duties was caring for young Tad Lincoln's goats, a duty they must have relished more than fighting Lee's Army of Northern Virginia.[23] On November 1, 1862, Lincoln penned a brief letter addressed "To Whom it may concern," in which he commended Captain David D. Derickson and the men of Company K for their service as guards at the White House and Soldiers' Home.[24] Captain Derickson (Company K, 150th Pennsylvania Volunteers) gained a certain notoriety for sharing Lincoln's bed at Soldiers' Home when Mary Lincoln was away.[25]

Dissatisfied with Lincoln's safety, Secretary of War Stanton, in December of 1863, ordered a cavalry detail assigned to the White House to specifically guard the president when he traveled about the area. Unlike Lamon, Stanton didn't seek Lincoln's approval but moved ahead on his own. Governor David Todd of Ohio had a special unit raised specifically to guard Lincoln. This unit, known as the Union Light Guard, was stationed near the White House on a piece of land known as the White Lot that adjoined the Treasury Department just to the southeast of the White House stables. The unit was meant to serve as a mounted escort to Lincoln as he traveled about the area.[26] Beginning in the spring of 1864, troopers from this unit accompanied Lincoln when he traveled between the White House and his summer residence at Soldiers' Home. In keeping with his fatalistic nature, Lincoln disliked the guard, feeling it unnecessary and intrusive, and would slip off failing to inform his guards or aides that he was leaving. It was during these trips that Lincoln was at greatest risk of being harmed.

In October 1864, Lincoln finally acquiesced to Lamon's and Stanton's urging for police protection. Lamon requested the District's police superintendent William Webb to supply four men from the Metropolitan Police force for assignment to the White House. Webb agreed, and on November 3, sent Sergeant J.R. Cronin and patrolmen A.T. Donn, T.F. Pendel, and A.C. Smith to Lamon. Subsequently, seven other members of the police force were assigned to the White House detail: W.H. Crook, Joseph Sheldon, W.S. Lewis, G.W. McElfresh, T.T. Hurdle, D. Hopkins, and John F. Parker.[27] While a total of eleven members of the police force eventually served as special bodyguards, there were never more than five members assigned to the detail at any given time.[28]

Police protection was afforded around the clock at the White House. On a hit-or-miss basis at least one officer accompanied Lincoln when he moved about the city visiting various sites—provided he did not evade such protection or forget to notify the guards. There is no known record that describes the duties and responsibilities of these bodyguards, and it remains unclear just what their precise duties were. From sketchy descriptions it seems their principal responsibility was to accompany the president while traveling to and from various sites, but not attend the president while inside these sites.

These forms of protection, however, were limited at best. While discouraging some would-be assassins, they could not have prevented a well-planned attack against Lincoln, and he knew it. Lincoln found such protection more of a discomfort than a help. He acquiesced to bodyguards and cavalry escorts only to mollify Stanton and Lamon. More in jest than seriousness, Lincoln is reported to have stated, "Some of [the cavalrymen] appear to be new hands and very awkward, so that I am more afraid of being shot by the accidental discharge of a carbine or revolver, than of any attempt upon my life by a roving squad of 'Jeb' Stuart's cavalry."[29]

Lamon and others thought Lincoln was especially vulnerable to would-be assassins as he traveled between the White House and his summer residence located in an idyllic rural setting three miles north of the White House. During the spring and summer months, beginning in 1862, Lincoln moved his family to a large two-story "cottage" located on the grounds of the Soldiers' Home. It afforded the Lincolns a respite from the heat and humidity of the city, and reduced their exposure to the numerous diseases that flared up during the hot summer months as a result of an inadequate sewage and sanitation system. Outbreaks of dysentery and typhus were regular events during the hot Washington summers.

Established by an act of Congress on March 5, 1851, the property was purchased with funds obtained by a levy on the officials of Mexico City as payment in lieu of pillage during the Mexican War. General Winfield Scott received $150,000 from the Mexican government that he used to establish a home for old soldiers. The original property consisted of a large, two-story farmhouse and two hundred acres of land that was owned by the wealthy Washington banker George Washington Riggs. A main administration building and two smaller cottages that became the residences of the establishment's administrators soon joined the Riggs farmhouse.

In 1858 President James Buchanan and his secretary of war, John B. Floyd, accepted an invitation to spend the summer months at the Home. In 1862, Lincoln, along with Secretary of War Stanton, followed Buchanan's lead and moved their families to the Home. The Lincolns occupied the Riggs farmhouse while the Stantons moved into a second cottage that had been used by Buchanan in the last year of his presidency. For three summers the Lincoln and Stanton families enjoyed the peaceful surroundings of the rural setting. It was both a retreat from the city and from the continuous stream of office seekers that seemed to harass the president daily.

While living at the Soldiers' Home, Lincoln would travel back and forth between the White House and the Home often alone and on horseback. Because of its remoteness and Lincoln's habit of riding alone, it proved to be the most vulnerable time during his presidency. It also proved to be a problem because of Lincoln's habit of occasionally failing to notify his staff of his movements. Lamon noted that Lincoln would frequently disappear "and before his absence could be noted he would be well on his way to his summer residence, alone, and many times at night."[30] It proved to be a troublesome habit that caused those concerned for his safety considerable anxiety.

On one of these occasions, Lincoln told Lamon of being "suddenly aroused . . . by the report of a rifle" as he approached the main gate leading onto the grounds of the Home. Someone had fired a rifle in the direction of the president. Lincoln spoke lightly of the incident, disturbed only by the fact that he had been "unceremoniously separated from his eight-dollar plug-hat."[31] Lincoln downplayed the incident, telling Lamon, "I can't bring myself to believe that any one has shot or will deliberately shoot at me with the purpose of killing me."[32]

While Lincoln showed little concern for his personal safety, he nonetheless, expressed a belief "that his career would be cut short by violence."[33] Lincoln's fatalistic views led him to believe that little could be done to prevent a determined assassin from carrying out a deadly attack, especially if the assassin were willing to risk his own life in the process. The trips to Soldiers' Home were clearly Lincoln's Achilles' heel that soon became obvious to anyone who took the time to reconnoiter the president as he traveled about. Among those who did observe his peculiar travel habits was a young Confederate officer by the name of Joseph Walker Taylor.

Taylor, known as Walker by his family, had served at Fort Donelson in the west where he escaped capture following the surrender of that fort in February 1862. Wounded just prior to his escape, Taylor made his way to Washington where he convalesced in the home of his uncle, Union Brigadier General Joseph Taylor, the brother of Zachary Taylor. Like many families during the war, the Taylors had members on both sides of the conflict.[34] Young Taylor knew his uncle would not betray him. While recovering from his wound, Taylor became aware of Lincoln's habit of traveling between the White House and the Soldiers' Home.

Fully recovered from his wound, Taylor headed for Richmond, somehow passing through Union lines. On reaching Richmond, Taylor requested an audience with Jefferson Davis. As the nephew of former President Zachary Taylor, young Taylor was closely connected to Davis through Taylor's cousin Sarah Knox Taylor, daughter of Zachary Taylor and first wife of Davis. Taylor was always welcome in the Confederate White House and could expect a warm reception almost anytime he was in Richmond.

After arriving in Richmond, Taylor made his way to the Confederate White House where Davis invited him to join him for breakfast. Joining the two men would be Colonel William Preston Johnston, son of Albert Sidney Johnston and Davis's top aide. Taylor told Davis that he had a plan that could change the entire complexion of the war. He proposed to capture Lincoln and bring him to Richmond. The audacity of the young officer's proposal did not appear to take Davis by surprise. He asked Taylor to explain:

> Lincoln does not leave the White House until evening, or near twilight, and then with only a driver, he takes a lonely ride two or three miles in the country to a place called Soldiers' Home, which is his summer residence.
>
> My point is to collect several of these Kentuckians whom I see about here doing nothing and who are brave enough for such a thing as that, and capture Lincoln, run him down the Potomac, and cross him over just where I crossed, and the next day have him here.[35]

Davis listened intently to the details of the plan and why it would prove successful. When Taylor finally finished Davis responded: "I suppose Lincoln is a man of courage . . . he would undoubtedly resist being captured. . . . I could not stand the imputation of having let Mr. Lincoln be assassinated." Davis then told his nephew: "No sir, I will not give my authority to abduct Lincoln."[36]

Jefferson Davis understood what those who were later accused of Lincoln's murder did not seem to understand: the line between capture and murder was extremely thin. Jefferson Davis was smart enough to know that any attempt to capture the president of the United States and carry him more than one hundred miles through occupied territory could result in the president's death or the death of someone close to him. Such attacks on the head of state were considered off limits. The war was only one year old and neither side felt the need for desperate measures. Black flag warfare had not yet raised its ugly head. Its time, however, was not far off.

Regardless of President Davis's initial disapproval, the idea of capturing Lincoln at Soldiers' Home continued to fascinate the Confederates. Colonel Bradley T. Johnson revived the plan in the winter of 1863–64. He proposed to gather two hundred crack Confederate cavalrymen and make a lightning strike to capture Lincoln at his summer cottage and carry him across the Potomac River into Virginia. With General Wade Hampton's approval, Johnson began gathering and equipping a raiding party. A series of events put the scheme on hold and Johnson did not pursue it. But the proposition still had life. In August 1864 it was passed on, with full approval of Confederate authorities, to Captain Thomas Nelson Conrad, who did not follow through when he found Lincoln well guarded. How John Wilkes Booth was brought into a Lincoln capture operation in July or August 1864 is unclear, but it also contemplated Lincoln's use of Soldiers' Home. The central point not to be overlooked is that by the summer of 1864 Confederate authorities were now willing to strike directly at Lincoln.[37]

Lincoln, more than his would-be protectors, understood the vulnerability of a president in an open society: "I long ago made up my mind that if anybody wants to kill me, he will do it. There are a thousand ways to getting at a man if it is desired that he should be killed."[38] These words proved prophetic on April 14, 1865. The day Lincoln was shot by Booth at Ford's Theatre, he had made use of both the cavalry troop and the police bodyguards at various times during the day and evening. Neither was able to prevent Booth from attacking him.

At the time of Taylor's visit with Davis, Booth was reaching stardom in a series of theatrical engagements in New York City. Booth was at his zenith, dazzling audiences while averaging over $650 a week.[39] The *New York World* announced that he was "an emerging star of real magnitude, and singular through fitful brilliancy."[40] The young actor agreed with the *World*'s assessment: "My goose does indeed hang high (long may she wave)," he wrote in December 1862.[41] To the handsome young Booth, all the world was a stage.

CHAPTER THREE

All the World's a Stage

> All the world's a stage,
> And all the men and women merely players;
> They have their exits and their entrances,
> And one man in his time plays many parts,
> His acts being seven ages.
>
> *As You Like It*, 2.7

John Wilkes Booth was born to fame. His father's acclaim as the country's most famous tragedian covered the family like a shower of sparkling meteors. His mother was a beautiful woman who was devoted to her children. Johnny, next to the youngest of six surviving children, was clearly the favorite. Both parents lavished affection on the young boy, encouraging "self-expression" and bravado. The other siblings showed little jealousy and shared their parents' love of their gregarious younger brother.[1] Of the four boys who survived to manhood, three, Junius, Edwin, and John, would become successful thespians. The youngest boy, Joseph, would become a doctor. Asia, one of two surviving girls, would acquire her father's deep love for literature and show a talent for writing. Only Rosalie, the oldest daughter, would withdraw from the Booth fame and display a "neurotic moodiness" for much of her life.[2]

John's view of life was filled with passion. It was a passion that was inborn, a product of his heritage nurtured by his father's libertarian views. The family ancestry shared many behavioral traits that led others to believe a touch of madness wound its way through the family. Junius Brutus Sr., progenitor of the American clan and John's famous father, was infamous for his erratic behavior. His recognition as a great tragedian, however, caused his peers to overlook his many aberrant acts. A spasmodic alcoholic, the elder Booth alternated between bouts of drunkenness and brilliance as he performed his way across the American stage. To his audiences he was a genius, and stories of his fits of crazy behavior only delighted them more.[3]

While a youth in England, Junius had played the role of Don Juan opposite several paramours in his private life. At least two of these dalliances resulted in pregnancies, costing his barrister father both money and pleadings before the English bar of justice. Junius's lothario traits were passed on to young Wilkes, whose romantic affairs are thought to have surpassed even his father's. But unlike his father, who left bastard children in his wake, John Wilkes Booth was considerably more careful—or lucky—as far as history can determine. Although several spurious claims of Booth's leaving offspring appear in the literature, none of them are supported by fact. When John Wilkes Booth died at the Garrett farm in 1865 he left several women to mourn him, but no sons or daughters.[4]

Junius's father, Richard, was somewhat of a disciplinarian with his son. He bore a past of his own that was not without trouble. At the age of twenty he had fled England for France, where he attempted to secure an enlistment in George Washington's rebel army and thereby free passage to America. Soliciting the aid of John Wilkes, England's famous agitator in the cause of American independence, Richard was rewarded for his efforts by being placed under arrest and returned to England and the care of his father.[5] Although Wilkes supported the Americans, he thought the boy was too young and too reckless to run off and fight in their revolution and notified the authorities of young Richard's whereabouts. Richard retained his admiration for America and Washington. In later years he achieved a mild notoriety by requiring his guests to bow before a portrait of George Washington that adorned his home in England.[6] Many years later, Junius Sr. was remembered for holding burials for insects on the family farm in Bel Air.[7] Such peculiar traits seemed to run in the Booth family.

Junius Brutus Booth was born in London in 1796, the middle of three children. He made his professional theater debut in 1813 at the age of seventeen, which was also the age at which he first impregnated a woman. Following a failed attempt to escape his responsibilities by fleeing to America, Junius and his father appeared in court where the elder Booth pleaded a settlement with the pregnant paramour. Following his reprieve, Junius continued his thespian pursuits on the English stage and soon rose to prominence. Within a few short years Junius was recognized as one of England's up-and-coming young tragedians. It was during this period that he met his first wife, Adelaide Delannoy, while on tour in Belgium. Junius returned to England with his new prize and married Adelaide on May 8, 1815.[8]

It took Junius all of five years and one son to return to his lothario's ways. In 1820, after five years of marriage, he took up with a young flower girl by the name of Mary Ann Holmes whom he met outside the Covent Garden Theatre in London. Junius was twenty-four and Mary Ann was eighteen. She was a beautiful girl who adored the great actor. Mary Ann and Junius fell in love and became traveling companions. In April 1821, the two lovers made their way to the small island of Maderia off the coast of Portugal. It was on Maderia that Mary Ann informed Junius that she was pregnant. Caught between a wife and a pregnant mistress, Junius once more began looking for an escape. The portrait of George Washington that hung in his father's house came back to him in a vision. Like father, like son, the lure of America called to the wayward Booth. Within the day he had secured passage on a ship bound for the United States. Junius swept up his pregnant mistress and set out for America. After a voyage of forty-two days Junius and his new love landed in Norfolk, Virginia.[9] The American progenitor of the soon-to-be-famous Maryland Booths had arrived in his new country with his pregnant Mary Ann and dreams of a new life. Two thousand miles away Adelaide and her young son Richard were unsuspecting of Junius's double life. Adelaide's ignorance would not last forever, however.

After two continents, two "wives," and two children, Junius was just beginning to hit his stride. A year after his arrival in America he sought a safe place of seclusion, a retreat from which he could launch his American career and keep his new wife and son from prying gossip—gossip he did not want to cross the Atlantic and reach Adelaide. He found his retreat on a beautiful piece of farmland twenty miles northeast of Baltimore near the little town of Bel Air, Maryland. Here he decided to settle with his young family. The date was June 4, 1824.[10]

As much as Junius's erratic behavior accompanied his professional life, there seemed to be little of it in his new family life. He was a faithful husband to Mary Ann and a doting father to their children. He settled his family into a two-story log cabin on an adjoining farm, then purchased the cabin and had it moved to his newly acquired property. He soon set about adding two wings to accommodate the large family that he and Mary Ann would bring into the world. In all there would be ten children including young Johnny who was born on the Bel Air farm on May 10, 1838. John Wilkes Booth was the ninth child born to Mary Ann Holmes and Junius Brutus Booth. All of the children were born out of wedlock. Of the ten, six would survive early childhood and grow into adults. Although Junius loved Mary Ann very much, he had failed to marry her. He could not, since he was still married to Adelaide. In the twenty years following his arrival in America, he returned to England and Adelaide on only two occasions, in 1825 and 1836. Adelaide would eventually find out about her husband's adulterous ways, but only after he had fathered ten children with Mary Ann.

In 1842, twenty-one years after Junius had arrived in America, his twenty-two-year-old son Richard visited him. It didn't take Richard long to learn of Mary Ann and the family on the Maryland farm. Richard wrote to his mother back in England telling her about his father and urging her to come to America as soon as possible and "establish his legitimacy." Adelaide would come, but she was determined to do more than establish Richard's legitimacy as Junius's son.

Adelaide arrived in Baltimore and was met by Richard, who had rented a furnished house for her. Adelaide's anger on finding her husband with his illegitimate children living a second life with Mary Ann did not upset her rational thinking. Writing home to her sister, Adelaide revealed her plans for her unfaithful husband: "He [Junius] is just about to commence his winter tour. I don't want to do anything to prevent him from making money, so I shall wait until he comes to Baltimore, and as soon as he arrives my lawyer will fall on his back like a bomb."[11]

Adelaide was true to her word. She waited for her husband to return from his acting tour and then pounced on him with fury. After a rancorous battle, waged almost exclusively by Adelaide, a divorce was granted in Baltimore on April 18, 1851. Three weeks later on young Wilkes's thirteenth birthday (May 10), Junius and Mary Ann were quietly married. Adelaide never returned to England, but remained in the United States never far from the Booths of Bel Air. She died in 1858 at the age of sixty-six and lies buried in New Cathedral Cemetery in Baltimore. On her tombstone are carved the words, "Wife of Junius Brutus Booth, tragedian." Such was the powerful image of this great icon of the American stage that even in death the spurned Adelaide wished to be remembered as his wife.

The first fifteen years of his life, young John would alternate between the Bel Air farm and a second home his father had purchased in Baltimore on Exeter Street. In 1851, the elder Booth decided to begin construction of a fine brick home close to the old homestead in Bel Air. His stature and finances had outgrown the log house and he decided to build a home more attuned to his fame and family. He named it Tudor Hall, a fitting title for the manor of a Shakespearean lord.

Junius would never see the home completed, however. He died on November 30, 1852, aboard a river steamer en route from New Orleans to a scheduled performance in Cincinnati, Ohio. A year later Mary Ann gathered up her three remaining children and moved into the unfinished construction. Junius Jr. and Edwin were in California, Joseph was away at boarding school, leaving only Rosalie, Asia, and John at home with Mary Ann.[12]

John and Asia grew inseparable during these years in the Maryland countryside. Described as extremely bright and strong-minded by all that knew her, Asia assumed a dominant role over her younger brother. She hovered over him, schooling and encouraging him in those things she felt important. Historian Terry Alford described their relationship together: "The two would pass their time in horseback riding, village dances, picnics, camp meetings and walks in the 'wild old woods' nearby."[13] It was an idyllic life.

Asia described her brother as an indifferent student who nevertheless survived each of the schools he attended. These included the private tutoring of Susan Hyde and Martin Kerney (1844–46), the Bel Air Academy in Bel Air, Maryland (1846–51), the Milton School for Boys in Cockeysville, Maryland (1851–52), St. Timothy's Hall in Catonsville, Maryland (1853), and Bland's Boarding Academy in York, Pennsylvania (1854). It was while a student at St. Timothy's Hall in Catonsville that John became a friend of the son of a Baltimore baker, Samuel Bland Arnold. It was also while a student at St. Tim's that young Johnny was baptized into the Episcopal faith. There still exists a record among the school's archives attesting to the baptism of Booth and his younger brother, Joseph, on January 20, 1854.[14]

While a student at the Milton School for Boys in Cockeysville, Booth experienced the tragic death of the father of one of his classmates. The father was killed by Black runaways who resisted efforts by the father to return them to slavery. So dramatic was the event to the young Booth that he wrote about it nine years later following a political rally in Philadelphia where he was visiting his mother and sister Rosalie.[15]

At the time Booth wrote about the incident he was in the ascendancy of his acting career, which was about to reach its zenith. He arrived in Philadelphia in December 1860, after spending more than a month in Montgomery, Alabama, where he learned of Lincoln's election as president on November 6. Toward the end of December, Booth attended a large rally in Independence Hall Square in front of the great state house.[16] Fears of disunion were growing daily. There was an air of anxiety everywhere as people began to fear the worst. The rally had been called to assure the people of the South that their Northern brothers were their friends. Abolition was not a policy shared by the majority of Northerners.

Apparently stirred by the oratory, Booth returned to his room where he sat down and wrote out the draft of a speech that he may have planned to give before the next rally. He was inspired. The speech is a long, rambling discourse on the crisis and its causes. But within the body of its rambling text, Booth's innermost passion is revealed: "There is a time when men should act for themselves and not under the guidance of a few political leaders who use them only for their own ends, I tell you Sirs when treason weighs heavy in the scale, it is a time for us to throw off all gentler feelings of our natures and summon resolution, pride, justice, Ay, and revenge, to take the place of those nobler passions in the human heart, respect, forgiveness and Brotherly love."[17]

Booth's call for revenge in place of "forgiveness and Brotherly love" would later bear bitter fruit. The crisis that had been coming for several months began to occupy more and more of his thoughts. Booth correctly perceived the problem when he asked and answered his own question: "What has been the cause of this secession—," he wrote, "why nothing but the constant agitation of the slavery question."[18] He continued on:

> The south has a right according to the constitution to keep and hold slaves. And we have no right under that constitution to interfere with her or her slaves.

> Instead of looking upon slavery as a sin I hold it to be a happiness for themselves and a social and political blessing for us. I have been through the whole south and have marked the happiness of master and man. True, I have seen the black man whipped but only when he deserved much more than he received.
>
> What right have you to exclude southern rights from the territories? Because you are the strongest? I have as much right to carry my slave into the territories as you have to carry your paid servant or your children.

The concept of slavery as a blessing for both the slave and the master was a common belief in the South. It was a blessing God himself ordained.[19] Booth continued:

> I believe country right or wrong, but gentlemen the whole union is our country and no particular state. We should love the whole Union and not only the state in which we were born. We are all one people and should have but one heart. Thank God I have a heart big enough for all the states.
>
> The South wants justice, has waited for it long. She will wait no longer.
>
> The South is leaving us. O would to God that Clay and Webster could hear those words. Weep fellow countrymen, for the brightest half of our stars upon the nation's banner have grown dim. Once out my friends, all will be dark and dreary.
>
> . . . The south has a right according to the constitution to keep and hold slaves. And we have no right under that constitution to interfere with her or her slaves.[20]

Near the end of the manuscript, Booth told of the incident involving his schoolboy friend, Tommy Gorsuch. Young Tommy's father, Edward Gorsuch, had been killed, some said murdered, while attempting to recover his runaway slaves from a Pennsylvania farmhouse. Booth ended his unfinished manuscript with the following account: "The fugitive slave law. Gentlemen, when I was a school boy, my bosom friend was a boy three years my senior named Gorruge [Thomas Gorsuch], he was as noble a youth as any living. He had two brothers grown to be men. And an old father who loved and was beloved by them. He was all that a man of honour should be. Two of his negroes committed a robbery, they were informed upon. They nearly beat the informer to death. They ran away from Maryland, came to this state [Pennsylvania]. The father, the two sons, the boy my playmate, came to this state under the protection of the fugitive slave law (not only to recover their property, but to arrest the thieves who belonged to them). . . ."[21]

Booth's speech stopped short at this point without finishing the story of Tommy Gorsuch's father. Today, we know the incident by the name given to it by the newspapers in 1851, the Christiana Riot. The incident in Christiana was a microcosm for the growing concern sweeping the nation over slavery. It was a dark harbinger of the violence that was becoming endemic in the decade leading up to the Civil War. Most important, Booth used it years later as an example of the unwarranted "constant agitation of the slavery question."[22]

Edward Gorsuch, young Tommy's father, owned several hundred acres of rich land north of Baltimore where he farmed wheat and corn with the help of several slaves. In September of 1849 four of Gorsuch's slaves made their escape across the border into the neighboring free state of Pennsylvania. Two years had passed with no word of the slaves. The matter had begun to fade from Gorsuch's mind when he received a letter from a man named William Padgett. Padgett, who earned the better part of his living as an informer on fugitive slaves, wrote Gorsuch that he had information about Gorsuch's runaways. Padgett had learned that all four lived not far away in the village of Christiana in Lancaster County, Pennsylvania. For a fee, Padgett would be happy to help Gorsuch in gaining their capture. Gorsuch accepted Padgett's offer and set out for Pennsylvania accompanied by his son Dickinson Gorsuch, his cousin Joshua Gorsuch, his nephew Dr. Thomas Pearce, and two of his neighbors, Nathan Nelson and Nicholas Hutchings.[23]

Padgett led the party to the home of a free Black named William Parker, where Gorsuch found two of his slaves. Parker was himself an escaped slave who had come to the area several years earlier. Parker had organized the local Blacks into an effective resistance group by teaching them to fight violence with violence. Shortly after arriving at Parker's house, Gorsuch and his posse found themselves confronting a large number of free Blacks from the surrounding area.

After several tense minutes of bantering back and forth between Parker and Gorsuch, violence erupted. Someone struck the elder Gorsuch with a club. Stunned, he fell to his knees. Seeing his father fall, Dickinson Gorsuch raised his revolver to shoot toward the attackers only to be struck across the arm with such force that the revolver was knocked to the ground. At that moment all hell broke loose. When calm eventually returned to the scene, young Dickinson Gorsuch lay wounded from a shotgun blast to the abdomen. Edward Gorsuch was found kneeling in a pool of his own blood. Protruding from his neck was the rusty blade of an old corn cutter whose handle had been worn smooth from years of use. Edward Gorsuch died within the hour. His son Dickinson would eventually recover from his wounds.

In the days following the fight at William Parker's house, the national press began to refer to the incident as the Christiana Riot. The Southern press made Gorsuch a cause celebre in their defense of slavery, demanding

Federal action. Following the arrest of several area Blacks and three White men who had refused to aid the Federal marshal on the scene, a sensational trial soon followed. The trial was turned into a test between two cultures: Southern versus Northern, slave versus free. In the end, freedom prevailed. The twelve jurors took only fifteen minutes to return a verdict of "not guilty."[24] Southerners were outraged, while Northerners celebrated.

Edward Gorsuch had been determined to carry on his way of life, even if it resulted in his death. To his Southern countrymen, "He died for law."[25] To Northern abolitionists, he died in an evil cause receiving his just reward. The death of Tommy Gorsuch's father touched the young John Wilkes Booth personally. While he would move on with his life, he would not forget what happened in Christiana.

The young boy eventually put death behind him and turned to brighter, gayer moments in his life. As he grew older he became even more handsome and more charming. He captivated all who crossed his path. John Deery, a close friend and owner of Booth's favorite billiard establishment in Washington, remembered Booth in later years: "John cast a spell over most men . . . and I believe over most women."[26] Others echoed Deery's assessment: "He was one of the best raconteurs to whom I ever listened. As he talked he threw himself into his words, brilliant, ready, enthusiastic. He could hold a group spellbound by the hour at the force and fire and beauty of him."[27] His brother Edwin would remark wistfully, "John Wilkes had the genius of my father, and was far more gifted than I."[28]

In 1874 Asia Booth Clarke wrote a memoir of her brother and her family.[29] In it she provides a sister's insight, painting a sympathetic picture while shedding light on the darker, more complex character of her brother. She loved to write and was an accomplished correspondent. Like all the Booth children, she inherited her father's love of classical literature and his personality quirks. Small trifles could send her off sulking. Her siblings were cautioned to leave her alone during these little fits. To one of her closest friends she wrote just before her twenty-first birthday, "Oh Jean, my Jean, all is vanity."[30] Vanity was clearly a Booth family trait.

Asia and John made a wonderful couple. Both were bright, witty, and full of life. John loved his older sister, and she adored him. In her memoir she wrote: "As a boy he was beloved by his associates, and as a man few could withstand the fascination of his modest, gentle manners. He inherited some of the most prepossessing qualities of his father, . . . he had the black hair and large hazel eyes of his mother. These were fringed heavily with long upcurling lashes, a noticeable peculiarity as rare as beautiful."[31]

But Asia's flattering description of her brother was not without its shadows. With his father dead, brothers June and Ned on tour, and young Joe away at school, it was a feminine world that surrounded young John. Its mores would bond him even closer to the Southern culture he would passionately adopt in his adult years. It had a certain political correctness that rejected democratic principles. Asia described how her younger brother bristled at the thought of the women of Tudor Hall dining at the same table as the White laborers. He would have none of it. It simply wasn't the Southern way. Asia may well have influenced her brother in his view of social graces. She wrote about the difference between Northern women and Southern ladies: "There were no 'Masters' and 'Mistresses' in the North. Thus [Northern women] unwillingly yielded, and forced themselves to encourage undue familiarity with those, too often the refuse of other countries, who had been in more servile bondage than the American slaves. Often grating under the insolent freedom of these ignorant menials whom they dared not even to call servants, northern women vaunted their love of equality and called themselves democratic."

Asia described her brother's first signs of "undemocratic feeling" when it came time to share their meals with the farmhands: "It was the custom for members of the family to dine and sup with the white men who did the harvesting. Wilkes had a struggle with his pride and knew not which to abide by, his love of equality and brotherhood, or that southern reservation which jealously kept the white laborer from free association with his employer or superior."[32]

According to Asia, "Wilkes made a compromise with his pride, as he termed it, and desired us, his mother and sisters, not to be present at the meals with the men." It was a short leap from this view of Northern crudity to the uncouth "Railsplitter" from the west. In Lincoln, John could only see an "ignorant menial" whose strange view of a republican democracy included the lowest forms of society at the dinner table. To John Wilkes Booth, Lincoln was a man who both ate his meals and blew his nose with his fingers.

Although aristocratic in character, Booth was not averse to a little sweat of his own, albeit aristocratic sweat. After his father died and the family moved into Tudor Hall, Booth tried his hand at farming. It was to no avail. While the spirit was willing, the body was not. He was not a sower but a reaper. Let others do the sowing. He had bigger plans.

In August of 1855 the seventeen-year-old Booth began his formal acting career. It was at the same age that his father first played upon the stage in England. Young John played the part of Richmond in *Richard III* at the Charles Street Theatre in Baltimore.[33] It was a flawed performance, perhaps premature, but the thrill had overtaken him. He played to tolerant reviews more out of respect for his father than for him. The truth was that his poor performance was due to poor preparation. Determined not to ride on his father's or brother's coattails, he billed himself as "J. Wilkes," reserving his full name until that day when he would do it credit and not embarrassment. He told Asia he would never be able to equal his father. Perhaps not, but he would come close, very close. Over the next ten years he would ascend to the heights of his father's profession and claim his own place among America's matinee idols.

By 1858 Booth had accepted a position paying eleven dollars a week with the Richmond Theatre in Richmond, Virginia.[34] He was still performing under the name "J. Wilkes." Booth was in the employ of the theater's owners during the 1858–59 season and was, therefore, well placed for one of the most dramatic events in American history, an event that was spawned from the violence of Christiana eight years before.[35]

On October 16, 1859, John Brown and his "liberation army" of eighteen men seized the United States armory at Harpers Ferry, (West) Virginia. Brown had sought to foment a major slave uprising throughout Virginia and elsewhere and to begin the final purge of slavery from American soil. A colonel in the United States Army, Robert E. Lee, and his handsome, young Lieutenant, James Ewell Brown "Jeb" Stuart, were sent to Harpers Ferry where they soon quelled the uprising and took Brown and other survivors prisoner.

Brown was placed on trial and charged with treason against the sovereign state of Virginia. The attack on a United States arsenal was treated as a state crime. After a trial of one week, Brown was found guilty and sentenced to hang on December 2, 1859. Two weeks after the trial ended, the Richmond Militia was ordered to Charlestown, (West) Virginia, the site of the hanging, to ensure order at the spectacle and to represent the capital city at the execution. Brown's hanging would be a special state event.

Booth was in Richmond fulfilling a theatrical contract at the time of the trial. On learning that a militia unit was about to travel to Charlestown, Booth was able to convince his military friends with his persuasive "force and fire and beauty" to allow him to join their ranks. Wearing a borrowed uniform, Booth climbed aboard the train and bundled with his new comrades as they made their way west into the Blue Ridge Mountains of Virginia.

During the next two weeks Booth took his turn standing sentinel and serving his adopted "state's cause." It was a wonderful feeling, and one that carried no threat of harm. It afforded Booth all the glory and none of the danger. On the ill-fated day of Brown's execution, Booth stood with the Richmond troops encircling the scaffold that the great abolitionist would ascend to meet his maker. Booth could not help but admire the fire and passion of the old man's commitment to his cause even if it was an evil cause. There was an attraction to Brown's death that fixated the twenty-one-year-old Booth. He told Asia that Brown was a man inspired, "the grandest character of this century!"[36]

Brown's hanging did not quell the unrest that ran throughout the country. It only served to incense the abolitionists and reinforced the fears of many in the South. To many in the North, Brown was a martyr; to those in the South, he was a harbinger of things to come. To Booth and his cohorts, Lincoln would soon replace John Brown as the hated symbol of abolition. In one of his fits of passion Booth told his sister, "*He* [Lincoln] is made the tool of the North, to crush out slavery, by robbery, rapine, slaughter and bought armies" (Booth's emphasis).[37] The comment about "bought armies" was a reference to the undesirable aliens of Europe who had made their way into the mainstream of America, in Asia's words, "The refuse of the other countries."

From 1861 through 1864 Booth continued to ply his trade of acting and emerged as a genuine star of the American stage. Under the "star" system, the finest actors and actresses toured the country performing at all the great theaters as headliners supported by local players who formed the theater's "stock" company. As a "star," Booth earned from hundreds to thousands of dollars a week including a percentage of the box office.[38] At the height of his career he earned $20,000 in one year, an amount equal to a quarter of a million today.[39] Booth's star tours took him around the country, from Boston to New Orleans, and as far west as Leavenworth, Kansas. Wherever he traveled and performed he was hailed as a good fellow and a great actor. By 1864 Booth had achieved all he could hope for in the field of acting. Freed of his father's shadow, his star now formed its own constellation.

The year 1864 saw changes in Booth, both in his professional and personal behavior. He began to experience difficulty with hoarseness. His throat problems have been attributed to a variety of causes ranging from improper care of his voice to bronchitis to syphilis, and are thought by some writers to be the reason Booth left his acting career.[40] His bouts of hoarseness were not persistent, however. His difficulty with his voice was episodic throughout 1864, and Booth appeared in several performances where several laudatory reviews made no reference to any difficulty with his voice or ability to project.

Speculation claimed that Booth developed a severe cold that eventually turned into bronchitis as a result of becoming snowbound in St. Joseph, Missouri, in January of 1864. Scheduled to perform at Ben DeBar's theater in St. Louis, Missouri, the following week, Booth was unable to travel by train because of the heavy snows.[41] He was able to hire a four-horse sleigh and travel sixty miles overland to St. Louis under extremely severe conditions.[42]

Although Booth does not write in his letters of contracting a cold or bronchitis, some writers have speculated that his prolonged exposure to the subzero weather during the trip to Breckinridge may have been the cause of his impaired speaking ability.[43] While this may be true, it did not force Booth from the stage. Booth performed as late as March 18, 1865, in the very theater where he would murder Lincoln, and where he received his usual laudatory reviews for his performance.

It was not bronchitis that saw John Wilkes Booth turn away from the stage in late 1864; it was his hatred for Abraham Lincoln and concern for his beloved South. Booth no longer had time for the stage. He was becoming consumed with only one passion, Abraham Lincoln. In 1860 he wrote: "Now that we have found the serpent that madens [*sic*] us, we should crush it in its birth."[44] The serpent was abolition. Four years later he was even more convinced that something great must be done if his beloved South was to survive. He became convinced that he was the one to crush the serpent's chief apostle, King Abraham Africanus.

Events were moving Booth and the Confederacy's leaders closer and closer together. The issuance of the Emancipation Proclamation "had raised to a new level of intensity the greatest fear of most southerners . . . a bloody slave uprising."[45] The proclamation's authorization to enlist Blacks into the Union army was viewed as "tantamount to granting them a license to murder, rape, and pillage their former owners."[46] Lincoln's call for emancipation was immoral—an act that threatened the life of every woman and child throughout the South.

Stephen Fowler Hale, secession commissioner from Alabama, proclaimed that abolition policies such as Lincoln's must lead to "amalgamation [of the races] or the extinction of the one or the other. Could Southern men submit to such degradation and ruin?"[47] William C. Harris, commissioner from Mississippi, answered for his state: "She had rather see the last of her race, men, women and children, immolated in one common funeral pile, than see them subjected to the degradation of civil, political and social equality with the negro race."[48]

Lincoln's heinous act calling for emancipation was the first step in stripping away the unwritten rule of "civilized warfare" that held political leaders immune from becoming military targets. As despicable as Lincoln's Emancipation Proclamation was to the leaders of the South, it would be followed by an even more heinous event that would place Lincoln in the center of the bull's-eye. A black flag was about to be raised.

CHAPTER FOUR

The Black Flag Is Raised

The purest treasure mortal times afford
Is spotless reputation.

Richard the Second, 1.1

One of Abraham Lincoln's great hopes for resolving the slavery crisis lay in his plan of compensated emancipation. Realizing that ending slavery by military force could come about only with great loss of life and national treasure, Lincoln wanted to shorten the war and accomplish emancipation by having the Federal government compensate slave owners by purchasing their "property." In his message to Congress on March 6, 1862, Lincoln pointed out that "any member of Congress, with the census-tables and Treasury reports before him, can readily see for himself how very soon the current expenditures of this war would purchase, at fair valuation, all the slaves in any named State."[1]

Lincoln believed that purchasing the slaves would save thousands of lives and millions of dollars. It was a simple case of common sense to Lincoln. His compensation plan was aimed at the Border States of Delaware, Kentucky, Maryland, and Missouri. These four slave states remained loosely tied to the Union. Maryland, Kentucky, and Missouri formed a broad buffer zone or "border" between the Northern states and those of the South. Their place in the Union was crucial and Lincoln and Jefferson Davis placed them high on their agendas. Davis hoped that these critical states would eventually secede and cast their lot with the Confederacy. To do so would prove the deathblow to reunion. This was especially true of Kentucky, the state of Lincoln's birth. Lincoln's connections with Kentucky ran deep. His three law partners were Kentuckians, as was his wife. Henry Clay, his "beau ideal," and Joshua Speed, his closest friend, were both Kentuckians.[2] Lincoln wanted Kentucky in the Union, but more than that, he needed Kentucky. Lincoln had said "to lose Kentucky is to lose the whole game."[3] Conversely, Lincoln believed that if Kentucky and her sister Border States were to declare against slavery by accepting compensated emancipation, the Confederacy was doomed to fail.

On July 12, 1862, he addressed an appeal to representatives of the Border States offering a plan for gradual emancipation: "Let the states which are in rebellion see, definitely and certainly, that, in no event, will the states you represent ever join their proposed Confederacy, and they can not, much longer maintain the contest."[4] On July 14, Lincoln followed his appeal by introducing his own draft of a bill that would result in compensation for slave property among the Border States. The bill called for the transfer of six-percent interest-bearing bonds of the United States Treasury to each state equal to the aggregate value of all the slaves within that state based on the census of 1860. The Congress would fix the price per slave. The transfer would be coordinated with emancipation in installments as slaves were set free, or the whole amount turned over at once if emancipation were immediate.[5] One day later, on July 15, a majority of Border State representatives rejected the proposal on the ground that "the Federal government could not stand the expense."[6] This, of course, was not true. As Lincoln pointed out in a letter to newspaper editor Henry J. Raymond following his March 6 message to the Congress, "one half-day's cost of this war would pay for all the slaves in Delaware, at four hundred dollars per head—that eighty-seven days cost of this war would pay for all [the slaves] in Delaware, Maryland, the District of Columbia, Kentucky, and Missouri at the same price."[7] Did anyone really believe that to continue the war would cost less money, let alone fewer lives, than purchasing all of the slaves in the Border States, thus isolating the Confederacy even further?

Frustrated in his efforts at compensation, Lincoln pulled the trigger on the Confederacy's slavocracy by issuing his preliminary Emancipation Proclamation on September 22, 1862. In it he declared, "All persons held as slaves within any state, or designated part of a state, the people whereof shall then be in rebellion against the United States shall be then, thenceforward, and forever free."[8]

What prompted Lincoln to issue his proclamation after seventeen months of war is arguable, but its effect, which became official on January 1, 1863, established several important objectives. First, by declaring those slaves who were covered by its provisions "forever free," it irrevocably linked any future reunion with emancipation. Second, it called for the enlistment of Black men into the Union army.[9] And third, it ended any thought of "restoration," or returning to conditions as they existed prior to hostilities. With the issuance of his proclamation, Lincoln closed the door to any hope of returning to the Union as it once was. Emancipation became the central issue of the conflict.

This irrevocable nature of Lincoln's action was one that Jefferson Davis understood. In his message to the Confederate Congress on January 12, 1863, eleven days after the proclamation became official, Davis said, "A restoration of the Union *has now* been rendered forever impossible." Davis went on to state that the proclamation was "a measure by which several millions of human beings of an inferior race, peaceful and contented laborers in their sphere, are doomed to extermination, while at the same time they are encouraged to a general assassination of their masters by the insidious recommendation 'to abstain from violence unless in necessary self-defense.'"[10] It was this last "recommendation" that caused the harshest reaction among the proclamation's critics. Both Davis and the British government decried the statement, claiming it was aimed at doing just what it asked slaves not to do, rise up and overthrow their masters using violence where necessary which, in reality, was everywhere.

Davis described the proclamation as the "most execrable measure recorded in the history of guilty man."[11] In retaliation for Lincoln's proclamation, he defiantly announced that he would deliver to state officials all commissioned officers of the United States Army that may be captured and they would be dealt with in accordance with each state's laws covering individuals who incite slave insurrection. Such laws carried the death penalty. Davis went on to say that enlisted men, however, would still be paroled as "unwilling instruments in the commission of these crimes."[12] Fortunately, cooler heads prevailed and Davis's bluster was never carried out. But the very act of declaring emancipation throughout the rebellious South was considered an act outside the bounds of civilized warfare. To Davis and his cohorts, the emancipation proclamation was an incitement to slave revolt with the inevitable consequence of the massacre of innocent women and children. Davis reduced Lincoln to a barbarian when he described his actions as "execrable." Such a person was not entitled to protection under the rules of civilized warfare.

While Lincoln's Emancipation Proclamation called for the enlistment of Blacks into the military, little happened until May 22, 1863.[13] On that date, the War Department established the Bureau of Colored Troops. The Southern reaction to the enlistment of Black troops was virulent. Black soldiers who fell into the hands of the Confederate military would not be treated as prisoners of war. Alarming incidents of Confederate atrocities involving Black troops began to filter north. Captured Black troops were often executed summarily or forced into slavery.[14] In a letter to Confederate general Richard Taylor, General Kirby Smith's assistant adjutant general S.S. Anderson stated what disposition should be taken in regard to Black soldiers by writing, "No quarter should be shown them. If taken prisoners, however, they should be turned over to the executive authorities of the States in which they may be captured, in obedience to the proclamation of the President of the Confederate States."[15] On hearing that Taylor's troops had taken Black soldiers as prisoners, Kirby Smith wrote to Richard Taylor: "I hope this may not be so, and that your subordinates who have been in command of capturing parties may have recognized the propriety of giving no quarter to armed negroes and their officers. In this way we may be relieved from a disagree-

Cottage Grove Public Librai

able dilemma."[16] The "propriety of giving no quarter" was akin to murder. Word of the "disagreeable dilemma" soon reached Lincoln. In July of 1863, Lincoln responded by issuing an "Order of Retaliation" which stated in part:

> The government of the United States will give the same protection to all its soldiers, and if the enemy shall sell or enslave anyone because of his color, the offense shall be punished by retaliation upon the enemy's prisoners in our possession.
>
> It is therefore ordered that for every [Black] soldier of the United States killed in violation of the laws of war, a rebel soldier shall be executed; and for everyone enslaved by the enemy or sold into slavery, a rebel soldier shall be placed at hard labor on the public works and continued at such labor until the other shall be released and receive the treatment due to a prisoner of war.[17]

Despite the threats, neither Davis nor Lincoln retaliated. Davis's message to his Congress and Lincoln's order of retaliation, however, are two examples that challenge the modern belief that the American Civil War was fought by gentlemen who exhibited only the highest standard of moral conduct in carrying out their duty. As the war progressed both sides began to adopt actions that, at a personal and governmental level, fell under the concept of black flag warfare. By the winter of 1864, the burdens of a cruel war began to bear heavily on both sides. As the weeks turned into months with no clear resolution in sight on either side, strategies began to change. Targeting the respective heads of state was no longer outside the boundary of acceptable warfare. By the end of 1863 it seems clear that Jefferson Davis and Abraham Lincoln were viewed as legitimate military targets, as evidenced by the events that took place in the first part of 1864.

In February of 1864 a daring plan was hatched in Washington aimed at the very heart of the Confederacy. The plan had its antecedents in the fall of 1863. By November of that year an estimated 13,000 Union soldiers were being held in prisoner-of-war camps in the Richmond area. These men were held at two principal sites, Libby prison in the heart of Richmond and Belle Isle prison camp located on an island in the James River immediately south of the city.

As reports began to filter into Washington it became clear that the conditions of these prisoners was appalling. With Lee hard pressed to feed his own army, Union prisoners were at greater risk of malnutrition and starvation. Not only were prisoners suffering from a shortage of rations, but word also reached Lincoln that the men were often subjected to brutal treatment by sadistic guards. To make matters worse, Mary Lincoln's brother, Captain David Todd, was one of the wardens in charge of Libby prison. Sergeant Charles Whitcomb, a Michigan cavalryman, told a House committee investigating the treatment of Union prisoners how Captain Todd had slashed him across his leg with a saber in an unprovoked attack simply because he hated Yankees.[18] Such treatment was believed common in Richmond's prisons. Lincoln felt increasing pressure to take action.

In May of 1863, during the Chancellorsville campaign, Major General George Stoneman was sent by the Army of the Potomac's commanding general, Joseph Hooker, on a raid behind Lee's lines in an effort to disrupt Lee's supply lines. Moving completely around Lee's army, contingents of Stoneman's cavalry breached the Richmond defenses and came within two miles of the center of the city. Several Union officers imprisoned in the city reported to their superiors following their exchange that the defenses protecting Richmond were so poor that Stoneman's men could have entered Richmond without opposition and burned it to the ground. One of these paroled officers, General August Willich, personally met with Lincoln on May 8 and told Lincoln about the defenses surrounding Richmond.[19] Impressed with Willich's story, Lincoln sent Hooker a telegram in which he stated, "There was not a sound pair of legs in Richmond, and our men, could have safely gone in and burnt everything & brought us Jeff. Davis."[20] Lincoln was not one to write idle thoughts. The idea of bringing out Jeff Davis was in Lincoln's head, and he favored the thought.

On February 6, 1864, Brigadier General Isaac J. Wistar, under the command of Major General Benjamin F. Butler, launched a cavalry raid against Richmond designed to breach the poorly manned defenses and enter the city freeing Union prisoners, destroy key facilities, and "capture some of the leaders of the rebellion," including Jefferson Davis.[21] James W. White, a prominent New York politician allied with Horace Greeley, wrote to Greeley following White's visit to Butler's headquarters shortly before the raid began. White stated that one of the objectives of the raid was to "first capture Davis and then blow up the Tredegar Ironworks."[22]

Butler was in command of the Department of Virginia and North Carolina at the time, and had made certain that both Lincoln and Secretary of War Stanton were fully aware of the planned raid against the Confederate capital and her leaders.[23] Wistar's raid was aborted, however, when his troops reached the key crossing points of the Chickahominy River and found them heavily guarded in anticipation of the Yankee raiders. Confederate intelligence had received detailed information about the raid and had ample time to prepare to meet it head on at the point where it had planned to cross the river.

Realizing that both the loss of surprise and the concentrated Confederate defense jeopardized his plan, Wistar ordered his forces to retreat. Despite the failure of this planned raid, it clearly demonstrated that black flag tactics were aimed at leaders of the Confederacy. Wistar's instructions to capture "the leaders of the rebellion" appeared in the Richmond papers claiming a plot existed "to liberate the prisoners and assassinate the President."[24]

While Lincoln was apparently disappointed at Wistar's failure, he was still in favor of attempting to rescue the imprisoned soldiers whose worsening condition weighed heavily on his mind. Within three weeks of the Wistar raid, a second plan emerged, this one from within the Army of the Potomac. Unlike the Wistar raid that had Butler's full support as commanding general, the second raid was opposed by the command structure of the Army of the Potomac. Brigadier General Judson Kilpatrick, commander of the Third Division of the Cavalry Corps, Army of the Potomac, proposed another raid against Richmond led by himself. Nine months earlier Kilpatrick, as part of the Stoneman raid, led a cavalry brigade to the very gates of Richmond only to fall back without attempting to enter the city. It was following this raid that Lincoln sent his telegram to Hooker telling him of Richmond's vulnerability and the lost opportunity to capture Davis. Kilpatrick's near success in May of 1863 must have impressed Lincoln enough to give him some hope of eventual success. Lincoln must have realized that burning everything in Richmond and capturing Jefferson Davis could not happen without the loss of civilian life. While capturing the commander in chief of an enemy force was within the laws of warfare, targeting civilians was not. Once again the black flag was raised.

Kilpatrick's proposed raid called for the same main objective as Wistar's earlier raid, namely the freeing of Union prisoners. Accompanying the Kilpatrick forces was a young cavalry officer, Colonel Ulric Dahlgren. Young Dahlgren was the son of Rear Admiral John A. Dahlgren, who was in command of the South Atlantic Blockading Squadron. The younger Dahlgren was personally acquainted with Lincoln and well liked by the president. Kilpatrick's plan consisted of a two-pronged approach with Kilpatrick attacking Richmond from the northwest while Dahlgren would slip around to the south of Richmond with five hundred men and attack from that point. Dahlgren would cross over the James River, free the Union prisoners at Belle Isle prison, and with his supplemented force enter Richmond from the south. One group of men, known as "Pioneers," armed with oakum, turpentine, and torpedoes, were assigned to burn the city.[25]

It was essential that the two forces coordinate their attacks if they were to be successful. Kilpatrick, however, met resistance and aborted his attack while Dahlgren became trapped north of the James River unable to find a fordable spot across the rain-swollen current. Cut off from Kilpatrick and unable to backtrack, Dahlgren tried to lead his troopers to the east around Richmond, only to run into a Confederate ambush. During a brief exchange of gunfire in which Dahlgren's small troop scattered, the young officer was shot from his saddle, dying instantly.

The raid would have been recorded as just another failure in Union efforts to breech the Richmond defenses except for one incredible error on the part of young Dahlgren. In a search of his body following his death, several documents were found that caused a sensation within the Confederate leadership and indignant denials from the Union military. Two of the documents contained written instructions detailing the raiders' objectives. These objectives could be explained in no other terms except black flag warfare. One document, with the heading "Headquarters, Third Cavalry Corps" and addressed to "Officers and Men," outlined the objectives of Dahlgren's attack. The troopers were to free the prisoners from Belle Isle and then, leading the contingent into Richmond, burn the city and capture Davis and his cabinet. A second document was more detailed, giving instructions: "The men must keep together and well in hand, and once in the city it must be destroyed and Jeff Davis and cabinet killed."[26] These papers were written in Dahlgren's hand.

One can imagine the havoc that would occur if thousands of brutally treated prisoners of war were turned loose in the capital of the Confederacy. Releasing such prisoners into the city of Richmond armed with oakum and turpentine could only prove disastrous for the civilian population of that city. Such action was viewed by most Southerners as an act of terrorism. Calling for the killing of Davis and his cabinet was nothing short of murder. The Confederate leaders were both outraged and delighted. Outraged at the barbarity of the proposed plan and delighted that such conclusive evidence had fallen into their hands—evidence that could be laid at the feet of President Lincoln.

The Confederates were quick to release the text of the orders and make photographic copies to prove their authenticity. It was a major propaganda coup for the Confederacy. Davis instructed Lee to give copies of the documents under a flag of truce to the Union army's commanding general, George Meade.[27] Meade's response was to distance himself as far as possible from the whole affair. He had not authorized the raid and did not support it in any manner. In responding to Lee's inquiry, Meade wrote, "In reply I have to state that neither the United States Government, myself, nor General Kilpatrick authorized, sanctioned, or approved the burning of the city of Richmond and the killing of Mr. Davis and cabinet."[28] Meade made it look as if Dahlgren had taken it upon himself to draft the orders and determine the objectives of his troopers once inside Richmond. Unfortunately Dahlgren was dead and unable to defend himself against such charges. Nevertheless, Meade's letter cleared everyone in the chain of command—beginning with Dahlgren's commander, Judson Kilpatrick, and extending up to President Lincoln—of any knowledge or hand in setting Dahlgren's mission as described in the documents.

The Confederate leaders weren't buying the Union denials. They knew the papers were genuine. The *Richmond Examiner* wrote an editorial that concluded that the contest between the two enemies had now become a "war under the Black Flag."[29] Lincoln's knowledge of the raid and his approval of it seem likely. Since General Meade had not approved of Kilpatrick's plan, but acquiesced to it, control was placed either within the War Department with Stanton or in the White House with Lincoln. In reality, both men had to know and had to have approved of the raid's objectives. Charges that the documents were forged soon surfaced, but neither Meade nor other officers in his command believed the documents were anything but genuine.[30]

The war was taking a sharp turn away from established principles of moral conduct. As the third year was drawing to a close, the Confederacy looked more favorably on strategies it may have once viewed as extreme and unacceptable. One month after the Union plot to sack Richmond and kill Jefferson Davis, another diabolical plot began to unfold, this one by the Confederacy under the guise of humanitarian benevolence. This time, evidence has come to light that places knowledge of the plan squarely on Jefferson Davis's desk. Its perpetrator was a Kentucky physician who had made his way to Canada as one of Jefferson Davis's agents. His name was Luke Pryor Blackburn, and he was widely recognized as an international authority on yellow fever and praised for his humanitarian efforts to quell several epidemics that had ravaged Southern coastal cities.

In the spring of 1864, Jefferson Davis established a group of agents in Canada whose purpose was to disrupt the war effort throughout the North and bring about Lincoln's defeat in the upcoming election. Davis selected Jacob Thompson and Clement C. Clay as his special commissioners to oversee the operation. The two men proceeded to Canada carrying drafts for one million dollars in gold[31] and a letter from President Jefferson Davis that read in part, "I hereby direct you to proceed at once to Canada, there to carry out such instructions as you have received from me verbally, in such manner as shall seem most likely to be conducive to the furtherance of the interests of the Confederate States of America which have been entrusted to you."[32]

It was Thompson's and Clay's charge to wreak as much havoc throughout the Northern states as they could, using a variety of resources. Joining Thompson and Clay were several prominent men from the Confederacy. Among these men was Dr. Blackburn, who decided he could better serve the Confederacy by using his medical knowledge against her enemies than by using it to help ease the suffering of her soldiers.

Born on June 16, 1816, in Woodford County, Kentucky, Luke Blackburn received all of the advantages of an upper-class family. He was educated in the best schools of Kentucky, graduating from Transylvania University with a medical degree in 1834 at the young age of eighteen. His medical interests soon centered on yellow fever and its etiology. During a yellow fever outbreak in Natchez, Mississippi, he instituted a rigid quarantine that was thought to have blunted the epidemic and saved the city from hundreds of deaths. In Louisiana he again performed great service during a yellow fever epidemic instituting another quarantine. By the outbreak of the Civil War he was among the leading authorities on the treatment of yellow fever.

Early in the war Blackburn received an appointment to the staff of Confederate General Sterling Price as his civilian aide-de-camp. In early 1863 he left Price's staff and was appointed by the governor of Mississippi as one of two commissioners to oversee the care of Mississippi's invalid soldiers. In August of 1863, Blackburn became a temporary blockade runner successfully carrying a shipment of ice from Halifax through the Union blockade at Mobile only to have the ship captured on its return to open sea. Mistaken by Union officials for a civilian passenger, Blackburn was released. He made his way back to Canada where he began to hatch a diabolical scheme to introduce biological warfare in the form of yellow fever into the Confederacy's arsenal of weapons against the North.

Although the cause and spread of yellow fever was misunderstood in the 1860s, the perception that it was highly infectious and easily spread among the population was widely accepted as fact. The belief that the disease was infectious led Blackburn to undertake a plan designed to infect selected populations in the Northern states as well as Union troops stationed in the coastal towns of Norfolk, Virginia, and New Bern, North Carolina. Added to Blackburn's targets was Abraham Lincoln. While history has treated Blackburn's yellow fever plot against civilian populations with skepticism, it was not only real, but one that was known at the highest levels of the Confederate government. The plan involved collecting and distributing clothing taken from victims who had died from yellow fever. The distribution included targeting civilian populations.

At the trial of the Lincoln conspirators in May of 1865, the question of introducing yellow fever into the North for the purpose of mass killing became an early focus of the prosecution. The government began its case by attempting to show that leaders of the Confederacy, including Jefferson Davis, were capable of diabolical schemes against civilians including arson and the spreading of disease. It was a short step from these sorts of atrocities to the murder of Abraham Lincoln.

While part of the testimony of the government's key witnesses against Jefferson Davis proved to be perjured testimony, not all of it was tainted or false. On Monday, May 29, a man by the name of Godfrey Joseph Hyams took the witness stand. Hyams was an inconspicuous sort of person. He was slight of build, had a dark complexion, and was afflicted with crossed eyes. He gave the appearance of being frail and weak. The press made a point of describing his features as "Israelitish" and pointed out to its readers that he was "of the Jewish persuasion."[33] What Hyams lacked in appearance, however, he made up for in his bite.

Hyams began by telling the court of a monstrous plot on the part of Confederate leaders to institute biological warfare against large segments of the Northern population. Hyams described how he was enlisted by one of Jefferson Davis's Canadian agents to distribute clothing believed to be infected with yellow fever into certain cities in the North. The object was to start an epidemic of the deadly disease that would prove devastating to Northern war efforts. It was, as Hyams put it, "directed against the masses of northern people solely to create death." Hyams's testimony named names and gave dates detailing the plot.[34] Despite his convincing testimony, Hyams has been lumped together with the other perjured witnesses, and his story has been characterized as another example of purchased testimony or simply ignored in all but two accounts of the assassination story.[35] He has been described as "an inglorious turncoat whose loyalties responded to money rather than a cause."[36]

Despite attacks against his character and truthfulness, Hyams's testimony accusing the Confederacy of a form of biological warfare does not stand alone, but is supported by numerous documents that lie scattered among historical archives and the testimony of at least eight different witnesses who tied Luke Blackburn and several other agents directly to a plot to induce deadly epidemics among civilian populations. Among those giving testimony confirming the plot were two important and high-ranking Confederate officials. Much of this material has been overlooked or considered too circumstantial to prove the case against Blackburn or give any credence to Jefferson Davis's direct knowledge of such a plot. But even without Hyams's damaging testimony, the case against Blackburn and his cohorts, including Davis, is compelling.

Blackburn's plot was initiated in April 1864 when a major yellow fever epidemic hit the Island of Bermuda with devastating force. Among the potential casualties of the epidemic was the Confederacy's blockade-running organization that used Bermuda as a major base of operations. The Confederates operated a wharf and office on the island under the command of Major N.S. Walker of the Confederacy's commissary department.[37]

While the epidemic raged, Blackburn left Halifax in Nova Scotia and arrived in Bermuda where he offered his medical skills to the Bermuda government. Welcomed by government officials, Blackburn set about his diabolic plan by carefully collecting the clothing and bedding of victims who had died from yellow fever. Packing the items into eight large trunks, Blackburn had them shipped back to Halifax, Nova Scotia. Before leaving for Bermuda in April, Blackburn had hired Godfrey Hyams to take charge of the trunks and safely import them into the United States. Blackburn's plan was for Hyams to take the trunks to Washington, Norfolk, and New Bern, where he would arrange for the clothing to be sold at auction, thereby gaining the widest possible distribution. As the clothing was spread amongst the civilian population, so would the deadly yellow fever, or so Blackburn believed. Included among Blackburn's targets was Abraham Lincoln.

A small black valise accompanying the trunks contained several expensive dress shirts that Blackburn had previously packed with the yellow fever clothing. Blackburn instructed Hyams to take the valise, along with a letter, to President Lincoln as a special gift by an anonymous benefactor. Blackburn believed that even if Lincoln did not choose to wear the shirts their mere presence would infect him with the deadly disease. Hyams, apparently afraid of the risk of taking such a "gift" to the White House, declined. The trunks were another matter, however, and Hyams would see to their transport.

Hyams carried out his assignment using the alias of J.W. Harris, shipping five of the trunks through Boston to Washington where he contracted with the auction house of W.L. Wall and Company to dispose of the infected clothing. Because Norfolk and New Bern were within the military lines of the Union army, Hyams had to contract the services of an army sutler to dispose of the infected clothing in those two cities.

Completing his task, Hyams returned to Canada where he reported back to Blackburn. Blackburn had promised Hyams he would pay him substantially for his work, but had yet to give Hyams any money other than a nominal sum to help carry out his grisly mission. Hyams had used that money to bribe the ship's captain to transport the trunks and the customs officers to allow the trunks to enter the United States.

Because Blackburn was scheduled to leave the next day for a return trip to Bermuda, he turned Hyams over to Jacob Thompson, telling Hyams that Thompson would see to his payment. Thompson agreed to pay Hyams $100 as a partial advance but only after Hyams secured a receipt from Wall showing that he had actually contracted for the sale of the clothing.

His initial effort at spreading disease accomplished, Blackburn returned to Bermuda on July 15 and again offered his services to the Bermuda government. Welcomed again, Blackburn set about securing another supply of infected clothing, this time filling three trunks with what he supposed was deadly contagion. He then contracted with a hotel keeper by the name of Edward Swan at St. Georges, Bermuda, to hold the trunks until the spring of 1865 and then ship them to New York, where they would be sold to unsuspecting New Yorkers in the same manner that they had been sold in Washington, Norfolk, and New Bern.

Blackburn's plot was exposed in April of 1865, however, when Hyams, disgruntled at not being paid for his work, walked into the United States consul's office in Toronto and offered to blow the whistle on several other of the Confederacy's clandestine operations. Hyams wanted both remuneration and a pardon for his valuable information. If the Confederates wouldn't pay, maybe the Yankees would.

After revealing the details of a Confederate plan to disrupt U.S. fishing off the Canadian coast, and the location of a Confederate "bomb house" in Toronto, both of which proved accurate, Hyams demands were met. On April

12, Hyams gave a detailed statement to U.S. officials about the Confederate yellow fever plot. Two days later, John Wilkes Booth assassinated Abraham Lincoln. Suddenly Hyams became an important witness for the U.S. government in their effort to directly place the blame for Lincoln's murder at the feet of Jefferson Davis and his Canadian agents. The yellow fever plot together with Hyams's claim that a valise of infected clothing was designated for Lincoln, pointed an accusing finger at Jefferson Davis. The government called Hyams to Washington, where he testified at the conspiracy trial of those accused of Lincoln's murder, giving the details of Blackburn's plot.

While the trial was taking place in Washington, authorities in Bermuda had independently received information about Blackburn's second inventory of trunks being held by Edward Swan on St. Georges Island. According to newspaper accounts in Bermuda, officials had been tipped off by a Confederate agent working in Major N.S. Walker's operation. Bermuda officials seized the trunks and charged Swan with violating Bermuda's health regulations. A hearing and trial subsequently held resulted in further exposure of Blackburn's plan to unleash yellow fever in the United States.

The proceedings in Bermuda, which coincided with Godfrey Hyams's allegations, persuaded Canadian authorities to act. On May 19 Blackburn was arrested in Montreal and placed on $4,000 bail.[38] Following a preliminary hearing he was charged with violating Canada's neutrality act and ordered held over for trial. Canada's chief witness was Godfrey Hyams. Hyams told of his recruitment by Blackburn and of his receiving the trunks in Halifax and of his taking the trunks through Boston, Philadelphia, and Baltimore to Washington. Hyams also told of Blackburn's repeated promises of money that never fully materialized, but that he eventually received $100 directly from Jacob Thompson. This payment of $100 by Thompson would eventually link Jefferson Davis with Blackburn's plot to wage germ warfare against the North.

During Blackburn's Canadian trial the prosecution dropped a bombshell into the proceedings when it introduced a deposition from William W. Cleary, Jacob Thompson's personal secretary and one of Jefferson Davis's key agents in Montreal. In his deposition, Cleary admitted knowing Blackburn and Hyams, having "met them on several occasions in Canada."[39] Cleary told the court that Blackburn had told him "that he had him [Hyams] employed to distribute . . . clothing which he had prepared, I think he said at Bermuda, infected with the yellow fever."[40] Cleary, however, claimed that Thompson had not given any money to finance Hyams, thereby keeping Thompson and his superiors clear of any direct involvement in the plot. Cleary's deposition left the impression that neither he nor Thompson, nor the leaders in Richmond, had anything to do with Blackburn's scheme. The Confederate commissioners and their superiors had clean hands. Blackburn was acting on his own.

The evidence against Blackburn, although circumstantial, was considerable. Those who were skeptical of Hyams's testimony could not ignore Cleary's deposition. The pro-Confederate *Montreal Gazette*, which initially had come to Blackburn's defense, had to admit at the end of the trial that the testimony of Hyams was true. The May 27 edition reported, "Mr. Cleary is a man of different character [from Godfrey Hyams], and we see no reason to question his deposition. . . . In the affidavit of Mr. Cleary, . . . we have for the first time, . . . reliable evidence to connect Dr. Blackburn with this affair. . . . It corroborates Hyams; . . . Dr. Blackburn must be held guilty of having attempted to damage the Federal cause by introducing yellow fever among the Federals by means of infected clothing. Such an act cannot be held to belong to civilized war. It is an outrage against humanity."[41]

The Canadian press reacted harshly toward Blackburn and those connected with the plot. The *New York Times*, which covered the story closely, reminded people that New Bern had been targeted by Blackburn the previous summer and had suffered one of the worst yellow fever epidemics in its history. A New Bern newspaper commented on Blackburn's plot after learning that their city had been targeted: "This hideous and long studied plan to deliberately murder innocent men, women and children, who had never wronged him in any manner, is regarded here as an act of cruelty without a parallel—a crime which can only be estimated and punished in the presence of his victims in another world."[42]

It mattered little that the New Bern epidemic, which killed two thousand people, was not caused by Blackburn's contaminated clothing shipped there in the summer of 1864. To Blackburn's thinking, the plot was successful, and his shipment of "yellow fever poison" worked, except it had killed many more civilians than Yankee soldiers.

Despite the evidence and the overwhelming public sentiment against Blackburn, he was acquitted of violating Canada's neutrality act on the grounds there was no proof that any of the trunks had ever been on Canadian soil and, therefore, did not violate its neutrality. The trunks had been carefully restricted to Halifax, and the Toronto court trying Blackburn concluded that it lacked jurisdiction in Nova Scotia.

In Washington, the trial of Abraham Lincoln's assassins began with an attempt by government prosecutors to link Jefferson Davis and his agents in Canada with organizing the plot to assassinate President Lincoln. Luke Blackburn was one of several links to the Confederacy and Jefferson Davis. The government issued orders for Blackburn's arrest but was unsuccessful in extraditing him during the conspirator's trial. When the government prosecutors failed to provide evidence that Davis had approved or even knew about Blackburn's diabolical plot they dropped interest in extraditing him to the United States. Meanwhile, the government shifted its attention to the eight defendants in the dock. The United States authorities soon forgot about Blackburn, and he faded away.

Had the U.S. government been more diligent it might have found the evidence it sought to confirm Blackburn's activities and show Jefferson Davis's knowledge, and therefore sanction, of the yellow fever plot. The evidence lay among the papers of Jefferson Davis that the government was in the process of collecting among the scattered archives in Richmond. Among these papers was a letter of damaging content by an Episcopal minister turned Confederate agent named Kensey Johns Stewart.

The Reverend Stewart served the Confederacy in a variety of capacities during the first three years of the war. In April 1861 Stewart was officiating at St. Paul's Episcopal Church in Alexandria, Virginia. On February 9, 1862, while Stewart was conducting Sunday services, a Union officer seated in the congregation demanded that a special prayer for the president of the United States should be read. When Stewart refused to comply, he was arrested and taken into custody. After a brief detainment, Stewart was released and fled to Richmond where he received an appointment as chaplain in the Sixth North Carolina Infantry. In late 1862 he was reassigned as chaplain for Union prisoners confined in Richmond hospitals. In March of 1863, Stewart traveled to England where he spent a year putting together a special edition of the Episcopal Prayer Book for the Confederacy in conjunction with the Reverend Robert Gatewood, who later became head of the Confederate army's intelligence office.[43] Stewart returned to Richmond in 1864 and, after a visit with Jefferson Davis, traveled to Canada where he became one of Davis's agents. In a letter to Secretary of War John A. Seddon dated October 25, 1864, Secretary of State Judah P. Benjamin wrote:

> The bearer Chaplain S.F. Cameron is employed with Mr. [Kensey Johns] Stewart on a secret service, according to an understanding with the President, and the Chaplain will want to pass through our lines on his way to Canada, accompanied by two friends.
>
> Will you give him the necessary papers to enable him to pass with his two companions, & oblige. Yours truly, J.P. Benjamin Sec. State[44]

The fact that Stewart was a prominent figure in the Confederacy's Canadian operation is also gleaned from a second letter that survived the Richmond fires written by Benjamin to Jacob Thompson. On November 29, 1864, Benjamin wrote to Thompson concerning a draft for $20,000 that was intended to finance Stewart's clandestine activities:

> I learn that an order on you for twenty thousand dollars, drawn by me on the 17th October, in favor of Mr. Stewart has not been received. . . .

> My present purpose is to explain to you that Dr. Stewart proposed to engage in the same business as that which you have controlled, and that as we supposed you would be returning home very soon, it was desirable that you should leave with him means sufficient to enable him to act with efficiency.[45]

Whatever Stewart's secret activities were, they were well known to Richmond and important enough to warrant a large sum of money to finance their undertaking.[46]

Two weeks after Benjamin's letter to Thompson, Stewart was in Toronto and wrote directly to Jefferson Davis. In his letter to Davis, Stewart complained about the "miserable failures" and "useless annoyances" that some of Davis's other agents were engaged in. Stewart pointed out that these ineffectual activities did little more than engender a "thirst for revenge" on the part of the Confederacy's enemies without having any real effect toward winning the war. In simpler words, Stewart felt Davis had a few loose cannons rolling around in Canada that should be spiked. Stewart bluntly wrote: "Your Excellency is aware that when a negro is slightly chastised, he hates you, but a *just* & thorough whipping humbles him." Stewart had the audacity to tell Davis that the time for "slightly chastising" his ineffectual agents was past and it was time for stronger action. Thompson and his cohorts needed a thorough whipping. Stewart then made a startling revelation. He called Davis's attention to one "inhumane & cruel" activity that he felt Davis should order stopped immediately:

> I cannot regard you as capable of expecting the blessing of God upon, or being personally associated with instruments & plans such as I describe below. As our country has been and is entirely dependent upon God, we cannot afford to displease him. Therefore, it cannot be our policy to employ wicked men to destroy the persons & property of private citizens, by inhumane & cruel acts. I name only one. *$100.00 of public money has been paid here to one "Hyams"* [emphasis added] a shoemaker, for services rendered by conveying and causing to be sold in the city of Washington at auction, boxes of small-pox clothing. . . . There can be no doubt of the causes of the failure of such plans. It is only a matter of surprise that, God does not forsake us and our cause when we are associated with such misguided friends.[47]

Stewart carefully avoided identifying Blackburn by name or of tying Thompson into the plot. But Stewart's reference to "$100 of public money" paid to "'Hyams' a shoemaker" is clear confirmation of Hyams's testimony given during the trial of the Lincoln conspirators. Stewart's letter not only confirmed Blackburn's plot, supporting Hyams's claim that Thompson paid him, but placed the whole affair squarely on the desk of Jefferson Davis. If Davis had no knowledge of Blackburn's activities before December 12, 1864, he certainly knew about them after receiving Stewart's letter.[48] Four months after Stewart's letter to Davis the trunks were not destroyed and the plot was still going forward despite Stewart's plea to Davis to order a halt to the project. More important, Hyams's veracity is vindicated by a man who probably despised him, the Reverend Kensey Johns Stewart.

The accusations against Blackburn are compelling. The testimony of the witnesses in the Bermuda hearing, the deposition of William W. Cleary during the Canadian trial, and the testimony of the Washington auction agent W.E. Wall and his assistant A. Bennett during the Lincoln conspiracy trial, fully support the details of Godfrey Hyams's claims. But most compelling in all of the evidence against Blackburn is the letter of Kensey Johns Stewart to Jefferson Davis, indicating Davis had full knowledge of the plot. Stewart, who along with Jacob Thompson, ranked at the top of Jefferson Davis's cadre of Canadian agents, knew of such a plot and attempted to convince Davis to order it stopped. This Confederate agent and close confidant of Davis clearly fingered Hyams as the hired disperser in a plan to unleash biological warfare by someone who was under Davis's control. That someone was Luke P. Blackburn. Yet four months later, the trunks containing "infected clothing" were still in Edward Swan's care awaiting the signal to ship them to New York.

Blackburn's motives, and those of his superiors, seem clear. Their ignorance of infectious disease in no way mitigates their guilt in attempting to unleash biological warfare against civilian populations. Indeed, they believed that Blackburn's trunks that had reached New Bern were responsible for the yellow fever epidemic that killed over two thousand people in that coastal town. Blackburn's small valise of gift shirts designed to infect Lincoln with a deadly disease show that he was a target of the Confederate operation in Canada. Black flag warfare had come of age.

Lincoln's Emancipation Proclamation, viewed as a call for slave insurrection, together with the Dahlgren Raid, may well have influenced Davis and his advisors to rethink what constituted legitimate military action. By inciting slaves to insurrection and ordering military actions that would result in untold civilian casualties, Lincoln had forfeited any protection he might have had under the accepted laws of war. If it is true that Lincoln sanctioned the killing of Davis and other members of his cabinet, he may well have placed himself at the center of the bulls-eye. It is important to understand, however, that it mattered little that Lincoln may not have targeted Davis; it was enough that Davis and his advisers believed that Lincoln had targeted them. Perception, after all, was reality. Among the best evidence that Jefferson Davis's view of black flag warfare had taken a dramatic turn came six months after Dahlgren's failed raid and while Luke Blackburn was still collecting infected clothing in Bermuda. It involved a Confederate agent by the name of Thomas Nelson Conrad.

In September of 1864 Thomas Nelson Conrad safely slipped into Washington for the purpose of "reconnoitering the White House . . . to ascertain Mr. Lincoln's customary movements."[49] Those were Conrad's words written twenty-eight years later. Conrad was a member of the Confederate Secret Service and he was on a mission, with Lincoln as the target. The mission had a clear connection with the Confederate leaders in Richmond.

Born at Fairfax Court House in Virginia, Conrad attended Dickinson College in Pennsylvania where he studied for the ministry. Following graduation he moved to Georgetown in the District of Columbia where he taught at the Georgetown Institute until his arrest in June of 1861 as a Southern sympathizer. At graduation ceremonies that year, Conrad had purposefully insulted the Unionists in the audience by instructing the music director to play "Dixie" at the close of festivities. Conrad was immediately arrested and imprisoned in the Old Capitol Prison in Washington. While a prisoner he made several important connections with other Confederate prisoners including a man by the name of "Bull" Frizzell. After several months Conrad was paroled and made his way to Richmond where he enlisted in Jeb Stuart's cavalry corps. A lay preacher, Conrad was appointed chaplain for the Third Virginia Cavalry (Wickham's Brigade, Fitz Lee's Division). He spent most of his time functioning as a "scout" before being tapped by Richmond to perform clandestine duty because of his intimate knowledge of Washington and his skill as a scout.

Conrad had lived in Washington for over five years and was familiar with the city and its environs.[50] He described his duties as a scout in a postwar memoir titled, *The Rebel Scout*:

> Stuart's scouts performed duties of three kinds: observing the Federal Army in camp, so as to be able to anticipate a movement; hanging upon the flank of the army when in motion, reporting line of march and number of corps; and crossing the lines into Washington and beyond, bearing dispatches, interviewing certain parties and securing information. The same scouts often discharged the first and second mentioned duty, but few ever went into Washington City. A college mate, . . . and myself were perhaps among the few who not only scouted within our line, but were frequently sent by President Davis and our general officers into Washington and sometimes into Canada.[51]

In 1864, Conrad was plucked from his position with Stuart and placed in the employ of the Confederate Secret Service. In September of that year he slipped into Washington on a plan to capture Lincoln and carry him to Richmond. As with other capture plots, Soldiers' Home became the ideal venue for snatching up Lincoln. In his memoir, Conrad explained his mission: "We had to determine at what point it would be most expedient to capture the carriage and take possession of Mr. Lincoln; and then whether to move with him through Maryland to the lower Potomac [Charles County] and cross or to the upper Potomac [Montgomery County] and deliver the prisoner to Mosby's Confederacy for transportation to Richmond. . . . [H]aving scouted the country pretty thoroughly . . . we finally concluded to take the lower Potomac."[52]

Conrad was a credible person, well placed in the Confederate order of things, and fully capable of carrying out such an operation. Conrad's mission, unlike those previously planned, appears to have been directed out of Judah Benjamin's office. In his memoir Conrad tells of receiving two letters from Jefferson Davis to Secretary of War James B. Seddon and Secretary of State Judah P. Benjamin. These letters directed the transfer of Conrad to the Secret Service department and provided him with the necessary funds to finance his operation in Washington.[53]

While in Richmond, Conrad received a second letter from Seddon on War Department letterhead, dated September 15, 1864, that directed Lieutenant Colonel John S. Mosby and Colonel Charles H. Cawood to "aid and facilitate the movements of Captain Conrad."[54] Mosby commanded the 43rd Battalion of Virginia Cavalry operating primarily throughout Loudoun County, Virginia, across the Potomac River from Montgomery County, Maryland. Cawood was in command of a signal corps camp in King George County, Virginia, situated across the Potomac River from Charles County, Maryland. These two areas represented the "upper Potomac" and "lower Potomac" referred to by Conrad in his memoir. The two Maryland counties were avenues into Washington that Confederate agents used with great success throughout the war. Both were potential escape routes for a capturing party carrying the president from his summer quarters at Soldiers' Home to Virginia and Richmond. Seddon's letter was just one more "dot" making up the overall picture that tied Davis and his subordinates to an effort to remove Lincoln from the presidency.

Conrad was careful not to write anything in his memoirs that directly connected Davis or Benjamin to his plot to capture Lincoln. While the correspondence transferring Conrad to the Confederate Secret Service and authorizing funds to finance his clandestine activities in Washington also make no mention of a plan to capture Lincoln and bring him south, it is simply not creditable to believe that Conrad would undertake such a daring mission on his own responsibility without Davis's full knowledge and approval.

To carry out his plan of capture, Conrad enlisted the help of three other individuals who were well known to him. Daniel Mountjoy Cloud had been a classmate at Dickinson College and good friend of Conrad.[55] The two men had worked together previously and were confident of each other's capabilities. The second man was John "Bull" Frizzell, who became friends with Conrad while both men were in the Old Capitol Prison in 1861. Conrad described Frizzell as a "broad-shouldered, rawboned, squareheaded sixfooter . . . always ready to 'cuss' out the Yankees and knock down a guard or a blackguard."[56] He wore a silver plate that covered a skull fracture suffered in an earlier adventure. Rumor had it that Frizzell had traveled to Harpers Ferry in 1859 to help capture John Brown and later cut off one of Brown's ears as a personal trophy.[57] The third man was Conrad's "halfbreed" servant named William. Conrad described him as "six feet in height, straight as an arrow, twenty-three years of age, . . . and bold as a lion."[58]

As with previous plots to capture Lincoln, this one also targeted Soldiers' Home as the likely place to snatch up the president. Conrad's scheme called for the four men to intercept Lincoln in his carriage as he arrived at the entrance to the Soldiers' Home. William would climb next to the driver and force him to divert the carriage along an escape route while Frizzell would jump inside and subdue Lincoln. Conrad would lead the carriage while Cloud covered the rear. The entourage would make its way over the Eastern Branch of the Potomac and head into southern Maryland along the Confederate line used by agents of the Confederate Secret Service. While there were many similarities between Conrad's plan and John Wilkes Booth's later plan, including the route of escape into Virginia, Conrad's operation appeared to be independent of Booth's.[59]

Conrad and Cloud stationed themselves in Lafayette Square, across from the White House, where they could observe Lincoln as he traveled to and from the Soldiers' Home as a part of his daily routine. With cold weather approaching, the president and his family would be moving back into the White House full time, leaving Soldiers' Home until the following spring. If Conrad and his men were to act, they had to act soon. Suddenly, without warning, Conrad noticed that Lincoln's carriage was accompanied by a troop of cavalry.[60] Conrad was stunned at this sudden development. He later wrote, "What can it mean? How long will it last? Have our plans been betrayed and our movements suspected?"[61]

Conrad scouted the White House for the next several days trying to find out if the cavalry escort was permanent and why it had been assigned to accompany Lincoln at this time. He arrived at an interesting conclusion for the sudden change in procedure—there must have been "another set of Confederates seeking the same end, and some one of them had given it away by some indiscretion."[62]

Indeed there were other plots afoot, but neither the War Department nor the National Police were aware them. At the time Conrad reconnoitered the White House, John Wilkes Booth was on his way to Canada and a rendezvous with Jefferson Davis's agents in Montreal. The cavalry troop assigned to accompany Lincoln on his trips to and from the Soldiers' Home was not new, however. It first began accompanying Lincoln in September of 1863, not in the fall of 1864 as Conrad had written. In any event, Conrad aborted the plan while musing that had Lincoln "fallen into the meshes of the silken net we had spread for him he would never have been the victim of the assassin's heartless, bloody and atrocious crime."[63]

Conrad's own account of his mission to Washington to reconnoiter Lincoln's movements for a capture operation seems authentic. The extant documents authorizing full support for his movements by Seddon and Benjamin suggest a direct link to Jefferson Davis for Conrad's capture plan. It is doubtful that these two secretaries would be supporting Conrad without the knowledge and approval of Davis. Of importance, Conrad's activities were financed with Secret Service funds. On January 10, two months after he had aborted his capture mission, Conrad wrote to Secretary of War Seddon stating that he had received four hundred dollars in gold from Secretary of State Benjamin to cover his expenses over the past four months.[64] Conrad further states in his letter that the gold was converted into one thousand dollars in Northern funds. This gold clearly financed his activity in Washington at the time he planned to capture Lincoln. The authorization of gold payments from the Secret Service fund required the approval of Davis.[65] That Lincoln was the target of a capture mission known by Davis seems certain.

The black flag efforts of Cipriano Ferrandini, Walker Taylor, Isaac Wistar, Ulric Dahlgren, Bradley Johnson, Luke Blackburn, and Thomas Conrad pale in comparison to the plot that was being devised in early 1865 by a man named Thomas Harney. Harney, an explosives expert in the Confederate Torpedo Bureau, was planning a mission to blow up the White House, taking Abraham Lincoln and members of his cabinet along with it.[66] The plot was set for April 1865 and, like Booth's plot, hoped to reverse the Confederacy's failing fortunes and gain her time to regroup. But the schemes of Harney and Booth were still in their formative stages in the fall of 1864 and would not reach fruition until April of the following year.

While Conrad was in Richmond organizing his capture scheme, John Wilkes Booth was in Baltimore meeting with two former friends, Samuel Bland Arnold and Michael O'Laughlen, and forming his own plot. Both Booth and Conrad looked to capturing Lincoln while he moved between his two residences and carrying him south to Richmond over the same southern Maryland route. Both would need the help of well-placed agents along the way. By the time Booth made his first visit to Charles County, Maryland, in November 1864, the Confederate command in Richmond must have been aware of his activities. Booth possessed certain attributes necessary for covert activity. Because of his profession and fame he could move about more freely and with less suspicion than most people. His fame and personality made him attractive to people such that he could get them to do things for him. He was intelligent, articulate, and above all, had a deep passion for the Confederacy and a hatred for Lincoln. While Booth was not a professional agent like Conrad, he proved better than Conrad in one important aspect: he did not abandon his mission. The year 1864 would mark a turning point in Booth's short but illustrious life. His last paid appearance occurred on May 28 with a matinee performance in *The Corsican Brothers* at the Boston Museum. Although he would appear three more times in benefits, his career was over.[67] He would turn away from the stage and toward the role he believed destiny had thrust upon him.

CHAPTER FIVE

The South Wants Justice

The South wants justice, has waited for it long. She will wait no longer.

John Wilkes Booth

Nine years since he first began his rise to stardom on the American stage, John Wilkes Booth's acting career had reached its peak during the 1862–63 season, and now, in 1864, it appeared to be in jeopardy. The throat problems that developed during the winter of 1864 did not prevent him from continuing his acting; other matters were pushing it backstage. Practically speaking, Booth's acting career ended with the 1863–64 season. His attention now turned toward his passion for the Confederacy. At the core of that passion was a hatred for Lincoln and his policies.

The year 1864 was also a fateful one for Abraham Lincoln. In the dark summer Lincoln penned a memorandum asking his cabinet members to sign the verso without reading its content: "This morning, as for some days past, it seems exceedingly probable that this Administration will not be re-elected. Then it will be my duty to so co-operate with the President elect, as to save the Union between the election and the inauguration; as he will have secured his election on such ground that he can not possibly save it afterwards."[1]

Lincoln's reference to the victor's having secured his election on grounds that would give up the Union referred to Major General George B. McClellan, the Democratic "Peace Candidate," whose own party platform called for a cessation of hostilities and restoration of peace. At the time, the war seemed to be stalemated. Sherman had disappeared into the dark abyss of Georgia, and his fate was uncertain as he approached the gates to Atlanta. The people of the North had no reason to believe he would be any more successful than McClellan had been on his way to capture Richmond two years before.

But Sherman wasn't McClellan. He took Atlanta on September 2, and two weeks later Phillip Sheridan gained a stunning victory in the Shenandoah Valley of Virginia when he defeated Jubal Early's army at the battle of Winchester. These two victories, coming just before the presidential elections, assured Lincoln's reelection. To the more astute, Lincoln's reelection assured the Confederacy's defeat—unless the results of the election could in some way be reversed or overturned.

While Lincoln's fortunes took on a renewed spirit of hope, John Wilkes Booth's grew darker and more sinister. In early 1864 Booth began to invest a part of his large stage earnings in the newly thriving oil business in Pennsylvania. "Petroleumania" was luring hundreds of entrepreneurs who had money to invest. Booth was among them. In January of that year he became partners with three friends, John Ellsler, Thomas Mears, and Joseph Simonds, in purchasing oil land in Venango County near the town of Franklin in northwestern Pennsylvania. The venture was short-lived, however, and proved unprofitable for Booth. Eight months later, at the end of September, events found Booth abruptly disposing of his oil interests and arranging his affairs as if his life were about to take a major change in direction. According to his partner Simonds, Booth lost $6,000 in the enterprise.

While the trial of the conspirators was taking place in Washington in May of 1865, Godfrey Hyams was telling the commissioners about his exploits shipping Luke Blackburn's trunks past customs in Boston and on to Philadelphia. A man with the unusual name of Cordial Crane was an official at the Boston Customs House. Upon reading Hyams's testimony, Crane's interest was aroused. He decided to check the register of the Parker House to see if Hyams or his alias, J.W. Harris, had registered at the hotel. Crane could not find either Hyams or Harris in the register but was startled to find that John Wilkes Booth had registered at the Parker House on July 26. Crane noted that three men from Canada and one from Baltimore also registered on that day. Crane copied the names of the five men and sent a letter to Stanton calling his attention to what he felt was a strange coincidence. Whatever Stanton thought of Crane's observation, he failed to follow up on it and simply filed the letter away.[2]

Booth's presence at the Parker House, however, did not escape the attention of the authors of *Come Retribution.* They concluded that Booth's presence at the same time three men from Canada and one from Baltimore were also present "has all the earmarks of a conference with an agenda."[3] Could Booth be meeting with Confederate agents from Canada? Soon after returning from Canada he closed out his business interests and began recruiting cohorts for his plan to capture Lincoln. The authors strengthen their theory by failing to find any trace among the various Canadian and Baltimore records for the four names on the Parker House register, leaving them to conclude that they were aliases.[4] One of the three "Canadians" that registered the same day at the Parker House also appeared on the register of the St. Lawrence Hall in Montreal. He used the name "H.V. Clinton," and while he registered at both hotels under that name, a search of Canadian and St. Louis records, both places that he listed as his home, failed to turn up anyone with that name. The authors suggest that H.V. Clinton was an alias of one of the Con-

Cottage Grove Public Librai

federate agents operating out of Montreal.[5] But there may be another explanation to account for Booth's visit to Boston in late July 1864.

A few months earlier, in the spring of 1864, Booth had been performing in Boston when he met a young girl named Isabel Sumner. Booth was twenty-six years old at the time, and Isabel was sixteen. Although young, Isabel seemed to have captured Booth's attention in a serious way. While in Pennsylvania tending to his oil business, and later in New York, Booth wrote several love letters to Isabel.[6] The two exchanged photographs and Booth gave her a gold ring bearing the inscription "J.W.B. to I.S." On July 24, just two days prior to his registering at the Parker House, Booth wrote a pleading letter to Isabel asking why she has been so silent lately. Fearing he has offended her, Booth ends his letter by writing, "I will come at once to Boston."[7] Booth's visit to Boston may have been nothing more than an opportunity to see his Isabel and smooth out any difficulties that may have developed in their relationship. Whatever happened between the two, they never took their relationship beyond a last visit together in New York City in August of 1864.

Booth's visit to Boston in late July may have involved both a meeting with Confederate agents and Isabel Sumner. Booth was certainly capable of handling a love affair and a clandestine operation at the same time. H.V. Clinton's appearance at both the Parker House and St. Lawrence Hall during this period can be viewed as supporting a meeting between Booth and Confederate agents from Montreal, but the evidence is purely circumstantial.

On August 7 Booth was in Philadelphia with his older brother Junius. From here Booth next went to Baltimore where he invited his old friends Michael O'Laughlen and Samuel Arnold to join him at Barnum's City Hotel. In his statement of April 18, 1865, Arnold remembered this meeting as taking place "about the latter part of August or the first part of September, 1864."[8] Arnold had to be mistaken, however, as Booth's meeting with Arnold and O'Laughlen had to have taken place sometime during the second week of August, shortly after Booth had been at the Parker House in Boston. According to Arnold's statement, the meeting adjourned and Booth said he would return in one month, presumably to go over the status of his capture plot. Booth failed to return in one month and sent Arnold a letter explaining that he was sick with erysipelas and would meet with them as soon as he was fully recovered.[9] This letter places Booth's first meeting with Arnold and O'Laughlen sometime before he contracted his illness. Booth's bout with erysipelas can be accurately placed before August 15 and running until sometime after August 28. On August 15, Asia Booth wrote in a letter to her friend Jean Anderson Sherwood that her brother was quite sick.[10] In an entry in his diary dated 28 August, Booth's brother Junius wrote, "John Booth ill 3 weeks with Erysipelas [*sic*] in the Right Elbow."[11] Since Arnold places his first meeting with Booth before Booth's illness, it must have occurred between August 7 and August 14. While previous accounts of Lincoln's assassination accept Arnold's statement that Booth's recruitment occurred around the end of August or early September, the meeting occurred much earlier, showing that Booth was already into his capture plan early in August 1864. Years later Arnold recalled the meeting at Barnum's: "I called upon him and was kindly received as an old schoolmate and invited to his room. We conversed together seated by a table smoking a cigar, of past hours of youth, and the present war, and he heard I had been south, etc., when a tap at the door was given and O'Laughlen was ushered into the room. O'Laughlen was also a former acquaintance of Booths from boyhood up, so he informed me. I was introduced to him and this was my first acquaintance with O'Laughlen. There was only one thing on Booth's mind now and he turned his undivided attention toward it. With the renomination of Lincoln for a second term as president, 'something decisive & great' must be done to save the slipping fortunes of the Confederacy."[12]

Arnold listened to his former school chum expound on the evils of Lincoln. After several minutes Booth got to the point. "Booth then spoke of the abduction or kidnapping of the President, saying if such could be accomplished and the President taken to Richmond and held as a hostage, he thought it would bring about an exchange of prisoners."[13] Booth told his would-be recruits that Lincoln was most vulnerable while traveling to Soldiers' Home and that it would be quite easy to capture him. Arnold and O'Laughlen listened to Booth's plan and when he was finished they nodded their approval. They would join Booth in his plan.

Just where and when Booth first began his operation to capture Lincoln is unclear, but the first positive evidence is the meeting with Arnold and O'Laughlen at Barnum's City Hotel during the second week of August. Joseph Simonds, Booth's partner in his oil investments, sensed that something was not right with Booth at this time. After receiving a letter from Booth, Simonds wrote back, "I hardly know what to make of you this winter—so different from your usual self. Have you lost all your ambition or what is the matter."[14] At the time Simonds wrote his letter Booth had not lost his ambition, he just redirected it toward another objective.

Following his meeting with Arnold and O'Laughlen, Booth spent most of August in New York City at the home of his older brother Edwin, recovering from the bout with erysipelas. Erysipelas is an infection caused by the bacterium *Streptococcus pyogenes.* In the age before antibiotics, it could prove fatal and even in modern times can be life threatening.[15] By September, however, Booth was fully recovered and made arrangements to deed part of his oil holdings to his brother Junius and sister Rosalie. At the same time that he divested himself of his oil stocks he ended his affair with young Isabel Sumner. Thoughts of love and wealth were rapidly fading from Booth's mind and were being replaced by a new project: an obsession to remove Abraham Lincoln from his "throne" of power.

Little analysis has been made of the sequence in which Booth recruited his conspirators. This sequence provides a clue to the importance of certain individuals to his plan. Arnold and O'Laughlen seemed obvious recruits. Both were Baltimoreans, both were old friends of Booth, and both had served in the Confederate army. They had been and perhaps still were soldiers fully capable of carrying out violent acts if called upon. Booth knew them and knew their views. They were "safe" recruits, ones Booth could rely on. It took little persuasion on Booth's part to convince the two to join him. Samuel Arnold was particularly beguiled by Booth's charm. Reflecting on their meeting years later, Arnold wrote: "I found Booth possessed of wonderful power in conversation and became perfectly infatuated with his social manners and bearing."[16] Apparently O'Laughlen felt the same way. Both men were Confederate patriots with little love for Lincoln. Arnold would justify their decision to capture Lincoln "as an act of honorable purpose, humanity and patriotism."[17]

With Arnold and O'Laughlen in the fold, Booth turned his attention south to Charles County, Maryland. Capturing Lincoln was only one part of the operation. Carrying him successfully to Richmond was the other. He would look to southern Maryland. Any plan to capture the president of the United States and carry him through occupied territory would require different capabilities to ensure even a modest chance of success. Firepower was essential. Muscle was necessary. An escape route was needed where one could find friendly help, or at the very least, no interference. Supplies would have to be safely provided along the way. Travel would be mostly at night, when the cover of darkness provided more protection. There were rivers to cross; guides would be needed—especially when traveling at night. Capturing the president could prove to be the easiest part of the operation. Successfully moving him south would be the hard part. Without help, the operation would stand a high probability of failure. Booth would soon get his help.

The key to any effort to reach Richmond lay in southern Maryland and her people. Here one could travel as safely as could be expected. Occupied by Federal troops, the area was also home to forces friendly to the Confederate cause, forces that had successfully outmaneuvered their enemies at nearly every turn for four years. The people of southern Maryland were as staunchly Confederate as the people of Richmond. Election returns for 1860 show that Lincoln received a grand total of six votes in Charles County and only one in Prince George's County.[18] So strong were the anti-Lincoln feelings in Charles County, for instance, that shortly after Lincoln's election in 1860 a special committee was formed that drafted a set of resolutions censuring the six voters. In a gesture of magnanimity, the committee agreed to "overlook their indiscretions for the present," but singled out one of them, perceived to be their ringleader, for expulsion. A special committee of four was appointed to visit Nathan Burnham and order him to leave the county by January 1, and should Burnham refuse to leave by that date, to "expel him *vi et armis.*"[19]

With their culture and economy tied so closely to the South, dozens of Charles County citizens offered their services to the clandestine efforts of the new Confederate States. Intelligence was vital to the success of Confederate operations. A communications link was established between Richmond and various points north as far as Canada. Within months, three lines had been established that ran from the southern boundary of Charles County bordering the Potomac River north to Washington and points beyond. The first line ran due north from Richmond through Bowling Green and Port Royal on the Rappahannock to a point on the Virginia side of the Potomac River known as Mathias Point. Here it crossed the river and continued on just east of Port Tobacco to Surrattsville. From Surrattsville it made its way directly into Washington. The second route crossed the Potomac a few miles to the east running north near Allen's Fresh at the mouth of the Wicomico River and on to Surrattsville then Washington. The third line was still farther to the east and ran along the western side of the Patuxent River

Of the three routes, it was the second one, passing near Allen's Fresh, over which John Wilkes Booth would finally choose to make his escape following his assassination of Abraham Lincoln. Closely attending this route were the principal leaders of Charles and Prince George's Counties. They were men whose names would have slipped into anonymity had it not have been for Booth: Thomas Jones, William Queen, Samuel Cox, John Surratt, Thomas Harbin, and Samuel Mudd. Each served the Confederacy as a member of its clandestine underground. For four years these men received, harbored, and ferried men, women, documents, and materiel between the North and Richmond. They were valuable agents to the Confederacy, many serving as important mail couriers along its routes.

Of the people serving as agents in southern Maryland, Thomas Jones ranked at the top. Jones had labored long and hard in service to the Confederate cause as the principal agent in charge of a mail courier route and of ferrying people across the Potomac River to Virginia. Jones was a good agent and an important part of the Confederate underground apparatus. Several years after the war had ended Jones published a memoir in which he wrote, "I entered with zeal into the Confederate cause."[20] Although an active agent, Jones managed to avoid arrest by the military authorities most of the time. In October 1861, however, he was not so lucky. Jones was arrested near Pope's Creek and thrown into the Old Capitol Prison in Washington charged with "disloyal practices."[21] Held for six months, he was eventually released after taking the oath of allegiance and returned home to Charles County, where he immediately resumed his activities in spite of his oath.

While researching his book on arbitrary arrests under the Lincoln administration,[22] historian Mark E. Neely Jr. uncovered a statement by George W. Smith of Bryantown, Maryland, accusing two men of subversive activities against the Federal government. Smith's statement reads in part: "The principal leaders in the secession party and those who have aided against the Government are, first, James A. Mudd; lives about one mile from Bryantown; has been conveying men and boxes supposed to contain munitions of war from Baltimore and different counties in the state to Pope's Creek on the Potomac. The men were strangers from Baltimore and other places. Mudd paid the expenses. . . . Thomas A. Jones of Pope's Creek, is the man who receives the men, arms and ammunition at that place and conveys them over to Virginia in his own boat and with his own negroes."[23]

Neely's attention was drawn to the name "James A. Mudd." He wondered if the first name could have been transcribed incorrectly. In a separate article, Neely asked, "Did Smith get the first name wrong? Was he a little off in his estimate of the distance from Bryantown (Samuel A. Mudd lived five miles north of Bryantown)? Who was Smith?"[24] Neely raised the possibility that James A. Mudd may actually have been Samuel A. Mudd. If so, Neely thought it raised interesting questions concerning the involvement of Samuel Mudd with Thomas Jones and his underground activities. Neely never answered the questions he raised in his article, concluding, "History may never know." Fortunately, we do know. George W. Smith was elected sheriff of Charles County in November of 1857. His opponent had been Sylvester Mudd,[25] Samuel Mudd's cousin, suggesting that the Mudds were his political rivals. In the 1860 census Smith is listed simply as "Hotel Keeper" in Bryantown, and records show that he received a liquor license on May 24, 1860.[26]

Smith correctly identified Jones's "munitions-runner" as James A. Mudd. He was not Samuel A. Mudd as Neely suspected, but the older brother of Samuel Mudd (1833–83), James Anthony Mudd (1830–1903).[27] James Mudd lived in the Bryantown District of Charles County, Maryland, along with his father, Henry Lowe Mudd, his brother Samuel A. Mudd, his brother Henry Lowe Mudd Jr., his cousin George D. Mudd, and his cousins Henry Mudd and Sylvester Mudd, who were George Mudd's brothers. The several Mudds, except for George Mudd, were strong Confederate supporters.[28]

The accusations against James Mudd in the fall of 1861 would resurface in the summer of 1863, only this time they would include his brother Samuel Alexander Mudd and their sister Mary Clare Mudd. Among the papers in the records of the provost marshal for the District of Columbia are two sets of charges filed by five runaway slaves of the Mudd family.[29] The charges accused Samuel Mudd and several of his neighbors, including his brother and his sister, with several disloyal acts including the shipping of captive slaves south to Richmond where they were forced to help build the defenses surrounding that city. Samuel Mudd was also accused of being part of a slave-capturing posse that apprehended a runaway slave by the name of George Hawkins and "beating him in a most unmerciful manner and then carrying him into the Rebel Lines."

The charges went further, however. Two of the slaves, Henry Simms and Richard Washington,[30] claimed that a quantity of arms and accoutrements were hidden by Samuel Mudd on his property, and while Union cavalry was searching the area, "Mudd's wife ran into the kitchen and threw a bundle of Rebel mail into the fire" to prevent its being discovered by searching soldiers. These charges were supported by another set of charges filed by three other Mudd slaves[31] who told the provost marshal that "Mr. Samuel Mud took from the house of Henry L. Mud some arms, that were made a present to Samuel Cox,[32] in the Rebel army, by the ladies in the neighborhood. Miss Mary Clare Mud [Samuel Mudd's sister] was one of the ladies. These arms were taken on the 6th of March by Mr. Baker, Mr. Wm. Simms, George Jarves. These arms consisted of swords. J. Smith took them to Centreville in a buggy."[33]

The provost marshal responded to the charges by dispatching a military detective, Captain John D. Johnson, to Charles County to investigate. Johnson filed his report after interviewing several persons in Charles County concerning the allegations. In the report he confirmed the slave-capturing allegations: "There is a patrol of citizens, who patrol the country around, for the purpose of apprehending fugitive slaves, which, when caught, are placed in jail, until such time as their owners shall call for them, and then being considered unsafe to roam at large, are taken and sent south, to make their escape more uncertain. This, I find, are the grounds upon which the charges are founded."[34]

Johnson continues his report by citing several individuals for various disloyal acts who are not named in the charges, and then concludes: "From information received, I am of the opinion that the majority of people, in the lower part of the state of Maryland, especially in Charles County, are disloyal, and that the loyal people, are detered [*sic*] from giving information, through fear. It is my impression it would be a good remedy to station a negro Regiment in their midst."[35]

If the majority of people were disloyal one wonders who Johnson interviewed and how he was able to separate the evidence of disloyal people from loyal people. Despite such difficulty, however, Johnson concludes that the slaves who were rounded up were "fugitive slaves" and therefore under the control of the fugitive slave law and purview of the "Charles County patrol." Johnson further explains that sending the captured runaway slaves south to Richmond was a reasonable remedy "to make their escape more uncertain." The Fugitive Slave Law was technically still in force within the state of Maryland since Maryland was still "loyal."

Clearly a slave-capturing patrol existed in Charles County whose task was to round up fugitive slaves and send them south back into slavery. Samuel Mudd and his brother Henry, along with other neighbors, were part of this "patrol." Johnson says nothing about the charges of beating George Hawkins "in a most unmerciful manner" or of hiding and smuggling arms or of destroying "Rebel mail" by Mrs. Mudd. But the record speaks to these charges elsewhere.

Samuel Mudd's activities tied him closely with the Confederate underground that operated throughout the area. While Booth and Mudd shared a common hatred for Lincoln, Mudd's reasons were considerably more personal than Booth's. By 1864, the Mudd family's wealth in slaves had been wiped out by the policies of Abraham Lincoln. The loss of slaves was soon followed by a loss in land values. Emancipation took away the slave labor that was essential to tobacco farming. The entire economy of Charles County saw the loss of slave property that totaled between eight and ten million dollars as a result of Lincoln's emancipation policies. When viewed from this perspective, the animosity toward Lincoln by the people of southern Maryland can be better appreciated. The climate was filled with bitter hatred for Lincoln. It was into this climate that John Wilkes Booth would come looking for help. But Booth had no contacts in southern Maryland. He needed an entrée into the clandestine world of Confederate operations in the area. He desperately needed a key connection. To find that connection he would first travel north to Canada.

Part Two

The Deed

Nor do I deem it a dishonor in attempting to make for her a prisoner of this man, to whom she owes so much of misery.

John Wilkes Booth, November 1864

We trust some bold hand will pierce his heart with dagger point for the public good.

LaCrosse Daily Democrat, August 29, 1864

CHAPTER SIX

The Key Connection

Misery acquaints a man with strange bedfellows.

The Tempest, *2.2*

In mid-October Booth visited with his mother at Edwin's house in New York City. The relationship between the two brothers had become seriously strained over their political differences. In her memoir Asia quoted Wilkes, "If it were not for mother I would not enter Edwin's house, but she will leave there if we cannot be welcomed, and I do not want her to be unhappy for me."[1] Asia told of "stormy words" between the two brothers. They were "the last unkind ones that ever passed between them."[2]

On October 16 he bid his mother goodbye and headed north to the Canadian province of Quebec. Two days later he registered at St. Lawrence Hall in Montreal, where he checked into room 150. St. Lawrence Hall had become the gathering place for Confederate agents in Montreal. Ostensibly Booth went to Canada to make arrangements to ship his theatrical wardrobe through the blockade to a Confederate port, but the length of his stay and his contacts while in Montreal suggest much more.

Booth was in Montreal a total of ten days, from October 18 through October 27. During that time he was seen in the presence of two men who were well-known Confederate agents based in Canada, George N. Sanders and Patrick C. Martin. Sanders was a Kentuckian who harbored a fanatical devotion for the Confederacy and an equally fanatical hatred for Lincoln. He had a history of associating with European revolutionaries. While in Europe awaiting his confirmation as United States consul in London, he advocated the assassination of Napoleon III (Louis Napoleon).[3] If true to form, Sanders undoubtedly urged Booth to go forward with a plot to assassinate Lincoln.

Booth's other contact in Montreal was Patrick Charles Martin. At least one reliable witness at the conspiracy trial testified to seeing Booth and Martin together in the fall of 1864.[4] Martin was a native New Yorker who had only recently been a liquor dealer in Baltimore. His career was not limited to liquor, however. Prior to the war he had extensive service at sea, where he had captained a variety of vessels. Following the outbreak of hostilities, Martin successfully ran the Union blockade on numerous occasions. His success soon made him a target of Federal authorities, and he escaped to Canada to avoid falling into Union hands. Once in Canada, Martin settled into more clandestine activities. He became one of the Confederacy's principal agents in Montreal, which became known as "Little Richmond."

A fellow Baltimorean, George P. Kane, who formerly served as police marshal for that city, had joined Martin in Montreal. In November of 1863 Martin and Kane had been involved in organizing a force of armed men to free Confederate prisoners being held at Johnson's Island, a Union prison camp located in Lake Erie just off of Sandusky, Ohio.[5] The prison held 2,600 Confederate soldiers. The bulk of these prisoners were officers who organized themselves and the other inmates into a cohesive group. One of the ranking Confederate officers in prison, Brigadier General James A. Archer, was able to smuggle a letter to Secretary of War James Seddon. Archer's letter was reminiscent of Union general August Willich's report to Lincoln in May 1863, in which he claimed the prison and city of Richmond were lightly defended and susceptible to attack. Archer wrote Seddon that Johnson's Island was weakly guarded and that taking over the prison camp would be relatively easy. Once in control of the camp, however, the prisoners would need some means to get off of the island. Archer asked for Seddon's help.[6] It was soon forthcoming.

Martin and Kane had devised a plan. It called for a force of armed Confederates to overpower the crew of the USS *Michigan* that was the only U.S. warship stationed on the Great Lakes near the prison camp. Once it was captured, the Confederates planned to turn the *Michigan*'s guns on the prison. Thus threatened, the prison guards would have no choice but to free the prisoners. Once freed, the prisoners would be carried off of the island and transported to Canada by boats commandeered on Lake Erie. From Canada they would make their way back to the Confederacy and Lee's army.

Kane and Martin met an advanced contingent of two dozen men in Montreal. They expected upwards of two hundred more to join them near Johnson's Island. The plan was abandoned when word of the raid somehow leaked, alerting Union forces that an attempt at overtaking the prison was brewing. The prison was reinforced and put on alert. Abandoning their plan to free the prisoners on Johnson's Island, Martin and Kane retreated to Montreal where they soon continued their covert operations against the United States.

A year after the aborted raid, Martin and Booth now met in another scheme designed to free Confederate prisoners. This time the daring plan involved exchanging a captured President Lincoln. Both operations were intended to free desperately needed Confederate prisoners of war—by force in the first instance and through an exchange agreement in the second. General Ulysses Grant had suspended the exchange of prisoners after he assumed command of the Union armies in March of 1864.[7] Grant knew that the North could replace its soldiers more readily than the South. By suspending prisoner exchange, Grant hoped to seriously deplete Lee's army of much needed men. By the fall of 1864 the strategy was working, and the Confederacy was experiencing a serious reduction in manpower. So serious was the problem that Confederate leaders contemplated enlisting slaves into the army. The growing numbers of Union prisoners in Confederate prisons was also putting an enormous strain on Confederate food supplies, which only made matters worse. Both sides looked to ways to liberate prisoners, not only to relieve the suffering but to help replenish frontline troops. Capturing Lincoln would give the Confederates the ultimate bargaining chip in forcing the North to reinstitute prisoner exchange.

Meeting with Martin in October, Booth made arrangements to ship his theatrical wardrobe through the blockade to a port in the South on one of Martin's vessels named the *Marie Victoria.* But Booth's business arrangements with Martin went beyond the shipping of his wardrobe. Booth needed help with his plan to carry the captured president through Charles County and across the Potomac River to Virginia. Where Booth came up with the idea to travel to Montreal and meet with Martin is unclear, but such a meeting must have been known at some point by the leadership in Richmond.

Martin appeared to be well connected with the Confederate underground in southern Maryland. He knew which individuals were capable of assisting Booth and which ones were most trustworthy. The Confederate mail line that began in Richmond and ended in Montreal passed through the heart of southern Maryland and involved some of the Confederacy's best agents. In order to help Booth, Martin prepared a letter of introduction to two of Charles County's more prominent Southern sympathizers, Dr. Samuel Mudd and Dr. William Queen.[8]

After providing Booth with this letter of introduction, Martin may also have given Booth the partial means to finance his recruitment efforts. When Booth returned to Washington from Montreal, he carried not only Martin's letter, but also a draft for $1,500 that he deposited in Jay Cooke's bank.[9] While the source of Booth's funds can not be positively established, Patrick Martin seems to be a reasonable source. Booth's income from acting was drying up, and his losses in the oil fields had been substantial. When the Confederate agents set up operations in Canada in May of 1864 they received a million dollars in gold from Confederate Secret Service funds to finance their operations against the United States. Some of this money may have been given to Booth while in Montreal to help underwrite his scheme to capture Lincoln. The fact that Booth returned from Canada and made a deposit in Cooke's bank within a week suggests that Martin had provided the funds. The amount of money was not trivial. In today's market, $1,500 is the equivalent of approximately $16,000 in current dollars. Booth disbursed all of this money between January 7 and March 16, the most active period of his recruitment activities, which further supports the notion that the funds were to support his capture plan.[10]

It is at the point of Booth's return from Montreal that the sequence of his recruitment furnishes a clue to the importance of Samuel Mudd to his overall operation. Samuel Mudd was just the sort of ally that Booth would need to carry out his plot. The location of Mudd's house was ideally situated along the escape route. If Booth were to avoid the soldiers occupying the area, he would have to travel at night, and he would need to know where the soldiers were located. Even riding hard all night from Washington he would not be able to get beyond the area where Mudd lived before daylight.[11] He would need a place to stay until nightfall. The fact that Mudd was a physician allowed him to move about the county without being harassed by the military. His contacts with other agents would allow him to gather information about the military in the area. All of these things would prove crucial to Booth in his plan to capture Lincoln and carry him south.

Martin's choice of William Queen and Samuel Mudd suggests Martin knew these two men not as friends, but as colleagues in clandestine operations. How else would Martin have known these two if not through the Confederate underground network? The fact that Martin's letter carried weight with these two men suggests their importance to Confederate operations in Charles County. As loyal Confederate operatives they could be trusted to help Booth in laying out his escape plan.

Armed with Martin's letter, Booth boarded the stagecoach in Washington for Charles County on Friday morning, November 11. Booth spent Friday evening at the Bryantown tavern where he was later met by Joseph Queen, a son of Dr. William Queen, and taken back to the elder Queen's house on Saturday.[12] The fact that Joseph Queen met Booth in Bryantown and brought him back to Dr. Queen's house suggests that prior arrangements had been made anticipating Booth's arrival.

The Queens lived approximately six miles south of Bryantown along the eastern edge of the Zekiah Swamp. On Sunday, Booth, Dr. Queen, and Queen's son-in-law John Thompson attended services at St. Mary's Catholic Church a few miles south of Bryantown. Also attending St. Mary's services that morning was Samuel Mudd.

Mudd's presence at St. Mary's Church on this particular Sunday supports the notion that he had come by appointment specifically to meet Booth. The Mudd family normally attended St. Peter's Church located two miles west of the Mudd farm and seven miles to the northwest of St. Mary's Church. The two churches lay in separate parishes. St. Peter's Church held mass every Sunday and had its own priest in residence, Father Peter B. Lenaghan.[13] Father Lenaghan married the Mudds, and their four children had been baptized at St. Peter's.[14] It seems more than coincidental that when Booth appeared at St. Mary's Church for the first time, Dr. Mudd was also present. It would prove to be a near fatal visit for Mudd.

Booth's presence at St. Mary's Church on Sunday morning is confirmed by several sources, the most important of which is Mudd himself. In a statement prepared prior to his arrest, Mudd wrote, "I was introduced to him [Booth] by Mr. J.C. Thompson, a son-in-law of William Queen, in November or December last."[15] Thompson was more specific in his statement, "On Sunday morning, this man Booth, Dr. Queen, and myself went to church in Bryantown, and I introduced Booth to Dr. Mudd." Thompson did not stop at this point, however. In answer to a second question as to whether he had ever seen Booth again Thompson answered, "I think some time, if my memory serves me, in December he came down there [Charles County] a second time to Dr. Queen's house." More on this second visit shortly.

Following Thompson's introduction of Booth that Sunday morning in November, Mudd gave this explanation of what happened next: "Booth inquired if I knew any parties in this neighborhood who had any fine horses for sale. I told him there was a neighbor of mine who had some very fine traveling horses, and he said he thought if he could purchase one reasonable he would do so, and would ride up to Washington on him instead of riding in the stage. The next evening [here Mudd means Sunday evening following church] he rode to my house and staid [*sic*] with me that night, and the next morning purchased a rather old horse."[16]

On this point, the veracity of Mudd's explanation begins to fall apart. While the evidence supports Booth's being introduced to Mudd at St. Mary's Church on Sunday morning and carrying a letter of introduction to him from Patrick Martin, it does not support Mudd's claim that Booth purchased a horse from Mudd's neighbor the next day. Three separate pieces of evidence place Booth back in Washington at his room in the National Hotel on Monday, November 14, the day Mudd claimed Booth bought the horse and rode him back to Washington.

George Washington Bunker, clerk at the National Hotel in Washington where Booth had a room, testified at the conspiracy trial that Booth was back in his hotel room on November 14. He supported his testimony with a memo prepared from the hotel register.[17] A second piece of evidence is found in a letter written by Booth to J. Dominic Burch, manager of the Bryantown Tavern where Booth spent the night of November 11. Booth's letter is dated November 14, 1864, and addressed from the National Hotel. In his letter Booth requests Burch to return an item left by Booth on the stagecoach.[18] This letter supports the conclusion that Booth not only was back in his hotel room on Monday, but that he returned from Bryantown by stagecoach and not on horseback as Mudd claimed.

A third piece of evidence, which proves that Booth could not have purchased the horse during his November visit as Mudd claimed, is found in the testimony of Thomas Gardiner. Gardiner was the nephew of George Gardiner, Mudd's nearest neighbor and the man from whom Booth purchased the horse. Thomas Gardiner testified at the conspiracy trial that he was present when Booth purchased the horse, and that his uncle had him deliver the horse to Booth at the Bryantown tavern "the next day."[19] While Gardiner could not swear to the exact day Booth bought the horse, he guessed that Booth bought it in the latter part of November and that he, Gardiner, delivered the horse the following day, a Tuesday. If Gardiner's memory was correct, Booth could not possibly have purchased the horse on that Monday in November, as Mudd claimed, and ridden it back to Washington.

If Booth did not purchase the horse from Mudd's neighbor at the time of his November visit, when did he purchase it, and why did Mudd lie about it? The answer can be pieced together from the testimony of John Thompson and John F. Hardy, another of Mudd's neighbors. Both Thompson and Hardy testified at the conspiracy trial about the events of Saturday, April 15. Hardy told the trial judges that Mudd stopped by his house late Saturday afternoon on his way home from Bryantown while Booth was still at Mudd's house resting. During his conversation with Hardy, Mudd told him that he had heard that Lincoln had been shot and that a man named Booth had shot him. Hardy went on to testify of having seen the man named Booth at St. Mary's Church on two separate occasions: "I saw him [Booth] some time before Christmas, at church, one Sunday. . . . Some time again I saw him at the same place, and asked if that was the same man; and the answer was 'Yes.'"[20] When Hardy was asked how long the two times were apart he answered: "I think about a month. I think it [the first meeting] was some time in November. . . . I think both times that I saw him there were before Christmas. . . . [I]t strikes me it must have been in November when I first saw him there."[21]

According to Hardy, Booth was in Charles County on two occasions, once in November, and a second time, in December. Although Booth was in Charles County a second time, did he meet with Mudd, and if so, what evidence supports a second meeting? The evidence comes from Mudd himself.[22]

Following Mudd's conviction he was sentenced to life in prison at Fort Jefferson in the Dry Tortugas, a series of small islands off of the Florida Keys. Mudd and conspirators Samuel Arnold, Michael O'Laughlen, and Edman Spangler were placed under a military escort assigned to accompany them to Fort Jefferson. In charge of the guard was Captain George W. Dutton, a member of the Veteran Reserve Corps. On Dutton's return to Washington after delivering his prisoners to Fort Jefferson, a reporter from the *Washington Evening Star* interviewed him. The following day an article appeared in the *Star* that quoted Dutton as having had a conversation with Mudd about his relationship with Booth.[23] On hearing about Dutton's claim, Joseph Holt, judge advocate general and the man in charge of the prosecution during the trial, called Dutton to his office and had him write out a report in the form of an affidavit. According to Dutton, Mudd had confided to him that he knew all along that the injured patient who came to his house the morning after Lincoln was assassinated was John Wilkes Booth, and further, he knew that Booth had killed Lincoln.

Dutton also claimed that Mudd admitted to having met with Booth and John Surratt and a man named Louis Wiechmann in December of 1864 at Booth's hotel room in Washington. This claim of a meeting between Mudd and Surratt had been made by government prosecutors to show that Mudd's involvement with Booth went deep into the conspiracy. Mudd's attorney Thomas Ewing had denied the meeting and introduction. Testifying at the trial, Wiechmann told the commissioners that he had been present at the meeting and spoke of Mudd's introducing Booth to John Surratt. Wiechmann had gotten the date of the meeting wrong, however, and Ewing seized the opportunity to attempt to impeach Wiechmann's damaging testimony. Wiechmann had told the commissioners the meeting took place on the fifteenth of January. Ewing produced several witnesses to prove that Mudd was nowhere near Washington during the month of January and was at home on the 15th and not in Washington as Wiechmann claimed. Ewing accused Wiechmann of lying. In his summation to the commission, Ewing said, "There is no reliable evidence at all that [Dr. Mudd] ever met Booth before the assassination except once on Sunday in November last."[24] The military commission thought otherwise. They believed Wiechmann. Ewing's attempt to disprove that the meeting ever took place seriously jeopardized Mudd's credibility at the time of the trial. Now Dutton's affidavit further eroded Mudd's credibility, claiming that Mudd knew his injured patient was Booth all along.

When Mudd received word of Dutton's affidavit he responded to it with an affidavit of his own. In his response, Mudd denied that he had told Dutton that he knew his patient was John Wilkes Booth. Surprisingly Mudd did admit to the meeting in Washington as described by Wiechmann and denied by Ewing. Mudd wrote that the meeting did not occur on January 15, 1865, as Wiechmann had claimed, but on December 23 two days before Christmas. Mudd seemed to justify his failure to admit to the second meeting at the time of his trial simply because Wiechmann had gotten the date wrong. It was this sort of technical evasion of the truth that got Mudd arrested in the first place.

In his affidavit, Mudd gave the details of the Washington meeting. In the course of his description he let slip a damaging admission. He told of a second meeting with Booth in Charles County a few days before the meeting on December 23 in Washington. This second meeting corresponded to the second time that Hardy claimed he saw Booth at St. Mary's Church shortly "before Christmas." In describing the Washington meeting, Mudd wrote in his affidavit:

> We [Mudd and Booth] started down one street, and then up another, and had not gone far when we met Surratt and Wiechmann. Introductions took place and we turned back in the direction of the hotel. After arriving in the room, I took the first opportunity presented to apologize to Surratt for having introduced him to Booth—a man I knew so little concerning. This conversation took place in the passage in front of the room (hallway) and was not over three minutes in duration. . . . Surratt and myself returned and resumed our former seats (after taking drinks ordered) around a centre table, which stood midway the room and distant seven or eight feet from Booth and Wiechmann. Booth *remarked that he had been down to the country a few days before, and said that he had not yet recovered from the fatigue. Afterward he said he had been down in Charles County, and had made me an offer to purchase of my land, which I confirmed by an affirmative answer* [emphasis added]; and he further remarked that on his way up [to Washington] he lost his way and rode several miles off the track.[25]

Mudd admits that Booth had been down in Charles County a second time during which the two men had met. Mudd states that Booth "had made me an offer to purchase of my land, which I confirmed by an affirmative answer." Booth's reason for returning to Charles County was to solicit the help of another Confederate agent by the name of Thomas Harbin. To do this, Booth needed Mudd's help.

Harbin, who worked as an agent for the Confederate Secret Service, maintained a signal camp in King George County on the Virginia side of the Potomac. He was a native of Charles County, however, and knew Mudd well. Both men lived within five miles of Bryantown. Before the war Harbin had served as Postmaster for Bryantown. Following the outbreak of hostilities he undertook handling the mail of the Confederate States government.

Among Harbin's "mail agents" were Samuel Mudd and John Surratt. These men helped to pass documents, newspapers, and letters between Richmond and points north. The process was simple. Letters from the Confederacy arrived by mail agent and were turned over to a trusted agent who saw that they received proper postage and handling by one of the friendly post offices in the area. The Federal postal system delivered the mail to the appropriate parties in the North. The reverse, of course, was also true in that local post offices handled mail from points north directed to Richmond. These letters were usually placed inside envelopes addressed to one of the mail agents in Charles County who saw that they were safely carried across the river to Virginia.[26] Harbin was among the several agents that dealt in clandestine mail and documents. Whether Booth, on hearing of Harbin and his exploits, asked Mudd if he would arrange a meeting between the two or whether Mudd volunteered Harbin is not known. What is known is that Mudd arranged a meeting between Booth and Harbin for Sunday, December 18.

Evidence that such a meeting occurred comes from Harbin himself. In an 1877 interview with newspaper columnist George Alfred Townsend, Harbin told of coming across the Potomac River from Virginia to meet with Booth in December. The meeting was set up by Samuel Mudd and took place at the Bryantown Tavern. Townsend describes what happened:

> After church that [December] day, Booth went into Bryantown a mile or two distant and in plain sight was introduced by Dr. Mudd at the village hotel to Mr Thomas Harbin who was the principal signal officer or [Confederate] spy in the lower Md counties.
>
> Harbin gave me all the particulars concerning Booth. He told me that at the tavern that Sunday it was Dr. Mudd who introduced him to Booth who wanted some private conversations. Booth then outlined a scheme for seizing Abraham Lincoln and delivering him up in Virginia.
>
> Harbin was a cool man who had seen many liars and rogues go to and fro in that illegal border and he set down Booth as a crazy fellow, but at the same time said that he would give his cooperation.[27]

Whatever Harbin may have thought of Booth, he agreed to join his conspiracy. The enlistment of Harbin into Booth's capture scheme was an important one. He would later prove vital to Booth's attempt to escape after crossing the Potomac River into Virginia.[28]

Following his meeting with Harbin, Booth returned to Mudd's house where he spent the night. The next morning Booth and Mudd rode over to George Gardiner's farm a short distance away where Booth purchased a horse from Gardiner.[29] It was distinguished by having lost one eye, which didn't effect its ability to carry a rider wherever he might need to go. Booth asked Gardiner to have the horse delivered by his nephew Thomas L. Gardiner to the Bryantown Tavern the next day, Tuesday.[30]

After taking possession of the horse in Bryantown, Booth visited the local blacksmith shop of Peter Trotter in the company of Dr. Mudd, where he had a new set of shoes made for his horse. When Trotter had finished, Booth and Mudd rode off together.[31] Having signed on Harbin and purchased a new horse, Booth rode back to Washington, where he checked into the National Hotel on Thursday, December 22. The following day Booth met again with Samuel Mudd, evidently by appointment, this time in Booth's room at the National Hotel.

Louis Wiechmann's account of the meeting in Washington at Booth's hotel room differed little from Mudd's later account. Whatever the details of the meeting, including how long it lasted and what was discussed, one thing is certain: as a result of Mudd's introducing John Surratt to Booth, Surratt agreed to join Booth as one of his band of conspirators. Booth now had four good men in tow: Sam Arnold, Mike O'Laughlen, Thomas Harbin, and John Surratt. Surratt, like Harbin, was an accomplished agent who enjoyed the confidence of the highest-ranking officers of the Confederate government.

John Harrison Surratt Jr. was the youngest of three children born to Mary Surratt and John Harrison Surratt Sr. Isaac, the oldest son, had gone to Texas before the war and enlisted in the Confederate army shortly after the shelling of Fort Sumter. Anna, the middle child, was closest to her mother, sharing the duties of running a household. At the outbreak of the war Anna was attending Catholic school in Bryantown. John was attending St. Charles College, a Catholic seminary located near Baltimore. It was here that John first met and became good friends with Louis Wiechmann, a friendship that would have grave consequences for the Surratt family in only a few short years. In August of 1862, John Surratt Sr. died, leaving Mary a widow with substantial debts. John and Anna returned home from their schooling at the time of their father's death to help their mother manage the tavern business.[32]

Located thirteen miles southeast of Washington, the Surratt Tavern was a natural stopping point for travelers passing through southern Maryland on their way to the capital. The tavern served as both a hostelry and residence. By 1862 it had become a center of secessionist activity. Its principal value lay in its location along the primary route into Washington and the Confederate sympathies of its owner. It served as the post office for the surrounding area, which made it ideal for receiving and distributing Confederate mail.[33]

John Surratt Sr. had served as postmaster until his death in August, and on his return from the seminary John Surratt Jr. replaced his father in this civil service post. Undoubtedly, it was at this time that John began working for the Confederate underground that was flourishing throughout the area. He was eighteen years old and a prime candidate for the army. His job as postmaster exempted him from Federal service while his underground activities satisfied his desire to serve the Southern cause without having to stand in the direct line of fire. It seemed he had the best of both worlds.

By the time Samuel Mudd introduced Surratt to Booth he was one of the Confederacy's better agents and had been granted considerable responsibilities as a courier between Richmond and points north. The tavern had become a "safe house" along the courier route between Richmond and Washington, a fact that had to involve the de facto cooperation of Mary Surratt.[34] All sorts of Confederate agents passed to and fro throughout the area, finding the tavern a safe place to stop over.

In November of 1863, John was removed as postmaster after serving thirteen months. In writing to a friend at the time, he said it was due to "disloyalty."[35] His removal had no effect on John's subversive activities, however. The Surratt Tavern remained a safe house and focal point for clandestine activity even without the post office. By the time of John's enlistment into Booth's conspiracy to capture Lincoln, his contacts were considerable. He brought credibility to Booth's operation, but more importantly, he brought the vital contacts along the courier route that Booth needed if he were to successfully make his way to Richmond with his grand prize. He was also in touch with Judah P. Benjamin, the Confederate secretary of state, which potentially gave Booth an ear in Richmond.

Thanks to Mudd, John Surratt was now in the fold. Indirectly Mudd was also responsible for Booth's next recruit, George Andrew Atzerodt, alias Andrew Atwood. Born in 1835 in the Kingdom of Prussia, Atzerodt emigrated with his parents in 1844 to the small village of Germantown in Montgomery County, Maryland. In 1857 Atzerodt and his brother John moved to the southern Maryland village of Port Tobacco where the two brothers went into the carriage-painting business. When the business failed soon after the start of the war, John went to Baltimore where he secured a position on the staff of James McPhail, provost marshal of Maryland. George, however, remained in Port Tobacco where he began a successful trade in ferrying men and materiel back and forth across the Potomac River for the Confederacy.

Soon after Thomas Harbin and John Surratt joined in Booth's conspiracy they paid Atzerodt a visit. Booth's newest recruits convinced Atzerodt to join with them. His knowledge of the river was important. Three days after Atzerodt's hanging in July 1865, the *Baltimore American* described his connection: "He carried on painting [carriages] in Port Tobacco until last fall [1864] when he met with John H. Surratt and a man named Harbew [Harbin]. Surratt induced him to join in the conspiracy of abducting the President. . . . Atzerodt's knowledge of men and the country in the vicinity of Port Tobacco, and, in fact, of all the counties bounding on the Potomac gave to the conspirators a valuable assistant. He was well acquainted with Herold . . . who was also engaged in the conspiracy. Surratt . . . sent for Atzerodt to come to Washington. . . . Surratt introduced Atzerodt to Booth."[36]

Booth's recruitment was proceeding well thanks to Samuel Mudd and his contacts. Next on Booth's list of recruits was David Herold. Herold was another member brought into the fold by John Surratt. As with Atzerodt, Herold was recruited in January. Twenty-two years old at the time, Herold lived with his mother and several sisters in a row house in the District of Columbia, a short distance from the entrance to the Washington Navy Yard located on Eighth Street. He was employed at the Navy Yard pharmacy. Herold's job at the pharmacy provided Booth with ready access to pharmaceuticals such as chloroform that might be needed to subdue a resisting president.

Cottage Grove Public Librar

Herold was an avid hunter and spent much of his free time chasing game birds throughout southern Maryland. His travels made him an expert in the geography of the region. This brought him into contact with the Surratt Tavern and John Surratt, and the two became good friends. When the Surratts moved to Washington in late 1864 Herold sometimes visited John at the boardinghouse on H Street. Booth needed a reliable guide and John Surratt knew just the man. There was no one who knew the back roads of southern Maryland better than Davey Herold.

The final recruit to Booth's inner circle came late in January, sometime around the twenty-first or twenty-second. He was a Confederate soldier whose most recent service had been with Mosby's famous partisan rangers. Lewis Thornton Powell, alias Lewis Payne (Paine), has been characterized by nearly every author on the assassination as the "muscle" of the team. He stood six feet, two inches tall, weighed 175 pounds, and at the young age of twenty-one was considered a powerful man. Like Arnold and O'Laughlen, Powell had served in the Confederate army.[37] At age seventeen he enlisted in Company I of the First Florida Infantry, known as the Jasper Hamilton Blues of Hamilton County, Florida. Powell served with the Army of Northern Virginia through its campaigns, culminating in the battle of Gettysburg. On July 2 he was wounded in the right wrist and taken prisoner. Removed to one of the army corps hospitals located at Gettysburg College, Powell served as a POW nurse during his recovery. While working at the corps hospital he met a young woman by the name of Margaret Branson.[38] "Maggie" Branson was an ardent Confederate sympathizer who went to Gettysburg to care for the Confederate wounded. According to Powell biographer, Betty Ownsbey, an intimacy developed between Powell and Branson that would later cause Powell to find his way to the Branson home in Baltimore where he would meet John Surratt.[39]

Powell eventually fled from the hospital in Gettysburg and tried to make his way back to the Second Florida. His travels took him to the home of a prominent Warrenton, Virginia, family named Payne. It was while resting at the Payne home that Powell made contact with members of Mosby's Forty-third Battalion of Virginia Cavalry and was soon accepted as a member of that famous command. Powell's name can be found on the muster rolls during 1863 and 1864. But on January 13, 1865, Powell is found riding into a Union encampment stationed at Fairfax Court House in Virginia. He had adopted the name of his Warrenton hosts and claimed to be a civilian refugee from Virginia. The provost marshal accepted Powell's story and sent him on to Alexandria, Virginia, with a pass. At Alexandria, Powell took the oath of allegiance and was released from further custody by the Union authorities.[40] Powell, now Lewis Paine,[41] left Alexandria and headed to Baltimore and the home of Maggie Branson, his Gettysburg hospital companion. Here the plot thickens.

On January 14, while Powell was on his way to Baltimore, John Surratt met with Thomas Harbin at Port Tobacco in Charles County, Maryland. The two men set out to buy a boat and see to its safe keeping in anticipation of using it to ferry the captured president across the Potomac River. They soon found a suitable boat in the possession of a local farmer named Richard Smoot. Smoot supplemented his income by ferrying passengers and contraband across the river.[42] Surratt and Smoot struck a deal, and Surratt and Harbin turned the boat over to George Atzerodt for safe keeping. Booth's recruitment of Surratt, Harbin, and Atzerodt was working out well. Having finished his business with Harbin and Atzerodt, Surratt returned to his mother's Washington boardinghouse and picked up his fellow boarder, Louis Wiechmann, and traveled to Baltimore where the two men checked into a local hotel.

During Surratt's trial in 1867, Wiechmann recounted the details of this trip with Surratt to Baltimore. In his testimony Wiechmann told of Surratt's having $300 in cash and telling him that he needed to meet with another man in the city on private business. Surratt did not or would not tell Wiechmann who the man was, but did tell him that he needed to see the man privately.[43] The prosecution attempted to show through Wiechmann's testimony that the man Surratt went to visit was Lewis Powell, alias Lewis Paine. It seems highly probable they were correct. Presumably Surratt had brought Powell living expenses to hold him over until called to Washington, which happened three weeks later.

On March 14, Surratt sent a telegram to his contact in Baltimore, David Preston Parr, a china dealer, to send Powell to Washington. Parr was another of the many people in Surratt's address book who worked as a Confederate agent. His Baltimore china shop was a Confederate mail drop.[44] It is likely that Surratt actually met with Parr and turned the $300 over to him with instructions to take care of Powell until further notice.[45] It is also likely that the $300 Surratt carried was given to him by Booth from the funds the actor had deposited in Jay Cooke's bank following his visit to Montreal in October.

Powell soon arrived at Mrs. Surratt's boardinghouse where he used the alias of the Reverend Wood. Booth was now convening his team in anticipation of his first strike. Booth was intent on abducting Lincoln from the presidential box at Ford's Theatre. Booth had called the team together to familiarize them with his plan and the layout of the theater. He had reserved the two presidential boxes, numbers 7 and 8, for the March 15 evening performance, ostensibly to treat his friends to an evening at the theater while making sure to point out several details of the layout.[46]

Following the play on the fifteenth, the group adjourned to Gautier's restaurant located a short distance from the theater on Pennsylvania Avenue between Twelfth and Thirteenth Streets. Here Booth, Surratt, Powell,

Atzerodt, Arnold, and O'Laughlen met in a private room to throw down oysters and discuss capturing Lincoln. Though less than seven months had passed since Booth first began pulling his team together, there was dissension in the ranks. Arnold and O'Laughlen were making noises about pulling out. Plans had been dragging too slowly to suit them. The talk centered on taking action and taking it soon before word leaked out about their plans. Too much alcohol led to arguments. Harsh words were exchanged.

In 1870 in a lecture given at the Montgomery County Court House in Rockville, Maryland, John Surratt told his entranced audience about that night: "Some hard words and even threats passed between [Booth] and some of the party. Four of us arose, one saying, 'If I understand you to intimate anything more than the capture of Mr. Lincoln I for one will bid you goodbye.' Everyone expressed the same opinion. We all arose and commenced putting our hats on. Booth perceiving probably that he had gone too far, asked pardon saying that he 'had drank too much champagne.' After some difficulty everything was amicably arranged and we separated at 5 o'clock in the morning."[47]

Surratt was being disingenuous. That violence might accompany their capture plan was understood by most. Although not a part of their plan, killing Lincoln was always a possibility. Despite the differences of opinion about the operation to capture the president, the team was still intact as evidenced by what occurred just two days later. Its failure ultimately resulted in a shift in plans.

CHAPTER SEVEN

A Shift in Plans

> The hour has come when I must change my plan. Many . . . will blame me for what I am about to do, but posterity, I am sure, will justify me.
>
> *John Wilkes Booth*

Two days after the all-night meeting at Gautier's restaurant, Booth stopped by Ford's Theatre. His fame as a star performer produced a regular stream of mail from admirers. A portion of this mail was addressed to Booth, in care of Ford's Theatre. Booth had no permanent or "home" address simply because he had no permanent home. For all of his fame, his name cannot be found among any of the standard records of the period. Born in Maryland, he regularly listed himself as being from Baltimore, yet he is not found among any Baltimore or Maryland records of the period. His name is not in any of the Baltimore city directories of the day, nor even the 1860 census for Maryland. There is no birth certificate and no death certificate.[1] Booth's home was wherever he happened to be at any given moment. John Ford's Theatre was, in some ways, Booth's home. The Ford brothers were good friends of Booth and believed him to be a bright and personable character who was admired by nearly everyone who knew him.

Stopping by the theater on the morning of the seventeenth, Booth apparently learned that Lincoln was scheduled to visit a group of convalescing soldiers at the Campbell Hospital located at the far end of Seventh Street near the District line.[2] Members of the Washington Theatre's stock company were scheduled to perform a play by the title of *Still Waters Run Deep*, for the soldiers at the hospital. Here was the very opportunity Booth had been waiting for. The stretch of road leading to the hospital was rural and lightly traveled. It was close to the Eastern Branch River Bridge that led into Maryland. Within minutes of snatching Lincoln, Booth and his cohorts could be across the river heading for southern Maryland. It seemed like a godsend to Booth. He quickly sent word to each of the men to come at once to a restaurant located near the hospital. They soon arrived: Arnold, O'Laughlen, Powell, Atzerodt, Herold, and Surratt. Booth's network worked perfectly. Despite their differences over strategy, they were all still in the game.

Booth sent Herold off in a buggy to Surratt's tavern in Surrattsville with the necessary paraphernalia that would be needed for the journey south—all except the food and liquor. Booth had sent those on to Dr. Mudd's house two weeks before.[3] Herold carried two double-barreled shotguns, two Spencer carbines, a pistol, ammunition, a knife, a length of rope, and a monkey wrench.[4] The weapons' usefulness was obvious. The rope would come in handy to string across the road to unseat any cavalry that might try to follow them: perhaps amateurish, but possibly effective. Even if such a booby trap failed to work, its mere discovery would force pursuing cavalry to negotiate the trail with caution, thus slowing them down. The wrench would be used to remove the wheels of the president's carriage so it could be safely secured on the boat used to ferry it across the river.

The plan was to overtake the president's carriage, capture Lincoln, and dispose of the driver. With the president secure, the captors would make a dash for the Eastern Branch of the Potomac River and, crossing over into Maryland, make a run through Prince George's and Charles Counties to the Potomac. In his Rockville lecture Surratt explained the plan:

> One day we received information that the President would visit the Seventh Street Hospital for the purpose of being present at an entertainment to be given for the benefit of the wounded soldiers. The report only reached us about three quarters of an hour before the time appointed, but so perfect was our communication that we were instantly in our saddles on the way to the hospital. This was between one and two o'clock in the afternoon. It was our intention to seize the carriage, which was drawn by a splendid pair of horses, and to have one of the men mount the box and drive direct for southern Maryland via Benning's bridge.[5] We felt confident that all the cavalry in the city could never overhaul us. We were all mounted on swift horses, besides having a thorough knowledge of the country; it was determined to abandon the carriage after passing the city limits. Upon the suddenness of the blow and the celerity of our movements we depended for success. By the time the alarm could have been given and horses saddled, we would have been on our way through southern Maryland towards the Potomac River.[6]

Booth told the others to wait while he rode over to the hospital to check things out. If they were to be successful they would need to have their timing down pat. A member of the cast scheduled to perform at the hospital was E.L. Davenport, a good friend of Booth. Booth arrived at the hospital and, finding his friend, pulled Davenport aside. What of the president? Davenport told Booth that the president had changed his plans at the last minute and was not expected to show up.[7] Booth was crestfallen. He returned to where the men were waiting with the bad news. The plan now aborted, the men returned to the city angered and with some trepidation as to possibly having been discovered. What if word had leaked and the president had been warned? Forewarned, the military would be looking for them. They were needlessly concerned. Their plot had not been discovered. Lincoln had simply changed his schedule at the last minute at the invitation of Indiana governor Oliver P. Morton. The Philadelphia *Inquirer* carried a story the following day explaining:

> A Rebel flag captured at Fort Anderson by the One-Hundred and Fortieth Indiana Volunteers was to-day presented to Governor Morton of that state in front of the National Hotel. A large crowd of people were in attendance.
>
> Governor Morton made a brief speech in which he congratulated his auditors on the speedy end of the Rebellion, and concluded by introducing President Lincoln whose purity and patriotism, he said, where confessed by all, even among the most virulent agitators (applause).
>
> The President addressed the assemblage.[8]

Although Lincoln was scheduled to appear at the performance at Campbell Hospital, he felt obligated to accompany Governor Morton to his meeting with the 140th Indiana Volunteers. Ironically, the meeting took place at the National Hotel where Booth was living at the time. Lincoln used the opportunity of the flag presentation to discuss the latest effort of the Confederacy to employ small numbers of slaves to fight in the Confederate army. In his Rockville lecture, John Surratt described the ending of the aborted capture scheme with a little pun: "To our great disappointment, however, the President was not there [on the road leading from the Campbell Hospital] but one of the government officials—Mr. Chase, if I mistake not.[9] We did not disturb him, as we wanted a bigger *chase* than he could have afforded us."[10] Surratt appears to have embellished his story. Chase was not on the road to Washington and neither were Surratt and the others. They were still at the restaurant waiting for Booth[11]

Surratt concluded his lecture by stating, "It was our last attempt." This may have been what Surratt wanted people to think to deflect any conclusion that his agreement to participate in Booth's conspiracy to capture Lincoln was totally separate from the conspiracy to assassinate him. But even John Surratt must have been aware that any attempt to capture the president of the United States was likely to result in the loss of life, not the least of which could have been the president's. Whether he believed it or not, Surratt, as were all of Booth's accomplices, stuck to his scheme to the very end. It was a "tar baby" from which none of them could pull away.

Returning to the city, the unnerved band of conspirators soon split up, going their separate ways. Surratt went on to Richmond to meet with Secretary of State Judah P. Benjamin on courier business that took him to Canada.[12] Powell headed for the Branson boardinghouse in Baltimore where he had been holed up earlier and where John Surratt had found him two months before. Arnold and O'Laughlen returned to their homes in Baltimore.[13] Atzerodt and Herold remained in Washington. Booth returned to Ford's Theatre on March 18 in a benefit performance for his friend John McCullough, playing Pescara in *The Apostate*.[14] On the twenty-first he was off to New York.[15] By the twenty-seventh he was back in Washington.[16]

The precise moment when Booth decided to change his plan of capture to one of assassination is not clear. Booth's capture operation was still an option in his mind as late as March 27 when he telegraphed Michael O'Laughlen to come to Washington immediately, "Get word to Sam. Come on, with or without him, Wednesday morning. We sell that day sure. Don't fail."[17] Booth's plans for this occasion never materialized. Still, Booth's telegram to O'Laughlen marks March 27 as the boundary for capture while April 14 marked the boundary for murder. At some point during these seventeen days, Booth decided to murder Lincoln. The precise day the plan changed is not clear, but sometime before April 14 Booth visited the home of William Seward and chatted with a household maid.[18] Was Booth casing the home in anticipation of assigning Powell the task of killing Seward?

It is also not clear why Booth went to New York following the aborted capture attempt, but New York was a focal point for Confederate clandestine activity in the northeast. A clue may be found in a statement by George Atzerodt. While held prisoner at the Washington Arsenal (Old Washington Penitentiary), Atzerodt was visited by Maryland provost marshal James McPhail and Atzerodt's brother-in-law John L. Smith.[19] During the visit Smith copied down a statement by Atzerodt[20] that contained several important revelations, including the following: "Booth said he had met a party in N. York who would get the Prest. certain. They were going to mine the end of Pres. House, next to War Dept. They knew an entrance to accomplish it through. Spoke about getting the friends of the Prest. to get up an entertainment & they would mix in it, have a serenade &c & thus get at the Prest. & party. These were understood to be projects. Booth said if he did not get him quick the N. York crowd would. Booth knew the New York party apparently by a sign. He saw Booth give some kind of sign to two parties on the Avenue who he said were from New York."[21]

Clearly Booth had a New York connection and a New York interest, but who and what is uncertain. The authors of *Come Retribution* proposed a clue to this possible connection. It came in the person of a man named Roderick D. Watson. Watson was a member of the Charles County gentry. What brought him to New York after the outbreak of the war was the Confederate underground. Watson became known to local Federal officials for his underground activities that included blockade running.[22] He was probably well acquainted with Patrick C. Martin, the man who put Booth in contact with Samuel Mudd. At least one record has survived that links Watson directly to John Surratt. A letter dated March 19, 1865, fits closely into Booth's visit to New York and into his plans to capture Lincoln. Watson had written to Surratt asking him to come to New York on important business. What business is not known. Booth also telegraphed Louis Wiechmann, Surratt's friend and a boarder at Mrs. Surratt's boardinghouse, asking for a "number and street" address. Surratt must have understood what Booth wanted and sent him the address of the Herndon house located on the corner of Ninth and F Streets, just around from Ford's Theatre. Booth needed the address to give to Lewis Powell who was currently in New York with him and would travel to Washington and check into the Herndon house where he would await Booth's final instructions.[23] His business in New York completed, Booth returned to Washington on March 25 and checked into the National Hotel. There were exactly nineteen days left before the target day.

What of Atzerodt's remarks about the "New York crowd" and a plot to "mine" the wing of the Executive Mansion closest to the War Department? Atzerodt's statement suggests that a plan was in the offing to "blow up" the president by placing explosives in a part of the White House at a time when the president would be meeting with his cabinet. In a single moment, a proper demolition would kill the president and members of his cabinet. Atzerodt alluded to Booth's concern when he told McPhail and Smith that "Booth said if he did not get him quick the New York crowd would."[24] Such a statement suggests that Booth apparently thought he might be upstaged and lose out in his attempt to get Lincoln himself. Could such a plan to blow up the White House have any credibility? It could, and it was real.[25]

Any plot to plant explosives in the White House would require considerable skills in both ordnance and access to the White House. Such a plan centered on Thomas Harney, who was employed in the Confederate Torpedo Bureau in Richmond in March 1865.[26] The Torpedo Bureau was under the command of Brigadier General Gabriel Rains and was involved in the development and deployment of a variety of explosive devices for use on land and in water. Rains had used such devices as early as May 1862 at Yorktown and to a devastating effect at City Point in August of 1864.[27] It is also clear that units from the Confederate Secret Service were directed by Rains out of the Torpedo Bureau. One of these units involved John Maxwell and R.K. Dillard, who served in Captain Zedekiah McDaniel's company in the Secret Service.[28] Maxwell and Dillard were responsible for placing a "horological torpedo" (time bomb) on a Union supply barge at City Point that destroyed a major part of Grant's supply base on August 9, 1864. The resultant explosion was devastating, killing 54 people and wounding 126.[29] According to

Rains, the two men operated under his authority.[30] It was from this bureau that Thomas Harney set out on a mission that had all the earmarks of a plan to blow up the White House.

Shortly before the evacuation of Richmond on April 2, Harney left the Torpedo Bureau with a cache of special ordnance and joined Mosby and his rangers who were still active in Fauquier County, Virginia. Mosby was the man to safely slip Harney and his experts into Washington so they could carry out their plan. Among the rangers assigned to escort Harney were several Marylanders who had come over to join Mosby's command. They had traveled the area on numerous occasions and were familiar with the routes into and out of the region. Harney was able to join Mosby but never made it to Washington. Arriving at Burke Station in Fairfax County, Harney, along with 150 of Mosby's men, ran into a Union cavalry regiment. In the ensuing skirmish Harney and three other men were captured and taken to Old Capitol Prison in Washington.[31]

Speculation that Harney was on a mission to fulfill the plot Atzerodt referred to in his confession is gleaned from a seemingly unrelated event that occurred in Richmond on April 4. When that city was evacuated on April 2, Colonel Edward Hastings Ripley, commanding the Ninth Vermont Infantry, set up his headquarters not far from the Torpedo Bureau. Ripley and his men were the first Federal troops to occupy the evacuated city. On April 4, Ripley granted an interview with a Confederate enlisted man who worked at the Torpedo Bureau by the name of William H. Snyder. Snyder had sought an interview with Ripley to alert him and his superiors to a plan that troubled Snyder. In his postwar memoir, Ripley described his meeting with Snyder: "He [Snyder] knew that a party had just been dispatched from Raine's [General Gabriel Rains's][32] torpedo bureau on a secret mission, which vaguely he understood was aimed at the head of the Yankee government, and he wished to put Mr. Lincoln on his guard and have impressed upon him that just at this moment he believed him to be in great danger of violence and he should take better care of himself. He could give no names or facts, as the work of his department was secret, and no man knew what his comrade was sent to do, that the President of the United States was in great danger."[33]

Is it possible that Snyder was referring to Harney and his expedition to Mosby? While Harney's mission may have been directed at other targets, Snyder's revelation and the timing of a plot against Lincoln emanating from the Torpedo Bureau in Richmond is remarkably coincidental. The two plans fit neatly together.

While Harney's plot may have been what Atzerodt alluded to in his statement to McPhail, there is no way to link Harney with the "N. York crowd." While news of the skirmish appeared in the *Washington Daily Morning Chronicle* on April 11, Harney's capture and imprisonment in the Old Capitol Prison was not mentioned.[34] Still, Booth could have found out about the failure of Harney's operation through any number of sources in the city. The fall of Richmond and Lee's surrender may well have caused Booth to conclude that capturing Lincoln no longer had a strategic purpose.

On the evening of April 11, one day after Harney's capture, a crowd of several hundred jubilant citizens assembled on the lawn of the White House to hear the president deliver an address. He promised a similar gathering the night before that he would comment on the great events now unfolding. The president stood on a small balcony and looked down upon the smiling faces below. There was an air of celebration and revelry among the throng as they pressed forward to hear the promised words of their president. Elizabeth Keckley, Mary Lincoln's seamstress and close personal friend, watched from inside a room on the second floor. She would remember the scene vividly, describing it three years later in her little book: "I looked out, and never saw such a mass of heads before. . . . Close to the house the faces were plainly discernible, but they faded into more ghostly outlines on the outskirts of the assembly; and what added to the weird, spectral beauty of the scene, was the confused hum of voices that rose above the sea of forms. . . . It was a grand and imposing scheme."[35]

The president explained his program of accepting the rebellious states back into the Union. First and foremost was Louisiana, deeply Southern, mostly Black, tightly bound to the commerce of the nation. A minority of residents who swore allegiance to the United States had adopted a new state government and constitution. The question under debate was whether or not this new government should be taken back into the Union or rejected in favor of a government dictated and controlled by others, mostly from outside her borders. Some wanted more from the new government while others wanted less.

The question of slavery in Louisiana had been answered by the new state constitution. It was abolished. But it stopped there. What would be next for the newly freed slave? Lincoln did not evade the issue: "It is unsatisfactory to some that the elective franchise is not given to the colored man. I would myself prefer that it were now conferred on the very intelligent, and on those who served our cause as soldiers. . . . Concede that the new government of Louisiana is only to what it should be as the egg is to the fowl; we shall sooner have the fowl by hatching the egg than by smashing it."[36]

Standing on the White House lawn listening to the president's words were John Wilkes Booth and Lewis Powell. It was all Booth could do to contain his rage. Hearing Lincoln speak of enfranchising Blacks, Booth turned to his companion and hissed, "That means nigger citizenship. Now, by God, I will put him through. That will be the last speech he will ever make."[37]

CHAPTER EIGHT

A Day of Jubilation

> He was almost boyish in his mirth. . . . *The Friday*, I never saw him so supremely cheerful—his manner was even playful.
>
> *Mary Todd Lincoln*

William T. Howell had waited nearly five weeks for his official appointment as Indian agent for Michigan. Lincoln appointed Howell on March 10, and he was confirmed by the Senate one day later. It was now April 14, and the appointment languished somewhere in the president's office. Lincoln sat down at his desk and penned a message to his commissioner of Indian affairs, William P. Dole: "Please do not send off the Commission of W.T. Howell, as Indian agent in Michigan, until the return of Mr. Harlan, and hearing from me again. Yours truly, A. Lincoln."[1]

Lincoln decided to delay Howell's appointment out of deference to his new secretary of the interior, James Harlan. Harlan had been nominated and confirmed as the new secretary on March 9, the day before Lincoln signed Howell's commission, and Lincoln wanted to give Harlan the opportunity to approve the appointment. It was little things like this that earned the president the respect of his cabinet members. Two weeks later, following Lincoln's death, Harlan withdrew the appointment and substituted Richard M. Smith for the position in his stead.[2] Had Howell's appointment gone through, his loyalty would be to a dead president. Smith, on the other hand, would now be indebted to Harlan.

Despite such mundane business there was a feeling of excitement everywhere, especially in the White House. April 14 was a day of jubilation. Lee's once powerful army was disbanded and the man who had brought about its demise was in town to visit with the president and attend a cabinet meeting for the first time. Ulysses S. Grant was the man of the hour, and a jubilant Lincoln wanted to show him off. Grant had not been popular with everyone at the time of his appointment as general of the armies. Lincoln thought differently. This general was different from all of the other generals rolled into one—he was a fighter. Under pressure from certain politicians to remove Grant, Lincoln tersely replied, "I can't spare this man. He fights!" On another occasion he mused, "He has the grit of a bulldog! Once let him get his teeth in, and nothing can shake him off."[3] Lincoln had been beset by a succession of generals who lacked the necessary combative spirit to carry the attack. McClellan, Lincoln once said, "had the slows." Grant was different. He was just what Lincoln had needed.

When Grant took command of the Union army he assumed responsibility for a battlefront reaching from the Atlantic coastline to the Rio Grande in Texas. His army consisted of twenty-one army corps of nearly 750,000 men operating in eighteen departments. It required administrative skills beyond any ever required before. The political landscape was covered with land mines that waited for the new commander's unsuspecting foot. Whatever Grant's shortcomings may have been, reluctance to fight was not one of them.

Also on Lincoln's desk this morning was a letter from James H. Van Alen.[4] According to Lincoln's secretaries, John G. Nicolay and John Hay, Van Alen had written to Lincoln urging him to "guard his life" and "not expose it to assassination as he had by going to Richmond."[5] Lincoln replied in a letter dated April 14, "My dear Sir: I intend to adopt the advice of my friends and use due precaution."[6] But as Lincoln knew, no amount of precaution could stop a determined killer. Putting Van Alen's letter aside, Lincoln could not help but smile, for today was a happy day, a day of revelry. His oldest son, Robert, was home on leave and would join the family for breakfast.

Lincoln, although a spare eater, was looking forward to breakfast this particular Good Friday. Robert had returned only the evening before from Grant's headquarters where he served as assistant adjutant general of volunteers. On graduating from Harvard University, Robert was intent on joining the Union army along with many of his fellow graduates. Mary Lincoln, when she heard of Robert's intentions, objected strenuously and appealed to her husband to persuade Robert not to volunteer. She could not bear another loss. Lincoln, caught between his son and his wife, compromised. He wrote a letter to Grant requesting his help. The most powerful man in the country was asking the second most powerful man for a favor. It was typical Lincoln: "Please read this letter as though I were not President, but only a friend. My son, now in his twenty-second year, having graduated from Harvard, wishes to see something of the war before it ends. I do not wish to put him in the ranks, nor yet to give him a commission, to which those who have already served long, are better entitled, and better qualified to hold. Could he, without embarrassment to you, or detriment to the service, go into your military family with some nominal rank, and I not the public, furnishing his necessary means? If no, say so without the least hesitation, because I am as anxious, and as deeply interested, that you shall not be encumbered as you can be yourself. Yours truly, A. Lincoln"[7]

Two days later Grant wrote back to Lincoln: "I will be most happy to have him in my military family in the manner you propose."[8] Grant appointed

Robert to the rank of captain in keeping with others on his staff. Robert served from February 11, 1865, until June 10, 1865, a total of four months. Although Lincoln volunteered to pay Robert's salary and expenses, he was spared the expense of his son's "necessary means." Grant saw to it that Robert was placed on the army's payroll.

Although he served only four months, Robert had the privilege of being present at Appomattox with the rest of Grant's staff when Lee surrender his Army of Northern Virginia. In conversation later that day with Speaker of the House Schuyler Colfax, Lincoln said: "Bob has just returned home and breakfasted with us. He was at the surrender of Lee, and told me that some of the rebel officers told him they were very glad the contest was over at last."[9]

Technically, of course, the war was not over. In fact, there were still nearly 175,000 Confederate soldiers scattered throughout the South who had not yet surrendered. The largest contingent was under the command of Joseph E. Johnston in North Carolina. Johnston's forces numbered 89,000 strong, although it was only on paper. A second major force of 50,000 men was located in the Trans-Mississippi region under Major General Kirby Smith. After Lee's surrender and with the government on the run, the remaining Confederate forces still at large were helpless to offer any serious continued resistance. Although they would remain in the field for a few more weeks, rational people knew the end had come.

But not everyone was rational. Jefferson Davis was now in Greensboro, North Carolina, where he had been forced to flee after the fall of Richmond. Operating out of a boxcar, Davis felt the war was not lost. There was still hope. He summoned General Joe Johnston to a war council, where he told Johnston he would call for raising new troops, rounding up deserters, calling in stragglers, refilling the depleted ranks. Battles could still be fought. There was fight left in the Confederacy. If Kirby Smith and Johnston could link-up, an impregnable defensive line could be established.

More rational heads prevailed, however. Johnston was blunt in his analysis. The only authority Davis had left was the authority to surrender the Confederacy. But he would have to authorize Johnston to negotiate with Union general William T. Sherman first. That done, Johnston would request a meeting with Sherman and see what terms Sherman would offer. Hopefully, Sherman would be as generous as Grant in offering peace to a defeated foe.[10] In any event, it was over.

Back in Washington, Friday mornings were set aside for meetings between Lincoln and his cabinet. Good Friday was no exception. The war would soon be over and the divided states would be united once again. United, but not restored. The momentous problem of bringing the seceded states back into their proper relation with their Northern counterparts was now at hand. At 11:00 o'clock, Lincoln greeted each of his secretaries as they arrived.

Present were Navy Secretary Gideon Welles, Secretary of the Treasury Hugh McCulloch, Acting Secretary of State Frederick Seward,[11] Postmaster General William Dennison, Attorney General James Speed, Secretary of the Interior John P. Usher, and Secretary of War Edwin Stanton. Joining the cabinet as its guest was General Grant.

The cabinet members found Lincoln in an exuberant mood. It was a very good day. The news that filtered in from all the fronts was optimistic. It was only a matter of time, even hours, before "Lincoln's War" would finally end. "The butchering," as Lincoln had called it, would soon be over. Every mother, both North and South, could go to bed knowing their boys would come home safely. It was almost exactly four years to the day since the bombardment of Fort Sumter had opened hostilities.

Several hundred miles to the south, in Charleston Harbor, a large crowd had assembled on the parade ground of the old fort. In the center a large white column rose high into the spring air. A large crowd of dignitaries stood transfixed around the column. At twelve minutes past 11:00 A.M. a band struck up the "Star Spangled Banner." Brigadier General Robert B. Anderson grabbed the halyard hanging from the column and, with tears streaming down his cheeks, hoisted "Old Glory" to the top of Sumter's great flag staff. As the flag reached the top, under orders from the president, a national salute was fired from every cannon and shore battery that had fired on the fort in 1861. April 14 was the anniversary of the surrender of Fort Sumter. Four years earlier, Major Anderson had been allowed to haul down his country's flag and surrender with honor in the face of the enemy. Four years later, Robert E. Lee was granted the same privilege. With this magnanimous gesture, Abraham Lincoln's policy of forgiveness was vindicated.

At the White House, Lincoln and his cabinet were meeting. Restoration was among the major topics under discussion. Grant listened as the politicians went to work. Tasks such as reopening post offices and establishing mail routes, reestablishing the Federal courts, preparing for and insuring elections at all levels, reestablishing trade and opening up ports, the collection of revenues, and what to do about the leaders of the rebellion had to be undertaken. On the question of restoring state governments Lincoln commented, "We can't take to running state governments in all of these southern states. Their people must do that, although I reckon at first, they may do it badly."[12]

When asked what he would do with the rebel leaders, Lincoln said that he would just as soon see them flee the country: "I should not be sorry to see them out of the country; but I should be for following them up pretty close to make sure of their going."[13] When it was pointed out that Davis's Confederate commissioner, Jacob Thompson, was in Maine and about to flee to England, Lincoln replied that it reminded him of a story. "There was an Irish soldier here last summer, who wanted something to drink stronger than water," Lincoln said. "He stopped at a drug shop where he spied a soda fountain. 'Give me plase a glass of soda water, an if yez can put in a few drops of whiskey unbeknown to anyone, I'll be obliged.'" "Now," Lincoln continued, " if Jake Thompson is permitted to go through Maine unbeknown to anyone, what's the harm?"[14]

Not everyone agreed. Stanton was among the group that felt the top leaders, certainly Jefferson Davis, should be arrested and tried for treason. Stanton, who weeks later would insist on a military trial for the accused conspirators, relented in Davis's case, saying that he would have no objection to handing him over to the civil authorities in Virginia.[15] Stanton believed the Confederacy's president should be tried in the civil courts for treason. There seemed no doubt that Davis would be captured and imprisoned.

One of the cabinet members asked if there was any word from General Sherman in North Carolina. Grant said he was expecting to hear something in an hour or two. At this point Lincoln told the men seated around the table that he expected the news to be good. He knew it would be good news because of a dream he had the night before. Lincoln said that it was a recurring dream, one that always followed a great or important event in the war. Welles asked what this remarkable dream was about. Lincoln told of being "in some singular, indescribable vessel . . . moving rapidly toward an indefinite shore." He had the dream just before the attack on Fort Sumter and the battles of Bull Run, Antietam, Gettysburg, Stones River, Vicksburg, and Wilmington. Lincoln told his cabinet members, "I had this strange dream again last night, and we shall, judging from the past, have great news very soon." Grant reminded Lincoln that Stone's River was no victory and "he knew of no great results that followed from it."[16]

The cabinet meeting broke up around two o'clock and Grant stayed behind to talk with the president. Lincoln had invited the general and his wife to attend the play at Ford's Theatre that evening with Mrs. Lincoln and himself. It would be a good time to relax and show themselves to the jubilant public. Grant accepted the invitation contingent on one condition. His wife, Julia, wanted to leave that evening and visit their children who were attending school in Burlington, New Jersey. Julia would later recall the occasion: "As soon as I received the invitation to go with Mrs. Lincoln, I dispatched a note to General Grant entreating him to go home that evening; that I did not want to go to the theater."[17] Grant told the president that if he were able to finish his paperwork early enough to catch the evening train, he and Julia would leave and visit the children.[18] It now seemed certain that Grant would be able to finish his work in time to catch the train. Lincoln said he was disappointed, but that he understood.

There are some writers who have suggested that Grant's decision not to attend the theater stemmed from an incident involving his wife, Julia, and Mary Lincoln. Julia Grant had been the target of a particularly nasty tirade by Mary Lincoln only weeks earlier. On March 23, Lincoln visited Grant at his military base at City Point, Virginia. Mary Lincoln accompanied her husband on the trip and the two stayed aboard the steamer *River Queen.* On March 25 Lincoln was scheduled to review part of the Union troops bivouacked in the area. Mary and Julia would travel to the review area in an ambulance provided by the army. Lincoln went ahead on horseback. When the two women arrived on the scene they saw the wife of the Fifth Army Corps commander, General Charles Griffin, riding alongside of the president. Mary Lincoln became extremely upset and visibly shaken. She considered Mrs. Griffin's presence with the president a serious breach of protocol. In her excited state, Mary tried to climb out of the ambulance. She had to be restrained for fear she would jump into the deep mud surrounding the ambulance. It was a humiliating experience for Julia, who was Mary's hostess.

The following day the incident was repeated when the two women were to join their husbands at the review of the Army of the James. Following lunch aboard Admiral David Dixon Porter's flagship, *Malvern,* Lincoln and Mary, General Grant and Julia, Admiral Porter, and Generals Philip Sheridan and Edward O.C. Ord went ashore two miles from the parade ground where elements of General Godfrey Weitzel's Twenty-fifth Corps were waiting to be reviewed by the president. Lincoln, accompanied by his generals, rode on horseback the two miles to the field. Once again the two women rode to the scene in an ambulance. Mary Ord, the attractive wife of General Ord, rode horseback behind Lincoln and the generals. Arriving at the parade ground, an aide accompanying Mary Ord had her join the president and officers as they rode in review of the troops. Mary Lincoln arrived on the scene to see Mary Ord riding beside the president. Immediately she became upset. "What does the woman mean by riding by the side of the President?" When Julia Grant attempted to calm her, she turned on her and began accusing her and her husband of coveting the White House and wanting to replace the Lincolns. "I suppose you think you will get to the White House yourself?"[19] The mild mannered Julia Grant must have felt humiliated, and yet when she wrote of the incident in her memoirs years later she excused Mary's behavior as due to her fatigue from all the traveling and to the unpleasant ride in the ambulance wagon.[20] Mary wasn't finished, however.

On seeing the ambulance with the two women arrive, Mary Ord broke away from the procession and rode over to join the women. Mary again flew into a rage. She believed the men in the ranks would think that Mary Ord was the president's wife while she sat behind the scenes in an ambulance wagon mired down in mud. It was too much for the first lady to take. She verbally abused Mary Ord, calling "her vile names in the presence of a crowd of officers," asking her how she dared to ride beside the president.[21] Mary Ord broke down in tears while Julia Grant continued to try and calm Mary Lincoln. The incident proved humiliating to everyone, especially the mild-mannered Julia Grant, who acted graciously throughout Mary Lincoln's tirade. In her memoirs, Julia Grant played down the incidents at the grand reviews, tactfully stating that they had been "embellished" by a member of Grant's staff.[22]

Some have speculated that the two incidents at City Point sufficiently traumatized Julia Grant that she told her husband under no circumstances would she attend the theater with Mary Lincoln and risk another humiliating confrontation. And yet the Grants had not seen their children for weeks. It seems unlikely that given the opportunity to catch an early train to New Jersey they would give up the opportunity to visit their children to attend the theater. Given Grant's schedule, the more likely scenario was that the Grants chose their children over the theater. It was not an unreasonable choice. Even so, Julia Grant had ample reason to view a night with Mary Lincoln with great distaste.

A great amount of speculation has also been written over what might have happened on the night of April 14 had Grant attended the theater with Lincoln. At least three writers have stated that had Grant been present Booth would not have been able to kill Lincoln. The presumption is that Grant would have been attended by a military guard that would not have allowed Booth to enter the box.[23] Theodore Roscoe in his study of the assassination wrote, "Bates [David Homer Bates, telegrapher in the War Department] should have known that General Grant, surrounded by military guards and aides, would have no reason for anxiety over his theater appearance." Roscoe pointed out that without Grant in attendance the theater party "would be deprived of the full-dress military escort customarily furnished for the public appearances of high-ranking Army leaders."[24] Roscoe was wrong. It simply was not true. Grant attended the theater on prior occasions without "full-dress military escorts" or "military guards and aides." In fact, on February 10, just two months before the fatal April 14, Grant and Lincoln attended Ford's Theatre to see John Sleeper Clarke[25] in a double performance of two comedic farces, *Everybody's Friend* and *Love in Livery*. During the performance Major General Ambrose Burnside joined them.[26] Lincoln and Grant remained to the end of the evening's performance. There is no evidence that guards were posted outside the box or a full-dress military escort attended the generals on this evening. Grant's absence from the theater on the night of April 14 left Lincoln no more vulnerable than on February 10 or on any of the other numerous times he attended the theater in Washington.

After chatting with Grant, Lincoln spent the next hour dealing with the human side of war. Among the visitors were Governor Thomas Swann, Senator John A.J. Creswell, and Edwin H. Webster, all of Maryland. Lincoln had asked the two politicians for a list of nominees for various state offices that required his approval. Webster, who was among the ten nominees, had accompanied Swann and Creswell on another matter. Webster hoped to convince Lincoln to pardon a Confederate prisoner, George S. Herron, who was the brother of a prominent Baltimore clergyman. Herron was a member of Company C, First Maryland Cavalry, and was a prisoner in Camp Chase, Ohio. He was seriously ill with dysentery, and his brother had made several prior attempts to get his release without success. Fearing his brother would die in prison, he turned to Webster for help. Webster now brought the case to Lincoln. Lincoln took Webster's petition and, turning it over, carefully penned across the back page, "Let this prisoner be discharged on taking the oath of Dec. 8, 1863. A. Lincoln."[27]

Senator Creswell had brought a request of his own for another Marylander. Benjamin F. Twilley was a Confederate prisoner who also wanted out and asked his friends to appeal to the kindhearted Lincoln. Twilley was a prisoner at Maryland's Point Lookout prison camp in lower St. Mary's County. Creswell had written on Twilley's original plea for amnesty, "I respectfully ask that the within named Benjn F. Twilley be discharged on the usual terms." Lincoln took the request from Creswell and, balancing it on his knee, penned the simple words, "Let it be done. A. Lincoln April 14, 1865."[28] Pardons were becoming a major part of Lincoln's daily business. Now that the war was essentially over, Lincoln was seeing a large number of requests on behalf of Confederate prisoners.

Lincoln signed several other pardons on the fourteenth. Among them was a young Confederate soldier who was awaiting execution. Lincoln signed the pardon and, turning to his young secretary Hay, said, "I think this boy can do more good above ground than under ground."[29] Lincoln wasn't through, however. Pardoning condemned soldiers was an act he took quite seriously. Lincoln commuted the death penalty for many soldiers for reasons completely unrelated to their offense or the situation at the time. One category that always received his reprieve involved young soldiers:

> Major General Meade, Army of the Potomac.
>
> I am appealed to in behalf of August Bittersdorf, at Mitchells Station, Va. to be shot to-morrow as a deserter. I am unwilling for any boy under eighteen to be shot; and his father affirms that he is under sixteen. Please answer. His Regt. or Co. not given me.
>
> A. Lincoln[30]

Lincoln was overwhelmed at times with the number of casualties piling up on both sides. With so much death he could not bring himself to be another cause added to those already at work. Speaker of the House Schuyler Colfax recalled a conversation with Lincoln in which he explained his thoughts: "Some of my generals complain that I impair discipline by my frequent pardons and reprieves; but it rests me after a hard day's work that I can find some excuse for saving some poor fellow's life, and I shall go to bed happy tonight as I think how joyous the signing of this name will make himself, his family and friends."[31]

Two other pardons, dated April 14, 1865, have recently been discovered among a collection of 760 cases that reside in the National Archives in Washington, D.C. Researchers Thomas Lowry and Beverly Lowry have reviewed over 37,000 court-martial cases and discovered 760 cases that contain notations in the hand of Abraham Lincoln.[32] Among these 760 cases are two dated April 14, 1865. The first case is that of an Alabama man, Bradford Hambrick. The charges against Hambrick claim he hunted down loyal citizens with dogs and compelled them to join the Confederate army. Hambrick was found guilty of threatening to shoot one man's wife and attempting to hang another man because he refused to wear a Confederate uniform. Hambrick was sentenced to one year in a penitentiary and fined $2,000. Hearing of Lincoln's magnanimity, Hambrick shot off a letter to Lincoln asking for a pardon. Expecting not to hear back from the Yankee president, Hambrick was surprised when he received a letter with the simple notation, "Pardoned. A. Lincoln April 14, 1865."[33]

The second case discovered by the Lowrys involved a Union soldier, Patrick Murphy, who had deserted from one regiment only to reenlist in another regiment. Murphy was found guilty of desertion and sentenced to be shot. As with all sentences of death, the file was forwarded to Lincoln for review. Murphy was a special case because on his file were written the words: "not perfectly sound." The court that had found Murphy guilty and sentenced him to death recommended clemency. Murphy's case traveled all the way from California through the tangled maze of military bureaucracy to reach Lincoln's desk on April 14. Lincoln studied the file and picking up his pen wrote, "This man is pardoned and hereby discharged from the service. A. Lincoln April 14, 1865."[34] Patrick Murphy would live.

One other incident during this hour on the fourteenth is worth noting. After taking care of several items of paperwork, Lincoln stepped into a small closet off of his office to wash his hands. Assistant Secretary of War Charles A. Dana found Lincoln there with his coat off and sleeves rolled up. Dana had received a dispatch from the provost marshal of Portland, Maine, which said that the Confederate agent operating in Toronto, Jacob Thompson, would be arriving in Portland that very night to board a Canadian steamer for Liverpool, England. Secretary of War Stanton had earlier told Dana to order Thompson's arrest, but on reflection told Dana to check with Lincoln and see what he wanted to do. Stanton probably remembered Lincoln's remarks during the morning cabinet meeting when asked what should be done with the various Confederate leaders, had said, "Frighten them out of the country, open the gates, let the bars down, scare them off."[35]

Dana read Lincoln the dispatch and asked him what he wanted to do.

Lincoln asked what Stanton had said. Dana said that Stanton wanted to arrest Thompson. Lincoln, shaking his head, said, "I rather guess not. When you have an elephant in hand, and he wants to run away, you better let him run."[36] Fourteen hours later, as Lincoln lay dying, Stanton would abandon Lincoln's policy and issue orders to track down and arrest Thompson along with every other member of the Confederate operation in Canada.[37] He was convinced that Jefferson Davis and his Canadian agents were behind Lincoln's murder.

By three o'clock Lincoln had finished his paperwork and joined Mary for a promised carriage ride. He had told Mary earlier in the day not to invite anyone else along. "I prefer to ride by ourselves today," he told her.[38] He wanted it to just be the two of them. Of course, the cavalry escort would accompany them, if for no other reason than to keep away the boisterous citizens roaming the city who were still celebrating Lee's surrender. The exact route the Lincolns took is unclear, but they eventually arrived at the Navy Yard in southeast Washington. It was a favorite spot for Lincoln. During the first three years of the war he visited the Yard at least sixty times, more than any other site in the Washington area except for the White House and the Soldiers' Home.[39] Most of these visits were to inspect naval vessels and witness various experiments with gunnery.[40] Lincoln had a fascination for weaponry and most things mechanical. Mrs. Lincoln had a special fondness for Mrs. Gustavus Fox, wife of the Navy Yard commandant to whom Mary sent freshly cut flowers on a regular basis.[41]

As with his previous trips to the Yard, Lincoln visited one of the Navy's several ships resting at anchor. On the fourteenth, he visited the ironclad *Montauk*. Dr. George B. Todd, surgeon on board the *Montauk*, described the visit in a letter to his brother: "The President and wife drove down to the Navy Yard and paid our ship a visit, going all over her, accompanied by us all. Both seemed very happy, and so expressed themselves, glad that this war was over, or near its end, and then drove back to the White House."[42]

Three days later, the *Montauk* would achieve dubious fame by serving as a prison ship for several of the accused conspirators charged with Lincoln's murder. On the twenty-seventh of April, the *Montauk* would receive the body of John Wilkes Booth for identification and autopsy.

After an hour the couple started back to the White House, chatting along the way about their circumstances and what the future now held. In a letter written seven months later Mary described their ride:

> He was almost boyish, in his mirth & reminded me, of his original nature, what I had always remembered of him, in our own home—free from care, . . . I never saw him so supremely cheerful—his manner was even playful. . . .
>
> During the drive he was so gay, that I said to him, laugh-

> ingly, "Dear Husband, you almost startle me by your great cheerfulness," he replied, "and well I may feel so, Mary, I consider *this day*, the war has come to a close"—and then added, "We must *both*, be more cheerful in the future—between the war & the loss of our darling Willie—we have both, been very miserable." Every word then uttered, is deeply engraved, on my broken heart.[43]

It was a little after five o'clock when the Lincolns arrived back at the White House. Richard Oglesby, Governor of Illinois, and General Isham Haynie[44] had stopped by to pay a visit. Finding the president absent, they had just started to leave when Lincoln's carriage pulled up. On seeing the two old friends walking away, Lincoln called to them. He invited them to join him in the reception room where they talked about things in general and where Lincoln took the opportunity to read from one of his favorite books of satire, *Phoenixiana* by John Phoenix.[45] Lincoln loved to read the satirical works of several popular authors of the day, John Phoenix being among them. Although he loved to read to his guests, his readings were not always well received by everyone. There were some who thought it undignified for a president to read satire, especially during such grave times. Lincoln thought some of his guests simply lacked the humor to appreciate his peculiar habit of reading aloud. But he was president, and he could read anything he wanted, even out loud to his captive guests.

Lincoln was having so much fun reading to his guests that he had to be called several times to dinner: "He promised each time to go, but would continue reading the book. Finally, he received a peremptory order from the butler that he must come to dinner at once."[46] Dinner lasted from 7:00 P.M. until 7:30 P.M. The substance of Lincoln's last meal is not known, but presumably he and Mary dined alone as Robert had retired early, exhausted from the continuous activity resulting from Lee's surrender.

Following dinner, Lincoln met briefly with Schuyler Colfax, Speaker of the House of Representatives. Colfax was leaving in the morning for California and wanted to go over a few political matters with the president. Almost as an afterthought, Lincoln told Colfax that Senator Charles Sumner had somehow gotten the gavel of the Confederate Congress when he was in Richmond and had intended to give it to Stanton. Lincoln told Colfax that he had told Sumner to give the gavel to the Speaker.[47]

At this point in the story it is necessary to question another doubtful occurrence that has crept into many of the books dealing with Lincoln's last day. It involves the reminiscences of one of the four bodyguards assigned to the White House detail, William Crook. In 1907 Crook published a little book titled *Through Five Administrations* about his experiences while serving as a security guard for five presidents.[48] In his book Crook told about an incident that occurred on the evening of April 14. He had come on duty at the White

House at 8:00 A.M. and was due to be relieved at 4:00 P.M. by John F. Parker, another member of the president's bodyguard. According to Crook, Parker was late in showing up, requiring Crook to stay on until Parker arrived.

Following dinner, which would place the alleged event close to 7:30 P.M., Crook writes that he accompanied Lincoln on his usual trip to the War Department where he visited with Stanton. The War Department was located in a building on the White House grounds along Seventeenth Street, a short walk from the White House. Crook wrote that the president had seemed more depressed than he had ever seen him before. While strolling across the White House grounds, the two came upon a group of men. The men appeared to be drunk as they passed by, causing Lincoln to remark, "Crook, do you know I believe there are men who want to take my life? And I have no doubt they will do it." Crook was taken aback and pressed Lincoln why he thought so. "Other men have been assassinated," Lincoln said. Approaching the War Department entrance, Lincoln continued, "I know no one could do it and escape alive. But if it is to be done, it is impossible to prevent."[49]

Arriving at the War Department, Lincoln met with Stanton. When Lincoln finally emerged from Stanton's office his mood had dramatically changed to one of happiness. Even so, Crook claimed that Lincoln "showed no enthusiasm for going" to the theater that night.[50] Lincoln would go, however, despite his desire to stay home because Mary Lincoln had insisted they go. Crook was alarmed and asked the president if he could stay on duty and go with him to the theater. The kindly president told Crook to go home and get his much needed rest. Reaching the portico of the White House Lincoln said, "Goodbye Crook." Crook later thought the parting strange. On every other occasion previously Lincoln had said, "Good Night, Crook." Crook concluded that Lincoln "had some sort of vague warning that the attempt [on his life] would be made on the night of the 14th."[51]

Crook's reminiscence has become a favorite among storytellers. But there are several difficulties with the account, making it unlikely that it ever happened. First is the timing. The Lincolns began their dinner a little late, just after 7:00 P.M. At 7:30 P.M. Lincoln met with Speaker Colfax. The only time Lincoln could have accompanied Crook to Stanton's office was between the end of dinner and Lincoln's 7:30 P.M. meeting with Colfax. In the interval between 7:00 P.M. and 7:30 P.M. there was not enough time to eat dinner, visit with Stanton, and return to meet with Colfax. Second is Crook's claim that Lincoln did not want to go to the theater that evening. In telling his story, Crook places the onus on Mary Lincoln, claiming she insisted they go to the theater even though Lincoln did not want to. According to Mary Lincoln, it was her husband who wanted to go to the theater while Mary wanted to stay home because of a headache that was causing her considerable discomfort. Two months after Lincoln's murder Mary wrote to Francis Carpenter, "his mind, was *fixed* [emphasis added] upon having some relaxation & bent on the theater." Mary agreed to go that night "so as not to disappoint her husband."[52]

Most damaging to Crook's veracity, however, is the finding of a statement by historian William Hanchett that quotes Stanton as saying that the last visit to his office by Lincoln was on the evening of Wednesday, April 12, not April 14.[53] Hanchett points out that no mention is made before the year 1907 by Crook or anyone else of Lincoln's visiting the War Department on the night of April 14, 1865.[54] Since publication of Crook's book, nearly every author has included the episode in writing about Lincoln's last hours.[55] Crook's reminiscence cannot be accepted, and while some of his observations are undoubtedly true, each must be scrutinized carefully before accepting them as an accurate part of the Lincoln assassination story. This includes the claim by Crook that John F. Parker, Lincoln's bodyguard, was several hours late in arriving for duty on the night of April 14, 1865.[56] It seems more likely that Crook was not even present when Lincoln sat down to dinner, suggesting that, contrary to Crook, Parker was already on the job having relieved Crook earlier in the evening.

Lincoln and Colfax ended their meeting at 8:00 P.M. Lincoln wished Colfax a safe journey. "Let me hear from you and I will telegraph you at San Francisco," Lincoln told the Speaker.[57] Waiting next to see the president was George Ashmun, congressman from Massachusetts. Ashmun wanted Lincoln's help in recovering a shipment of confiscated cotton for one of Ashmun's constituents. Ashmun had also wanted an appointment with Lincoln for himself and his friend Judge Charles P. Daly to discuss a second matter. Lincoln apologized to Ashmun, telling him that he had to leave for his theater appointment, but would see him first thing in the morning. The play at Ford's Theatre was scheduled to begin at 8:00 P.M., and the president and his wife were already late.[58] He took a small card from his pocket and penned his final note: "Allow Mr. Ashmun and friend to come in at 9 A.M. to-morrow. A. Lincoln."[59]

The president's carriage waited at the front portico. Seated beside the driver, Ned Burke, was Charles Forbes, the president's personal valet and messenger. John F. Parker, the evening bodyguard, had gone ahead to the theater where he would meet the carriage on its arrival and escort the president and first lady into the theater. There would be no cavalry escort this night. The president was adamant about not allowing the escort to accompany him and Mrs. Lincoln to church or to the theater.[60] As the carriage made its way along the curved driveway leading from the portico, Mary Lincoln told the driver to stop by the residence of Clara Harris on the corner of Fifteenth and H Streets across from the White House. Here they would pick up Major Henry Rathbone and his fiancée, Miss Harris.

The young couple had not been Mary's first choice to go with them to the theater. General and Mrs. Grant were. When the Grants turned the president down, he turned to Major Thomas Eckert, assistant secretary of war. Eckert also turned Lincoln down. He had no interest in accompanying them to a theater and feigned work as an excuse for not going. Mrs. Lincoln finally settled on Clara Harris and Major Rathbone.

It was twenty minutes past eight when the carriage pulled away from the Harris residence and headed toward Ford's Theatre.[61] A chill was settling over the city and the damp night air indicated rain was about to start falling soon. Mary took the president's arm in her own and placed her hand over his. She noticed that his hands were bare. Mary was constantly admonishing him to wear gloves whenever they were out in public. It simply wasn't proper for the president of the United States to appear in public without gloves. Stuffed in Lincoln's coat pockets were two pairs of white kid gloves. Mary simply didn't have the heart to scold him this evening. He was so happy. She had never seen him so supremely cheerful.

CHAPTER NINE

Decision

Our cause being almost lost, something decisive & great must be done.

John Wilkes Booth

Abraham Lincoln was enamored with the performing arts. While a young man in New Salem, Illinois, he had been introduced to the plays of William Shakespeare by the village blacksmith, Jack Kelso.[1] His fondness for Shakespeare became so great that he committed whole plays to memory, and like the literature of the Bible, they became a favorite source of material for his fertile mind.[2] Lincoln's taste in the theater was broad, ranging from tragedy to comedy, but it was the plays of Shakespeare that he found most compelling.

On a cold March night in 1863, Lincoln visited Ford's Theater to see James W. Hackett as Falstaff in Shakespeare's *Henry the Fourth*.[3] The following day Hackett sent Lincoln a copy of a book he had recently published containing critical essays on Shakespeare and Shakespearean actors. Lincoln wrote to Hackett acknowledging receipt of the book and took the opportunity to comment on one of his favorite subjects, *Macbeth*: "Some of Shakespeare plays I have never read; while others I have gone over perhaps as frequently as any professional reader. Among the latter are Lear, Richard Third, Henry Eighth, Hamlet and especially Macbeth. I think nothing equals Macbeth. It is wonderful."[4] Lincoln then offered his own critique of the great bard: "Unlike you gentlemen of the profession, I think the soliloquy in Hamlet commencing 'O, my offence is rank' surpasses that commencing 'To be, or not to be.'"[5]

Like Macbeth, Lincoln was himself a tragic figure of enormous proportion whose life and death would have fit supremely into a Shakespearean tragedy. His love of *Hamlet* and *Macbeth* was in keeping with his fatalistic view of life. His visits to the theater allowed him to find solace in the powerful stories of Shakespeare's tragic figures. It was a solace that was shared by John Wilkes Booth.

Lincoln visited several of Washington's major establishments during the four years of his presidency. He attended Ford's Theatre on at least thirteen occasions prior to the night of April 14.[6] On one of those occasions he saw John Wilkes Booth perform in a play titled *The Marble Heart.*[7] His most recent visit had been on the night of February 10, 1865, just two months before his death, when he saw the comedy *Love in Livery* starring Booth's brother-in-law, John Sleeper Clarke. It was on that night that Lincoln was accompanied by Generals Grant and Burnside and the three men sat in the presidential box without benefit of guard or attendant.[8]

Following Lincoln's murder eight weeks later, much ado would be made of an unprotected president. Some would see dark conspiracy in the absence of a guard.[9] But there was no conspiracy or dark secret in the practice. The president along with his generals wanted no interference from such trappings. The absence of a guard on the night of February 10 is consistent with the notion that guards were not used inside buildings. Access to the president was reasonably easy.

Ford's Theatre was an impressive building located on Tenth Street between E and F Streets not far from the president's house. It was situated in the middle of the block diagonally across the street from the Metropolitan Police headquarters. The theater was large for the period, measuring 75 feet across the front by 100 feet in depth. It had three floors and contained offices and a sitting room or lounge. It was one of Washington's premier theaters and a favorite of the president and his wife.

The theater had been built in 1833 as the First Baptist Church of Washington. In 1859, the First Baptist congregation merged with the Fourth Baptist congregation and built a new, grander church only three blocks away, giving up the Tenth Street structure. Fiscal pressure resulted in a decision by church elders to sell the old building, and in 1861 John Ford was granted a five-year lease on the property with an option to purchase it outright at the end of that period. It proved to be a very profitable move for Ford. The church was already a theater of sorts able to accommodate a variety of performances. War had swelled the population of the city with younger men who craved most any form of entertainment.

The first year Ford rented the building to George Christy for his famous Christy's Minstrels. Ford leased the building to Christy as a test of the Washington market.[10] He was already one of the country's leading theatrical entrepreneurs who owned establishments in Baltimore and Philadelphia. He had never experienced failure. Satisfied the market would prove a financial success, Ford closed down the theater in February of 1862 and began a major renovation in anticipation of reopening it as Ford's Theater. The newly renovated theater opened on March 19 only to be gutted by fire nine months later. Determined to go on, Ford rebuilt the theater and went back into production in August of 1863. For the next nineteen months the theater hosted 573 performances to the delight of Washington crowds.[11] It was a great success, ensuring Ford and his two brothers top rank among the nation's theatrical entrepreneurs.

The theater became a second home to the country's most famous actors and actresses, including John Wilkes Booth. But despite its being one of the major theaters in the country, Booth appeared at Ford's Theatre in only thirteen performances on three separate occasions between 1863 and 1865. His last performance was on March 18, 1865, as Pescara in *The Apostate.*[12] The performance occurred the day after Booth's aborted plan to capture Lincoln while visiting Campbell Hospital. Booth's performance on the eighteenth belied later accounts that he had been forced to abandon his illustrious career because of chronic throat problems. Twenty-four days after this performance he would return to Ford's for one last visit, when he would play the most infamous role of his brilliant career. So much of Booth's life had been intertwined with theatrics that fantasy became mingled with reality on more than one occasion. At the height of his career, Booth began preparing for his greatest role. It was a role he was well prepared for, having lived it many times over in his mind.

Booth had been up late the night of April 13. He had caroused through the city, stopping by several of his favorite watering holes. By 2:00 A.M. he returned to his hotel room where he took time to write a letter to his mother before retiring: "Everything is dull; that is, has been till last night. (The illumination.) Everything was bright and splendid. More so in my eyes if it had been a display in a nobler cause. But so goes the world. Might makes right."[13]

Booth would write a second letter later in the day. While the first letter was for only his mother's eyes, the second letter was for posterity. It was written to the editor of the *National Intelligencer* and was meant for the entire world to read. Booth would give the letter to a fellow actor, John Matthews, with instructions to deliver it to the *National Intelligencer.* Unfortunately, the letter would not survive.

Shortly after 10:00 A.M. on April 14, Booth was seen having breakfast at the National Hotel with two young ladies.[14] Following breakfast he walked a short four blocks to Ford's Theatre where he chatted a few minutes with Harry Ford, John Ford's brother and business partner.[15] Booth next picked up his mail that had been delivered to the theater.[16] Sometime between 10:00 and 11:00 A.M. a messenger arrived at the theater from the White House requesting the presidential box be reserved for that evening. The president and his wife would be attending the evening performance. The theater had eight private boxes located on either side of the large stage, four at ground level and four at the upper level or dress circle. The president used the two upper boxes located to the right of the audience whenever he and his guests attended the theater. A simple partition that separated the two boxes was removed on such occasions, creating one large box. Access to the two boxes was through an outer door that led to a small vestibule. The vestibule had two doors that led into the separate boxes. This arrangement created an ideal situation for Booth. He could enter the vestibule, thus shielding himself from the audience seated in the dress circle while separating him from the inner box. Here he could wait in darkness until the moment he chose to act. The box, with its vestibule, was ideally situated for Booth's plan. He needed only to secure the outer door to the vestibule so no one could follow behind him. He did this at some point during the day, probably during a second visit to the theater around 6:00–7:00 P.M. when he was seen stabling his horse behind the theater.[17]

Sometime between 3:00 and 6:00 P.M., Harry Ford personally arranged the president's box. He placed three velvet-covered chairs, a velvet-covered sofa, and six cane chairs in the box. From his office on the third floor, he brought a large velvet-covered, walnut rocking chair that he placed in a corner of the box close to the balustrade. The rocking chair was placed such that the curtains decorating the opening of the box hid the president from the audience while giving him a clear view of the stage. The chair was placed opposite the inner door leading from the vestibule into the box. Ford also placed two American flags on staffs at each end of the box and draped two more American flags over the balustrade. He then set a blue Treasury Guard flag on the center post dividing the two boxes. Directly beneath the blue flag hung a large framed portrait of George Washington.[18]

It was during Booth's morning visit to the theater that he learned that Lincoln and Grant would be attending the evening performance. Here was the opportunity he had waited for. The time and the place were perfect. Booth was thoroughly familiar with Ford's and had free access to the place. He could move about the theater without arousing suspicion. He would use the opportunity to visit the box later that evening and make his preparations to secure the outer door.

Between 12 noon and 1:00 P.M., Booth stopped by the stables of James W. Pumphrey, where he made arrangements to rent a horse for his escape later that night. He told Pumphrey he would stop back around 4:00 P.M. that afternoon to pick up the horse. During his chat with Pumphrey, Booth said he was stopping by Grover's Theatre to write a letter.[19] The day before, Booth had paid a visit to Grover's Theatre asking the manager, C.D. Hess, if he intended to invite the Lincolns to his theater to celebrate the rededication of Fort Sumter. Booth had already made up his mind to assassinate the president. All he needed was opportunity.

Hess told Booth he planned on inviting President and Mrs. Lincoln, but had not yet sent a message to the White House. By the time Hess's invitation arrived, the Lincolns had already made arrangements to go to Ford's.[20] In either case, Booth was well acquainted with both of the theaters' layouts and their owners. Either theater would serve his purpose.

Before going to Grover's, Booth paid a second visit to Mrs. Surratt at her boardinghouse. At approximately 2:30 P.M., one of Mrs. Surratt's boarders, Louis Wiechmann, returned from Howard's Livery Stables, where he rented a buggy at Mary Surratt's request. She needed to go to Surrattsville and asked Wiechmann if he would drive her there. She gave Wiechmann $10 and sent him to Howard's to rent a buggy. On his return, Wiechmann found Booth and Mary Surratt standing by the fireplace in conversation. A few minutes later Booth left and Mary Surratt and Wiechmann rode down to Surrattsville.[21]

Mary carried a small package wrapped in brown paper and tied with a string that had been given to her by Booth with instructions to deliver it to John Lloyd, the tavern keeper. It contained Booth's field glass, although Mary later claimed she did not know what was in the package. She also carried a message from Booth. The message would send her to the gallows. She told Lloyd to "have those shooting irons ready that night,—there would be some parties call for them."[22] While Lloyd's testimony would tighten the noose around Mary's neck, it would prove controversial to those advocates of Mary's innocence who pointed out that Lloyd was a drunk and spoke only to save his own neck. In short, he lied. But another condemned conspirator, George Atzerodt, corroborated Lloyd's claim that Mary had told him to have the guns ready. In his statement made while imprisoned at the Arsenal, Atzerodt claimed, "Booth told me that Mrs. Surratt went to Surrattsville to get out the guns (two carbines) which had been taken to that place by Herold. This was Friday."[23] Atzerodt's statement is devastating to claims of Mary's innocence. Atzerodt could have only gotten such information from Booth himself sometime during their evening meeting in Lewis Powell's room.

The fact that Booth came to Mary Surratt's boardinghouse on the afternoon of April 14 with a package that he wanted Mary to carry to Surrattsville can only mean that he had visited her earlier in the day and learned of her plans to go to the tavern that very afternoon. How else would Booth know of her trip unless he had visited her earlier in the day? Whatever the reason for her trip that fateful afternoon, Mary gave Booth's package to Lloyd, and the message that would help send her to the gallows.

At some point in the afternoon Booth stopped by the Kirkwood Hotel located on the corner of Twelfth Street and Pennsylvania Avenue. Early that morning George Atzerodt had registered at the Kirkwood under instructions from Booth. Atzerodt would be assigned the task of killing Andrew Johnson, who was staying at the Kirkwood until he could find more suitable quarters befitting a vice president. The fact that Atzerodt had registered at the Kirkwood Hotel at least three hours before Booth had learned that Lincoln would be attending Ford's that night suggests that Booth had prior knowledge that the Lincolns would be attending a theater that evening. Which one of Washington's several theaters was not clear, but the Lincolns usually attended Ford's or Grover's. April 14 was the anniversary of the surrender of Fort Sumter to Confederate forces in 1861. Sumter's rededication on April 14 was a day for national celebration. Extending an invitation to the president was good business.

While at the Kirkwood, Booth took a small card from his pocket and wrote out a terse message that he left with the desk clerk. The card read: "Don't wish to disturb you; are you at home? J. Wilkes Booth." The clerk placed the card in the box of William A. Browning, personal secretary to Andrew Johnson. Browning returned from the capitol building to the Kirkwood House sometime around 5:00 P.M. to find the card in his box.[24] Browning, who had met Booth on several occasions prior to his coming to Washington, assumed the card was meant for him, but after Lincoln was killed, believed it was intended for Johnson.[25] Most authors have accepted Browning's conclusion that the card was meant for Johnson and not for himself. Some even suggest that Booth was attempting to implicate Johnson in Lincoln's assassination.[26] This seems unwarranted by simple logic. If Booth intended for Atzerodt to murder Johnson, why would he try to implicate him in Lincoln's murder? Booth was more than likely calling on Browning to find out Johnson's schedule for that evening to facilitate Atzerodt's assigned task. Booth was simply using Browning as his "locator." Browning's absence meant that Booth would have to take his chances that Johnson would be in his room that evening.

At 4:00 P.M. Booth ran into fellow actor John Matthews on Pennsylvania Avenue between Thirteenth and Fourteenth streets. Booth was carrying the letter he had written earlier in the day at Grover's and addressed to the editor of the *National Intelligencer.* According to Matthews's testimony given two years later during the impeachment hearing on Andrew Johnson, Booth asked Matthews to deliver his letter to the *Intelligencer* the next morning unless he later told Matthews not to.[27] This latter instruction was an important qualification suggesting that Booth was covering his bases in case the assassination did not take place. Matthews agreed without knowing its contents or Booth's plan. It was a small favor for a good friend. When Matthews awoke on Saturday morning to find that Booth had murdered the president, he tore open the envelope and read the letter. Shocked by what he read, Matthews claimed to have reread the letter, carefully absorbing its contents. Alarmed that he might be implicated in some way with his good friend, Matthews immediately burned the letter and told no one about the incident.[28] Sixteen years later he would attempt to reconstruct the letter from memory for an article published in the *Washington Evening Star* of December 7, 1881.

The letter that Matthews reconstructed is nearly identical to the "to whom it may concern" letter that Booth wrote in November of 1864 and left in the safekeeping of his sister Asia.[29] It is not plausible that Matthews could have remembered the text of so long a letter sixteen years after he had read it. Historian James O. Hall concluded, correctly I believe, that Matthews probably used Booth's "to whom it may concern" letter in reconstructing much of the *National Intelligencer* letter that he had destroyed.

While Booth and Matthews stood on the avenue chatting, an open carriage passed by carrying General and Mrs. Grant. Matthews later described the incident: "Why, Johnny, there goes Grant. I thought he was coming to the theater this evening with the President. 'Where?' he exclaimed. I pointed to the carriage; he looked toward it, grasped my hand tightly, and galloped down the avenue after the carriage."[30]

Matthews's account of Grant's riding by in a carriage and Booth's galloping after it squares with an account given by Horace Porter, Grant's aide,[31] several years later in which Porter told that a man strongly resembling Booth rode past the carriage looking intently at Grant. Julia Grant remembered the incident more vividly, having become alarmed by the man who looked into the carriage. She told of having lunch with General Rawlings's wife and young daughter on the afternoon of April 14. Four men came into the dining room and sat opposite their table. Julia Grant noticed that one of the men kept staring at her. Both she and Mrs. Rawlings agreed there was "something peculiar about them." Julia described the incident that occurred later in the day while riding with her husband to the train depot: "As General Grant and I rode to the depot, this same dark, pale man rode past us at a sweeping gallop on a dark horse—black, I think. He rode twenty yards ahead of us, wheeled and returned, and as he passed us both going and returning, he thrust his face quite near the General's and glared in a disagreeable manner."[32]

Booth's whereabouts for the next few hours are not clear, but he stabled his horse behind Ford's theater and probably had supper. Around 6:00 P.M. he returned to the theater. It was now dark as the actors had finished their rehearsal and were off to supper. Making his way to the box, Booth entered the vestibule and closed the outer door. He took a knife from his pocket and carefully cut a small square in the plaster wall just large enough to receive the end of a pine brace. He carried with him the upright section of a music stand that he had found back stage. He now placed one end of the piece of wood into the hole cut into the wall while placing the other end against the door. The effect was to brace the door so that anyone trying to push it open from the other side would only wedge the piece of wood more tightly in the wall. Satisfied with his work, he removed the stick, placed it on the floor by the molding where it wouldn't be noticed, and cleaned up the small pieces of plaster.

By 7:00 P.M. he was at the Herndon House where he met with Powell, Atzerodt, and Herold to go over the final plan. Booth had stashed Powell at the boardinghouse after bringing him down from Baltimore. Atzerodt was missing and Booth sent Herold to get him at the Kirkwood Hotel and bring him to Powell's room.[33] With his team of assassins assembled, Booth went over each person's assignment. Powell "would go up to Seward's house and kill him."[34] Atzerodt was to kill Andrew Johnson in his room at the Kirkwood Hotel. Herold would accompany Powell as his street guide and then lead him out of Washington to a rendezvous point in Maryland. Booth reserved the president for himself. Whatever else happened that night, the president must die. The final countdown had begun.

CHAPTER TEN

Sic Semper Tyrannis

Though this be madness, yet there is method in't.

Hamlet, 2.2

Darkness had settled over the city cloaking its hidden recesses from prying eyes. The celebration of Lee's surrender was marked by brilliant illuminations of most of the government buildings. Even the brightest lanterns, however, could not reach the back alleys where the city's underclass roamed. It was Good Friday, a holy day reserved for the remembrance of man's sin against God—but it was joy, not sin, that was on the minds of the people this glorious night. Jubilation was everywhere as the victors celebrated the joyous news of Lee's surrender five days before.

At John Ford's theater a special benefit performance was scheduled for America's leading lady, Laura Keene. Miss Keene would receive the lion's share of the house receipts as payment for her star performances on the stage. This night would prove to be especially lucrative for Miss Keene, who would play to a packed house. Earlier in the day word had been sent to the *Evening Star* and *National Intelligencer* that the president and his wife would attend the theater that evening. Handbills were printed announcing the special event.[1] Among the guests would be Ulysses S. Grant, the hero of the hour. It would be an opportunity for the people to see the two great leaders together. Grant, however, would not attend.

It was a few minutes past 9:30 P.M. when Booth made his way up the narrow alley leading to the rear of Ford's Theatre. The alley was known by the people who lived in the area as "Baptist Alley" from its long association with the church that had once occupied the structure. Booth moved slowly past several shacks that lined the passageway. The dim glow of candlelight leaking from one of the small shacks helped guide him as he quietly moved toward the rear of the building. A wooden door led from the rear of the stage into the alley. Reaching the door, Booth dismounted and gently tapped against its surface so as not to disturb the performance that was in progress. The door opened slightly and a man stepped outside. It was Edman Spangler, a stagehand who also worked as a carpenter-handyman around the theater.

Spangler was an old friend of the Booth family. In 1852 he worked as a carpenter in helping build the Booth home in Bel Air. Spangler now worked at the theater shifting scenery between acts. The two men whispered briefly. Booth asked Spangler to watch his horse while he went inside for a few moments. Although Spangler was busy with the play, he couldn't refuse his charming friend. Once Booth entered the theater, however, Spangler would call for young Joseph Burroughs to watch the horse while he returned to his work behind the stage. Burroughs worked as a general do-all around the theater, passing out flyers, carrying messages, and selling peanuts to patrons. He had earned the name "John Peanuts."[2] Spangler turned Booth's horse over to Burroughs who soon stretched out on a small bench that stood next to the building.

Stepping inside the rear of the theater, Booth took hold of a metal ring fastened in the floor and carefully lifted a trapdoor exposing a set of steps leading down into a basement beneath the stage. Descending the stairs, he felt his way across the dirt floor to the opposite side, where he came upon another set of steps. Climbing these he pushed open a second trapdoor that led back to the floor he had just been on, only now he was on the other side of the backstage area. In this way Booth was able to pass from one side of the stage to the other without being seen or interfering with the play in progress immediately in his front. The maneuver required a familiarity with the theater and the underground layout of the building.

Having passed to the other side of the stage, Booth made his way through a side door that led into a narrow alley. The alley ran between the theater and an adjoining saloon before emptying onto the sidewalk in front of the theater. Booth's familiarity with the theater served him well. He was able to leave his horse at the rear of the building while making his way unnoticed to the sidewalk in its front. In this way, his horse was safely positioned in the rear of the building in readiness for a fast getaway.

It was a few minutes before ten o'clock and the play was near the halfway point. Booth checked the time and entered the saloon next door. Here he ordered a whiskey and water and, after bantering with the barkeep, left by the front door.[3] Emerging onto Tenth Street, Booth turned to go into the theater. John Buckingham, the doorkeeper was standing in the doorway leading into the small lobby when Booth walked up. Booth nodded and asked Buckingham the time. He told Booth to check the clock located in the lobby of the theater.[4] Buckingham was well acquainted with Booth and paid little attention as the famous actor came back out and then went back in again. After entering the theater the second time, Booth made his way to the stairs at the north end of the lobby that led up to the dress circle on the second floor.[5]

Arriving at the top of the stairs, Booth found the circle filled with people. Several persons were standing against the rear wall watching the play unfold on the stage below. Booth paused, leaned against the wall, and surveyed the scene. After a few minutes he began to make his way across the rear of the circle. Pausing a second time, Booth took in the surroundings. Near the far

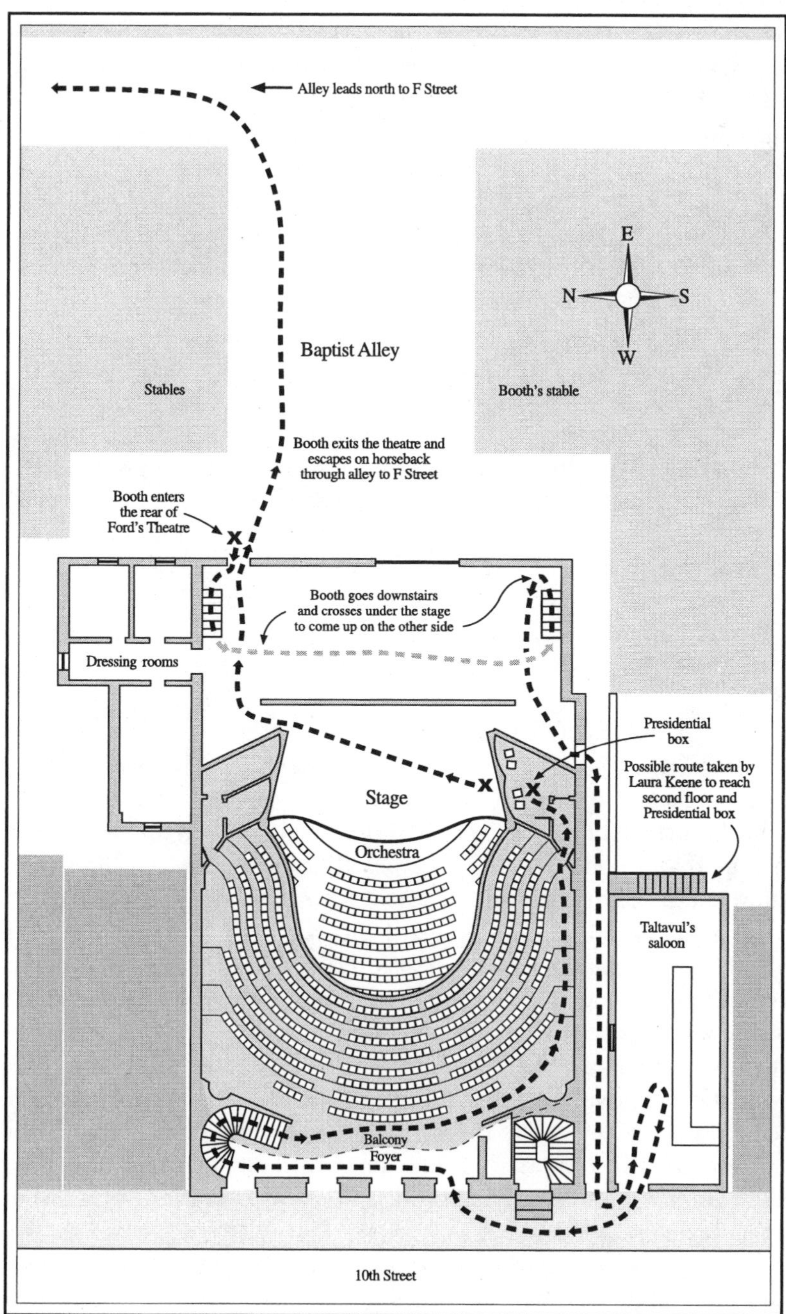

Ford's Theatre: Path of John Wilkes Booth as he moved from the rear alley of the theater to the presidential box and back out of the theater following his assassination of President Lincoln.

side of the circle a Union officer, Captain Theodore McGowen of the Veteran Reserve Corps, sat in a chair, arms folded laughing at the comedy below. Booth began walking toward the closed door. As he came closer to the box he found his path blocked by McGowen. The officer pulled his chair forward making room for Booth to pass. McGowen later recalled what happened:

> I was sitting in the aisle leading by the wall toward the door of the President's box, when a man came and disturbed me in my seat, causing me to push my chair forward to permit him to pass; he stopped about three feet from where I was sitting, and leisurely took a survey of the house. . . . He took a small pack of visiting-cards from his pocket, selecting one and replacing the others, stood a second, perhaps, with it in his hand, and then showed it to the President's messenger, who was sitting just below him. Whether the messenger took the card into the box, or, after looking at it, allowed him to go in, I do not know; but, in a moment or two more, I saw him go through the door of the lobby leading to the box, and close the door. . . . I know J. Wilkes Booth, but, not seeing the face of the assassin fully, I did not at the time recognize him as Booth.[6]

The "messenger" was Charles Forbes, personal valet and footman to the president. Forbes had accompanied the president and his party to the theater, taking a seat at the end of the row, which placed him closest to the outer door of the presidential box. Forbes scrutinized the card and then nodded indicating Booth could go into the box. The officer turned his attention back toward the actors on stage.[7]

Assigned as the president's guard this particular evening was Officer John F. Parker, a member of the Washington Metropolitan Police Force. Parker was one of four officers assigned to guard the president around the clock. He was scheduled for night duty on April 14 and had reported to the White House where the man he relieved, William Crook, told him the president and Mrs. Lincoln were preparing to go to Ford's Theater. Parker proceeded ahead, arriving at the theater before the presidential party, and was there when the Lincolns arrived. He apparently saw them into the theater and to the box. After that it remains unclear just what Parker's duties were or where he had gone.

One thing is clear, Parker was not stationed outside the box, and when Booth came, he did not have to pass a police guard. The only person who stood between Booth and the inner passage to the president's box was Charles Forbes. Forbes was not a policeman and had no duties pertaining to the president's personal safety, only to his comfort.

Having satisfied Forbes that his business was legitimate, Booth passed through the outer door and found himself standing in the vestibule of the two boxes. Booth's first act was to take the piece of wood that he had secured earlier in the day from a music stand and wedge it between the outer door and the wall, securing one end into the notch he had cut into the plaster. The acute angle formed by the wall and the door ensured that no one would be able to push the door open from the outside. The door secure, Booth knelt on one knee and peered through the small hole cut just above the doorknob. He could make out the side of a rather large rocking chair directly opposite the door. Seated in the rocker was the president.

Frank Ford, the son of Harry Clay Ford, has refuted the commonly held assumption that Booth had drilled an observation hole in the inner door during the afternoon. In a letter concerning the planned restoration of the theater in 1962, Mr. Ford wrote: "The hole was bored by my father, Harry Clay Ford, or rather on his orders, and was bored for the very simple reason it would allow the guard, one Parker, easy opportunity whenever he so desired to look into the box rather than open the inner door to check on the presidential party."[8]

Whether Booth drilled the hole or whether a member of Ford's staff did, it served Booth's purpose. Using the hole, he was able to catch a glimpse of the interior of the box to make certain Lincoln was seated in the rocker directly beyond the door and not somewhere else in the box. Booth would have only a brief moment to act if he was to catch those in the box by complete surprise. Rising to his feet he drew the small derringer from his vest pocket and set the hammer at full cock. The moment had arrived.

On the stage was a lone actor, Harry Hawk. The play in progress, *Our American Cousin*, was a spoof on British aristocracy and American "coarseness." Just the type of humor Lincoln especially enjoyed. After all, he was characterized for most of his political life as the crude, rough-edged westerner who lacked the social graces necessary to be president. Hawk played an American backwoodsman who was visiting his English cousins. Hawk's character was that of a coarse, uneducated bumpkin whose English host, Mrs. Mountchessington, had mistaken him for a wealthy suitor for her daughter. His part was filled with comic lines that showed his farcical nature. Lincoln could well identify with Hawk's character, having spent his early years among the bumpkins of the prairie.

Mrs. Mountchessington had been carefully scheming to unite Hawk's character, Asa Trenchard, with her daughter Augusta. As the end of scene 2, act 3, approached, Mrs. Mountchessington discovers that Asa is not the wealthy cousin she had thought but rather an uncouth American with nothing to offer her own ambitions but "hisself." She indignantly upbraids Asa after sending her daughter offstage, "I am aware, Mr. Trenchard, you are not used to the manners of good society, and that, alone, will excuse the impertinence of which you are guilty." Not quite the fool portrayed, Asa calls after her as she exits the stage, "Don't know the manners of good society, eh? Well I guess I know enough to turn you inside out, old gal—you sockdologizing old man-trap." It was a carefully placed laugh line meant to bring a burst of laughter from the audience. It always worked that way. The audience roared with laughter.

Booth grasped the knob and, turning it slowly, pushed the door open, stepped forward, raised the derringer, and squeezed the trigger. The muzzle, not more than two feet from the president's head, erupted with a loud explosion as the small sphere of lead shot from its throat. The ball, not larger than the tip of a little finger smashed into the base of the president's skull. It passed diagonally from left to right, plowing through the gelatinous substance of the president's brain before lodging behind his right eye. The concussive force fractured the orbital socket. The numbing effect was instantaneous. The president's body went limp as he slumped in the rocker, his head dropping forward with his chin pressed against his chest.

After a few seconds, the laughter fell away. Harry Hawk instinctively looked up at the box. A small puff of bluish smoke floated over the balustrade and hovered in midair over the stage. A shrill scream coming from inside the box startled the audience. A loud thump, another scream, and the body of a man swinging his legs over the flag-draped balustrade fell onto the stage. In sliding over the balustrade Booth's spur became entangled in one of the flags, causing him to land off balance on the hard stage below. The awkward fall resulted in his breaking the small bone in his left leg a few inches above the ankle.

Landing in a crouch, Booth quickly rose, turned toward the stunned audience, and thrust both of his arms in the air. The consummate thespian, Booth yelled to the audience, "Sic semper tyrannis." Standing center stage was a confused Harry Hawk. His humorous lines had drawn loud laughter from the audience; not loud enough, however, to disguise the sharp report of the gunshot. Hawk stood frozen as the man he recognized as his friend turned and, pushing past, ran stage right, disappearing behind the set.

Booth lunged toward the rear door, bumping into another figure standing in his path. Slashing with his knife, he pushed the figure aside. The door swung open before him and he rushed through it. Not ten feet away was his horse, its reins still held by the young Burroughs lying on a wooden carpenter's bench. Startled, the boy jumped to his feet only to feel a sharp pain to his head as the butt end of a bowie knife crashed down on his skull. Grabbing the reins, Booth swung himself up into the saddle. Young Peanuts Burroughs crouched on the ground clutching his head in pain. Booth pulled hard on the reins, dug his spurs deep into the animal's side, and galloped down the dark alley. He turned his horse to the left and, passing through an open gate, galloped up the narrow alleyway emerging onto F Street. He turned to his right and headed east for the Navy Yard Bridge and Maryland.

The deed was done. The tyrant was killed. Abraham Lincoln could burn in hell. *Sic semper tyrannis!*

CHAPTER ELEVEN

The Wound Is Mortal

He committed a monstrous crime in making war upon us, and his death was no more than just punishment for the crime.

William Starr Basinger, Savannah Volunteer Guards

The young officer told the ward master he would be absent for a few hours this evening. As army surgeon he was in charge of the commissioned officers' ward at the hospital at Armory Square in Washington. The demands of his duties gave him little time to enjoy the pleasures that were available in the wartime capital. Charles Leale had been an admirer of President Lincoln for some time, and after hearing the president give one of his impromptu speeches, he became even more enamored with him. When he read in the afternoon paper that Lincoln would attend Ford's Theatre that evening, Leale decided to take the evening off and go to the theater for no other reason than to catch a glimpse of his commander in chief.[1]

A general order was still in effect that all men in uniform must carry a pass authorizing their presence in the District of Columbia. Since uniformed soldiers were frequently challenged as they moved about the city, officers found it more convenient to change into civilian clothes before embarking on any social activity. In this way they avoided the overzealous challenges by the provost marshal's staff. Leale hurried back to his room and changed into a suit before proceeding to the theater.[2]

Word of Lincoln's scheduled visit had spurred ticket sales, and Leale could get a seat only in the dress circle, or "first balcony," not far from the outer door leading to the president's box. He tried to get a seat in the orchestra section where he could get a better view of the box and hopefully see the president. However, the orchestra was already sold out by the time he arrived. Still, he was happy with his balcony seat. It proved to be ideally situated.

The audience was in an upbeat mood. The play had many humorous lines, and the audience was generous in its laughter. Midway through the opening act the crowd began cheering and clapping their hands in a thunderous ovation. Only a few rows behind Leale, the president and Mrs. Lincoln were making their way toward the box. Leale turned to find himself looking directly at the president. "I had the best opportunity to distinctly see the full face of the president, as the light shone directly upon him," Leale wrote, and then added sadly, "I was looking at him as he took his last walk."[3]

President Lincoln, Mrs. Lincoln, along with their two guests, Major Henry Rathbone and Miss Clara Harris, slowly made their way across the back of the dress circle to the far side of the theater. Leale described what happened next: "The party was preceded by a special usher, who opened the door of the box, stood to one side, and after all had entered closed the door and took a seat outside, where he could guard the entrance to the box."[4] The "usher" mentioned by Leale was not really an usher, nor was he associated with Ford's Theatre or the president's security. He was Charles Forbes, the president's personal valet and messenger.

After a few minutes the audience sat down, and the actors returned to their performance. Leale kept looking over at the box hoping for glimpses of the president. At one point he noticed a disturbance at the outer door of the box. A man was talking with the "usher," persuading him to allow him to enter the box. After a brief moment the man was allowed to enter.[5] A minute later the sharp report of a gunshot was heard. Suddenly a man dropped from the front of the balustrade and landed on the stage amid screams from the box. Righting himself, the man shouted to the audience and ran across the stage, disappearing behind the scenes. It all happened in a matter of seconds.

Most of the audience seemed confused at what had taken place. Leale, however, reacted immediately. Hearing the screams from the box, he started to make his way toward the outer door that was only a few feet from where he had been seated. Forcing his way through the crowd he reached the door and tried to open it by pushing inward. The door would not move. It was rigid as if it had been nailed shut. Leale heard someone yelling on the other side to stop pushing against the door. His attempt to force the door open only served to fix the wooden brace more firmly in the wall notch that Booth had cut earlier in the day. Rathbone was struggling to remove the brace but Leale's weight against the door made his efforts impossible. Finally, when Leale stepped back, Rathbone was able to remove the brace and open the door. Forbes was still standing by the door but let Leale pass once he explained that he was an army surgeon.[6] Following close on the heels of Leale was Dr. Albert F.A. King, a Washington doctor who was also sitting in the dress circle near the outer door to the box, and a third man, William Kent, a government employee who had been sitting beside King.

Leale found Rathbone standing inside the door clutching his arm. Rathbone asked Leale to attend to it, but Leale quickly evaluated the situation and put Rathbone in the "treatment later" category. Clara Harris, Rathbone's fiancée and companion that night, described the scene in a letter to a close friend eleven days later: "Henry has been suffering a great deal with his arm, but it is now doing well,—the knife went from the elbow nearly to the shoulder, inside, cutting an artery, nerves & veins—He bled so profusely as to make him very weak—My whole clothing as I sat in the box was saturated literally with blood, & my hands and face—you can imagine what a scene—Poor Mrs. Lincoln all through that dreadful night would look at me with horror and scream, Oh! My husband's blood—My Dear Husband's blood—which it was not, though I did not know it at the time. The president's wound did not bleed externally at all—the brain was instantly suffused."[7]

Reaching the inner box, Leale approached the rocker where Lincoln sat slumped; his wife holding him upright so he wouldn't fall forward onto the floor: "As I looked at Lincoln he appeared dead. His eyes were closed and his head had fallen forward. He was being held upright in his chair by Mrs. Lincoln who was weeping bitterly."[8] Leale felt for a pulse. There was none. He then moved Lincoln to a recumbent position on the floor and, removing his hands from the president's head, noticed traces of blood. Leale thought Lincoln had been stabbed in the neck or back.

Dr. Charles Taft, another army surgeon, was seated in the orchestra below. He had come onto the stage directly beneath the box. Announcing that he was a doctor, he was lifted from the floor and boosted up to the level of the balustrade by Thomas Bradford Sanders. Grabbing onto the flag draped over the balustrade, he climbed into the box. Following directly behind Taft was Lieutenant James Bolton, a member of the District's provost marshal's guard.[9] Counting the four original occupants, there were now ten individuals in the confined area of the double box.

Taft immediately began to assist Leale, who was leaning over the wounded man's body. Using a borrowed pen knife, Leale cut Lincoln's collar off and then split his shirt and coat open from his neck to his elbow. Leale quickly examined the exposed area. There was no knife wound, no cut artery, no blood. Lifting one of Lincoln's eyelids Leale noted the left eye was dilated, indicating neurological damage. He next ran his fingers through Lincoln's thick hair. He found the wound. A small entry hole on the back part of the head behind the left ear. A small clot of blood plugged the hole. Leale carefully removed the coagulated material and Lincoln began to breathe more rhythmically. Removing the clot had relieved the pressure that was suppressing the president's respiration.

Leale suddenly became aware of another person kneeling beside the prostrate body of the president. It was Laura Keene, the actress for whom the evening benefit had been scheduled.[10] Someone in the box had called for water, and Keene, who was standing in the wings looking up at the box, grabbed a pitcher of water from the special green room just offstage. She asked Thomas Gourlay, the stage manager, to lead her to the box. It was impossible to maneuver through the large crowd still milling about the downstairs area. The lobby staircase was completely blocked by people. Gourlay led Keene through a rear passage that exited through a backstage door into the alleyway that separated the Star saloon from the theater. Here the two climbed a staircase that led up to the lounge area on the second floor. From this point, Gourlay and Keene passed through a door that opened onto the dress circle near the entrance to the box. Gourlay had to clear only a short pathway to the outer door.

Keene asked Leale if it would be all right to hold Lincoln's head in her lap. Leale explained: "While we were waiting for Mr. Lincoln to regain strength, Laura Keene appealed to me to allow her to hold the President's head. I granted the request, and she sat on the floor of the box and held his head in her lap."[11]

William Kent, a government employee, also remarked about the incident, "Laura Keene came up in the meantime, and the President's head was raised to rest in her lap."[12] Laura Keene preserved the dress with the president's blood on it. However, several persons raised doubts about the stains, stating that the president's head wound did not bleed. Taft seemed emphatic, "At that time there was no blood oozing from it." However, it is clear that the head wound did bleed. Leale described running his separated fingers through the president's hair matted with his blood. Each time Leale removed the clot that formed in the entry wound blood oozed out.

Someone asked Leale if the president should now be moved to the White House, where he could be made more comfortable. The three doctors conferred. They were in agreement. It would be too dangerous to move the president the seven blocks over rough Washington streets. All three felt he should be moved from the theater. A closer place would have to be found. Someone suggested Taltavul's saloon next door. According to Taltavul, he said it would not be right for the president to die in a saloon.[13] It is easy to see that Taltavul was not an entrepreneur.

Leale said that as soon as the president gained sufficient strength he should be taken "to the nearest house on the opposite side of the street."[14] The doctors conferred again and decided the president was strong enough to move. Leale explained: "We decided that the President could now be moved from the possibility of danger in the theater to a house where we might place him on a bed in safety. To assist in this duty I assigned Dr. Taft to carry his right shoulder, Dr. King to carry his left shoulder and detailed a sufficient number of others, whose names I have never discovered, to assist in carrying the body, while I carried the head going first."[15]

The "others" whose names Leale never discovered were four soldiers from Thompson's Battery C, Independent Pennsylvania Artillery. Stationed at Camp Barry on the outskirts of the city, the four soldiers decided to visit the city and take in a play. They were sitting in the dress circle at the time the president was shot. Their names were Jacob J. Soles, John Corey, Jake Griffiths, and William Sample.[16] With the three doctors at the head and shoulder area, the four soldiers gently picked up the president's torso and legs.

With Leale in the lead, the body of President Lincoln was "borne on loving hands" through the balcony area to the lobby stairs. At this point they were joined by two soldiers who had been helping to manage the large crowd of stunned people filling the dress circle. Years later they would step forward and add their names to those of their four comrades. They were William McPeck and John Weaver. At the head of the stairs the men reversed the body and took it down the steps feet first. Emerging from the theater into the darkness they were greeted by a solemn crowd standing still in shock. As the body of the president slowly made its way into the street the multitude parted, opening a path to the other side. The bearers were joined at this point by ten members of the Union Light Guard, who had been notified to report to the theater immediately. They had been assigned to serve as escort duty at the White House but were used as mounted orderlies.[17] The soldiers formed a corridor through which the president's body was carried.

As the group slowly made its way into the street, Leale began to look around for a house where they could safely lay the president in bed. The house directly across the street from the theater was dark, no one was at home. Then a dim light appeared on the steps of a brick house diagonally across the street from the theater's main entrance. A man stood at the top of the stairs holding a small candle. Young Henry S. Safford had been reading in the front room of William Petersen's house when he heard a commotion outside shortly after 10:30 P.M. Going to the front door, he heard someone say that the president had been shot. Just then he noticed a group of men carrying the body of the president out from the theater. Safford described the scene: "Suddenly those carrying him seemed in doubt as to where they would take him." Safford, "realizing the cause of their hesitation," cried out, "Bring him in here, bring him in here."[18] Leale nodded to the others and they carried the president's body up the steps and into the front door of 453 Tenth Street. Safford directed the group into a small bedroom located at the far end of the narrow hallway.

The house where Lincoln was carried was owned by a German-born tailor named William Petersen. Born Wilhelm Petersen on August 16, 1816, in Hanover, Germany, Petersen immigrated with his young wife to the United States in 1841. He was twenty-five years old, she was twenty-two. In 1849 Petersen purchased a lot on Tenth Street nearly opposite the Tenth Street Baptist Church and built a three-story brick house. The entrance to the house was above street level and was reached by a curving stairway of ten risers. There was a basement entrance in the front that led to Petersen's tailoring shop that was located in the front basement room.[19]

The Petersen family consisted of mother and father and seven children ranging from the age of three months to sixteen years.[20] In addition there were nine other residents of the house who were boarders. Included among the nine were Henry Ulke and Julius Ulke, both photographers, who on

Saturday, April 15, 1865, visited the room minutes after Lincoln's body had been removed. Setting up their wet plate camera, they took one of the most haunting photographs in history. The scene showed the bed moments after Lincoln's body was removed; a blood-soaked pillow hung over the side, evidence of the ghastly scene that had taken place.

The large number of people who lived in the house were accommodated in eleven rooms. The basement area had two rooms, the first floor contained a front and back parlor and a rear bedroom, the second floor consisted of three rooms, and the third floor contained three rooms. On entering the front of the house on the first floor, a narrow hallway passed the two parlors on the left before ending at the doorway to the rear bedroom. It was this rear bedroom where Lincoln was carried and placed on a bed. The room measured nine and a half feet wide by seventeen feet long and had a small dresser and two chairs in addition to the bed. The front parlor would serve as a mourning room for the duration of the deathwatch while the rear parlor would serve as the war room for the government of the United States. Here Stanton would assume control of the only two activities the government would concern itself with for the next eight hours, assassination and war, in that order.

The bed in the rear room was too small to hold the president's long body. Removing the foot of the bed was not possible without breaking the bed, which would render it unusable. So the body was laid diagonally across the bed, placing the head nearest the door and the feet nearest the wall. The bed was pulled away from the wall so that the doctors could move freely around three sides. Leale made the president as comfortable as possible, then asked that everyone leave the room except the medical doctors so that a careful physical examination could be made. The room soon emptied except for Mrs. Lincoln, who had followed directly behind the president. Leale tactfully explained the situation to Mary Lincoln and she moved to the front parlor where she waited.[21]

Leale, with help from the other doctors, stripped Lincoln's clothes off and examined his naked body. No other injuries could be found, only the small hole in the back of his head. Leale noted that Lincoln's extremities were extremely cold and ordered several hot water bottles, hot blankets, and ingredients to make a "sinapism," the medical term for a mustard plaster.[22]

After carefully arranging the bed covering, the doctors sent for Mary Lincoln and placed her in a chair at the president's head. Mary was grief stricken. She kissed her husband several times, pleading with him to speak just one word to her.[23] It was no use. Despite her pleadings, Lincoln lay comatose, unresponsive to all stimuli. Mrs. Elizabeth Dixon, wife of Senator James Dixon of Connecticut, comforted Mary Lincoln. Elizabeth Dixon had been asked to come and be with Mary by Robert Lincoln after he arrived at the house. She stayed by Mary's side all through the night, escorting her back to the White House following Lincoln's death.[24]

Mary's pleadings were distracting to the doctors. They asked Mrs. Dixon, to take her to the front parlor and keep her there. Leale continued to remove the small clot that kept forming in the small hole in Lincoln's skull. A small piece of skull acted much like a valve blocking the flow of blood through the opening. Each time Leale displaced the small fragment and cleared the clot he noticed a marked improvement in the President's respiration and pulse. At this point the doctors agreed there was little that could be done other than make the president as comfortable as possible. The deathwatch began.

Now that the president was stabilized Leale sent a note to the Reverend Phineas T. Gurley, pastor of the New York Avenue Presbyterian Church where the Lincoln family worshiped. The church was only a few blocks from the Petersen house. Leale also sent word to Surgeon General Joseph K. Barnes, Surgeon Willard Bliss (Leale's superior at the Armory Square Hospital), Dr. Robert K. Stone (the president's family doctor), and each member of the cabinet, telling a young soldier to go first to Secretary Stanton's house and bring him at once.[25]

Earlier that afternoon, Ellen Stanton had reminded her husband that they had been invited to go with the Lincolns to the theater that evening. Stanton told his wife to decline the invitation if she wished. Stanton was very much opposed to the president's theatergoing and had no interest in accompanying him. On the way home from his office he stopped by the home of Secretary of State William Seward to see how he was recovering from injuries sustained in an earlier carriage accident. After a short chat with Seward, Stanton returned home where he was greeted by a group of War Department clerks who had come to serenade him. There was a great spirit of joy among everyone. The feeling of victory seemed almost boundless.

Following the serenade, the singers began to move away in the direction of Ford's Theatre, where they would wait for the president and the first lady to emerge so that they could serenade their commander in chief. It was a few minutes past ten o'clock when Stanton locked up the house and went to his bedroom. His wife looked in on the children, who had bedded down a few hours before. They were peacefully asleep.[26]

As Stanton began to undress he was startled by his wife's scream from the floor below, "My God! Mr. Seward has been murdered!" Stanton's first reaction was one of disbelief. He had left Seward a little over an hour ago, and he was resting comfortably despite his serious injury. Stanton quickly pulled on his clothes and hurried downstairs. An excited messenger stood in the front hallway, hat in hand. It was true. Seward had been murdered. Stanton rushed outside where a carriage stood near the door. Climbing aboard, he told the driver to hurry to the Seward house.[27]

As Stanton arrived at the Seward home, Gideon Welles appeared simultaneously. Welles was also preparing for bed when a messenger yelled up to him that Lincoln had been shot and Seward murdered. Welles asked where the president was shot. The messenger said at Ford's Theatre. Welles told the man that he must be mistaken. Seward was confined to bed and could not possibly be at the theater with Lincoln. There seemed to be great confusion. He decided to go to Seward's house immediately. Hurrying on foot he found a large crowd gathering outside. Welles pushed his way into the house and made his way to Seward's bedroom. He met Stanton at the door. The two secretaries found Seward lying in bed attended to by Seward's family physician, Dr. Tullio S. Verdi. The bed sheets were saturated with blood. In an adjoining room, Seward's son, Frederick, lay unconscious, his skull fractured. There was blood everywhere.[28]

At the very moment Booth was making his way into the president's box at Ford's Theatre, Powell was forcing his way into Seward's home. An ex-druggist's clerk, Powell used the ruse of bringing an important medicine from Seward's doctor, Tullio Verdi. A black servant, William Bell, admitted Powell into the house. Bell said that he would take the medicine to the convalescing Secretary, but Powell insisted he was instructed to deliver it personally. Powell pushed past Bell and began to make his way up the stairs when Frederick Seward appeared. The two men argued, Powell insisting that he must personally give the medicine to the Secretary. Fanny Seward, the Secretary's young daughter, was in her father's room tending to him. She opened the door to see what the commotion was all about. The alert Powell looked at her and asked, "Is the Secretary asleep?" Fanny answered without thinking, "Almost."[29] Fanny Seward had inadvertently told Powell where Seward was resting. Frederick Seward stepped in front of Powell to block his way and Powell turned to leave. He had descended no more than a few steps when he erupted. Aiming his revolver at Frederick Seward, Powell pulled the trigger. The gun misfired. He then used the gun to bludgeon Seward, fracturing his skull and leaving him comatose on the floor. A wild melee ensued. Within minutes five members of the household were injured, three critically. George Robinson, Seward's nurse, Emerick Hansell, a State Department messenger, and Augustus Seward, William Seward's eldest son, suffered various wounds from Powell's large bowie knife. All five would survive the attack, but they would carry the scars of Powell's assault for life.

Although Stanton and Welles found Seward seriously wounded, he was alive. Satisfied that he would survive, the two men decided to go to the theater immediately. As they emerged from the house they were besieged by several people who told them it was too dangerous. Stanton and Welles hesitated for only a moment and then climbed into the carriage that had brought Stanton to Seward's house. At this point Major General Montgomery Meigs joined the pair along with District of Columbia Supreme Court Justice David Kellogg Cartter. Meigs climbed into the carriage next to Stanton and Welles while Cartter climbed up alongside the driver. As they were about to depart, Major Thomas Eckert rode up on horseback.[30] Eckert tried to persuade

Stanton from going near Tenth Street. There were thousands of people milling in the streets and it would be too risky.[31] Welles and Stanton ignored Eckert's pleas and ordered the driver to hurry. Eckert followed closely behind. Arriving at Tenth Street the men were told that the president was no longer in the theater. He had been taken to a house across the street. Welles later described the scene in his diary:

> The President had been carried across the street from the theater, to the house of a Mr. Petersen. We entered by ascending a flight of steps above the basement and passing through a long hall to the rear where the President lay extended on a bed, breathing heavily. Several surgeons were present, at least six, I should think more. . . . The giant sufferer lay extended diagonally across the bed which was not long enough for him. He had been stripped of his clothes. . . . His slow, full respiration lifted the clothes with each breath that he took. His features were calm and striking. I had never seen them appear to better advantage than for the first hour, perhaps, that I was there. After that, his right eye began to swell and that part of his face became discolored. . . . The night was dark, cloudy, and damp, and about six it began to rain.[32]

It was "a little past eleven" when the two secretaries stepped down from their carriage and made their way into the tailor's house.[33] A few miles to the southeast a lone rider galloped up the long incline of Harrison Road (now Good Hope Road) east of the Anacostia River. Cresting the hill he slipped past the lonely pickets who were standing guard, protecting the city against its enemies. No one could get into the city without being challenged. Leaving the city was another matter.

Viewing the president, Stanton became alarmed. The president's labored breathing was like a death rattle to the secretary. He knew the president's life was slipping away with each passing minute. No doctor need tell him the wound was mortal. Mrs. Lincoln was in the front parlor attended by two ladies who were among her closest friends. She was in a state that alternated between semiconsciousness and near hysteria. Her grief was overwhelming. Her husband had cared for her and protected her from all who disliked her and would abuse her. Soon she would be alone. The one true comfort of her life was slowly passing away from her and no matter how hard she tried to reach out and pull him to her, it was futile. Although Stanton disliked Mary Lincoln, he felt compassion for her at this dreadful moment. Leaving her in the front parlor, he set up his acting government in the rear parlor.

For the next several hours Stanton assumed the role of acting president. He was without constitutional authority, but such times called for action, not debate. The succession to the presidency should the president and vice president be incapacitated fell first to the Senate president pro tempore and then to the Speaker of the House.[34] The secretary of war was not within reach of acting president.

Often maligned for his vigorous pursuit of the war, Stanton now fulfilled his enemies' characterization as a usurper of power. In truth, he stepped into the breach at a moment of national crisis and brought a steadying influence. Both the president of the United States and his secretary of state seemed to be dying and the belief that a major conspiracy was still in the process of unfolding was widespread. And why shouldn't it be believed? As the hours passed it became more evident that conspirators were popping up all over the place in what clearly looked like a plot to overthrow the constitutional government by assassination. Welles summed up the general belief when he said, "Damn the Rebels, this was their work."[35]

Stanton set up a makeshift office in the rear parlor where he and Judge David Kellogg Cartter began taking testimony to the night's grizzly events. They sat at a small table in the rear parlor with one of the army clerks acting as a recorder. It was a few minutes before midnight when the first witness began telling his story. It soon became obvious that recording the narrative by longhand was too cumbersome and would slow the process. General Christopher Columbus Augur walked out onto the front stoop and called out for someone who knew shorthand. Albert Daggett, a clerk with the State Department, was standing on the balcony of the house next door. He knew someone who was proficient in the art of phonography, a fellow border in the large rooming house. His name was James Tanner. Tanner had been standing on the balcony only moments before and had gone back inside his room that was just inside the large window that led onto the balcony. The General told Daggett to get Tanner and send him next door immediately.[36]

Corporal James Tanner had just turned twenty-one ten days earlier. At the tender age of eighteen he became a battle-hardened veteran. At the second battle of Bull Run on August 30, 1862, he suffered terrible wounds when a Confederate shell exploded near where he lay, its shrapnel tearing his legs apart. After he was taken to a field hospital, his legs were amputated below the knees. He was eventually fitted with artificial legs, and after a long rehabilitation period he returned to service in 1864 in the Ordnance Bureau of the War Department.[37]

Tanner had been at Grover's Theatre that night and learned of Lincoln's assassination when the owner interrupted the play to announce the tragic news. Like others he left the theater and made his way back to his rooming house on Tenth Street opposite Ford's Theatre. Tanner rented the second-story front room. It had a balcony that overlooked the street, and Tanner and his fellow boarders would frequently come out onto the balcony and spend their leisure time watching the people as they passed by. Now, the balcony afforded a front row seat to the events unfolding beneath it. Tanner had been on the balcony with Daggett watching the huge crowd that continued to fill the area between E and F Streets. He had stepped inside briefly just as General Augur had emerged from the Petersen house calling for a phonographer.

When Tanner entered the Petersen house he was taken straight back to the rear parlor where Stanton and Cartter were sitting. Tanner described the scene: "I found Secretary Stanton sitting on one side of the library [parlor] and Chief Justice Cartter of the Supreme Court of the District at the end. They had started in to take what testimony they could regarding the assassination, having some one write it out in longhand. This had proved unsatisfactory. I took a seat opposite the Secretary and commenced to take down the testimony."[38]

For the next hour and a half Tanner hurriedly copied down every word. By 1:30 A.M. the last witness had been interviewed. There were six witnesses in all, and all six had been an eyewitness to the shooting in the theater. Tanner apparently listened to the substance of the testimony as well as the words. Two days later in a letter to one of his fellow phonographic students living in Syracuse he wrote: "In fifteen minutes I had testimony enough down to hang John Wilkes Booth, the assassin, higher than ever Haman hanged."[39]

By the end of the testimony there was more than enough evidence to order the arrest of Booth. Still Stanton hesitated, and his hesitation became sufficient to lead some future writers to weave his delay into a sinister web of conspiracy. By delaying, his critics claimed, Stanton allowed Booth to slip free of the confines of the city and make his escape. This was nonsense, of course. No amount of celerity on Stanton's part could have trapped Booth within the city or at any point immediately outside the city. By the time the first bit of evidence was being heard Booth and Herold were arriving at the Surratt tavern in Surrattsville some thirteen miles away. Years later, historian Otto Eisenschiml would write that Stanton had deliberately taken steps to allow Booth time to escape the military's defenses ringing the city. Eisenschiml claimed there "was an interruption of all telegraphic communication between Washington and the outside world, lasting about two hours."[40] Eisenschiml was mistaken. While a commercial telegraph line was disabled for two hours, the military lines remained open and functioning.[41] Proof of this is seen in a telegram that was received in the War Department telegraph office dated 11:00 P.M., April 14, and a second outgoing telegram dated 12:00 midnight, April 15, which Eckert himself sent to General Grant.[42] The first telegram that Stanton sent went out at 1:10 A.M. to New York Police Chief John Kennedy.[43] All three of these telegrams show that the military telegraph was functioning during the critical hours immediately following Booth's attack on Lincoln. Eisenschiml's suggestion that "there might be a traitor in the ranks of the telegraphic corps" was nothing more than poor research on his part.

Stanton was engaged in considerably more than hearing the testimony of the six witnesses who appeared at the Petersen house early Saturday morning. He was issuing orders to his subordinates throughout the country. By the time Horace Greeley's *Daily Tribune* hit the streets of New York a dozen dispatches had been issued. One fact that most writers ignore is that Stanton did not listen to the testimony of each witness in its entirety or continuously. He was interrupted constantly and had to make numerous decisions and issue orders. Coupled with this was his compulsion to visit the president at periodic intervals between midnight and 1:30 A.M. when the testimony finally ended.

Tanner began to transcribe his phonographic notes and, as he stated later, did not finish the transcription until 6:45 A.M., just thirty-seven minutes before Lincoln was officially declared dead, and while Stanton was sitting by the president's side on his deathwatch.[44] Even so, Stanton must have gleaned early on that Booth was the culprit, but how early is not clear. Stanton's first dispatch was filed at 1:30 A.M. at the end of the testimony session. It did not hit the telegraphic wires until 2:15 A.M. As of this dispatch it wasn't known whether the assassin of Lincoln was the same person who attacked Seward. Stanton's telegram to Dix read, in part, "About the same hour an assassin, whether the same or not, entered Mr. Seward's apartment, and, under pretense of having a prescription, was shown to the Secretary's sick chamber."[45]

In his second dispatch filed at 3 A.M. Stanton mentioned Booth as the possible assassin: "Investigation strongly indicates J. Wilkes Booth as the assassin of the President."[46] By the time this dispatch reached the public through the newspapers Booth and Herold were safely at Dr. Mudd's house beyond the immediate reach of Stanton and his soldiers.

Outside of the Petersen house considerable action was unfolding. Shortly before eleven o'clock John Fletcher walked up to Pennsylvania Avenue from his stables one block south. He had rented one of his horses to Davy Herold and warned the young man that he was to bring the horse back on time. Herold was two hours overdue, and Fletcher feared that he had taken the horse and ridden off with no intention of returning him. Fletcher's timing was fortuitous. As he approached the avenue he caught sight of Herold one block away. Herold had accompanied Powell to the Seward house earlier in the evening. Waiting outside, Herold heard the screams resulting from Powell's attack and decided to flee the scene, leaving Powell to fend for himself. Now he was slowly trotting along Pennsylvania Avenue near Fourteenth Street. Fletcher shouted for Herold to return the horse, but Herold, wheeling around, spurred the animal up Fourteenth Street away from the avenue and Fletcher.[47]

Watching Herold riding off on his horse, an angry Fletcher turned and ran back to his stables, where he mounted his own horse and set out after Herold and his rented horse. Fletcher had once overheard Herold and his sidekick George Atzerodt talk about a place across the river in southern

Maryland called White Plains. He suspected that Herold was probably headed there now. Herold often visited the area on hunting trips. Fletcher had little else to go on. It was a good hunch.

Only an hour earlier Atzerodt had come by the stable to pick up his horse and had asked Fletcher to join him for a drink at the corner saloon. Fletcher thought Atzerodt somewhat of a disheveled lowlife who was usually tipsy when he came to the stables. Still, it didn't hurt for him to join the German in a drink, especially since the German was paying. Returning to the stables, Atzerodt mounted his horse. It was a rather spirited little mare that showed a feisty demeanor. As Atzerodt was about to leave he turned to Fletcher and said that his horse would be "good upon the retreat" this particular night.[48] The comment meant nothing to Fletcher at the time, but he would remember it later that night when he visited army headquarters.

Fletcher arrived at the Navy Yard Bridge a little after 11 P.M. where he was stopped by the military pickets guarding the bridge. In charge of the night guard was Sergeant Silas T. Cobb. Cobb asked Fletcher his business, and Fletcher told the sergeant that a young man had recently ridden off with one of Fletcher's horses. He gave the guard a description of Herold and asked if he had by chance tried to pass over the bridge. Cobb acknowledged that a man fitting the description had passed over the bridge only minutes before. In fact, two men had passed over the bridge only minutes apart. Fletcher concluded the second man was Herold and probably assumed the first man was his pal George Atzerodt.

Fletcher asked Cobb for permission to cross over into Maryland and continue his pursuit of Herold. Cobb told Fletcher he could cross but could not return before morning. Fletcher pleaded his case with Cobb, saying that he had no intention of staying on the other side until morning. He had a stable to manage and needed to return as soon as possible. Cobb held to his rule. Fletcher could leave but he could not return until morning. There was little if any threat to the city by people leaving it, only the imagined threat from people entering. Cobb had his orders.[49]

Fletcher, frustrated and angry, turned his horse around and headed back to his stables. After taking care of his horse he walked the short distance to police headquarters located on Tenth Street near Ford's Theatre.[50] The crowd had not dissipated but was still milling outside the Petersen house where the dying president was being cared for. Inquiring at police headquarters about a possible stolen horse, Fletcher was told that the police had, in fact, picked up a stray east of the capitol building near Lincoln Hospital earlier in the evening. They had taken it to the Twenty-second Army Corps Headquarters stables where it was being held. On duty that night at the police headquarters was Charles Stone. Stone told Fletcher he would accompany him to look at the horse. The two men walked over to the stables where Fletcher was shown the saddle that had been on the abandoned horse. It was not one of his saddles, nor was it the saddle used by Davy Herold. But Fletcher recognized the saddle. It belonged to the disheveled little German that had tossed down a whiskey with him earlier that same evening. He momentarily forgot the man's name but told General Augur that he had the name written on a card back at his stables. Augur told Fletcher and Stone to retrieve the card and bring the name to him at once. Returning to his stables, Fletcher pulled the card from a ledger book he kept in his office. Written on the card was the name *George A. Atzerodt.*[51]

Fletcher was next taken to the stable where the stray horse was held. It was a large brown horse that had only one eye. Fletcher had seen both the horse and the saddle before, always in the possession of George Atzerodt. Fletcher did not know what to make of the situation. He had assumed that Davy Herold and George Atzerodt had fled over the Navy Yard Bridge earlier in the evening, but here was Atzerodt's saddle and a horse he had used on occasion in the past. Was it possible that someone else had gone over the bridge instead of Atzerodt? Still, it seemed likely the two friends were together somewhere in southern Maryland. Atzerodt, of course, had not crossed over the Navy Yard Bridge ahead of Herold. That rider was John Wilkes Booth. But at midnight the army had information that would prove extremely valuable within the next few hours. Herold and Atzerodt were linked together, and one or both were now believed to have fled into southern Maryland. It would take only linking the two of them to John Wilkes Booth to alert authorities that southern Maryland was the likely place to search. That linkage would shortly occur on Saturday morning.

As dawn was breaking over the disconsolate capital, Washington's Provost Marshal James O' Beirne had sent one of his detectives, John Lee, to the Kirkwood Hotel located at Twelfth and Pennsylvania Avenue to guard Andrew Johnson just in case there was a wider conspiracy whose work was not finished. When Lee arrived at the Kirkwood Hotel he questioned the clerk and barkeep Michael Henry about any events or persons that might raise his suspicions. Henry was more than cooperative. He did believe there was a "suspicious appearing character" who had registered in room 126 on Friday morning.[52] Lee asked Henry to take him to the room. Henry was unable to unlock the door since there was only one key to the room and the boarder had taken it with him. No matter, Lee forced the door open and entered the room. There he found several items, including a coat. In its pocket was a small bankbook with the owner's name carefully penned inside, *J. Wilkes Booth.*[53] On the desk register was the name of the man who had rented the room a day earlier, *George A. Atzerodt.*[54] It was a major break in the investigation.

The authorities began to piece their information together. Clearly Herold was linked to Atzerodt, and now Atzerodt was linked to Booth. As a result of Fletcher's information, Augur suspected that Herold went over the Navy Yard Bridge minutes behind a second man sometime around 11 P.M. As a result of Fletcher's information, Augur ordered a troop of the Thirteenth New York Cavalry under the command of David D. Dana sent over the bridge into southern Maryland. Dana was assigned to Company E, Third Massachusetts Heavy Artillery, stationed at Fort Baker on Good Hope Hill near Union Town. This was the same Fort Baker that Herold and Booth passed a few minutes after 11 P.M. during their flight from Washington.

Dana proceeded to the small village of Piscataway located six miles to the southeast of Surrattsville. Arriving at 7:00 A.M., Dana learned from the troops stationed there that Booth and Herold were not seen in the immediate area and, therefore, must have taken the Surrattsville road in the direction of Bryantown. Dana then headed for Bryantown twelve miles to the southeast of Piscataway.[55]

Arriving in Bryantown shortly after noon on Saturday, April 15, Dana set up his headquarters in the Bryantown Tavern.[56] Dana told his men to start gathering up any and all suspicious characters including anyone thought to be a Southern sympathizer. The last part of the order was problematic since nearly everyone in the county was a Southern sympathizer if not an outright Confederate agent of one sort or another. Dana's orders left few residents outside the military's dragnet.

Back in Washington, the crowd outside of the Petersen house continued their vigil. Inside, the group of men surrounding the president were now becoming fatigued. The tenseness and emotional drain was beginning to show. The deathwatch had already lasted several hours longer than the most optimistic estimate called for. Time slipped slowly past, each tick of the clock measured against the failing pulse of the president. A sense of grief weighed heavily on all that were present. The emotional wailing of Mary Lincoln was distressing to even the most hardened heart.

The deathwatch was drawing to an end. Shortly before seven o'clock Mary Lincoln was sent for one last time so that she may see her husband before the end. Leale described the tragic scene: "As she entered the chamber and saw how the beloved features were distorted, she fell fainting to the floor. Restoratives were applied, and she was supported to the bedside, where she frantically addressed the dying man. 'Love,' she exclaimed, 'live but one moment to speak to me once—to speak to our children.'"[57]

The distraught woman was led away to the front parlor as those in the room pressed a little closer to the bed. Seven o'clock came and went. The pauses between beats and breaths grew longer, and when they resumed, feebler. Sitting opposite Leale at the head of the bed was Surgeon General Barnes. Dr. Stone sat on the edge of the foot of the bed. Robert Lincoln stood beside Senator Sumner, who placed his arm around him. As Leale held the president's hand he placed his forefinger over its pulse. For nearly a minute he felt nothing. Not even the slightest surge or movement. The breathing stopped. Leale looked across at Barnes, and the two men seemed to close their eyes in unison. It was over. Barnes carefully crossed Lincoln's hands across his breast and whispered, "He is gone."[58]

To those in the room it seemed as though several minutes passed in utter silence. The group of solemn men simply stared at the lifeless form lying on the bed. Then Stanton quietly said to Gurley, "Doctor, will you say anything?"[59] Gurley nodded and knelt by the bedside and waited as each of the men sank to their knees. All placed their hands on the bed along with Gurley as if to connect with the lifeless form beneath the coverlet. Gurley began to speak. He asked that God accept his humble servant Abraham Lincoln into His glorious Kingdom.[60] When he finished, Stanton, tears streaming down his cheeks, spoke the six words that would become immortalized, "Now he belongs to the ages."[61]

On returning to his church at New York Avenue and Thirteenth Street, Gurley went straight to his study and sitting at the large oak desk began writing a poem to ease his own grief:

> Thy name shall live while time endures,
> And men shall say of thee,
> He saved his country from its foes,
> And bade the slave be free.[62]

CHAPTER TWELVE

Surrattsville

I am pretty certain that we have assassinated the President and Secretary Seward.

John Wilkes Booth

As Stanton and Welles were making their way to Ford's Theatre, a horse and rider were seen racing hard across the capitol grounds in the direction of the Eastern Branch of the Potomac River.[1] The exact route is not known, but within a few minutes the rider arrived at the Eleventh Street Bridge located next to the Washington Navy Yard in southeast Washington. The distance from Ford's Theatre was just over three miles.

Guarding the bridge were two soldiers from the Third Massachusetts Heavy Artillery stationed at Fort Baker.[2] The rider galloped up to the gate that blocked passage across the wooden bridge. The sentry raised his hand and called for the rider to stop. He reined in his horse. In command of the detail on duty that night was Sergeant Silas T. Cobb. Cobb challenged the man sitting astride his sweating mount: "Who are you sir?"

"My name is Booth."

"Where are you from?" Cobb asked.

"The city," the rider answered, steadying his horse. The sergeant noted the horse's sweaty flanks indicating he had been ridden hard.

"Where are you going?"

"I am going home." He replied. "To Charles County."

"What town are you going to?"

"I do not live in a town." The rider seemed in a hurry.

Cobb took hold of the bridle to steady the horse from its nervous prancing.

"You must live in some town." Cobb remarked.

"I live near Beantown," came the reply. "It is a dark road and I thought if I waited til now that I would have the moon to help me."[3]

Sergeant Cobb hesitated, then nodded to the private. The gate swung open as the Sergeant stood to one side, letting go of the bridle.

"All right, you may pass, but you cannot come back across before daybreak."

"I have no intention of returning," the rider said as he began walking his horse across the open bridge.

It is curious that Booth gave his real name and destination to Cobb, and yet the military never took advantage of this information. Perhaps Booth slipped up because he was in an excited state having just murdered the president. Still, it could have proved to be a fatal slip. Booth's statement that he was headed for "Beantown" indicated that he planned to go to Dr. Mudd's house only minutes after shooting Lincoln and not by accident as most authors claim. Mudd lived only three miles east of the small village known as Beantown.

Once across the bridge Booth turned onto Harrison Road, which would take him into southern Maryland. Riding hard up the steep incline leading out of the city he had only one more checkpoint to pass before he would be free of any hindrance. At the top of the hill the road passed between two forts. Back in Washington Stanton was just arriving at the Petersen house.

At the bridge Cobb had just returned to the guardhouse when a second rider galloped up. Cobb went through the routine a second time. The rider identified himself as "Smith." He told Cobb he had overstayed his visit with a lady of the evening. Cobb understood. It was an easy thing to do. Cobb then asked him his destination. The rider told him he was headed for his home in "White Plains." It was located approximately six miles to the southwest of Mudd's house, well away from Booth's intended direction. White Plains was the same place that Fletcher remembered hearing Herold and Atzerodt discuss on previous occasions.[4] As with the first rider, no threat was seen. Cobb waved the man across the bridge, warning him as he had the first rider that he could not return before morning.

Cobb had violated his orders by allowing Booth to pass over the bridge. It was a technical violation. The threat to Washington was over and passage to and from the city was relaxed. Although General Augur would dress down Cobb, he was never charged or formally reprimanded for his failure.

Once past the two forts at the top of Harrison Road the way was clear. It was a little past 11:00 P.M. when the hard riding Booth passed the forts and headed south toward Surrattsville. There was no challenge. There couldn't be. No word had passed from the city that something desperate had taken place. The sentries on duty may have heard the hoof beats far in the distance, but so what? It mattered little that some citizen was making his way at this late hour out of the city.

Sometime around midnight Major George Worcester, the commanding officer of Fort Baker, received a telegram from Augur's headquarters ordering him to deploy his troops between the two forts "and form a continuous line of telegraph pickets, . . . it is supposed that one of the assassins is still in the city."[5] By posting soldiers as "telegraph pickets," the two forts remained in voice contact with one another by simply shouting messages from one guard to the next.

Booth had told the guard at the bridge that he was headed for "Beantown." To be sure, he would go to Beantown, but first he made another stop. Riding past the forts, Booth continued on for another five miles until he reached the high ground south of the city at a spot known as Soper's Hill. Here he stopped and waited for Herold and Powell. He hallooed softly but no one answered. Soper's Hill seems to have been the spot Booth designated as a rendezvous point for the four men to meet. Herold, following his arrest, told the detectives that he first ran into Booth at Soper's Hill on the night of April 14. Herold had put the time at approximately 11:30 P.M., which fits nicely with other known times along the road to Mudd's house.[6]

Within minutes of when Booth stopped, Herold galloped up. He had been five minutes behind Booth most of he way. Herold did not know where Powell was and probably told Booth that they became separated on their way out of the city. Atzerodt was on his own. Booth could not afford to delay any longer. There was no way of knowing whether a cavalry force was in their rear or not. Besides, Booth needed to have his leg looked after. The fracture of the fibula in his left leg likely prevented Booth from using the stirrup. This would have forced him to ride with his left leg dangling free while he clutched onto the horse's mane with one hand to help steady himself and keep from falling. The two men galloped off in the direction of their next stop, the Surrattsville Tavern.

The road to Surrattsville was direct and Davy Herold knew it like the back of his hand. With the moon to help them, he led the way. Herold had been along this very road dozens of times, often stopping at the tavern for friendly conversation and whiskey. It was to the Surratt tavern that Booth had sent Herold on March 17 in anticipation of Lincoln's capture. Herold had carried weapons to the tavern, and when Booth failed to show up with the captured president Herold deposited them with John Surratt, who had come down to the tavern from Washington. Surratt had shown John Lloyd, the tavern keeper, where to hide the two carbines so they would be safe. Above the attached kitchen was an unfinished loft. The joists of the second floor were exposed where the area above the kitchen joined the house. Between the exposed floor joists Lloyd shoved the two carbines as far back as he could. He also shoved a box of shells in the same space.[7] In this way the two guns were safely out of sight but ready to be pulled out at a moment's notice.

The Surratt tavern was located thirteen miles southeast of Washington at the small village crossroads known as Surrattsville. It was ideally situated along the main road that fed into southern Maryland. From Surrattsville, a traveler could chose his route depending on his destination. The tavern provided a convenient rest stop, and since 1862 it had provided a safe stop for the numerous persons moving through the region on clandestine business. It was the only safe house along the Confederate underground routes through southern Maryland that was identified by its actual name.[8] It proved of vital importance to underground activities thanks to one of the Confederacy's better agents, John Harrison Surratt Jr.

The tavern was owned by Mary Elizabeth Surratt, a forty-two year old widow whose husband, John Harrison Surratt Sr., had died in August of 1862. Mary's husband had been troubled his entire adult life by alcoholism and bad debts. Which was cause, and which was effect, wasn't clear. Still, he managed to acquire nearly four hundred acres of good land in Prince George's County, a ten-room tavern and hotel, and a ten-room, three-story brick house in Washington, D.C. In 1852 he secured a license to sell liquor at his new tavern and in 1854 was appointed postmaster. Even though he piled up substantial debts, he left the Washington townhouse unencumbered.

John and Mary, together with their three children, Isaac, born 1841, Elizabeth Susanna, born 1843, and John Jr., born 1844, lived a normal life for their time. Mary had even acquired a few slaves, not a trivial acquisition nor unusual for the times. By August of 1862 she had lost her slaves, presumably runaways, and had lost her husband. Her older son, Isaac, was serving in the Confederate army while her younger son John was away at seminary school. In 1859 John Jr. had entered St. Charles College in Howard County, Maryland.[9] Here John became a good friend of another seminary student by the name of Louis J. Wiechmann. Wiechmann would eventually wind up a boarder in Mary Surratt's Washington boardinghouse from where he would become a close observer of John and Mary's dealings with Booth.

When John's father died, John Jr. abruptly ended his seminary training and returned home to Surrattsville to help his mother weather the storm. John took over his father's role as postmaster and helped his mother run the tavern. He also attended to other business, namely Confederate espionage. John was young, bright, and energetic. He had a flair for adventure and a devotion to the Southern way of life so prevalent in the region. The Confederates needed men like John and a place to do business like the tavern. It was a perfect match. Within a short period of time John was traveling between Richmond and points north as a courier carrying documents for the cause. His activities brought him into direct contact with high-ranking members of the Confederate government.[10] The tavern was soon visited on a regular basis by all sorts of people: rogues and scoundrels, adventuresome men and women, all plying their skills on behalf of Jefferson Davis. John carried out his spy activities skillfully, for he was never arrested during the war by the Federal authorities, nor was his mother's tavern closed down.

Saddled with her husband's debts, Mary Surratt attempted to deal with them as best she could. Unfortunately, they were too large to be settled easily. After two years of keeping the tavern afloat and her finances out of bankruptcy, Mary decided to lease the tavern and move into Washington where she could at least derive a steady income by renting out her extra rooms to boarders. It would prove to be a fatal move. Within the year she would be dead.

In October of 1864 Mary began moving furniture into the H Street house. In November she moved herself and her daughter Anna and son John. In December she leased her tavern and Prince George's property for five hundred dollars a year to a man named John Lloyd who, like her husband, had a fondness for alcohol. Even so, Lloyd would pay his rent and keep the tavern in business both for innocent travelers and Confederate agents. John Surratt Jr. still maintained control over the premises as far as clandestine activities were concerned. He used the tavern regularly as a stop in his travels between Richmond and the North and made sure his compatriots found it a welcome stop also.

In November, Mary welcomed her son's schoolmate, Louis J. Wiechmann, as one of her boarders. Four weeks later, in December, another friend of John's would show up. He was John Wilkes Booth, who needed just the sort of friends that could be found at the H Street boardinghouse. Samuel Mudd first introduced Booth to John Surratt on December 23 on Seventh Street only a few blocks from the boardinghouse. Booth soon became a regular visitor of Mary and her houseguests. Included among the guests who visited the house were Booth, George Atzerodt, Lewis Powell, and Davy Herold.[11]

In preparing to capture the president following his visit to Campbell Hospital on March 17, Booth had sent Herold to the Surratt tavern with several items that would be needed in the escape. Included were two carbines, side arms, ammunition, a rope, and a monkey wrench.[12] Herold had waited at the Surratt tavern for Booth and his hostage most of the afternoon and early evening of the seventeenth. When Booth failed to show up, Herold rode south five miles to the village of T.B. where he stayed the night at Thompson's tavern.[13] The following day Herold began riding back in the direction of Surratt's tavern. On the road he met John Surratt and George Atzerodt who told him the planned abduction had failed when Lincoln did not show up at the hospital as planned.

Surratt took the weapons and other materials back to the tavern where he showed Lloyd where to hide the rifles between the joists over the kitchen. The rifles remained there until the night of April 14. The hidden weapons merely added to the evidence that would prove deadly to the widow Surratt.

On the evening of April 10, Mrs. Surratt asked Wiechmann if he would drive her in Mr. Booth's buggy down to the Surrattsville Tavern the next day. Wiechmann agreed, but when he went to Booth's hotel room the next morning to borrow the buggy, Booth told him he had sold the carriage. Booth then gave Wiechmann ten dollars and told him to rent a buggy at one of the local stables. Wiechmann secured the buggy, and sometime around noon he and Mary headed out for the tavern.

Soon after crossing over the Navy Yard Bridge Wiechmann and Mary encountered John Lloyd and his sister-in-law riding into Washington in another carriage. The carriages passed and came to a stop. Lloyd climbed down and walked back to where Wiechmann and Mary Surratt were waiting. The two began talking in hushed tones. While Wiechmann could hear that they were talking, he could not discern their words.[14] Apparently Lloyd could not understand Mary at first either. She tried to guard her words, and when Lloyd failed to understand her she became more explicit. Three months later John Lloyd would take the witness stand and claim that Mary Surratt told him to have the "shooting irons" (carbines) ready, as persons would be by to pick them up.[15] Lloyd told Mary that he didn't want the guns at the tavern, as he feared that it would be searched by the military and the guns discovered. Mary was not interested in Lloyd's misgivings. Just have the "shooting irons" ready to go. The two parted, and Wiechmann and Mary continued on to the tavern where Mary hoped to meet with a man named John Nothey who owed her money for seventy-five acres he had purchased from her husband several years earlier. After arriving at the tavern Mary sent word to Nothey to come meet with her at the tavern. Nothey came and presumably discussed his debt with Mary, but neither Nothey nor Mary later gave any indication of what they discussed or had agreed to.[16]

Three days later, on Good Friday, April 14, Mary and Louis made another trip to the tavern, a trip that would seal the widow's fate. In the morning mail Mary Surratt had received a letter from one of her husband's creditors, George Calvert, who wanted his payment for the land John Surratt had purchased in 1852 and on which he had built his tavern. Calvert noted in his letter that Nothey was willing to settle his debt with Mary. Calvert then insisted that Mary settle her debt with him.[17] Calvert pressured Mary to pay up or face legal consequences. Since Nothey owed Mary for the land he had purchased from her husband, Mary sought to collect payment to settle her debt with Calvert. Mary later told authorities that she decided to visit Nothey at Surrattsville and collect her money. Wiechmann had gone to work on the morning of April 14 only to find that Stanton had issued a directive that permitted anyone wishing to attend Good Friday services to be "relieved from duty for the day."[18] Wiechmann took advantage of Stanton's directive and attended services at St. Patrick's church, returning afterwards to the Surratt house for dinner.

Mary again asked Wiechmann if he would hire a buggy and take her to Surrattsville. Wiechmann said he would and left to make arrangements. On his way out he bumped into Booth, who was coming up the front steps to the house. The two men greeted one another and went about their respective business. When Wiechmann returned with the buggy he found Booth and

Mrs. Surratt still talking in the front parlor. Booth soon left and Mary came out to join Wiechmann. As she was about to enter the carriage she remembered the package Booth had asked her to carry to the tavern. Returning to the house she picked up the package. According to Wiechmann, Mary said the package contained "glass."[19] Wiechmann assumed the package contained dishes wrapped in paper.[20] In fact, the package contained Booth's field glass that he would pick up later that night on his flight from Ford's Theatre.

It was around 4:30 in the afternoon when Wiechmann and Mary arrived at the Surrattsville tavern. John Nothey was nowhere in sight. Mary had failed to make arrangements to meet him there, further weakening her argument for the trip on Friday afternoon.[21] Lloyd was also absent when Mary arrived. He had gone to Upper Marlboro to attend the trial of a man who had attacked him at the tavern some time earlier. Mary took Booth's package and went into the tavern to wait for Lloyd to return. The trial in Upper Marlboro had been postponed, but the gregarious Lloyd decided to hang around town for a while playing cards and drinking.[22] Mary decided to wait for Lloyd.

It was a little after five o'clock when Lloyd arrived back at the tavern. He pulled around to the rear of the kitchen and began to unload the wagon. Mary came out to where he was parked. "Speak of the devil and his little imps appear," she said derisively.[23] Lloyd was unamused. It was at this point that Mary told Lloyd about the guns. Lloyd quoted her exact words during his testimony on the witness stand, "Mr. Lloyd, I want you to have those shooting-irons ready: there will be parties here to-night who will call for them."[24] Lloyd was pressed for details. His testimony suggested that a precise message was passed along—nothing casual or suggestive. Whiskey and guns. He said she had actually said more, "give them a couple bottles of whiskey."[25] The prosecution then asked about the monkey wrench and rope. Lloyd restated his testimony: "No: the rope and monkey wrench were not what I was told to give him. I gave him such things as I was told to give by Mrs. Surratt." The prosecutor then underscored Lloyd's damaging testimony: "She told you to give him the carbines and whiskey and field-glass?" Lloyd answered: "Yes, Sir."[26] Unknown to the prosecutors at the time but subsequently revealed was a statement by George Atzerodt confirming Lloyd's testimony. On May 1 following his arrest, Atzerodt told Maryland provost marshal James McPhail, "Booth told me that Mrs. Surratt went to Surrattsville to get out the guns which had been taken to that place [Surratt's tavern] by Herold. This was Friday."[27]

The field glass became an important item. It was the tangible piece of evidence that tied Mary directly to Booth and supported the prosecution claim that Mary had gone to Surrattsville on Friday at Booth's behest. Lloyd was recalled to the witness stand later in the trial and questioned further about the package Mary had handed him. Lloyd repeated his earlier statement that it was a field glass. He said he had handed it to Herold the night of the assassination when the two men arrived at the tavern.[28] Two years later, at the trial of John Surratt, Lloyd went into detail about the field glass: "It was a double glass [binocular]." The glasses were unusual in that they had a special mechanism to change the ocular lenses by rotating a small, knurled knob located near the viewing end. Lloyd was directed by the prosecutor to "turn that little screw there and tell us what you see then." Lloyd replied, "Marine, Theatre, Field," and "Marine" again.[29] A Paris optical maker named Chevalier in 1860 had patented the unusual mechanism, and it was found only in his field glasses.[30]

Although Mary had claimed that her visit to Surrattsville was an effort to see John Nothey, she made no effort to see him. If her trip had been to recover money owed her, it was soon forgotten. Having finished her task, Mary and Wiechmann were ready to return to Washington. Just one small detail needs to be mentioned. The wagon they had traveled in was damaged. A spring coil had come loose from its attachment. Mary asked Lloyd if he could fix it so that they could return to the city. Lloyd said he would try. He took a rope and securely fastened the broken coil to the wagon, temporarily making the wagon serviceable. While Lloyd may have been drinking that afternoon, he was not too drunk to repair the broken wagon, and he accomplished it effectively and with little trouble. When Mary left the tavern on the evening of April 14, Lloyd was primed and ready for a visitor later that night.

Normally it took a little over two hours to make the trip to Surrattsville from Washington on horseback. Riding hard, however, that time could be cut in half. It was a few minutes past midnight when Booth and Herold reached the crossroads near the tavern. They turned into the dirt lane leading up to the tavern door located on the side of the frame house. Booth sat slumped in his saddle grimacing with pain. The pain in his leg radiated into his lower back. Riding had become increasingly difficult. The adrenaline rush that had carried him across the stage and over the Navy Yard Bridge had long ago worn off.

Herold slid off of his horse and, climbing the porch steps, began pounding hard on the wooden door. Once, twice, three times. Inside the tavern an inebriated Lloyd had fallen asleep. Herold's pounding soon aroused him. Opening the door he peered into the surrounding darkness. At the end of the porch he could make out a man sitting astride a horse. Standing in the doorway was a second man. This second man pushed his way past Lloyd and reached for a bottle of whiskey still sitting on the bar where Lloyd had left it earlier. Grabbing a glass, he poured himself a drink and then carried the bottle out to the mounted rider. Passing Lloyd he said in a hurried voice, "Lloyd, for God's sake, make haste and get those things."[31] Lloyd turned and made his way through the hall and up the stairs to the loft over the rear storeroom. He knew immediately what "those things" were. Later, during his interrogation by detectives, he would be asked a critical question: "He had not before that said to you what 'those things' were?'" Lloyd was clear in his answer, "He had not." Lloyd continued his answer with a telling statement, "From the way he spoke, he must have been apprised that I already knew what I was to give him."[32] Here is a crucial clue often overlooked in the standard histories. Not only did Lloyd understand what Herold meant by "those things," but also Herold knew that Lloyd would understand.[33] How did Herold know that Lloyd would understand his order? Only if he had been told beforehand that Lloyd had been informed about the guns and persons needing them later that night. This could only have come from someone who knew that Lloyd had been "apprised" earlier in the day.[34] That someone could only have been Mary Surratt. The noose tightened a little more.

Lloyd returned with the two carbines and a field glass. Herold took one of the guns. Booth was offered the other. He refused it. His leg was broken and he couldn't place his foot in the stirrup. He needed both hands to hold onto his horse. He slung the strap of the field glasses over his shoulder and took a heavy swig from the bottle Herold had passed up to him.[35] Finishing his drink, Booth handed the bottle back to Herold, who returned it to Lloyd. Carbine in hand, Herold swung himself back into his saddle and began to wheel his horse around in the direction of the road. Booth edged his horse forward slightly and, looking down at Lloyd, said, "I will tell you some news if you want to hear it. . . . I am pretty certain that we have assassinated the President and Secretary Seward."[36] The two men then galloped off in the direction of the small community known locally as Beantown.

CHAPTER THIRTEEN

Dr. Mudd

> About 4 o'clock on Saturday morning, the 15th, two persons came to my house. . . . I never saw either of the parties before, nor can I conceive who sent them to my house.
>
> *Dr. Samuel A. Mudd*

By the time Booth and Herold left the Surratt tavern the moon was approaching its zenith, bathing the countryside in light. Heading south, the two men soon came to the village of T.B., where the road divides, one fork heading east to Horsehead, the other continuing south to Beantown. Either road would take them to their next destination, the home of Dr. Samuel Mudd. There they would find safety and succor and Booth could have his painful leg cared for. Spurring their horses the two men continued on the road toward Beantown. Once at Beantown the road turned east, passing St. Peter's Catholic Church where the Mudd family regularly worshiped. Two miles beyond was the farm of Samuel Mudd.

It was four o'clock when Booth and Herold rode up the dirt lane leading to the home of Dr. Mudd. Twilight was still an hour away. Herold dismounted and walked up to the door. Knocking loudly, he listened for some sound of movement. Within a few moments the door opened. Peering through the opening was a man in a long, white nightshirt holding a candle. The man standing outside spoke first. His companion had injured his leg and needed medical attention. Seated on a horse a few feet away sat a bearded man, a large shawl wrapped around his shoulders resting high on his neck. The door swung open and the two men were invited inside.

Mudd examined the injured man's leg, determined it to be broken, and told the patient's companion to help him up the stairs to one of the bedrooms. Here the doctor made an incision in the boot, carefully removed it from the tender leg, and set the broken bone, splinting it with pieces fashioned from a hatbox. The injured man was put to bed and the doctor went about his business, later riding into the village of Bryantown to purchase a few sundries. While in town he learned about the assassination. On returning home at five o'clock he saw the two men about to leave. The companion asked for directions that would take them west to the parsonage of a local minister. Pointing the two men in the right direction, Mudd went into his house, where his wife told him some disturbing news. She noticed that the injured man was wearing a false beard. She had seen it come loose as the man struggled down the stairs as he was preparing to leave. Earlier in the day the man had asked for a razor and shaved off his handlebar moustache.

Mudd's suspicions were aroused. He and his wife discussed whether he should return to town and notify the soldiers stationed there about the suspicious nature of the two visitors. Mrs. Mudd, fearful for her safety and that of her children, asked her husband not to leave them alone. Mudd decided not to go into town but to stay with his wife and children. He would notify the soldiers later, telling them everything he knew about the visit of the two strangers. They had been at his house no more than twelve hours.

This is the story Dr. Mudd told. This is the story he would have the world believe: an unsuspecting doctor who innocently provided medical care to an injured stranger in need of help. But there are too many fingers pointing in the direction of Mudd's guilt. When John Wilkes Booth arrived at the home of Samuel Mudd in the early morning hours of April 15, it was the fourth time these two men had met. The meetings were neither accidental nor innocent. They were part of a conspiracy to remove Abraham Lincoln as president of the United States and commander in chief of the Union army. Mudd's decision not to notify the soldiers on Saturday was based more on self-preservation than fear of his two guests.

Easter Sunday saw a welcome change in the weather. The intermittent rain that had fallen for the past two days gave way to clearing skies. George Mudd had decided to attend Easter services at St. Peter's Catholic Church instead of St. Mary's where he was a member. St. Peter's was located less than two miles from Samuel Mudd's home in Beantown. George had accepted an invitation to have dinner at the home of his cousin, Henry Lowe Mudd, Sam's father, and St. Peter's was only a few miles from Henry's plantation.

Sam and George were second cousins sharing the same great-grandfather.[1] They also shared a common profession in medicine. George, seven years Sam's senior, had graduated from the University of Maryland Medical School in Baltimore in 1848. A few years later he sponsored Sam as a candidate at the same school. Sam graduated with his medical degree in March 1856.[2] Both men had established their medical practice in the community surrounding Bryantown. Medicine was one of the few things the two men agreed on. Sam was a strong Confederate sympathizer and member of the Confederate underground that operated in Charles County. He harbored an intense dislike for Lincoln and an even stronger dislike for his antislavery views. George Mudd, on the other hand, was a strong Unionist and supporter of the Federal government. The two families learned to tolerate each other's views and got along reasonably well. Aside from his Union sympathies, George Mudd was a respected member of the Charles County community.

Following Easter services on April 16, George started out for Henry Mudd's house. Riding along the dusty road, he was soon joined by his cousin. The two men talked as they rode. News of the assassination seemed to be on everybody's lips that morning. Sam had heard about it in Bryantown on Saturday afternoon, and passed it along to his neighbors John Hardy and Francis Farrell on his way home.[3]

As the two men rode along the road, Sam told George about the two men who visited his home the day before. He told his cousin that he was suspicious of their behavior, especially the injured man. He became worried that the two men might have something to do with the events in Washington. Sam asked George if he would go into Bryantown and tell the military about the two strangers.[4] Sam's anti-Lincoln views and his work for the Confederate underground suggested he knew much more than he was telling. By asking George to inform the soldiers, Sam probably hoped to downplay the importance of the two men's visit. Sam was in trouble, and George must have suspected as much. Because of his reputation as a Unionist in this heavily Confederate community, George was above suspicion with the Federals, and Sam probably thought if George were to tell the soldiers it would go better. As the two men approached the lane leading up to Sam's house, George told his cousin he would mention the matter to the authorities who had set up their headquarters in Bryantown. The two men parted, and Sam returned home while George continued on to Henry Mudd's house a half mile away.

Monday morning George rode into Bryantown where he talked with the officer in charge, Lieutenant David D. Dana of the Thirteenth New York Cavalry.[5] George told Dana what his cousin had told him about the two suspicious strangers who had come to his house. Dana did not act immediately on the information but waited until Tuesday morning to tell the newly arrived Lieutenant Alexander Lovett about the two men who had been at Samuel Mudd's house. Lovett had been ordered by Major James O'Beirne, a District of Columbia provost marshal, to pick nine troopers and two of O'Beirne's detectives, William Williams and Simon Gavacan, and go to southern Maryland and look for Booth.[6] O'Beirne was responding to a request from one of his men whom he had earlier sent to Surrattsville. On Sunday, April 16, O'Beirne dispatched Captain George Cottingham along with detective Joshua Lloyd[7] to Surrattsville after Cottingham had told O'Beirne that he had heard that Surratt and Herold frequented the area around the Surratt tavern.[8] O'Beirne told Cottingham and Lloyd to head for Surrattsville and search the area. After tracking down John Lloyd and arresting him, Cottingham sent word back to O'Beirne that he needed help to continue his search.[9] O'Beirne responded by sending Lovett, the two detectives, and the nine troopers from the Provisional Cavalry stationed in the District of Columbia. The contingent set out Monday evening and arrived at Surrattsville by way of Piscataway that same night. Tuesday morning, April 18, Lovett, along with Williams and Gavacan, arrived in Bryantown where they checked in with Dana.[10]

Dana filled Lovett in about his conversation with George Mudd. When Lovett found out that Dana had not followed up with Samuel Mudd he sent for George Mudd, and with the three detectives—Williams, Gavacan, and Lloyd—set out for Mudd's house. It was near noon when Lovett and the three detectives, along with George Mudd, arrived at the Mudd home. Mudd was away from the house working in his fields. Lovett and the other men went inside and talked to Mrs. Mudd while her husband was sent for. George Mudd waited outside by the front door for Sam to return.[11]

Mrs. Mudd told much the same story that George Mudd had told Lovett on Monday morning in Bryantown. She told Lovett that the two men stayed most of the day, leaving about five o'clock on Saturday afternoon. Her story added little to what George had reported—with one rather surprising revelation. Mrs. Mudd told Lovett about a strange incident that occurred just before the injured man left the house Saturday evening: "I heard them moving around the room and in a short time they came down. . . . When they came down I was standing in the hall at the foot of the stairs. Tyler [Booth] wore heavy whiskers; these proved to be false, and became partly detached as he came down the stairs."[12]

Listening to Mrs. Mudd's strange tale, Lovett asked nothing more about the "detached" whiskers. At this point Mudd arrived and joined his wife in the front room. Lovett asked Mudd to tell him about the two strangers who had visited on Saturday. Mudd later wrote out his account of what happened: "About 4 o'clock on Saturday morning, the 15th, two persons came to my house and commenced rapping very loudly at the door. After they had knocked twice more, I opened the door, . . . they told me they were two strangers on their way to Washington, that one of their horses had fallen by which one of the men had broken his leg. I examined the injured leg, . . . there was one bone broken about two inches above the ankle joint. He wanted me to fix it up any way, as he said he wanted to get back, or get home and have it done by a regular physician. I took a piece of the bandbox and split it in half, . . . and took some paste and pasted it into a splint."[13]

Mudd described the injured man for the detectives: "I suppose he would weigh 150 or 160 pounds. His hair was black and seemed somewhat inclined to curl; it was worn long. He had a pretty full forehead and his skin was fair. He was very pale when I saw him, and appeared accustomed to in-door rather than out-door life. He had whiskers, and also a moustache."[14] It was a remarkably accurate description.

Mudd described the injured man as having whiskers but made no mention that his wife had told him that the whiskers were false. This was curious since Mudd had no way of knowing that his wife had told Lovett about her suspicions. Surely such information would prove vital to the military authorities searching for Booth. Mudd went on with his story: "After breakfast the older one [Booth] asked for a razor and some soap; which he got; and on my giving him the articles which I had prepared, a short time afterward, I noticed that his moustache had disappeared."[15]

While Mudd told Lovett about Booth's shaving off his moustache he still did not mention that his wife had noticed that Booth's whiskers were false. Lovett would later testify at Mudd's trial that Mudd was evasive in his answers.[16] Lovett claimed that Mudd seemed reluctant to volunteer any information except in response to specific questions. He felt as if he were pulling teeth to get information from Mudd. It wasn't until Lovett returned to the Mudd house on Friday, April 21, that Lovett finally asked Mudd if he had noticed whether or not the whiskers were false.[17] Even then, Mudd failed to tell Lovett that Mrs. Mudd had seen the whiskers come loose from Booth's face. He simply told Lovett he could not tell if the whiskers were natural or false.

Mudd once again described for Lovett the events of Saturday, telling that his patient wanted to hire a carriage or buggy to continue his journey. Mudd and Herold rode over to Oak Hill where Mudd's father lived and asked Mudd's younger brother if there was a carriage available. His brother told him there were no suitable carriages available. Unable to secure a conveyance at Oak Hill, the two men then rode on toward the village of Bryantown four miles to the south.[18]

As they approached Bryantown, Herold suddenly turned his horse around and told Mudd that he was going back to the house to get his friend. Mudd continued into Bryantown where he said he purchased several items. It was while in Bryantown that Mudd heard news of the assassination: "I first heard of the assassination of President Lincoln at Bryantown. My object in going there was to purchase some articles that were needed by the family; and I thought I would at the same time see about some nails that were intended for immediate use. I purchased at Mr. Beans some calico & some pepper, for which I paid him. I got back to my house between 4 & 5 o'clock."[19]

Finishing his business in Bryantown, Mudd started back home. On the way back he stopped by the house of one his neighbors, Francis R. Farrell. Visiting Farrell was a man named John F. Hardy, another of Mudd's neighbors. Hardy later testified during the trial that Mudd told him and Farrell that Lincoln had been assassinated and that the assassin's name was Booth.[20] Mudd then continued home.[21] When he arrived he found his two guests in the process of leaving. Mudd later claimed he spoke briefly with the two men, giving them directions to the home of Reverend Lemuel Wilmer before returning to the house.

There is something not quite right about the time frame of Mudd's trip into Bryantown. Mudd's statement that he returned home between 4 and 5 P.M. is contradicted by the testimony of his neighbor, John Hardy. Mudd and

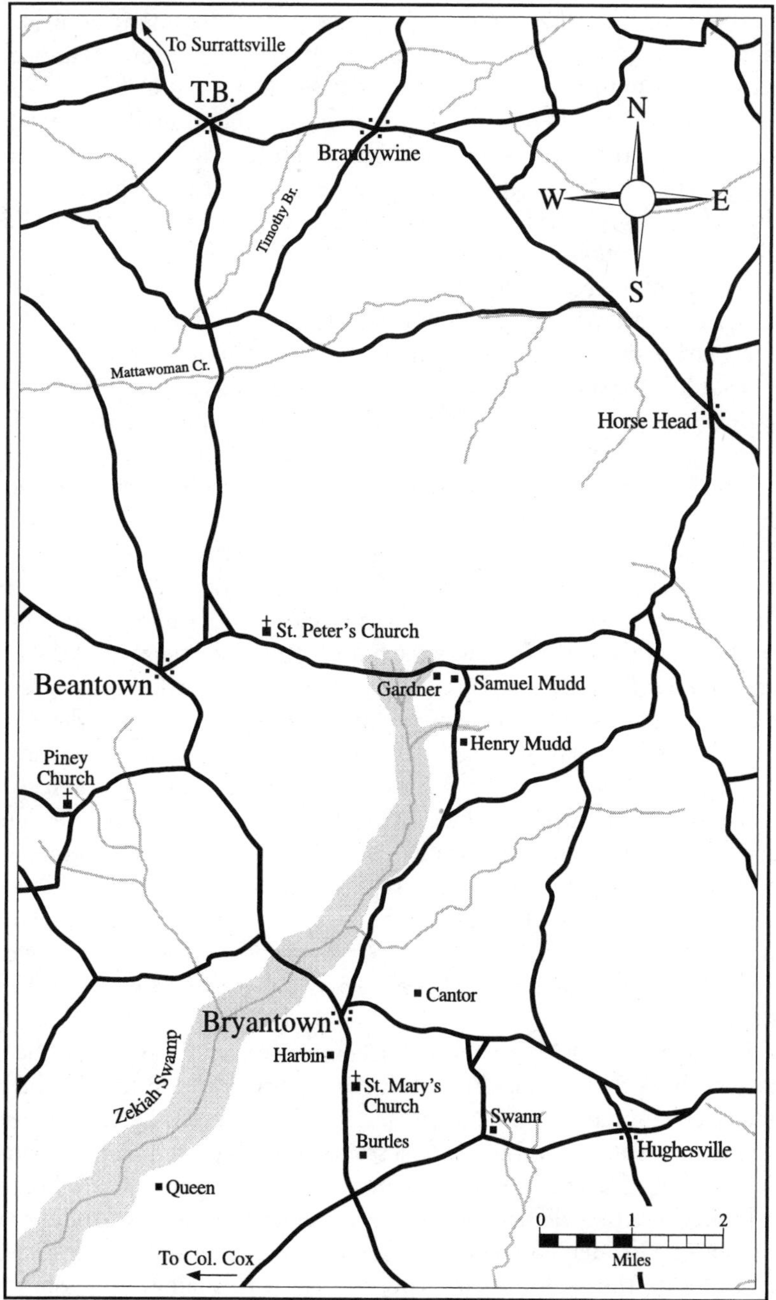

Bryantown area (neighborhood of Samuel A. Mudd).

Herold left for his father's house immediately after the noonday meal. According to Hardy's testimony, Mudd didn't return from Bryantown until close to sunset. Hardy told the prosecution that Mudd arrived at Farrell's house "very near sundown." When asked to be more specific about the time, Hardy said, "I do not think the sun was fifteen minutes high on that Saturday evening."[22] Hardy's statement helps to fix the time with some precision. Sunset for Saturday, April 15, 1865, occurred at 6:44 P.M.[23] This would place Mudd at Farrell's house around 6:30 P.M. When Hardy was asked how long Mudd was at his place Hardy replied, "I do not think he staid ten minutes."[24] If Hardy is correct, Mudd could not have returned home until after 7 P.M., not between 4 and 5 P.M. as he claimed. This presents a substantial discrepancy from Mudd's statement. Mudd was probably in Bryantown for no more than thirty minutes. If we allow two and a half hours for the round trip to Bryantown, there are as many as three hours unaccounted for.

The answer to Mudd's unexplained absence may lie a few miles south of Bryantown. Booth and Herold posed a serious problem for Mudd. He had to find a way to get them out of his house and safely through the county and over the Potomac River into Virginia. With soldiers now searching the area, the only safe time to travel was at night. The closest place after Mudd's house where Booth could find safety was the home of another member of the Confederate underground, a man by the name of William Burtles. Burtles lived a mile and a half due south of Bryantown in a remote hollow east of the Zekiah Swamp. He called his place Hagan's Folly.[25] Burtles was thoroughly familiar with the swamp and would have no trouble directing the two men to the home of another agent, Samuel Cox. Cox was one of the respected leaders of Charles County society. A major owner of land and slaves,[26] he commanded respect from nearly everyone in the region, and most important, he was an ardent Confederate. At the start of the war he commanded a company of local volunteers organized to defend Maryland should she decide to secede along with her sister states. It was this activity that earned Cox the title of "Captain."[27]

By the spring of 1865 Cox had become a seasoned veteran of the underground wars that rumbled through the county. Early in the war he had been suspected of aiding the enemy and had been visited by Union troops searching for weapons. In June 1861 a troop of one hundred Federal soldiers landed at Chapel Point in Charles County and marched to Cox's home at Rich Hill, where they demanded the surrender of arms believed to be stored in the house. Cox denied having any such store of arms, and after a search failed to locate the weapons the troop returned to their waiting ship and sailed back up the Potomac to Washington while Cox checked the marsh near his house to make sure the weapons were still safe.[28] Seven months later, in January 1862, Cox was visited again, this time by members of the Excelsior Brigade's 70th New York Infantry under the command of Colonel William Dwight. Dwight had been tipped off by one of Cox's slaves, a man named Jack Scroggins, that Cox had "secreted a large amount of ammunition and arms" at his house and in an adjoining marsh.[29] After fingering his master, Scroggins sought refuge in the camp of the 70th New York at Hill Top, a small village located ten miles northwest of Cox's home. Scroggins believed his act of patriotism earned him a safe haven among Lincoln's soldiers.

Cox went to the camp and demanded the return of his slave. Denied at first by members of the regiment who sought to protect Scroggins, the men were ordered by one of their officers to turn him over after Cox promised not to harm Scroggins. The Union army was a year away from fighting a war to emancipate slaves and the Fugitive Slave Law remained in force. Many soldiers stationed in Charles County had little sympathy with slave owners but were often compelled by their officers to turn over fugitive slaves. Such was Scroggins fate. As repugnant as it was to most Union soldiers, enforcing the law was still the official policy of the Lincoln administration. It remained the policy in an effort to keep the Border States loyal, and Maryland was an important case in point. Lincoln deemed it essential that Maryland, along with Kentucky and Missouri, remain in the Union.

Having secured Scroggins from his protectors, Cox tied him behind his horse with a rope and began the ten-mile trip home. At some point he sped up, forcing Scroggins to run behind the horse until he literally ran out of his shoes. Arriving back at Rich Hill around 11 P.M., Cox tied the exhausted and bleeding Scroggins to a tree outside his house. For three hours Cox alternated with his overseer, Franklin Roby, and neighbor John Robertson whipping Scroggins to a point where only the "collar-band and wristbands" of his "new cotton shirt" were left. Sometime around 3:00 A.M. the badly beaten Scroggins was cut loose from the tree and left on the ground to die. Scroggins lived for another fifteen hours before succumbing to his brutal beating.[30]

If Booth were to get over the river safely, Cox would be the person to arrange it. But Booth had to get to Cox's place first, and that would require negotiating the dangerous Zekiah Swamp. Here is where Burtles could play a major role.[31] Mudd could easily have made the trip between Bryantown and Burtles and still have ample time to counsel with Burtles about how to handle Booth before returning home near sundown. After first conferring with his brother, Mudd went into Bryantown to reconnoiter the situation. When Mudd arrived in Bryantown and found it crawling with troopers, it short-circuited his plan to send the two fugitives off in an orderly fashion. Now he must get them off his place and fast. Burtles was the likely answer to Mudd's problem.

When Mudd returned home at sundown he had been absent for over six hours. He more than likely filled Booth in on the situation, telling him about the soldiers in Bryantown. They would have to leave immediately and make their way to Burtles's place on their own. The darkness would be both a blessing and a problem. Moving south in the dark would be a hindrance, but the cover of darkness would help shield the pair from Union soldiers who might be roaming the area. Mudd gave careful directions, making sure that Booth and Herold circled east around Bryantown in a wide arc, avoiding the troops stationed there. He would later concoct a story about finding his two guests in the processing of riding west in the opposite direction toward Parson Wilmer's place.[32] This was compatible with his story that the pair had stopped by his house on their way to Washington. If successful, it would throw the soldiers off of Booth's track long enough for Cox to put the pair across the river. Once across, Mudd's problems would be behind him.

Forty years later Nettie Mudd wrote about that fateful night and her father's plight. In her book, Nettie claimed her father had wanted to go back into Bryantown after Booth left and tell the military authorities about the two "strangers" and the suspicions they aroused. But Mrs. Mudd pleaded with her husband not to leave her alone as she feared the men might return and do her and the children harm. According to Nettie Mudd's account, the doctor decided to stay with his wife and leave the telling to a later time.[33] Nettie's story is inconsistent with the facts. Mudd had already left his wife and children in Booth's care for over six hours without apparent apprehension. Having learned in Bryantown about the president's murder, he felt no apprehension about the two men left alone with his wife. He made no attempt to hurry back to his house, stopping at Francis Farrell's place instead for what appears to be idle talk. The following morning he rode to church services at St. Peter's, leaving his wife and children alone once again. If Mudd did fear for his wife and children's safety as he claimed, he could have taken them along with him or left them at his father's house, which he would pass on his way into town. Certainly they would be safe there and Mudd could pass his vital information on to the soldiers in a timely way. Mudd had to know this information was critical since Booth and Herold had left his house within the hour and would be only a short distance away. By waiting until Sunday before passing the information along to his cousin, Mudd allowed Booth to gain a full day over pursuing troops. As it turned out, Mudd's information wasn't passed on to the soldiers in Bryantown until Monday, giving Booth almost two full day's head start on the military stationed there.

On learning that Booth had a broken leg, Lovett returned to General Augur's headquarters on Thursday, April 20, and informed Colonel Henry H. Wells, provost marshal for the defenses south of the Potomac, of the important information. Wells immediately went to Stanton, informing him that Booth's leg was broken and that he was last seen in the Bryantown area. Stanton ordered Wells to go to Bryantown and follow up on the information that he had received from Lovett.[34] Wells boarded a steamer and headed for Chapel Point, where he secured a horse and set out for Bryantown. In the meantime, Lovett was ordered to return to Bryantown to take up the hunt. On Friday morning he set out for Bryantown. Feeling something wasn't quite right about the doctor's answers, the lieutenant stopped by Mudd's house a second time.

Mudd repeated much of the same information that he had given Lovett during their first meeting. Lovett noticed that Mudd seemed nervous and flushed as if suffering under some apprehension. Lovett's suspicions were again aroused. He had seen enough. Lovett told Mrs. Mudd that his men would have to search the house. At this moment, Mudd recalled an important piece of evidence. He remembered the boot that he had removed from the injured man's leg. Mudd told his wife to go upstairs and bring down the boot.[35] Mudd explained that it had been accidentally shoved under the bed and was only later discovered while cleaning the room. After the Tuesday conversation with Lovett, Mudd must have known that the boot was a vital piece of evidence. Assuming Mudd was telling the truth when he said he had forgotten about it, why hadn't he taken it immediately to Lovett when he did find it "under the bed"? When Lovett took the boot from Mrs. Mudd and examined it, he noticed an inscription on the inside of the upper margin of the boot. The inscription read, "J. Wilkes."[36] Lovett showed Mudd the inscription and asked him if he had not noticed it when he cut it from the man's leg. Mudd said he had been unaware of the writing. There was more. Now believing that the injured man was John Wilkes Booth, Mudd still had not mentioned that his wife had told him that Booth was wearing false whiskers. Lovett finally popped the question to Mudd, asking him if the injured man might have been wearing false whiskers. To Lovett's surprise Mudd replied, "I did not pay sufficient attention to his beard to determine whether it was false or natural."[37]

Lovett must have found it hard to believe that Mudd would have forgotten so important a piece of information. He was sufficiently cynical of Mudd's response that he decided to take him into Bryantown for further questioning by Colonel Henry H. Wells, his superior, who had just arrived from Washington. Noticing that Mrs. Mudd was upset that her husband was being taken into custody, Lovett assured her that her husband would return as soon as they had finished questioning him.

Mudd, Lovett, and the three detectives mounted their horses and headed along the road to Bryantown. The group had not gone very far when Lovett asked one of the detectives to show Mudd a photograph of Booth. Mudd examined the picture and said that he did not recognize the man in the photograph. Perhaps there was a slight resemblance around the eyes, but nothing more.[38] Seventy-two years later, historian Otto Eisenschiml would claim the photograph was not of John Wilkes Booth, but his brother Edwin.[39] Eisenschiml had found the photograph of Edwin among the trial exhibits in the War Department files. It was labeled "Exhibit No. 1, John Wilkes Booth."

Eisenschiml claimed that the government deliberately switched photographs of the two brothers to entrap certain individuals in their web of conspiracy, the principal one being Samuel Mudd.[40] Eisenschiml's claim became a part of the conspiratorial mythology concerning Dr. Mudd's alleged innocence.

While the two Booth brothers bore a strong resemblance, Edwin was clean shaven—while Wilkes wore a prominent moustache. Why Eisenschiml assumed that the photograph in exhibit 1 was the same photograph shown to Mudd on the way to Bryantown is unexplained other than by inference that if the government would stoop to such tricks during the trial, they would surely stoop to such subterfuge in rounding up "innocent" victims of a government conspiracy. Eisenschiml's argument has been picked up by nearly every author since and repeated as additional evidence that Mudd was innocent of any culpability with Booth. Eisenschiml's theory fails, however, because subsequent research into the photograph labeled exhibit number 1 and the photograph shown to Mudd while en route to Bryantown were photographs of John Wilkes Booth and not his brother Edwin (see chapter 19 for a full discussion of this evidence).[41]

After arriving in Bryantown, Mudd wrote out a statement in which he finally acknowledged knowing Booth: "I have seen J. Wilkes Booth. I was introduced to him by Mr. J.C. Thompson, a son-in-law of Dr. William Queen, in November or December last. . . . Booth inquired if I knew any parties in this neighborhood who had some very fine horses for sale. I told him there was a neighbor of mine who had some very fine traveling horses, and he said he thought if he could purchase one reasonable he would do so. . . . The next evening he rode to my house and staid [*sic*] with me that night, and the next morning he purchased a rather old horse, but a very fine mover of Mr. George Gardiner, Sr., who resides but a short distance from my house."[42]

Mudd then wrote: "I have never seen Booth since that time to my knowledge until last Saturday night."[43] With this statement Mudd made the most serious lie of all those he had told to the military detectives interrogating him. He now found himself in the most dangerous situation of his life.

CHAPTER FOURTEEN

Here in Despair

With every man's hand against me, I am here in despair.

John Wilkes Booth

Samuel Mudd stood beside the stable located in the rear of his house. The sun had finally set, covering the area in darkness. It was time for the two men to move on. Mounting their horses, Booth thanked Mudd for all his help. The two men wheeled their mounts and rode off to the southeast following a small farm road that led through the tobacco fields and ran near the edge of the Zekiah Swamp. Herold would lead the way. He knew the countryside much better than Booth, or so he told him. Mudd stood watching as the two riders disappeared into the darkness of the night. An hour later they were seen at Oak Hill, the plantation of Mudd's father. Henry Mudd lived only a half mile to the southeast of his son's home. Herold may have become lost momentarily after leaving Mudd's house. One of the elder Mudd's former slaves, a man named Electus Thomas, met Herold in the road leading up to the house. Herold appeared to be confused. He asked the old man which direction the sun rose and which direction it set. Electus "told him as near as he could get at it."[1] Herold gathered himself up and rode back to where Booth was waiting. Having oriented themselves east from west, the two men made their way to the east around Bryantown, making sure to keep a safe distance between themselves and the military.

Now in total darkness, the two men had trouble navigating and found themselves lost a second time. They eventually came to the house of a man named Joseph Cantor.[2] They were still to the east of Bryantown. Cantor too could be trusted. Like his neighbors, he had no use for Yankees. Cantor pointed the pair down the Cracklingtown Road to where it intersected with the road leading from the small village of Hughsville. Burtles's place was just a short journey to the west of the intersection. By traveling this way the pair would remain well east of Bryantown and swing south of the village. So far everything was going well despite their temporarily getting lost. They had been now riding for close to two hours.

As Booth and Herold approached the juncture of the two roads they saw the light from a cabin. It was the home of a free Black by the name of

Oswell Swann. Swann was one of the few free Blacks who lived in the area. He had managed to purchase a small farm situated along the Cracklingtown Road just west of the village of Hughsville. Swann was a savvy man. As a free Black living in a pro-Confederate region, he had to be. He knew all of the principal players in Charles County and also knew how to avoid trouble. His friendship with George Mudd probably served him well on more than one occasion. George Mudd held the mortgage that allowed Swann to buy his own farm. It was around nine o'clock when Booth and Herold came across Swann standing outside his cabin.

By now, Booth and Herold were not sure of where they were or the direction to Burtles's house. Booth's leg was causing him considerable pain. He asked Swann if he had anything to drink. Swann brought the pair food and some whiskey. Booth then asked Swann the way to William Burtles's house, telling him he would pay him two dollars if he would lead them there.[3] It was an easy two dollars. Burtles lived less than two miles from Swann's cabin. The three men started out for Burtles's house but after a short distance Booth asked Swann if he knew the way to Cox's house. Booth offered Swann another five dollars if he would lead them directly to Cox's.[4] Did Swann know the way? He did, but it would mean the three men would have to cross the Zekiah Swamp. Cox's home, known as Rich Hill, was on the western side of the great swamp. Getting across it required an expert guide, especially at night. Booth upped the fee, offering Swann another five dollars for his help. Swann agreed. He would guide them to Cox's plantation for twelve dollars.[5] He had little choice. If he had refused they would have used his services anyway at the end of a gun. At least this way he would make twelve dollars. The authorities would not hold him culpable for following a White man's order (there were still a few advantages to being Black). The three men headed south. Bryantown, now cloaked in darkness, lay a few miles to the north.

With Swann as their guide, the two men arrived at the home of Samuel Cox shortly after twelve o'clock on Sunday morning. They had been traveling for over six hours. Booth sat astride his horse as Herold dismounted and went up to the front door. Realizing that everyone was probably sound asleep; he knocked loudly against the wooden door. Within a minute or two he could hear movement. On the second floor directly above the door was a large window. In the pale cast of the moonlight Herold could just make out a face peering through the imperfect glass. It was the young adopted son of Captain Cox, Samuel Cox Jr. Herold could hear footsteps on the staircase coming toward the door. Booth sat astride his horse beneath the bows of a large Ailanthus tree, his inflamed leg dangling free of the stirrup.

The door opened slowly as a dim candle flickered its feeble light through the narrow opening. Herold spoke first. He and his friend needed shelter and something to eat. The man leaned forward, extending his candle toward the horse and rider sitting under the Ailanthus tree. To his right a Black man stood nearly invisible in the darkness. The occupant nodded his head. Herold turned back to help this companion slide down from his horse. Placing his arm around Herold's shoulder, the two men entered the house, leaving the Black man squatting in the thick grass beneath the tree. He was not welcome inside.

It was a few minutes past midnight when Booth and Herold entered the home of Captain Samuel Cox. Cox had organized a small rifle company before the Yankees arrived and shut down the local militia. Among his "recruits" were many of the able-bodied men of Charles County. During the trial one of the witnesses made a revealing statement that Samuel Mudd had been part of Cox's local militia; "a company gotten up in Bryantown."[6] When the war broke out, the local militia stood ready to defend Maryland should the state secede. But instead of secession Maryland chose to remain in the Union. It was a choice many felt was coerced. The local militia units were disbanded, several members fleeing south to serve in Lee's army while others stayed behind to serve in the underground.[7] Cox was one of the more important ones to stay behind.[8] He was an authority figure in the area and, as such, commanded respect from all around. From most Blacks in the area he commanded fear. Jack Scroggins's fate had not gone unnoticed. Cox was squat in build and had a round, heavily muscled face. He had a full head of hair and his beard was short-cropped running from ear to ear, his upper lip clean shaven in Brethren style. He gave the appearance of a no-nonsense patrician.

Inside Cox's house the fugitives gained a much-needed respite from their difficult travel through the swamp. They had covered nearly ten miles over difficult terrain and were tired. Although Booth had rested at Mudd's house during most of the day, the constant pain in his leg and back had sapped his strength, leaving him worn and hurting. Cox gave the two men food and drink and allowed them to rest. They talked for nearly five hours before Cox told them they would have to leave. No matter, Booth wanted to get across the river and closer to safety as soon as possible. Cox would see that they were put into good hands. It was essential to get the two fugitives to a secure place before patrols started combing the area.

With the first light of dawn beginning to break, a man appeared at Cox's door. His name was Franklin Roby, Cox's overseer and farm manager. Cox told Roby to take the two men to a place where they would be safely concealed until he could send help to them. It was a small pine thicket located two miles to the southeast of his home. The thicket was located just over the boundary of Cox's property. The crafty Cox was still mindful of what would happen if the two fugitives were found on any part of his land. Cox would later be gathered up as a result of the dragnet that would sweep through the county. He would protest as usual, admitting that two strangers stopped by his house but that he refused them entry and sent them on their way. One of his former slaves, now in his employ, would swear the captain told the truth.[9] Oswell Swann would tell a different story.

Swann would later tell the soldiers that the two men had been invited inside Cox's home and stayed for four or five hours.[10] Swann was caught both ways. A free Black, he nonetheless had to live and work in the area and Cox was an important man, one whose word was seldom crossed. It would have been just as easy for Swann to agree with Cox and his lady servant. The problem was that the military had asked Swann first what happened and only later asked Cox's servant. If Swann was going to lie, he would have had to get his story straight ahead of time, and that didn't happen. There is no evidence to suggest that Swann suffered as a result of his testimony against Cox, but then there is no evidence that Cox himself ever suffered beyond a brief stay in the Old Capitol Prison as a result of Swann's revelations. Cox returned home still a force within the county.

At daybreak the party broke up. Swann received his payment and made his way through the swamp back to his cabin. Roby picked up Booth and Herold and led them to the pine thicket and told them to lie low; someone would soon come and take care of them. It was important to get them across the river as quickly as possible. But nothing could be done until nightfall. The two men remained in the thicket the entire day wondering what would happen next. They had placed their lives in Cox's hands as well as Swann's. One slip of the tongue or careless word and the area would be swarming with Yankees.

Back at Rich Hill, Cox sent word to Thomas A. Jones, his foster brother and one of the Signal Service's most trusted and effective agents. For the first two years of the war, Jones had lived in a house located on a high bluff overlooking the Potomac River.[11] Years later he described the scene: "My small one-story house was built upon a bluff about eighty feet high. I could stand in my back yard and look up the river until my view was cut off by Maryland Point, seven or eight miles distant; while down the river I could see the water almost as far as the eye could reach."[12] It was the ideal location for a signal station, a fact not overlooked by the Confederacy. Jones was enlisted into the Confederate Signal Service (secret service) and placed in charge of the courier agents that trafficked contraband mail through Charles County. "I entered with zeal into the Confederate cause," Jones wrote in his memoir. For four years he oversaw the flow of Confederate mail through Charles County and personally arranged for ferrying a continuous stream of agents and enterprising men and women across the river. Throughout this time he was arrested only once, in 1861, and after several months in the Old Capitol Prison he was released after swearing an oath to uphold the Constitution of the United States. Such oaths meant nothing to Jones or his friends, and he immediately returned to his clandestine work. In 1863 Jones moved into a small cottage that he called "Huckleberry," not far from his old home overlooking the Potomac. He continued his work ferrying men and materiel over the river.

In December of 1864 Jones became aware of a plan to capture the president. The plan involved the famous actor John Wilkes Booth and one of the Confederacy's better agents, John H. Surratt Jr. Jones understood that the captured president was to be carried from Washington over the Navy Yard Bridge into southern Maryland and then through Prince George's and Charles Counties until the Potomac was reached. From here the captors and their prize hostage would cross the river into Virginia and head for Richmond, where the president would become the guest of Jefferson Davis and his cabinet. The plan to capture Lincoln never took place, and Jones concluded its failure was a result of "the wretched condition of the roads during the latter part of the winter and early spring, due to mild weather, frequent rains and constant hauling over them of the heavy army wagons."[13] Four months later, he learned that the plan had changed and that Lincoln had been assassinated.

On Saturday evening, April 15, as Booth and Herold were leaving Dr. Mudd's company, Jones was talking to two Federal soldiers. The soldiers had warned Jones to keep a close eye on his skiff, as there were "suspicious characters somewhere in the neighborhood who will be wanting to cross the river." They further cautioned the crafty Jones, "if you don't look sharp you will lose your boat."[14]

The following morning, Easter Sunday, a knock came to Jones's door. It was Samuel Cox Jr. Jones invited the boy into his house and listened to his message. Captain Cox had sent his adopted son to ask Jones to come right away as the Captain needed to talk with him about "seed-corn." Jones sensed that something was up. "Even had I not heard the evening before of the assassination of Mr. Lincoln, knowing Cox as I did, I would have been sure he had sent for me to come to him for something of more importance than to talk about the purchase of seed-corn."[15]

The two men mounted their horses and rode to Rich Hill three miles to the northeast of Huckleberry. Cox met Jones at his front gate. He told his son to take care of the horses. Cox and Jones then walked off into the field in front of the main house. Standing where no one could possibly hear their conversation, Cox told Jones about his two visitors. Then he asked Jones if he had heard the news. Lincoln was shot. Jones said he had heard. There was a minute of silence before Cox spoke again, "Tom, we must get those men who were here this morning across the river." Jones replied, "Sam, I will see what I can do, but the odds are against me. I must see these men; where are they?"[16]

Cox told Jones about the pine thicket. He had given the men some food and a pair of blankets, and oh yes, he had arranged for a signal by which an approaching friend could be recognized. It was a "peculiar whistle." Jones was troubled. It would be a difficult and hazardous task. "It was with extreme reluctance I entered upon this hazardous enterprise. But I did not hesitate; my word was passed."[17]

At his hiding place among the pines Booth suddenly sat up. He thought he had heard something on the far side of the thicket. He picked up one of the two Colt revolvers that had been carefully placed by his side on his blanket and pointed to Herold to pick up the carbine. From somewhere off in the darkness the two men heard a strange whistle. It was the whistle Cox had told them to expect. Herold got up and slowly made his way out of the small enclosure where the two men were resting. A short distance in front of him he saw a man standing still as if waiting to be recognized.

"Who are you, and what do you want?" Herold asked.

"I come from Cox. He told me I would find you here. I am a friend; you have nothing to fear from me," Jones replied in a low voice.[18]

Herold motioned to Jones to follow him, and the two men made their way into the thicket undergrowth where Booth was waiting. Jones later described the scene: "He was lying on the ground with his head supported on his hand. His carbine, pistols, and knife were close beside him. A blanket was drawn partly over him. His slouch hat and crutch were lying by him. He was dressed in dark—I think black—clothes; and though they were travel stained, his appearance was respectable. . . . He wore a moustache and his beard had been trimmed about two or three days before."[19]

Jones was mistaken about one thing. Booth did not wear a moustache. He had shaved it off two days before while at Dr. Mudd's house.[20] Jones told Booth he and Herold would have to stay put until the right moment presented itself when they could be placed on the river. In the meantime Jones would keep them supplied with food and information. They could build no fires, and the horses that were grazing nearby would have to go. They were too dangerous to leave around where they would surely raise suspicions. Their presence was too easily detected by sound and smell. Besides, they would have to be fed during their stay, which would make Jones's job that much more difficult and dangerous. Cox would later tell Jones that he saw Herold lead the two horses into the Zekiah Swamp and a few minutes later heard two reports of a pistol. He assumed that Herold had shot the horses and left them to sink in the quicksand of the swamp. A few days later Cox went to the spot where he thought Herold had taken the horses but could find no trace of the animals. The captain assumed the horses had slipped beneath the surface of the water and were pulled down in the swampy quicksand without a trace.[21] Whether or not Herold disposed of the horses as Cox suggested isn't known. The horses were worth a good bit of money, as were their saddles and accoutrements. Some believed that they died of old age pasturing on one of the many Charles County farms.

The long waiting now began. Booth and Herold huddled in the pine thicket while Jones visited them daily, bringing food and newspapers. Booth

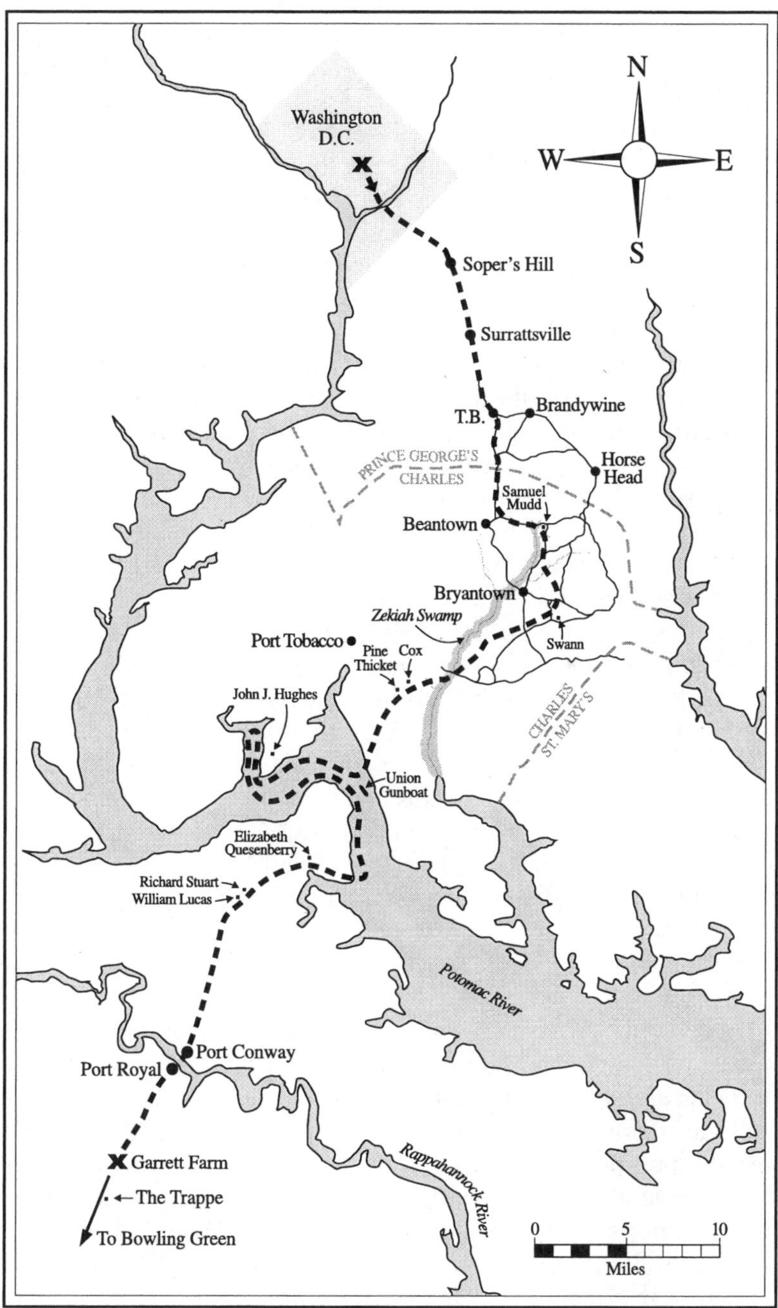

Booth's escape route from Washington, D.C., to the place of his death at the Garrett farm near Port Royal, Virginia.

now had time to rest and reflect on the events of the past few days. He searched the newspaper for his letter to the *National Intelligencer.* It would explain his actions. He could not find it. What he did read in the papers disturbed him. He was not given the slightest benefit for having struck down the great tyrant. The *Baltimore Clipper* described Booth's act in vile terms: "Whilst we mourn over these fiendish acts . . . cowardly and vile . . . whilst we shrink with horror from the contemplation of atrocity so fearful and startling, the thought will occur of the utter madness that could have prompted the authors of these crimes."[22]

"Cowardly and vile, . . . atrocity . . . utter madness. . . ." Were these newspaper writers themselves mad? How could they have so misjudged his act? It was neither cowardly nor vile. It was an act of heroism, of liberation, an act of patriotism ridding the country of its hated Caesar. Booth wrote in a little memorandum book that he carried with him: "I struck boldly and not as the papers say. I walked with a firm step through a thousand of his friends, was stopped, but pushed on. A col. was at his side. I shouted Sic Semper before I fired. In jumping broke my leg. I passed all his pickets. Rode sixty miles that night, with the bone of my leg tearing the flesh at every jump."[23]

This was perhaps a little exaggeration, but it was not too far from the truth. Booth was stopped by Lincoln's messenger, Charles Forbes, at the door to the box. The man with Lincoln in the box was a major, not a colonel (Major Henry Rathbone). All reports indicate that Booth shouted something after he fired his derringer, not before. He rode thirty miles, not sixty. And the bone never broke the skin. It was not a compound fracture. Still, Booth was right to think that his act was not cowardly. One of stealth perhaps, but not cowardly. While Booth may have been fanatic in his cause, he was not a madman. There is a difference. A century of writing has cast Booth as mad and his act one of insanity. These writers are wrong. To assassinate Lincoln took considerable fortitude. It was a calculated act of war, even if driven by hate.

Booth wrote: "Our cause being almost lost, something decisive and great must be done." Does Booth mean "our Confederate cause?" And what about "being *almost* lost." Clearly Booth felt the cause was not lost yet. There was still time to save the cause. What could have been more decisive than to murder the president of the United States and commander in chief of its military forces? Booth was clearly angered that these papers, even these Northern, Lincoln papers, could not see his act as "bold," "decisive," and "great." Truly Booth must have felt as King Lear did: "I am a man more sinn'd against than sinning."[24] He must have wondered what it had all come down to: "After being hunted like a dog through swamps, woods, and last night being chased by gun boats till I was forced to return wet, cold and starving with every man's hand against me, I am here in despair. For doing what Brutus was honored for, what made Tell a hero. And yet I for striking down a greater tyrant than they ever knew am looked upon as a common cutthroat."[25]

While Booth lay nursing his ego, venting his defiance, Thomas Jones was hard at work. Each day he would ride to the small community of Allen's Fresh where one could be sure to find the cavalry. Here he could learn the news of the massive manhunt. Each day was the same. The countryside was in a frenzied state as rumors passed from tavern to tavern. Booth was here. Booth was there. Booth was everywhere. To make matters worse, the government had announced reward money totaling $100,000 for the apprehension of those involved in the president's murder.

On April 16, Captain Thomas H. Hines, another of Jeff Davis's agents, while on his way to Canada, stopped at a bar in Detroit where he was falsely identified as Booth. Holding a crowd at bay with his revolver, Hines made his escape on a ferry over the Detroit River into Canada.[26] On April 19, Booth was reported on the train passing from Reading to Pottsville in Pennsylvania.[27] On April 20, passengers arriving from Point Lookout, Maryland, on the western shore of the Chesapeake Bay reported that a man fitting Booth's description attempted to cross the Potomac River near that place.[28] With so many false sightings, Jones had to be careful. All of the reports of Booth's whereabouts just might result in a false sighting in the area and cause a search by local cavalry.

On Tuesday Jones rode into Port Tobacco. It was the day most people came into the village to conduct business. It was a good time to do a little reconnaissance. Stopping by the local barroom at the Brawner Hotel, he made the acquaintance of Captain William Williams, a military detective who had spent the morning at Dr. Mudd's house listening to the doctor tell of his two guests. Williams invited Jones to have a drink with him, and Jones obliged. A crafty detective, Williams knew the ways of getting information innocently given. But Jones was wily too. He had managed to stay out of Federal prisons during much of his service to the Confederate cause. Williams turned to Jones and said, "I will give one hundred thousand dollars to any one who will give me the information that will lead to Booth's capture." Without hesitation Jones replied, "That is a large sum of money and ought to get him if money can do it."[29]

Williams was a sharp detective and probably knew of Jones's reputation locally. Williams tried to loosen Jones up with a promise of big money. But Jones was no fool. Jones knew that Williams was in no position to give him one hundred thousand dollars—or twenty dollars for that matter. The two men lifted their glasses in salute to each other and swallowed the last of their whiskey. Jones had to keep his fugitives under cover. The time was still not right.

On Thursday, April 20, Jones made his daily trip to the village of Allen's Fresh near the mouth of the Wicomico River.[30] Like Port Tobacco, it was a good place to pick up information and monitor the local troops in the area. Jones finally hit pay dirt. While he was sitting in the local establishment, word came that Booth and Herold were sighted in St. Mary's County a few miles southeast of Allen's Fresh. Within minutes the cavalry troop was mounted and riding hard to the southeast. Jones knew it was now or never. Waiting until the last of the troopers rode out of sight, he mounted his horse and rode hard for the pine thicket. It was dusk when he left Allen's Fresh, and darkness had settled in by the time he arrived where Booth and Herold were hiding. The moon would not rise until sometime around 2:00 A.M., giving them full cover of darkness.[31]

Jones gathered up the two men and told them it was time to cross the river. Booth was lifted onto Jones's horse and the three men began the slow journey. Jones moved out ahead to make sure the coast was clear. He would then signal for them to make their way to where he was waiting. He had come this far and didn't want to fail so close to the end. It was around 9:30 P.M. when the trio reached Huckleberry. Jones told the two men to wait by the barn some fifty yards from the house while he went inside to get food and make sure his former slave, Henry Woodall, had left the boat hidden in the grass near the shore. The two friends had fished the river numerous times together, and both men had labored on the land for so long that any distinction of race had long ago faded away.

When Jones entered the house he saw Woodall seated at the table eating. Jones asked Woodall whether he had had any luck fishing for shad. Woodall said he had. Did he leave the boat where Jones had asked him to leave it? He had. The Black man knew what Jones meant. They had talked about keeping a skiff safely hidden in a grassy creek out of sight. Henry would take care of it, making sure he was seen each evening plying the shore around Pope's Creek. The more conspicuous the better. Nothing suspicious in that. Jones gathered up some food and slipped back outside. No one asked any questions.[32]

Handing the meager victuals to Herold, Jones led the pair down the long descent to the river. The path was steep and narrow in spots, too steep for a horse. They would have to make the final descent on foot. With Booth leaning on Herold, Jones led them down the trail. The sound of the water lapping against the sandy shore guided them as they approached the river.

Reaching the shore, Jones found his boat right where Woodall had said he left it. It was a large, fourteen-foot, flat-bottom skiff painted a leaden grey. There were three oars carefully tucked under the seats. Jones helped Booth crawl into the stern and gave him one of the oars, which he would use as a rudder by sculling over the stern. Herold seated himself at midships and carefully slid the oar pegs into the pivot holes in the gunwales. Jones took a small candle from his pocket and, shielding it with one of the oilskin overcoats he carried, lit the wick. From his other pocket he took a small wooden box no larger than a match safe. Inside was a compass. He handed Booth the compass and, holding the candle over it, showed Booth the course to steer. “Keep to that and it will bring you into Machodoc Creek,” he said. “Mrs. Quesenberry lives near the mouth of this creek. If you tell her you come from me I think she will take care of you. Be sure to hide the light.”[33]

Jones started to push the boat out into the river when Booth spoke: “Wait a minute old fellow.” Booth took several bills from his pocket and offered them to Jones. Jones carefully counted out eighteen dollars, the cost of his boat. He knew he would never see it again. Then Booth spoke, his voice choked with emotion, “God bless you, dear friend, for all you have done for me. Good-bye.”[34] Jones nodded and pushed hard, sending the boat out into the dark waters of the river. He stood silently listening to the rhythmic lapping of the oars as they dipped into the water. With each stroke the sound became fainter and fainter. After a few minutes only the sound of the water gently washing onto the sandy beach could be heard. Jones heaved an audible sigh. He breathed in deeply, filling his lungs with the cool night air. Suddenly he felt as if a great weight had been lifted from his chest.

CHAPTER FIFTEEN

The Roundup

> LIBERAL REWARDS will be paid for any information that shall conduce to the arrest of either of the above-named criminals, or their accomplices.
>
> *War Department Poster*

It was a little after 10:00 P.M. when George Atzerodt walked into the bar of the Kirkwood House and ordered a glass of whiskey. Not far from where he stood was the room of Andrew Johnson, the new vice president. Johnson had taken a room at the Kirkwood House until he could find a more suitable residence for himself and his family. Atzerodt denied later that he agreed to murder Johnson.[1] But at the assigned hour of 10:00 P.M. he was at the Kirkwood House and he was armed. If Atzerodt had no intention of murdering the vice president he was certainly in the right place at the right time to do it.

Atzerodt stared at the yellow flame coming from one of the gas jets above the bar. He had been drinking for the better part of the day, and everything around him appeared hazy. Picking up his drink, he swallowed the bitter liquid in a single gulp and, shoving the glass across the bar, turned and left the hotel without saying a word. The barkeep was used to a more garrulous Atzerodt. He sloughed it off as too much drink.

His courage evaporated, Atzerodt mounted his horse and galloped down the avenue in the direction of the capitol. As he passed Tenth Street he saw several soldiers and civilians running in the direction of Ford's Theatre.[2] Could Booth have gone through with his plan? Had he really killed Lincoln? Now Booth would find him and kill him too for failing to carry out his end of the plan. He spurred his horse and galloped east until he reached the Pennsylvania House located on C Street between Sixth and Four and a Half Streets. The Pennsylvania House was Atzerodt's favorite hotel whenever he needed a place to bunk. It was also one of his favorite watering holes. Entering the bar he ordered another whiskey and, swallowing it, headed back out the door. He next returned his horse to the stables of Kelleher and Pywell where he had rented it that afternoon.[3]

For the next three hours Atzerodt wandered aimlessly about. In one of many moments of anxiety he tossed his knife into the street, where it landed beneath a carriage step.[4] Walking down to Pennsylvania Avenue he climbed aboard a horse trolley and rode to the Navy Yard, where he tried to talk an old acquaintance into letting him share his room with him. The man refused, telling Atzerodt to go back to his own hotel and stay there for the night.[5] Atzerodt climbed back on the next trolley and returned to the Pennsylvania House. It was now 2:00 A.M. and he was tired. The effects of his drinking had finally worn him down. Checking into the hotel, Atzerodt was assigned to room 53 where he flopped into bed with four other patrons who were sound asleep.[6]

At 6:00 A.M. Atzerodt awoke, pulled on his boots, grabbed his rumpled hat, and left the hotel. He walked out without paying his bill. His mind was still clouded by Booth and what the man might do to him for not "putting Johnson through." He had decided it was time to get out of the city. Twenty-five miles to the northwest was the small community of Germantown in Montgomery County, Maryland. Twenty-one years earlier George's father, Henry Atzerodt, had come to the sleepy Maryland community from Germany and purchased a farm along with his brother-in-law Johann Richter. Henry Atzerodt eventually sold his interest in the farm to Johann and moved his family to Virginia while Johann continued to work the farm with his son Ernest.[7] Ernest Hartman Richter, or Hartman as he was known to his family, eventually took over the farm from his father and continued farming in the peaceful Maryland community.[8] Over the years Atzerodt visited his cousin at the old family homestead. Now he decided he would be safe there.

Setting out on foot, Atzerodt headed for Georgetown, located to the west of the city. From here he could catch the stage to Rockville which would take him close to his destination. By the time he reached the bridge that crossed over Rock Creek, Abraham Lincoln's body was being loaded aboard an ambulance for transportation to the White House.

Arriving in Georgetown, Atzerodt stopped by the general store of Mathews and Company located on High Street (now Wisconsin Avenue) where he pawned his revolver for ten dollars.[9] His next stop was at the home of the widow Lucinda Metz where he was given breakfast. Lucinda had spent her early years in Germantown where Atzerodt had come to know her. He had grown hungry from the long walk, and he knew he could count on her for breakfast.[10] His appetite satisfied, Atzerodt walked two blocks to the Montgomery House where he bought a ticket and boarded the stagecoach for Rockville.

Atzerodt's first problem came only a few miles up the pike on the road to Rockville. Army pickets stationed at the military road that serviced several of the forts on Washington's northern border were stopping traffic headed out of the city and searching all wagons and suspicious characters. The stage was held up along with the rest of the traffic. Atzerodt, ever personable and friendly, got out of the stage and began walking to the head of the line. He was either incredibly brash or incredibly stupid, but such a behavior tended to make him seem less suspicious.

Reaching the head of the line he struck up a conversation with several of the soldiers standing picket. The officer in charge, Sergeant Lewis L. Chubb of the Thirteenth Michigan Light Artillery, had received verbal orders to pass no one out of the city. This order was soon amended around 1:00 P.M. directing the guards to search every wagon, arrest anyone looking suspicious, and record the names of everyone allowed to pass through the pickets. Atzerodt soon engaged the sergeant in friendly conversation and bought him and his men a round of hard cider with the money he had picked up pawning his revolver.[11]

At the head of the long column of travelers was a farm wagon driven by William Gaither. Gaither had traveled into Georgetown the night before with a load of butter and eggs and was on his way home when he became caught up in the blockade. Atzerodt bid the soldiers goodbye and turned his attention to Gaither. The two men chatted amiably and Atzerodt wound up buying Gaither two glasses of hard cider. The farmer would later recall that Atzerodt was a friendly sort, quite polite to everyone, and generous with his money. He described the German as "kind of a Jewish-looking man, about 5 feet 8 or 10 inches tall, lightish complexion, sandy moustache."[12] The pickets soon cleared Gaither, and Atzerodt climbed up alongside the farmer as if they had been traveling together all along. It was that simple. Two and a half weeks later Sergeant Chubb was court-martialed on two counts: drunkenness and disobeying orders. After hearing the testimony and weighing the evidence, the court ruled that Chubb was not guilty on both charges.[13]

It was near dusk when Atzerodt and Gaither arrived at the turnoff to Gaither's farm three miles north of Rockville. Here the main road heading north forked, sending off a tributary to the west. Having reached the end of his free ride, Atzerodt climbed down from the wagon and bid his new friend goodbye.[14]

Atzerodt was now within eight miles of his final destination. He had traveled the first twenty miles without a major incident, riding past Stanton's pickets much the way Booth and Herold had ridden past the pickets the night before. Located near the fork in the road where he climbed down from Gaither's wagon was a tavern and blacksmith shop owned by John Mulligan.[15] Atzerodt had time to drop in and have a drink or two. With the balance of his ten dollars he did not have to rely on the hospitality of the tavern keeper.

From Mulligan's Atzerodt continued on foot, eventually arriving at the old Clopper Mill a few miles south of Germantown. Atzerodt knew the miller, Robert Kinder, from his many visits to the area and decided to beg a place to sleep for the night. Kinder obliged Atzerodt and told him he could sleep in the mill by the fireplace.[16] The miller would spend the next six weeks in Old Capitol Prison for his kindness. It was midnight when Atzerodt fell sound asleep.

Easter Sunday broke clear and sunny after a week of rain. Atzerodt's fear had subsided substantially as he started out once again on foot along the final stretch toward the home of his cousin. He had not gone far into his walk when he stopped by the house of Hezekiah Metz, a mile down the road from the old mill. The affable Metz invited Atzerodt to join the family for the noonday meal and the gregarious German was more than happy to oblige.[17] During the dinner the conversation turned to the assassination.[18] Atzerodt soon joined in. Yes, the president was assassinated. Seward's throat was cut but he did not die. Rumor was that Grant was also assassinated. Atzerodt seemed clear in his answers: "If he was killed, he must have been killed by a man that got on the same train or the same car that he did."[19] To the other guests Atzerodt seemed nervous as he talked. The very subject of Lincoln's murder had excited him.

The dinner over, Atzerodt thanked his host and set out on the final leg to his cousin's farm. It was three o'clock in the afternoon when George arrived at the Richter farmhouse.[20] For the next three days he strolled around the farm doing odd jobs to earn his keep. It was good to be back with his cousin on the old homestead. He planned on staying as long as his cousin would have him. On Wednesday, April 19, George crawled into bed along with two hired hands that were helping Richter put in the spring crops. The night was clear and the spring chill had become noticeable only after the sun had gone down. George was soon fast asleep.

Around 5:00 A.M. Atzerodt was abruptly awakened by a rude shaking. Standing over him was a blue-clad officer shoving the cold barrel of an army .44 against his head. Ordered to get up and get dressed, he was roughly pushed down the stairs into the front hall where several soldiers stood with their weapons drawn. A frightened Richter, still dressed in his nightshirt, stood shaking between two cavalrymen. Their uniforms were covered with mud, giving evidence of hard riding. Sergeant Z.W. Gemmill of the First Delaware Cavalry was looking for a recent visitor to the area who had been talking knowingly about the assassination, about Lincoln and Seward, and about General Grant. After a brief conversation Gemmill was satisfied Atzerodt was the man they were looking for.

Atzerodt and Richter were taken under military guard to Monocacy Junction just south of Frederick, Maryland. From Monocacy Junction they were taken to the small village known as Relay on the outskirts of Baltimore. At Relay they were placed on a special military train and taken to Washington. It was Thursday, April 20, and Atzerodt had been at large for just over five days. He would never see a free day again. Just how the troopers managed to find Atzerodt at Richter's house is an example of how widespread and efficient the military's dragnet was. It was a series of fortuitous circumstances that brought the little German into custody.

Atzerodt's good luck turned bad on Wednesday, April 19, but he didn't know it. One of the guests that had joined the Metz family for Easter dinner was Nathan Page. Following Easter dinner Page ran into another local farmer by the name of James Purdom. Purdom worked as an army undercover detective passing information about his neighbors to the military. Page told Purdom that a suspicious character was staying at the Richter farm and that the man spoke of the assassination as if he knew more than the papers reported. Purdom took note of Page's information and later that evening passed it on to one of his army contacts, Private Frank O'Daniel of the First Delaware Cavalry stationed at Monocacy Junction.[21] Purdom asked O'Daniel to pass the information on to his sergeant, George Lindsley.

It was near midnight when O'Daniel returned to camp and reported his conversation with Purdom to Lindsley.[22] Lindsley immediately took the information to his commanding officer, Captain Soloman Townsend.[23] After a short delay, Townsend called Sergeant Z.W. Gemmill to his tent and instructed Gemmill to pick six troopers and go to Richter's house and check out Purdom's information.[24] Gemmill rounded up the disgruntled troopers and headed south toward the farm of James Purdom. With Purdom as guide, the soldiers arrived at the Richter farm and dragged the "suspicious character" from his bed. Within the half hour, the posse had taken Atzerodt, Richter, and two other farm hands into custody and was heading back to Monocacy Junction.[25]

Shortly after Atzerodt's capture a second group of men rode up the long lane leading to the house of Hartman Richter. This second group had come from Baltimore under orders from Provost Marshal James L. McPhail. McPhail, acting on a tip from Atzerodt's own brother, John Atzerodt, sent out a posse to the Richter farm. John Atzerodt was McPhail's deputy and had been on an assignment in Charles County when Lincoln was shot. On learning that the government was looking for his brother, John Atzerodt telegraphed McPhail suggesting he check out the Richter farm in Germantown. By the time McPhail's men reached the Richter farm it was too late. Atzerodt was already in custody. McPhail's men would lose out on the $25,000 reward money that had been allotted for Atzerodt's capture.[26]

McPhail's office was in the thick of the hunt for all of the conspirators. Three days earlier, on Monday, April 17, he had engineered the arrests of Samuel Arnold and Michael O'Laughlen. McPhail's efforts were a model of efficient detective work. Following the abortive capture plot on March 17, Sam Arnold had returned to Baltimore frustrated with Booth and his antics. He applied for a job as clerk in the store of John W. Wharton at Fortress Monroe, Virginia. Arnold reported to work on Sunday, April 2.[27] At the time Lincoln was shot Arnold was working at Fortress Monroe apparently oblivious to what Booth had done.

Early Saturday morning government detectives were searching Booth's room at the National Hotel in Washington. Among several items found in a trunk in the room was a letter addressed to Booth which was signed "Sam" and carried the address "Hookstown." Neither "Sam" nor "Hookstown" registered with the detectives in Washington at the time of the letter's discovery. Hookstown, it turned out, was the name of a small community in northwest Baltimore where Sam's father, George William Arnold, had purchased a farm in 1848. When Samuel Arnold returned home from Confederate service in 1864, he spent part of his time living on the old farm. At the time Arnold wrote his letter to Booth from "Hookstown" he was staying at the old Arnold farmhouse in northwest Baltimore.[28]

Arnold's arrest, however, did not come about as a result of the incriminating letter, as most written accounts have assumed. McPhail was unaware of the letter or its contents on Saturday morning when he sent two of his detectives in search of Arnold. After McPhail received word shortly after midnight on Friday, April 14, that Lincoln had been shot by John Wilkes Booth, one of his detectives, Voltaire Randall, told McPhail that Sam Arnold and Booth were old friends. Perhaps there was a connection. McPhail also remembered that Michael O'Laughlen had lived across the street from the Booth family in Baltimore. McPhail was a shrewd enough detective to realize that these two Baltimoreans just might be connected to Booth—and if not, they might know where to find him. He immediately telegraphed the War Department in Washington before word of the "Sam" letter reached Baltimore: "Sir: Samuel Arnold and Michael O'Laughlen, two of the intimate associates of J. Wilkes Booth, are said to be in Washington. Their arrest may prove advantageous."[29]

McPhail didn't wait for Washington to respond. He swung into immediate action. As a former Confederate soldier, Arnold was required to register his address with McPhail's office.[30] Checking his register, McPhail found "Hookstown" next to Arnold's name. Still unaware of the "Sam" letter, McPhail sent Randall and a second detective by the name of Eaton Horner to Hookstown to find Arnold. At Hookstown the two detectives learned from a "colored woman" that Arnold had taken a job at Fortress Monroe in Virginia. Randall and Horner returned to Baltimore where they visited Arnold's father at his bakery located a half mile from McPhail's headquarters.[31] It was at this time that the detectives learned of the "Sam" letter from the morning papers. They were now convinced that Arnold was a conspirator in Lincoln's murder. Arnold's father confirmed that his son was working at Fortress Monroe, Virginia. Randall and Horner set out Sunday morning for the fort.

On reaching the fort, the two detectives found Arnold and placed him in custody. It was a major collar and showed how efficient McPhail had been in his investigation. He was well ahead of his counterparts in Washington. The *Baltimore Clipper* ran a brief note under the byline "Fort Monroe, April 17: Two detectives arrived here this morning from Baltimore, Md., and arrested the clerk of a sutler store at this place on suspicion of having been in some way connected with the assassination of the President."[32]

After taking Arnold into custody, Horner began questioning him about his relationship with Booth. Stonewalling at first, Arnold soon realized that the detectives knew a great deal about him and the relationship as a result of the damaging "Sam" letter. Arnold began talking freely. He told Horner about a Dr. Mudd of Charles County, Maryland, whom Booth had visited in November 1864. Booth, he said, carried a letter of introduction from someone in Canada. Horner later testified at the conspiracy trial about his arrest and questioning of Arnold, telling the court of Arnold's statement about the letter of introduction. When Horner was asked whom the letter was directed to, he answered bluntly: " [Arnold] said that [Booth] had a letter of introduction to Dr. Mudd and to Dr. Queen."[33] Before Horner left the witness stand he was cross-examined by Mudd's defense counsel, Thomas Ewing. Ewing attempted to soften the damaging testimony against his client. He asked Horner if he did not mean to say that Booth had a letter of introduction to Dr. Queen or Dr. Mudd. Horner was clear in his answer, "I understood him to say *and* Dr. Mudd."[34] The statement was devastating to Mudd's case.

Horner's testimony about a letter of introduction to Dr. Mudd is supported by the statement of another conspirator, George Atzerodt. Shortly before he was hanged, the local papers published a statement by Atzerodt that they described as a "confession." The *Baltimore American* wrote under the headline "Confession of Atzerodt": "Atzerodt said Booth was well acquainted with Mudd, and had *letters of introduction to him* [emphasis added]. Booth told Atzerodt about two weeks before the murder that he had sent provisions and liquor to Dr. Mudd for supplying the party on their way to Richmond with the President."[35]

Returning to Baltimore with Arnold, Horner handed him over to McPhail. McPhail had Arnold write out a statement for the record. McPhail turned a copy of Arnold's statement over to Stanton. Attached to the copy of the statement was a note by McPhail: "Note.—Besides this written statement of Arnold's, he verbally communicated the fact that Booth was the correspondent of Doctors Mudd, Garland, and Queen."[36]

There is a second point, albeit subtle, that emerges from Arnold's arrest. It is this. Arnold told the authorities on April 17 about the letter of introduction, a full day before the military detectives first visited Mudd at his farm or had even heard the name of Dr. Mudd. Arnold could not possibly have learned about Dr. Mudd from anyone connected with the investigation in Baltimore. Government detectives did not learn of Dr. Mudd until Sunday afternoon when George Mudd visited Lieutenant Dana in Bryantown. Arnold could have learned about Mudd from only one source, John Wilkes Booth. This point has been lost in the histories of Lincoln's murder. Those who claim we would never have heard of Dr. Mudd if Booth had not broken his leg have missed this important point. Regardless of whether Booth had availed himself of Dr. Mudd's medical services or not following his murder of Lincoln, Arnold's statement linking Mudd and Booth through a letter of introduction would have sent detectives to Mudd's house in search of the doctor. It was Booth's cohorts, Samuel Arnold and George Atzerodt, that pointed the finger at Mudd early in the investigation.

The "Sam" letter contained a reference to another of Booth's friends whom the government added to their list of suspects: a man by the name of "Mike." Arnold had written in the "Sam" letter, "I called also to see Mike, but learned from his mother he had gone out with you, and had not returned."[37] Washington was as much in the dark about "Mike" as they were about "Sam." But McPhail was ahead of Washington here also. He had known the O'Laughlen family for thirty years, and his office was located only a short distance from the O'Laughlen home. McPhail's earlier investigation had turned up the name of O'Laughlen as well as Arnold.

Word soon reached the O'Laughlen family in Baltimore that the authorities were looking for their son Mike. On Monday, April 17, O'Laughlen made arrangements to turn himself in to the Baltimore police to spare his mother the pain of seeing her son arrested in her home. By the evening of the seventeenth, Samuel Arnold and Michael O'Laughlen were in the custody of McPhail and on their way to Washington. That same evening detectives were making their way to the boardinghouse of Mary Surratt armed with new information and new questions for the lady of the house.

Government detectives first visited Mary Surratt's boardinghouse around 2:00 A.M. on the morning of April 15. This visit occurred only three and a half hours after Booth had shot the president and while he and Herold were en route to Dr. Mudd's house near Beantown. While the name of John Wilkes Booth would not be released officially until 3 A.M., the visit to Mary Surratt's house at 2:00 A.M. shows that government detectives were already aware that Booth was the assassin and that Mary Surratt's boardinghouse was linked to Booth. Such speed requires explanation.

According to his testimony during the conspiracy trial, Detective James A. McDevitt went to the Surratt boardinghouse along with his partner John Clarvoe and two other detectives, Daniel Bigley and John Kelly, shortly before 2 A.M. on the fifteenth.[38] McDevitt was looking for John Surratt and found Louis Wiechmann instead. Years later McDevitt claimed that he had been out that night on a "scouting expedition" when he received a tip from an unnamed actor who told him "to keep an eye on Mrs. Surratt's house on H Street."[39] Information had also come into police headquarters from James P. Fergueson, the bartender of the saloon next to Ford's Theatre on the side opposite the Star Saloon. Fergueson told detectives that John Surratt was often in the company of Booth.[40] Thus the name of John Surratt was linked with that of Booth early on the morning of April 15. McDevitt visited Mary Surratt's house looking for her son John.

McDevitt and his colleagues searched the house thoroughly, looking for any sign of John Surratt or Booth. According to Wiechmann's later testimony, McDevitt told him that John Surratt was the suspected attacker of Seward.[41] Wiechmann told the detectives that Surratt was in Canada. Mary Surratt confirmed Wiechmann's statement by telling the detectives that she had received a letter from her son in Montreal that very day. Asked to produce the letter, Mary couldn't find it.[42]

Wiechmann later wrote in his memoirs that when he asked McDevitt why they came to Mrs. Surratt's house so soon after the assassination, McDevitt had said that "a man on the street" told him, "if you want to find out all about this business go to Mrs. Surratt's house on H street."[43] The identity of this mystery informant, however, remains obscure.

Satisfied that John Surratt and Booth were not at the house and nothing more could be done just then, the detectives returned to their headquarters leaving the occupants of the house in a state of high anxiety. After all, Booth had been a frequent visitor and was a friend of John Surratt. What the detectives did not know—and what Mary Surratt did know—was that several others in Booth's cabal were also visitors to the house and only hours earlier Booth had been at the boardinghouse and asked Mary to take a package and message to Surrattsville for him.

The next two days were ones of frightful anxiety for the members of Mary's boardinghouse. Following breakfast on Saturday morning, Louis Wiechmann had gone to police headquarters with another of Mary Surratt's boarders, John Holohan. The two men became voluntary "witnesses" and were subsequently authorized to accompany detectives John McDevitt and Daniel Bigley on a futile mission to Canada in search of John Surratt. As two of Mary Surratt's boarders, these men were initially under suspicion, especially Louis Wiechmann. But Wiechmann was proving to be the government's key informer, and after he was held in custody for a brief period he became the government's "star" witness. His long association with John Surratt, his knowledge of all of the boarders and visitors to the Surratt house, and his role in escorting Mary Surratt to and from Surrattsville on two occasions made him crucial for the government's case.

With Wiechmann and Holohan away and John Surratt missing, Mary was left alone at her boardinghouse along with the three other women: Honora Fitzpatrick, seventeen years old; Anna Surratt, twenty-two years old; and Olivia Jenkins, Mrs. Surratt's fifteen-year-old niece who was visiting with her. At 11:00 P.M. on Monday, April 17, five military detectives appeared at Mary's door. Colonel Henry H. Wells, provost marshal for the defenses south of the Potomac, now had received several snippets of information from different sources that all had a common connector—541 H Street. Wells told Colonel H.S. Olcott to order a search of the Surratt house and to arrest all of the occupants. Major H.W. Smith of Augur's Twenty-second Army Corps,

Captain W.M. Wermerskirch, R.C. Morgan, Eli Devoe, and Charles W. Rosch arrived at the house around 11 P.M. Smith informed Mary Surratt that they had come to arrest her and "all in your house, and take you for examination to General Augur's head-quarters."[44]

While Smith waited for the ladies to gather their things, one of the more fortuitous events for the government occurred. A "peculiar knock" was heard at the front door. Wermerskirch opened the door to find a tall man with a pickaxe on his shoulder standing in the doorway. The man was taken aback by the uniformed men standing in the hallway. Somewhat startled, he told the officer that he must have the wrong house. When challenged as to whose house he sought, the man answered, "I came to see Mrs. Surratt." He was told he was at the right house and to step inside. The stranger was Lewis Thornton Powell (alias Lewis Paine). Powell had fled the Seward house on Friday evening and disappeared into the void of Washington. Now, three days later, he showed up at the home of Mary Surratt.

The *Baltimore Clipper* for Thursday, April 20, was a bestseller. It carried the complete text of a letter Booth had left with the local Washington newspaper that began, "To Whom It May Concern." The paper also carried a detailed description of the events at Mary Surratt's boardinghouse on the night of April 17:

> Late last night R.C. Morgan of New York made a lucky strike in working up the assassination plot. Acting as one of the special commissioners of the War Department under Mr. Orcutt [Olcott], he visited the residence of Mrs. Surratt, on H street, between Ninth and Tenth [actually between Fifth and Sixth].
>
> The women were put under arrest and sent to headquarters for examination,—Then a search of the house was made,—Papers and correspondence of a most important character were found, but the most important event transpired while search was being made in the garret.
>
> A peculiar knock was heard at a lower outer door. The expert at once entered and opened the door, when a large man confronted him with a pick ax in his hand. Stepping aside, the man entered rapidly and Morgan then closed the door upon him and quickly locking it, put the key in his pocket.
>
> The stranger, here discovering something was wrong, turned and remarked that he had made a mistake—was in the wrong house, etc. "Who did you wish to see," he was asked. "I came to see Mrs. Surratt," said he. "Well, you are right then. She lives here," was replied.
>
> He nevertheless insisted upon retiring, but a pistol was pointed at him and he was ordered into the room adjoining. His

pick-ax was taken from him and he [was] ordered to sit down. Here a lengthy questioning and cross-questioning took place.

He stated he was a refugee from Virginia; was a poor man's son; had been brought up on a farm; did not know how to read; had always been kept hard at work, because his father was poor, and then showed his oath of allegiance, which he had in his pocket; said he had worked on the horse-railroad here [horse-drawn trolley system in Washington].

When asked where he lived, he boggled a little. When asked where he slept last night, he said, "Down the railroad"—When asked where the night before and Friday, he was still more embarrassed, and equivocated considerably. He said he came to this house to dig a drain for Mrs. Surratt; that he was to work at it early in the morning, and thought he would come in before he went to bed, as she would not be up in the morning.

It is proper to state that up to the questioning of where he stayed, no suspicion had been excited that he was other than a veritable laborer; but the fact of his coming at so late an hour led to suspicion that he might know something of the family connections.

Surratt himself having disappeared with Booth, a glance at his boots covered with mud disclosed them to be fine ones; his pants, also very muddy, were discovered to be of fine black cassimere. His coat was better than laborers usually wear and nothing but his hat indicated a refugee.

He was further questioned and on saying that he had no money he was searched and twenty-five dollars in greenbacks and some Canadian coins found on his person, a fine white linen handkerchief with delicate pink border, a tooth and nail brush, a cake of toilet soap and some pomatun [hair pomade], for all of which he tried to give a plausible account, though bothered a good deal about his taste for the white handkerchief in his possession.

Here his hat was examined and found to have been made of a fine gray or mixed undershirt of his own, which he had taken off to make a hat of, cut out in Confederate soldier style, and not sewed up but pinned. This led to the conviction that he had lost his hat, and other circumstances fixed suspicion that he was the assassin of the Seward family.

The Secretary's [William Seward's] negro doorkeeper [William Bell] was sent for without the knowledge of what was wanted, came into the room and was seated, the gas having been turned down previously. After he was seated the gas was turned on brightly, and without a word being spoken, the poor boy started as if he

The last photograph taken of Lincoln in Springfield, Illinois, before leaving for Washington. By C.S. German, February 9, 1861.

The Passage through Baltimore, by Adalbert Volck, March 1861.

Above left, Allan Pinkerton, ca. 1875. Head of Pinkerton's National Detective Agency. (Courtesy of James O. Hall.) *Above right,* Believed to be the encampment on the White House grounds of Company K, 150th Pennsylvania Volunteer Infantry. From a stereoview by E. and H.T. Anthony, no. 1311, c. 1862. Unpublished. (Author's collection.)

View of Soldiers' Home, c. 1862. Anderson Cottage (left) served as the "Summer White House" for the Lincoln family from 1861 to 1865. From an unmarked stereoview. Unpublished. (Author's collection.)

Above left, The Booth family house in Baltimore. (Courtesy of Richard Sloan.) *Above right*, The photograph of John Wilkes Booth known as Gutman No. 35. This photograph was sent to Captain George W. Dutton in command of the guard at Aqueduct Bridge in the District of Columbia to help in the search for Booth. *Carte de visite* photograph, c. 1863, by Silsbee, Case and Company, Boston. (Massachusetts Historical Society.)

Tudor Hall. The Booth Home near Bel Air, Maryland, built in 1851-52. The Booth family moved into the house in 1853. (Photograph by the author.)

Above left, Samuel Bland Arnold. 1865. (Library of Congress.) *Above right*, Michael O'Laughlen Jr. 1865. (Library of Congress.) *Below*, Barnum's City Hotel. One of Baltimore's finest hotels, Barnum's served as the site for the Democratic National Convention between 1832 and 1852 and later became the principal meeting place for anti-Lincoln forces. It was here that Cipriano Ferendini worked as a barber and where John Wilkes Booth met with Samuel Arnold and Michael O'Laughlen during the first week of August in 1864 to enlist them in his plot to capture President Lincoln. (Photograph by William Chase, author's collection.)

Above left, Samuel Alexander Mudd. (Surratt House and Museum Library.) *Above right*, Thomas H. Harbin. A Confederate agent who was introduced to John Wilkes Booth by Samuel A. Mudd on December 18, 1864, at the Bryantown Tavern. As a result of the meeting Harbin agreed to help Booth in his scheme to capture Lincoln. (Courtesy of James O. Hall.)

Bryantown Tavern, c. 1870. Where John Wilkes Booth stayed and where Samuel A. Mudd introduced him to Thomas H. Harbin on December 18, 1864. The Thirteenth New York Cavalry set up headquarters in the tavern on Saturday, April 15, 1865. Now a private residence. (Courtesy of Robert W. Cook.)

Above left, David E. Herold. (Library of Congress.) *Above right,* George Andrew Atzerodt. A resident of Port Tobacco, Charles County, Maryland, Atzerodt avoided arrest while ferrying men and materials across the Potomac River throughout the war. Atzerodt was assigned to kill Vice President Andrew Johnson. (Library of Congress.)

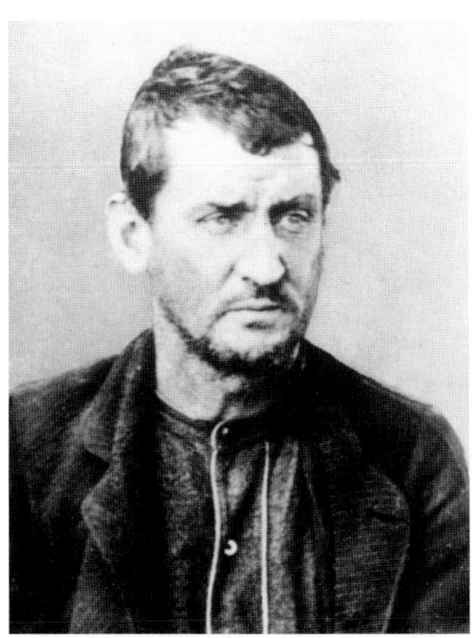

Above left, Edman Spangler. (Library of Congress.) *Above right,* Lewis Thornton Powell, alias Lewis Paine. A member of Mosby's Rangers, Powell was assigned to assassinate Secretary of State William H. Seward. (Courtesy of Betty Ownsby.)

Mary Elizabeth Surratt, c. 1852. Mary Surratt operated the boardinghouse on H Street and owned the tavern in Surrattsville, Maryland. Both establishments served as safe residences for Confederate agents. Mary Surratt was hanged as a conspirator in Lincoln's death. (Courtesy of James O. Hall.)

John Harrison Surratt Jr. Posing in his uniform as a Papal Zouave, c. 1870. (National Archives.)

The Surratt boardinghouse, located at 541 (now 604) H Street, Washington, D.C. Booth visited this house on several occasions, and Lewis Powell and George Atzerodt boarded here. Mary Surratt and Lewis Powell were arrested here on the night of April 17, 1865. (Photograph by the author.)

Above left, John T. Ford, c. 1864. From a *carte de visite* photograph. (Author's collection.) *Above right*, Harry Clay Ford, c. 1864. From a *carte de visite* photograph. (Author's collection.)

Ford's Theatre draped in mourning the day of Lincoln's funeral in Washington, D.C., April 21, 1865. From an unmarked contemporary stereoview by Alexander Gardner. (Author's collection.)

The presidential box at Ford's Theatre. From a contemporary stereoview by Alexander Gardner. (Author's collection.)

View of the rear of Ford's Theatre showing Baptist Alley. Booth used the stage door shown in the picture. (Photograph by the author.)

The Surratt tavern in Surrattsville, Maryland. Booth and Herold stopped here near midnight on April 14, 1865, to pick up a carbine, a field glass, and whiskey on their way to Samuel Mudd's house. (Photograph by author.)

Above, Huckleberry. The home of Thomas A. Jones at the time he hid Booth and Herold in a pine thicket. Jones, Booth, and Herold stopped here briefly the night of April 20 on their way to the Potomac River. (Photograph by the author.) *Right*, Thomas A. Jones. Jones was the chief agent of the Confederate Secret Service in southern Maryland. Under instructions from Samuel Cox Sr., Jones cared for Booth and Herold from April 16 through April 20 when he placed them in a small boat and sent them across the Potomac River toward Virginia. (Thomas A. Jones Collection, Charles County Community College, La Plata, Maryland.)

Left, Samuel Cox Sr. Booth and Herold stopped at Cox's plantation home, Rich Hill, around midnight on April 15, 1865. Cox saw to their safe hiding in a pine thicket not far from his home. (Courtesy of James O. Hall.) *Above*, Rich Hill. The home of Samuel Cox Sr. (Photograph by the author.)

The home of Samuel Alexander Mudd near Beantown in Charles County, Maryland. Booth was a houseguest of Dr. Mudd in November and December 1864. Booth and Herold arrived at Mudd's house at 4:00 A.M. on Saturday, April 15, and stayed until 7:00 P.M. that same evening before traveling to the home of Samuel Cox Sr. (Courtesy of James O. Hall.)

Cleydael. The home of Dr. Richard H. Stuart. Booth and Herold were brought to Cleydael by one of Thomas Harbin's agents on the evening of April 23. Stuart fed the two fugitives and sent them to the cabin of William Lucas. (Photograph by the author.)

William Rollins of Port Conway, Virginia. Rollins and his wife, Bettie, furnished Union soldiers with vital information that led the search party to Willie Jett in Bowling Green, Virginia. Jett then led the Union soldiers to Richard Garret's house where Booth and Herold were hiding out. (Courtesy of James O. Hall.)

Site of the ferry slip at Port Royal, Virginia, c. 1935. Booth and Herold, along with four Confederate soldiers, landed here shortly before noon on Monday, April 24. (Surratt House and Museum Library.)

Above, The farmhouse of Richard Garrett, c. 1935. The last stop for Booth and Herold. The house collapsed by 1939 and today the site is located in the median strip of U.S. Highway 301. (Surratt House and Museum Library.) *Below*, Old Capitol Prison and its wooden annex, Carroll Prison. Nearly everyone arrested under suspicion of being involved in the assassination of Lincoln was held in Old Capitol Prison. Mary Surratt and Samuel Mudd were held here before being transferred to the Washington Arsenal. From a stereoview, c. 1866. (Author's collection.)

Officers' quarters, Fort Lesley J. McNair, 1984. Surviving part of the original Washington Arsenal. The trial was held on the third floor of this building. (Photograph by the author.)

Woodcut engraving showing the transfer of conspirators to the Old Penitentiary at the Washington Arsenal. Engraving inaccurately depicts Mary Surratt wearing a hood. She was never hooded. *Frank Leslie's Illustrated Newspaper.* (Author's collection.)

The military commission that sat in judgment of the conspirators together with the prosecution team. Left to right: Colonel David R. Clendenin, Colonel Charles Tomkins, General Thomas M. Harris, General Albion Howe, Colonel James A. Ekin, General Lew Wallace, General David Hunter (president), General August V. Kautz, General Robert S. Foster, John A. Bingham, Colonel Henry L. Burnett, and Judge Advocate General Joseph Holt. (Library of Congress.)

Hanging of the conspirators on July 7, 1865. Photograph by Alexander Gardner. Left to right: Mary E. Surratt, Lewis Powell, David E. Herold, and George A. Atzerodt. (Library of Congress.)

The deathbed scene in the Petersen house. Photographer Julius Ulke, a boarder in the Petersen house took this haunting photograph, minutes after Lincoln's body was removed. (Courtesy of Richard Sloan.)

Sketch of the death bed scene in the Petersen house from *Harper's Weekly*, May 6, 1865. (National Park Service.)

A fragile memorial to the slain president. A cross set among dessicated leaves under a glass dome forms a memorial altar popular in Victorian America. From an E. & H.T. Anthony stereo card produced shortly after Lincoln's death. (Author's collection.)

The only known photograph of Lincoln lying in state. The casket rests in the rotunda beneath the dome of New York's City Hall. The photograph was discovered in 1952 in the Illinois State Historical Library in Springfield, Illinois. Photograph by Jeremiah Gurney Jr. (Illinois State Historical Society.)

The Lincoln funeral car draped in mourning cloth as it sat in the U.S. Military Railroad yards in Alexandria, Virginia. Two members of the Veteran Reserve Corps stand guard. (Smithsonian Institution, National Museum of American History, Commerce.)

The hearse used by the city of Springfield for its funeral procession. The hearse was lent to Springfield for Lincoln's funeral by the city of St. Louis. (Illinois State Historical Society.)

Funeral services held in the East Room of the White House on April 19. All of the windows, mirrors and chandeliers were draped in black silk. From a contemporary print, *Harper's Weekly*, April 20, 1865. (Author's collection.)

The funeral procession of Abraham Lincoln on its way to the U.S. Capitol as it marches up Pennsylvania Avenue in Washington, D.C. (Library of Congress.)

The public vault in Oak Ridge Cemetery, Springfield, Illinois. The bodies of Abraham Lincoln and his son Willie Lincoln were placed in this public vault at the time of the Springfield funeral. The six civilians are members of the Springfield community charged with establishing a final burial place for Lincoln and his family. From a *carte de visite* photograph. (Author's collection.)

> had been shot, and the *pseudo* laborer started also and turned deadly pale.
>
> The recognition was instantaneous and mutual. On being asked why he seemed so affected, the negro immediately answered: "Why at's the man wot cut Massa Seward," and moving for a moment uneasily and with his eyes intently fixed on the prisoner he continued: "I does't want to stay here no how."
>
> Major Seward [William H. Seward, youngest son of William Seward] and sister [Francis "Fanny" Seward] were sent to identify him this morning and did so completely. His identification is absolute, and he is now a prisoner on board a monitor. All of the circumstances connected with his arrest and detention are of the most marvelous character.
>
> The detectives would not have been at the house but for the fidelity of a freedman, a poor colored woman, and the merest accident divested him of his well assumed character of a poor laborer.[45]

Two important points are gleaned from this account. The first is Powell's ability to deal effectively with the detectives' questioning, which runs counter to his characterization as a "dull-witted" person. One must assume that Powell went to Mary Surratt's house not knowing detectives would be there and was caught off guard in an anxious moment. Despite this, Powell produced a cover story that was as good as could be expected under the circumstances.

The second revealing statement in the paper's account explains why the military detectives went to the Surratt house intent on arresting the inhabitants: "The detectives would not have been at the house but for the fidelity of a freedman, a poor colored woman. . . ." This "freedman" was Susan Mahoney Jackson, a Black woman who had been hired by Mary Surratt just three weeks earlier. According to her testimony during the trial of John Surratt two years later, Mrs. Jackson was taken to General Augur's headquarters where she was questioned. She told of seeing John Surratt earlier that day at the boardinghouse, a clear contradiction of Mary Surratt's claim that her son was in Canada.[46] In fact, her son was in Elmira, New York, on a mission for Confederate general Edwin G. Lee.[47] Mrs. Jackson's statement, however, gave the detectives further cause to look with suspicion on Mary Surratt and her house.

Mary was called into the front parlor where she was asked if she knew the man who had come to her door or had ever seen him before. Did she ask him to dig a drain for her? She seemed alarmed and, raising her arm in the air, declared, "Before God, sir, I do not know this man, and I have not seen him before, and I did not hire him to come and dig a gutter for me."[48] Her denial bode poorly for Powell and for herself. The fact that Lewis Powell sought out Mary Surratt's house of all places in the District suggested that she could offer him safe haven. She said that she did not recognize him when in fact he had been a visitor and boarder in her house. The authorities believed she was trying to cover up something more serious. Certainly her daughter Anna and Miss Fitzpatrick had known Lewis Powell from his visits with the two ladies. Mary would also deny knowing Davy Herold although he too had been a visitor to her house on more than one occasion. To deny knowing Powell only added more water to Mary's sinking ship. Lewis Powell and the four ladies were taken into custody to General Augur's headquarters.

Perhaps the least known of the accused conspirators was Edman Spangler. Spangler worked as a carpenter and stagehand for John Ford and was a longtime friend of Booth. He had worked as a carpenter on the Booth home in Bel Air in 1853. Spangler, along with several other members of John Ford's staff, was taken into custody on the morning of Saturday, April 15. Spangler gave a statement that said little more than that he was well acquainted with Booth, that he had been asked by Booth to hold his horse in the alley behind the theater, and that he passed the job on to "Peanuts" Burroughs because he had work to do. Spangler also told his interrogators that he saw a man run out the rear door of the theater a few minutes after he heard a shot. Spangler was released on Saturday only to be arrested again on Monday, April 17, and taken to the Old Capitol Prison, where he had the dubious distinction of being the first of the soon-to-be indicted conspirators to be arrested and jailed. The jail records list him simply as "accomplice."

On Monday, April 24, Dr. Samuel Mudd was taken into custody at his home near Beantown and transported to Washington where he was placed in the Old Capitol Prison along with the other conspirators. In less than eight days the government had rounded up several hundred individuals and, culling through them, winnowed it down to ten persons believed to be directly involved in the assassination of Abraham Lincoln. Of the ten, seven were now in prison: Edman Spangler, Samuel Arnold, Michael O'Laughlen, Mary Surratt, Lewis Powell, George Atzerodt, and Samuel Mudd. Of the three still at large, two would be in custody within forty-eight hours. Only John Surratt Jr. would make his escape, but only for a little over a year. He would be arrested in Italy, escape a second time, and be recaptured at Alexandria, Egypt. Returning to the United States, Surratt would stand trial in a civil court. The jury would be unable to reach a verdict and Surratt would be released.

The government had moved swiftly and with a certain degree of success. But still at large was the nation's number one fugitive. General Winfield Scott Hancock, commander of the Middle Military Division encompassing the District of Columbia, Maryland, and the border counties of Virginia, issued a special broadside appealing "to the Colored people." Hancock reminded Blacks that Lincoln was assassinated "simply and solely because he was your friend." He appealed to them: "Go forth and watch, and listen, and inquire, and search, and pray, by day and by night, until you have succeeded in dragging this monstrous and bloody criminal from his hiding place."[49] It was asking a great deal.

Forty-five miles south of the Old Capitol Prison in a small pine thicket, John Wilkes Booth rested, ignorant of the roundup that was taking place all around him. He would eventually read about the arrest of his seven friends. While he would write many revealing things in his little memorandum book, he would say nothing about his companions now facing a hangman for his act. They were not his worry. His only worry now was the river that separated him from Virginia and safety.

Part Three

The End

I have too great a soul to die like a criminal.

John Wilkes Booth

CHAPTER SIXTEEN

Virginia at Last!

> To night I try to escape these bloodhounds once more. Who, who can read his fate. God's will be done.
>
> *John Wilkes Booth*

Night sounds travel far over water. Whispers seem to glide through the air and strengthen as they slip across the surface. The two men sat in the small boat afraid to speak, uncertain what ears might be listening off in the darkness. The only sound was that of the water as it gently lapped against the sides of the boat. Booth sat hunched over in the stern peering into the black distance trying to pick out some object that would tell him where they were. It was less than three miles across the river at the narrowest point from where they set out. The wind was blowing out of the northwest and helped them along, but the tide was against them for most of the way.[1]

Neither the wind nor the tide caused the two men to veer suddenly off their course; it was most likely a Union gunboat. As they approached the Virginia shore they were suddenly startled to see a large shadow rising up out of the water. It was a ship. A Yankee ship. Anchored just offshore in a direct line with their boat and their destination at Machodoc Creek was the USS *Juniper*.[2] Herold quickly veered the skiff upriver, desperately working to move out of the vision and earshot of the gunboat's watch.

The two men had come perilously close to running into the Union ship. Had they been sighted it would have been over for sure. Booth's luck was still holding out. Hours later an exhausted Herold pulled the skiff into the mouth of Nanjemoy Creek some six miles up river. After hours of struggling against current and wind they were back on the Maryland side not far from where they started several hours earlier. It was too late to attempt another crossing this night. Besides, the two men were exhausted after hours on the river. They would slip into the mouth of the Nanjemoy and come ashore on its eastern bank at a place called Indiantown. It was a large farm owned by Peregrine Davis and farmed by his son-in-law John J. Hughes. Davy Herold knew the area well. He had hunted the land on many occasions and had become friends with the owner.

On the day after his arrest Herold was questioned by Judge Advocate

General Joseph Holt and his assistant, John A. Bingham, on board the monitor *Montauk*. He managed to evade most of the questions and give the impression that he was nothing more than an innocent bystander in Booth's conspiracy. But in answer to one of the questions about his habit of hunting in southern Maryland, he revealed his extensive knowledge of the area while describing his visits there. He told his interrogator that he frequented Charles County, often stopping at Peregrine Davis's farm. Herold had been in the habit of visiting there for the past five or six years.[3]

Hunting was a passion with Herold. Every fall he would take two or three months and hunt the fields of Charles County in search of partridge. The area around Nanjemoy creek was among the most beautiful in all of southern Maryland. The tidal waters were lined with grasses of many varieties. Joe Pye weed filled the landscape with its tall purple flowerheads that were a favorite of wild bees. Dozens of species of waterfowl habited the area. It was easy to lose oneself in the serenity of the surrounding countryside. But not this day.

Davis's farm was a favorite stop during Herold's hunting visits. Now he would visit the farm one last time. It was early morning on Friday, April 21, when the two men came ashore and made there way to Hughes's house. A century later, in an interview with historian James O. Hall, George Hughes, the grandson of John J. Hughes, would tell of the family tradition surrounding that visit. Booth and Herold did go into the Hughes house.[4] But, it was too dangerous for them to stay in the house overnight. The area was swarming with Federal troops. Hughes gave them food and drink; then he let them hide out on the property until they could retry the river.[5] For some reason they did not try to cross Friday night, or if they did try, they again aborted their attempt. Perhaps gunboats were still in the area patrolling the river. The next opportunity came on Saturday, April 22. Herold continued his story: "That night, at sundown, we crossed the mouth of Nanjemoy Creek, passed within 300 yards of a gunboat, and landed at Mathias Point [Virgina]."[6]

After nine days of running and hiding Booth and Herold had finally reached Virginia. It was still a dangerous situation, but the river had put them out of direct reach of the searching authorities. When Thomas Jones had handed Booth the small-boxed compass, he pointed the course to Machodoc Creek on the Virginia side. Holding his candle close to the face of the compass Jones told Booth to seek out a Mrs. Quesenberry. "If you tell her you come from me I think she will take care of you," he told Booth.[7]

Elizabeth Quesenberry was another of the Confederate faithful who served the cause. She lived in a small house located on the inlet where Machodoc Creek emptied into the Potomac River. When Booth and Herold reached the Virginia shore early Sunday morning on the twenty-third, they missed their intended target. Aiming for Machodoc Creek, they landed at Gambo Creek located a mile upriver from the mouth of Machodoc Creek.

Pulling the boat ashore, Herold helped Booth hobble to a safe spot in the underbrush. Here he would wait while Herold tried to find Mrs. Quesenberry and obtain her help. Elizabeth Quesenberry was a thirty-nine–year-old widow who lived with three minor daughters. Herold made his way to Quesenberry's house at approximately one o'clock on Sunday afternoon. Mrs. Quesenberry was not at home when Herold arrived, and he asked one of the young daughters if she could be sent for. After nearly an hour she finally appeared. Mrs. Quesenberry later told her story to the authorities. It was the same story others had claimed they were told. Herold told her he and his brother were escaped prisoners of war and that his brother had broken his leg in a horsefall. Could she furnish them with a wagon? She refused. It isn't clear just how much of Mrs. Quesenberry's statement is truthful. Booth and Herold were among friendly sympathizers. They had no need to lie about their circumstances. Jones had told Booth to expect help, and he got it. Mrs. Quesenberry sent for Thomas Harbin and Joseph Baden. Harbin arrived at Mrs. Quesenberry's around three o'clock and agreed to take the two men off of her hands. She gave Harbin food for the two men and sent him off in the direction of Gambo Creek.[8] Harbin was well acquainted with Booth, of course, having been introduced to him at the Bryantown Tavern by Dr. Mudd. The introduction would now pay off handsomely for Booth. Without Harbin's help, the two men would have been stranded on the Virginia shore.

Booth told Harbin they wanted to go to Dr. Stuart's house. Stuart was living at his second home, located fifteen miles inland from his plantation-style mansion on the Potomac River. He called the summer home Cleydael after an ancestral home in Belgium. Booth and Herold would need horses. Harbin sent for one of his subordinates, William Bryant. Bryant brought two horses with him and agreed to take the men to Stuart's house.[9]

A few weeks after she helped Booth and Herold, Mrs. Quesenberry was arrested and taken to Washington. Although never jailed, she was interrogated and gave a statement. Toward the end of the statement she said, "I did not report it [Booth and Herold's visit] to any government officer as I had no opportunity to do so. I heard that after they left Dr. Stewart's [*sic*] they had crossed the Rappahannock at Port Royal and that soldiers were in pursuit."[10] The Confederate grapevine was still intact and functioning well. Mrs. Quesenberry was being fed news at regular intervals thanks to Thomas Harbin and his camp of agents.

Bryant, with Booth and Herold in tow, arrived at Cleydael shortly after dark, around eight o'clock according to a statement later made by Stuart.[11] Stuart admitted to seeing the two men along with William Bryant and a "Mr. Crisman." Herold was dismounted and, as usual, did all the talking. He told Stuart they had come from Maryland and needed accommodations for the night. Stuart told Herold it would be impossible to provide them lodging. His house was full up with his immediate family and other guests.[12] He had no spare room for the strangers. Herold then told Stuart that the other man, his brother, had a broken leg and needed aid. He told Stuart "that Dr. Mudd had recommended him." Stuart was curt: "I said that nobody was authorized to recommend anybody to me."[13] Stuart was suspicious. He must have known about the assassination, and from the extensive network that existed in King George County, must have known that Booth and Herold would be headed across the river. Stuart revealed as much in his statement when he said: "The man with the broken leg said very little; he did not say who he was; they kept urging me so that at last I said 'I do not want to know anything about you.' . . . He pressed me saying 'If you will listen to the circumstances of the case, you will be able to do it.'"[14]

Stuart was cautious with his interrogators. By telling them that he did not want to know anything about his visitors he hoped to show that he was not a willing abettor in aiding Booth and Herold. Stuart, however, seemed well aware of who the men were: "I was suspicious of them. I did not know but they might be some of the characters who had been connected with the vile acts of assassination here in Washington, which I heard of a few days before—the previous Tuesday; this was a Sunday. I was suspicious of the lame man (Booth). He desired to tell me something I did not care to hear. . . . He said he had a fall and broken his leg; he said Dr. Mudd set it. . . . They said Dr. Mudd had recommended them to me."[15]

Stuart was trying to cover himself by sounding unsure of his visitors: "They inquired who could send them up to Fredericksburg. I said I could not possibly do it. I was asked if I knew who could do it. I told them I had a neighbor near there, a colored man who sometimes hired his wagon, and probably he would do it if he was not very busy; and it would be no harm to try. . . . I agreed to give them something to eat & they walked into the house to get it. . . . the men had finished their meal, & I remarked 'the old man is waiting for you; he is anxious to be off.' . . . They got up immediately and went out."[16]

Following Stuart's orders, Bryant took Booth and Herold a short distance from Stuart's house to the cabin of a free Black by the name of William Lucas. Lucas lived with his wife and six children in a small cabin near the border of Stuart's farm.[17] Booth needed a place to sleep and transportation to the Rappahannock River since Bryant would not leave his horses with the two fugitives. After Stuart's rebuff, Booth was in no mood to plead for help. He gave the unfortunate Lucas no choice. At one point Booth reached behind his back and pulled out his large bowie knife, saying to Lucas, "Old man, how do you like this?"[18] He then told Lucas that he and his friend would sleep in the cabin for the night.

Booth and Herold bedded down for the night while Lucas and his family slept outside. When morning came Booth asked Lucas to take him in his wagon to Port Conway on the Rappahannock. Port Conway was located on the north shore of the Rappahannock River ten miles to the south of Stuart's home. It was the safest place to cross the river, a fact that Harbin undoubtedly told Booth before sending him on to Stuart's house. Lucas tried to argue against going with Booth. He complained that his wife was sick and he didn't want to leave her for so long a period. Booth was losing his patience. His manner was growing increasingly ugly when Lucas's son Charley stepped in and said he would take the pair in his father's wagon. When Lucas asked if Booth intended to take his horses and wagon without pay, Booth asked how much he received for driving to Port Conway. The old man said ten dollars in gold or twenty dollars in greenbacks. Booth paid the $20 in greenbacks to Mrs. Lucas.[19] Despite his threatening demeanor, Booth was generous. Charley Lucas hitched up the pair of horses, and after Booth was helped into the wagon, the three men set out for Port Conway. According to William Lucas it was around seven o'clock on the morning of April 24.[20]

Before departing, Booth wrote out a note to Stuart on a page he had cut from his little memorandum book. It was meant to insult Stuart for his inhospitable treatment. Booth underscored his displeasure by writing Stuart, "It is not the substance, but the manner in which a kindness is extended that makes one happy in the acceptance thereof."[21] Booth then quoted a line from *Macbeth:* "The sauce in meat is ceremony; meeting were bare without it." To add insult to injury, Booth attached $2.50 to the note in payment for the food Stuart begrudgingly gave him.[22] Booth signed the note "Stranger."

Charley Lucas reached Port Conway sometime around ten o'clock.[23] Once an important port of commerce, the village had all but been abandoned to the ghosts of a thriving past. It lay at the confluence of two major highways that carried goods north and south as well as east and west. In colonial days, large hogsheads of tobacco made their way from the surrounding countryside to the village, where they were picked up by merchant vessels heading to foreign ports. While tobacco was still the lifeblood of the region, it had long flowed into other veins, leaving Port Conway dry. The community was now reduced to a few residences, a store, and an abandoned warehouse. William Rollins and his wife owned the small store. Rollins had only recently married a young girl by the name of Bettie who tended store for the occasional customers who found themselves in need of odd staples.[24]

Herold helped Booth out of the wagon and over to a pier where he could rest comfortably. Swollen and throbbing, his leg continued to be a source of severe pain. Lucas bid good riddance to his passengers and headed back toward his father's cabin. Port Conway had a small ferry that was operated from the Port Royal, or far side, of the river. Booth and Herold could see the ferry barge sitting on the far bank unattended. After setting Booth on the pier, Herold hallooed for anyone who might be around. William Rollins appeared shortly and greeted the two men. Apparently unknown to Herold was the fact that Rollins, like so many of those who handled Booth, was the signal corps agent at this point along the river.[25] He asked what he could do for them. Herold repeated the old story that he and his "brother" were soldiers recently surrendered by General Lee. The brother, whom he introduced as James W. Boyd, had injured his leg defending Petersburg. Herold's choice of an alias fit nicely with a set of small initials (J.W.B.) Booth had inked into the skin on his left hand when still a young boy. Herold told Rollins they were headed for Orange County and needed to cross the river. Could Rollins take the pair over in his boat? They offered Rollins ten dollars to guide them to Orange County Court House. If not, they would pay him two dollars to take them in his wagon to Bowling Green.[26] Rollins said he could take them across the river but they would have to wait until he set out his nets. The shad were running now and they would wait for no one. Rollins knew that the two men could wait, his fish could not. He told Herold he would be back in a while. Rollins then rowed out into the river with his Black helper, and the two men began tending their nets.

While Booth and Herold sat waiting for Rollins to return, three men approached the pier on horseback. They were dressed in Confederate army uniforms. Booth sat quietly as the gregarious Herold once again assumed the role of spokesman. He made his way to where the trio had stopped. Two of the soldiers had dismounted and were looking for Rollins as he set his nets in the river. They were looking for the ferry to take them across.

Herold walked over to the men and, slapping the haunch of one of the horses, introduced himself as David Boyd. He told the soldiers the other man was his brother James. He had hurt his leg at Petersburg.[27] Where did the soldiers come from? he asked. They told Herold that they had recently been with Mosby and had stood down with the rest of his command only a few days earlier. They were on their way to Caroline County just over the river. The youngest soldier was Absalom Bainbridge. He was seventeen and had been a private in Company B of the Third Virginia Infantry. The next youngest was William S. Jett. Eighteen years old, Willie Jett had served as a private in Company C of the Ninth Virginia Cavalry. Seated on the horse and senior in rank and age was Mortimer Ruggles. Ruggles was a lieutenant who had served as second in command to Thomas Nelson Conrad in his spy operation in northern Virginia.[28] Ruggles was the son of Major General Daniel Ruggles. General Ruggles had been assigned duty as commissary general of prisoners in the closing weeks of the war. Born in Massachusetts, Daniel Ruggles had married a Virginia woman and settled in the Fredericksburg area. At one point Mortimer Ruggles had served as an aide on his father's staff. By the closing days of the war all three men had wound up with Mosby.

On hearing the men had served with Mosby, Herold brightened up. Here were men who could be trusted. "I will tell you something," he said. "We are the assassinators of the President. That man sitting there is John Wilkes Booth."[29] Herold had gotten their attention. They now looked hard at him and his "brother" sitting on the pier. Herold said they needed help. They wanted to cross the river and needed a place to stay. Could the soldiers help? The man still on horseback was listening intently as Herold spoke. The two younger men turned toward the officer as if looking for a sign. He gave it with an approving nod of his head. They would help.

It was near noon when the ferry started back across the river from the Port Royal side. A free Black named James Thornton operated it. Reaching the Port Conway side, Thornton looped a restraining rope around one of the posts sunk deep into the bank of the river. Ruggles gave up his mount to Booth and climbed up behind Bainbridge. Herold rode double behind Jett.[30] There was a sixth passenger on Thornton's ferry whom most authors have overlooked. His name was Enoch Mason, and he had served as a courier in King George County with the Fifteenth Virginia Cavalry.[31]

Mason lived not too far south of Dr. Stuart's summer home at Cleydael. Like Ruggles, Jett, and Bainbridge, Mason was traveling south away from his home in King George County. Jett apparently wanted to go to Bowling Green to visit with Izora Gouldman, the daughter of Henry Gouldman, who operated the Star Hotel in Bowling Green. Jett had interests in Izora that would eventually fade away. But for now he wanted very much to see her. Bainbridge was on his way to visit the Clarke family, whose son Joseph had served with him during the war. Ruggles was apparently following his two younger comrades. Mason later claimed that he was going to Bowling Green to try and buy a wagon. The sale was never consummated, and he returned north of the Rappahannock two days later on the twenty-sixth.[32] While the presence of these four Confederate soldiers in the area was not suspect, the direction they were traveling was. All four lived north of the Rappahannock, not south. Was it possible they had been detailed from Mosby to King George to look for the assassins of Lincoln and proffer whatever help they could?

Mason's presence at this crucial time has led the authors of *Come Retribution* to speculate about his actions. They suggest that Mason might have been reporting to his contacts at Milford Station where the Confederacy operated a telegraph that was still operational and guarded by the remnants of the Ninth Virginia Cavalry.[33] If Booth and Herold were being handled under orders from Confederate sources, word of their movement needed to be known. Mason was just one of the many little informational dots that filled the landscape covering Booth's escape.

The ferry with its six passengers landed on the Port Royal side of the river around two o'clock. The sun would be setting in a little over four hours and Booth needed a place to stay.[34] Jett suggested they try the home of Randolph Peyton and his two sisters, who lived in a large house only two blocks from the ferry slip. Jett knew the family, or perhaps most important, the family knew Jett.[35]

Arriving at the house, Jett found the two sisters, Sarah Jane and Lucy

Peyton, alone. Their brother Randolph was away on business. Sarah Jane and Lucy were both spinsters. Jett told the ladies about the two soldiers from Maryland. They were good Confederate men. One of the men was recovering from a wound received at Petersburg. Could they spend the night at their house and rest? At first the ladies felt obliged and thought it would be all right, but looking the two men over had second thoughts. They demurred, explaining to Jett their brother Randolph was away and not expected to return for another day. It would not be appropriate to have two strange men, even though they may be Confederate soldiers, stay the night in the spinsters' home. Jett accepted their reasoning.

Returning to where the men were waiting astride their horses, he told them they would have to move on. He knew of two other possibilities. Just down the road was the farmhouse of Richard Garrett; failing that, there was Gouldman's hotel farther along in Bowling Green. Jett knew of Richard Garrett, having seen him at the courthouse while on duty in the area. The Garretts were a hospitable family. Jett felt sure the two men would be welcome at their place.

The five of them passed through the few remaining houses along the road toward Bowling Green and headed south in the direction of Garrett's farm. It was now close to three o'clock on the afternoon of April 24. Booth and Herold had been on the run for ten days. They would soon have to run no more. Their journey was nearing its end.

CHAPTER SEVENTEEN

The Cavalry Arrives

> The Major-General commanding directs that you detail twenty-five men, well mounted, to be commanded by a reliable and discreet commissioned officer, to report at once to Col. L.C. Baker.
>
> *Lieutenant A.R. Sewall*

U.S. highway 301 passes over the Rappahannock River not more than a hundred yards from where the old ferry ran between Port Conway and Port Royal. Vestiges of the original site remain as a boat ramp on the Port Royal side where local sportsmen can float their boats onto the gently meandering river. The village of Port Royal gives the modern-day traveler the appearance of a mini-Williamsburg waiting to happen. Old wood-frame homes, their brick chimneys slowly crumbling, sit as dying symbols of an earlier, more prosperous era. Many of the homes appear abandoned.

Three miles south of Port Royal the median strip of the divided highway broadens to a point where two hundred feet of dense underbrush and scrub pine separate the northbound and southbound lanes. The site sits out in the middle of nowhere, identifiable only by a state highway marker whose black letters have slowly faded to a dull gray.

On special Saturdays in the spring and fall of each year a large bus pulls off of the highway and empties its cargo of avid enthusiasts onto the gravel shoulder of the northbound lane. With its leader in front, the line of people snakes its way through the underbrush to the center of the median strip. There is a heightened anticipation among the group as they carefully step through the tall grass. The leader cautions his followers to walk with care, looking out for stickers and other nasty weeds. Arriving at a small clearing the people gather around an old iron pipe sticking a few inches above the ground. Attached to the top of the pipe is a small plastic sleeve. Inside the sleeve is a card containing the following words: “Exact northeast corner of the Garrett farmhouse as ascertained by Bob Bergantino. The Garrett farmhouse fell in on itself in the late-1930’s. This stake courtesy of the Surratt Society.”

Invariably the group falls silent as it senses the history that played out here. A woman, in her forties, clutches a small locket suspended from a chain around her neck. Inside the locket is a picture of John Wilkes Booth. She has followed his footsteps into every nook and cranny of his short, infamous life. Such is the strange and bizarre fascination this story holds.

The stake marks the site of the farmhouse of Richard Garrett. Here in the first hours of dawn on April 26, 1865, John Wilkes Booth died, twelve days after murdering the president of United States. Both men died unaware of their killer. Both men gained immortality because of their deaths. John Wilkes Booth's death brought an end to a tragic period in American history and marked the beginning of another.

When the three Confederate soldiers and their two companions arrived at Richard Garrett's farm on the afternoon of April 24 it was just after three o'clock. Willie Jett once again assumed the roll of sponsor. Jett asked the elder Garrett if the two soldiers could rest for a day or two at his house before pushing on. The lame man, James Boyd, had been injured at Petersburg in the closing moments before that city was abandoned. He was tired and worn out from his wound. The old man did not hesitate. Of course the man could stay, and he would be welcome to the hospitality of a Virginia gentleman and his house. Jett was much obliged and thanked Garrett. He and his friends would leave now along with the injured man's companion, but they would return the next morning. They had other business to attend to. The four men returned to the main road and headed south toward Bowling Green, leaving Booth standing on the porch.

The four men had traveled three miles when they came to a small log building located just off of the road to Bowling Green. Known locally as the Trap, it was run by a woman named Carter, who had four daughters. Mrs. Carter and the four Carter sisters had a reputation in the area that attracted men. Today was no exception. The four men dismounted and spent the next hour or so "visiting" with the Carter sisters while Mother Carter provided the drinks. Having finished their business, the four men continued on their journey to Bowling Green.[1] The passing dalliance would ultimately prove fatal to Booth and Herold.

Shortly after sundown the men arrived at the Star Hotel in Bowling Green where Jett and Ruggles decided to rest for the night. Herold and Bainbridge continued on past Bowling Green to the farm of Mrs. Virginia Clarke where they stayed the night.[2] Back at the Garrett house Booth was displaying his usual charm by entertaining the Garretts and Miss Lucinda Hollaway, Mrs. Garrett's sister. Lucinda was a schoolteacher whose intellect was the perfect foil for the handsome houseguest. Booth's spirits were buoyed. Making use of a pillow provided by the elder Garrett, Booth had slept for several hours. When he awoke, he felt invigorated.[3] The throbbing in his leg had subsided appreciably. Things were beginning to look up.

Tuesday morning dawned bright and shiny. Spring was in the air and nowhere was it more beautiful than in Virginia. The redbud trees were covered with deep pink blossoms, which formed a showy contrast against the white sprays of the sarvis trees. The usual sharp chill of early spring had been replaced by a balmy freshness.[4] The air was filled with the smell of moist earth and floral renewal. Booth felt better than he had felt in nearly two weeks. It was the first night he had slept in a bed, dry and comfortable, since he stayed at Dr. Mudd's nine days earlier.

Coming up the road on their return from Bowling Green were Davy Herold and his two friends from Mosby's command. Ruggles was in the lead with Herold and Bainbridge in the rear. Willie Jett had decided to stay on in Bowling Green and court the sixteen-year-old Izora Gouldman. The fighting was over, and it was time to return to loving. Booth sat on the Garrett porch watching the three men slowly ride up the lane toward the house. He hallooed to the men, and young Davy hallooed back. Davy could tell Booth felt better, and that made him feel better. Bainbridge pulled up to the porch, where Herold slid off his mount and joined Booth on the porch as the four men shook hands one last time. Booth thanked the soldiers and "God blessed" them once again as they rode out toward the main gate and turned in the direction of Port Royal. Things were indeed looking better.

It was late afternoon when Ruggles and Bainbridge approached the village of Port Royal. As they made their way over the top of the hill they could see the small village before them. Off in the distance they could just make out the ferry barge in the middle of the river. Ruggles pulled up abruptly. Along the shore near the ferry slip he could make out what looked like several horses and men. The ferry barge was also loaded with horses and men. The two soldiers stared hard. Sure enough, there before their eyes was a troop of Union cavalry: twenty or thirty horsemen. The two horsemen instinctively turned around and, pressing their spurs into the flanks of their mounts, began racing back in the direction of the Garrett farm.

The troopers, under the command of Lieutenant Edward P. Doherty, consisted of a select group chosen from the Sixteenth New York Cavalry stationed in Washington. Joining Doherty and his men were two former army officers, Luther B. Baker and Everton J. Conger. Baker and Conger had served in the First District of Columbia Cavalry and had mustered out early in 1865, joining the staff of Colonel Lafayette C. Baker as members of the organization he called the National Detective Police. The Sixteenth New York was serving as part of the Defenses of Washington under the Twenty-second Army Corps. For much of the last two years of the war they scouted throughout much of northern Virginia and Loudoun County on the trail of the elusive Mosby. Their service was not wholly without combat, however, having lost twenty-one men in battle. How this particular detachment of troopers came to be so close to the two fugitives on the twenty-fifth is an ironic tale in itself. Like so many of the incidents in this greatest of all manhunts, it began on a false premise.

On Monday, April 24, as Charley Lucas brought his wagon up to the ferry slip at Port Conway, a strange turn of events was taking place in Washington. The War Department telegraph office was located on the first floor of the War Department building near the east wing of the White House. To Lincoln, it was the war room, center of all information. On the morning of April 24, with Booth still at large, Lafayette Baker was visiting Major Thomas Eckert at the telegraph office. Eckert, who was in charge of the office, had been going through the night's telegrams looking for news from Sherman, who was closing in on Confederate general Joe Johnston in North Carolina. While Baker and Eckert were talking, a telegram was received from the Federal station at Chapel Point in Charles County.[5] It was close to 11:00 A.M. Major James R. O'Beirne, provost marshal of Washington, had taken several men and headed for Charles County, where he was scouring the coastal area looking for information about Booth and Herold. O'Beirne interviewed one of the local farmers who told him that his son had seen two men crossing the Potomac River on Sunday morning, April 16. O'Beirne assumed the two men had to be Booth and Herold. It was, of course, a case of mistaken identity. Booth and Herold were at that time safely tucked away in the pine thicket under the watchful eye of Thomas Jones. They would not attempt to cross the Potomac for four more days. The men crossing the river on Sunday, April 16, were in all probability Thomas Harbin and Joseph Baden. James Owens, an employee at the Newport Tavern, located near the mouth of the Wicomico River, admitted to his interrogators two days after Booth was killed that he rowed Harbin and Baden across the Potomac River on April 16.[6] Owens's information came too late.

Eckert handed the telegram to Baker. Baker read the telegram and immediately headed for Stanton's office located in the same building. Stanton and Baker conferred. It seemed clear to both men that it was Booth and Herald who slipped across the Potomac to Virginia. Stanton had no doubt that the two men who left Mudd's house Saturday evening were Booth and Herald. It would have taken them until Sunday morning to reach the river. It made good sense. This was the first positive piece of evidence to come into Stanton's office since Lovett brought news of Booth and Herold's being at Dr. Mudd's.

Stanton immediately wrote out an order to General Augur, who already had sent elements of the Thirteenth New York Cavalry off to lower Maryland and Bryantown.[7] Stanton told Augur to provide Baker with twenty-five troopers, an officer, and a vessel to transport the men down the Potomac to Belle Plaine on the Virginia side of the river where they could begin the search for Booth and Herold. While the sighting was a week old, it was the first definite news the military had in their search. Dana and his men would remain in Bryantown, their chance having slipped away days earlier when Booth and Herold were holed up at Mudd's house.

The man Stanton entrusted this latest information to was one of the war's most notorious characters. Lafayette C. Baker's past was shrouded in confusion due to his penchant for lying. He had served as provost marshal of the War Department, colonel of the First District of Columbia Cavalry, and finally, under the title "Agent, War Department." Baker soon gained the confidence of both Stanton and Seward and served as head of his small investigative unit, the National Detective Police. Later he referred to this unit as the United States Secret Service.[8] Baker himself did not ride after Booth. He would entrust that task to his closest confidants. The man Baker would hand pick to command his posse was a combat veteran, Colonel Everton Judson Conger. Baker had picked Conger from among several officers in the Veteran Reserve Corps to take command of the chief's own regiment, the First District of Columbia Cavalry.[9]

Although Baker was the commanding officer of the First District of Columbia Cavalry, he rarely was with the regiment. Command devolved to Conger, and when Baker was told he could have twenty-six troopers from the Sixteenth New York, he wanted one of his own men in charge, if only nominally. He selected Everton Conger. Conger was a battle-tested veteran, having served in the West Virginia Third Cavalry where he had twice been wounded; later, with the First District of Columbia Cavalry, he received a third, more serious wound. While on a cavalry raid near Richmond on June 24, 1864, Conger was shot in the hip.[10] He was returned to Washington where he convalesced. When he was finally recovered, Baker assigned Conger to his office with the National Detective Police. Conger was a competent, no-nonsense soldier whose record showed numerous successes. Baker had picked the best man in his office to accompany the Sixteenth New York in its pursuit of Booth.

Baker had summoned Lieutenant Edward P. Doherty of the Sixteenth New York Cavalry to his office along with Conger. Doherty would be in immediate command of the twenty-six troopers assigned from the Sixteenth New York. To this group Baker would add his cousin Luther B. Baker. In calling on Doherty, Baker wanted to introduce Conger to him and go over their instructions.

When Baker first learned that Booth was the assassin, he commandeered the photographic facilities of the surgeon general's office. During the early hours of Saturday, April 15, he had several photographs of Booth reproduced for distribution to his agents. Just which image of Booth—and how it came into the hands of the military searching for him—has been the cause of confusion among several writers. Baker's use of the surgeon general's photographic facilities is learned from a letter written by Assistant Surgeon General Charles H. Crane that survives today in a private collection. In his letter Crane writes, "We still have hope that the murderer Booth will be captured. I send you his picture. We had a number struck off in our "gallery" last Saturday [April 15] to distribute throughout the country."[11] The "gallery" was the name of the surgeon general's photographic facility, and the picture Crane included with his letter is a particular image known today as "Gutman No. 35." The photograph had been taken by the Boston firm of Silsbee, Case and Company as one of two views shot during the same sitting. It subsequently became known as the "wanted poster view" because it was used on several of the wanted posters put out by the government.[12]

Now that he had Stanton's approval, Baker called Conger, Lieutenant Doherty, and Captain Joseph Schneider of the Sixteenth New York into his office to go over the search party's instructions and give the men photographs of Booth to be used in the search. Captain Schneider later stated, "I saw Captain Doherty[13] have some circulars and photographs in his hands."[14] These were the images Baker had made in the surgeon general's "gallery" and were carried by Conger and the Sixteenth New York as it searched for Booth.

In 1937, historian Otto Eisenschiml was the first to suggest Lincoln's murder was a great conspiracy involving Stanton and Baker. Among his many misleading claims, Eisenschiml wrote that the photographs used by the prosecutors at the trial of the conspirators and those distributed to the search party were not of John Wilkes Booth. In examining the trial exhibits located in the War Department files at the time of his research, Eisenschiml discovered a photograph of Edwin Booth in place of John Wilkes Booth. Eisenschiml concluded erroneously that Stanton and Baker had engineered a photographic switch giving Conger and Doherty a copy of Edwin Booth's photograph instead of his brother John. The purpose of this devious switch, according to Eisenschiml, was to confuse identification efforts, thus allowing Booth time to escape. Crane's letter belies Eisenschiml's claim and confirms subsequent research that has shown that the picture carried by Conger and Doherty was a picture of John Wilkes Booth and not of his brother Edwin.[15]

Shortly after sundown on Monday, April 24, troopers from the Sixteenth New York Cavalry boarded the steamer *John S. Ide.* Accompanying the soldiers were Conger, Baker, and Doherty. The men safely aboard, the steamer headed down the Potomac forty miles to an abandoned military base known as Belle Plaine located near the western boundary of King George County, Virginia. Belle Plaine was only twelve miles as the crow flies from Port Conway. The men were unloaded at 10:00 P.M. and headed south toward the Rappahannock River. On reaching the river, they swung east toward Port Conway.[16] They began beating on doors and dragging bewildered residents from their house at gunpoint. Two men—one lame—were they here? Talk! The tactics were frightening. They were meant to be. The troopers were tired, hungry, and in enemy territory. Rebels had murdered their president. They were not interested in clever interrogation tactics. The local people were not about to risk their lives or their homes to protect two fugitives on the run. It was not hard to get the truth.

At one point the party separated into two groups to facilitate covering the area. The two posses came together again at Port Conway just before noon on Tuesday morning, April 25. Here they found William Rollins tending his nets. Conger had arrived first and had taken the opportunity to take a short nap before the others arrived. He was exhausted and suffering from his old wounds. Just before reaching Port Conway, Doherty and Baker had questioned Dick Wilson, the free Black who had helped Rollins with his fish nets when Booth and Herold were trying to negotiate their way across the river. Wilson had seen two men fitting Baker's description the day before. Doherty and Baker had one of the troopers wake Conger. Now the three men squared off at William Rollins.

Intimidated by the cavalrymen, Rollins talked freely. Two men had crossed the river the afternoon before. Yes, one was lame. Baker showed Rollins a photograph of Booth. The injured man looked like the one in the photograph. Rollins had noticed one difference, however. The man who crossed on the ferry did not have a moustache.[17] One other point Rollins made. The two civilians had crossed over on the ferry with some Confederate soldiers. One was a fellow named Willie Jett. Did Rollins know where they were headed? No, he didn't.[18] Then Rollins's young wife entered into the conversation. Bettie Rollins knew that Jett was "sparking" the Gouldmans' young daughter, Izora.[19] Gouldman operated the Star Hotel in Bowling Green. Conger was told that if he wanted to find Willie Jett he might look for Izora Gouldman. Izora was a very pretty girl. Jett had probably already forgotten about the war and the two men.

Conger told Rollins to get his horse. He would have to guide them to Bowling Green. Rollins hesitated. He told Conger he would do it, of course, but could Conger make it look like he was under arrest. Rollins had to be careful of his neighbors. Helping Yankees was not something he wanted to show on his resume. Conger agreed. Just get the damn horse and hurry. The troopers sensed they were getting close. On Monday morning they were five days behind Booth and Herold, now it appeared they were less than a day behind. They were closing the gap and Conger could smell success.

Conger put three troopers in Rollins's boat and told them to cross the river and bring the ferry back over. Within thirty minutes the ferry was back on the Port Conway side of the river. It took five complete passes, totaling three hours, before all twenty-six troopers and their horses could be carried over to the Port Royal side. The time was costly, and Conger and his comrades were impatient. As each contingent was unloaded it collected its horses and sat waiting for the next load. Doherty had instructed his sergeant, Boston Corbett, to wait on the far side of the river and keep the men together after they had crossed. This was the scene that Ruggles and Bainbridge saw as they crested the hill leading into Port Royal. Blue bellies and lots of them. The two Confederates were savvy soldiers. It was a search party, no doubt about it. The puzzling question is why Ruggles and Bainbridge risked their paroles to return and warn Booth. It could have cost the Confederates dearly.

When the last load of men and horses made their way across the river, the troopers mounted up and started south toward Bowling Green. As Doherty and Baker headed up the long rise that led out of the village they noticed two horsemen standing on the crest of the hill in the far distance. They appeared for only a few seconds, then quickly vanished behind the horizon.[20]

Ruggles and Bainbridge had come dangerously close to riding into the Sixteenth New York as it rode out of Port Royal. Turning back, the two Confederates reached the Garret place where they found Booth relaxing on the porch. Ruggles wasted no time in alerting Booth of the approaching troopers, then headed out at a gallop. Booth's pleasant demeanor quickly changed. Yankee cavalry had ruined his day. The two men were on their own now. Ruggles had done all he could. Booth and Herold gathered themselves up and headed toward the wooded area as Jack Garrett watched in puzzlement. The two strangers seemed excited.

Another thirty minutes and the young Garrett knew why. The Sixteenth New York came riding toward the Garrett farm, dust flying everywhere. Reaching the far end of the lane that led from the main road to the house, the posse continued riding past. Within a few minutes they were gone, leaving only clouds of dust in their wake. Garrett turned around and looked over toward the woods where he saw Davy Herold slowly emerge from the underbrush. The young man turned and motioned for his "brother" to come out of the woods. The two men slowly made their way back to the front porch where a suspicious Jack Garrett was standing.

Watching the two make their way back toward the house, Jack Garrett started to have a bad feeling about his father's houseguests. Booth was especially anxious to be taken to Orange Court House, which lay approximately fifty miles west of the Garrett place.[21] Jack Garrett had led Booth to believe he would take him there the next day, but he was now becoming increasingly wary of the two men after seeing their reaction to the Yankee cavalry galloping past. Garrett began to suspect foul play. Fearing the two men might steal the Garretts' horses during the night, Garrett told them they would have to sleep in the tobacco barn. He said that if the Yankees were to catch the pair inside his father's house, they might well burn it to the ground. Garrett was not making up a lame excuse. The Yankees might well burn the house if the two Confederate fugitives were found hiding in it. Booth agreed. He had little choice. He and Herold would bed down in the tobacco barn. To make sure they would stay there, the Garret brothers placed a lock on the barn door and decided to sleep in a corncrib nearby, taking turns watching the barn.[22]

About three miles south of Garrett's the troopers came to the Trap. The men reined up and Conger, Baker, and Doherty went inside. They found the Carter ladies inside. Baker began questioning them but was having little luck. The Carter ladies were not very communicative. Loose talk could seriously hurt their business. They had no personal grudge against Yankees. In fact, the better part of business was color-blind. Blue or gray, it didn't matter, but it wasn't a lady's place to talk about her clients. Then the wiley Conger decided to try a ploy. He explained that the reason they wanted to find these men and arrest them had nothing to do with the war. It seems one of the men had beaten and raped a young girl. It was an outrage that could not go unpunished. Conger hit a nerve. It was indeed an outrage.[23]

The Carter ladies loosened up. Yes, four soldiers had visited them the day before on their way home. But none of the men appeared to be lame. To be sure, they all could walk just fine, even with their boots off. One of the men lived locally, a young man named Willie Jett. He was one of the four. They didn't know where they were headed except in the direction of Bowling Green. There had been a reference to a Mrs. Clarke (Baker thought the name was "Graham").[24] Perhaps some of the party might be at her house. The ladies then said that three of the men had returned the next day heading toward Port Royal. Willie Jett, however, was not one of them. The men thanked the ladies and went back outside. A brief discussion followed. Should they return to Port Royal and retrace their steps or continue on to Bowling Green. It wasn't clear if Booth had been to the Trap or not. Doherty wanted to continue on. Jett had been at the Trap for certain. Doherty's reasoning was that even if Booth had not accompanied Jett and the others to the Trap, Jett would know where Booth was. A bird in the hand was worth two in the bush. Doherty's argument won. The men agreed to go to the Star Hotel where they hoped to find Jett.[25]

It was near midnight when the Sixteenth New York approached the small village of Bowling Green. A half mile outside of town the troopers stopped. Baker and Doherty along with ten or eleven troopers dismounted. Conger remained on his horse. The rest of the unit stayed with the horses. Arriving at the hotel on foot, the troopers quietly surrounded the building with orders to make sure no one escaped. With their weapons drawn, the three officers climbed the wooden steps of the porch and began pounding on the hotel door. Getting no response, Conger and Doherty walked around to the rear of the house where they found a Black man. Doherty asked the man where Willie Jett could be found. The man said that Jett was in bed in the hotel. Conger then inquired where the room was located. Doherty next pounded on the rear door. Within a few minutes a woman opened the door. It was the proprietor's wife, Mrs. Gouldman. She escorted the two men into a front parlor. Doherty asked where her son was sleeping. She led the men to an upstairs bedroom where her son and Jett were sleeping together in a bed. Rousing Jett from his sleep, the men took him back downstairs and began questioning him.[26]

The eighteen-year-old Willie Jett did not need any coaxing. He knew the game was up. Jett asked Conger if he could speak to him privately. Doherty and Baker agreed to leave the room. Jett was willing to cooperate with the search party. Like Rollins, though, he was afraid to give the appearance of cooperating with Yankees. He told Doherty that the men they were looking for were holed up at a farmhouse up the road on the way to Port Royal. He would lead him there but did not want to appear to be a willing accomplice. Conger obliged. Jett was allowed to go back upstairs and get dressed before joining the troopers.

CHAPTER EIGHTEEN

Tell Mother I Die for My Country

Poor Booth, to think that he fell at last. Many a true heart in the South weeps for his death.

Kate Stone

The cavalrymen waiting in front of the hotel were slumped in their saddles, half of them asleep. They had been riding for over twelve hours without rest. Cavalrymen knew how to sleep astride a horse. It was something they learned early in the war. Their brief respite was suddenly broken when the three officers came out of the hotel with Willie Jett in tow. The four men mounted their horses and the troop started back in the direction of Port Royal. Richard Garrett's farm was located ten miles to the north of Bowling Green. They would backtrack to the Garretts' with Jett leading the way.

When the troop arrived at the lane leading into Garretts' place, Doherty gave the signal to pull up. Conger and Baker took Jett and proceeded ahead of the column so as not to alert anyone to their presence. On reaching the gate that blocked the lane leading up to the farmhouse, the men dismounted and waited for Doherty and the rest of the men to come up. The three men conferred briefly and Doherty gave the signal for his men to split into two groups and surround the house. Doherty then told his men to draw their pistols and proceed carefully. Booth and Herold were believed to be in the farmhouse.[1] Jett and William Rollins were left under guard at the gate. It was a few minutes after 2:00 A.M., Wednesday morning. The scene was cast in total darkness. The moon was new and at its lowest illumination of the month. The darkness favored the prey more than it did the predator.[2]

Doherty tethered his horse to a tree as Conger and Baker climbed the steps leading to the porch. They began pounding heavily on the front door. After several minutes the door opened, revealing the dim light of a candle. An old man peered through a crack in the door. He started to ask the men what they wanted. Before he could get the words out of his mouth he was rudely grabbed by the front of his nightshirt and dragged outside.

"Where are the men that were here today?" One of the soldiers barked.

The old man was flustered and shaken. He said that the men who had been there had gone to the woods.

"Liar!" someone barked back. "Where are they?"

Richard Garrett could do little more than stammer. One of the officers yelled to the soldiers who were waiting near their mounts. "Bring a rope, hang the damned old rebel and we will find the men afterwards. We'll stretch the truth out him." Baker yelled to no one in particular.[3]

As one of the men prepared to toss a rope over the branch of a large locust tree in the front of the house, Jack Garrett stepped forward. He had been sleeping in the corncrib while his brother kept watch over the two men in the barn. Hearing the commotion at the house he came over to see what was the matter. He had feared that the two men had gotten out of the barn and were trying to steal the Garretts' horses. When he saw the Yankee cavalry he knew there was trouble. His poor father stood trembling in his nightshirt, about to be strung up from a tree in the front yard. Garrett suddenly realized the two fugitives were something more than they had let on. The suspicions that had caused him earlier to padlock the two men inside the tobacco barn were verified.

With the Yankee cavalry in his front yard, Jack Garrett had more to worry about than his father's house being torched. His father was about to be strung up. He had to act quickly. "Wait!" He hollered. "I will tell you what you want to know." Garrett tried to free his father from the cavalryman's grip. "Don't injure father," Jack said. "The men you want are in the tobacco barn."[4] Conger quickly motioned to Doherty, who waved his men toward the barn not more than a hundred feet from the house. Garrett's youngest son, William, now appeared and Baker told him to get the key to the barn. The younger Garrett returned with the key. Baker grabbed the candle from the old man and told William Garrett to come with him.[5] The two men approached the barn door, and Baker told Garrett to unlock it and go inside and get the arms from the two men. Garrett balked, saying they would shoot him if he went in. Baker was unsympathetic, telling Garrett if he didn't go in *he* would shoot him.

After a few minutes Garrett came back out, visibly shaken. He said the man had refused to give up his arms and had ordered him out or he would shoot him.[6] Booth next tried to finesse the situation by engaging Baker in conversation. Baker would have none of it, telling Booth that he must surrender or the barn would be set on fire. Booth requested time "for reflection": "Captain, that's rather rough. I am nothing but a cripple, I have but one leg, and you ought to give me a chance for a fair fight."[7] Baker relented. He gave Booth five minutes to come out.[8] Booth was trapped and he knew it. There was no chance for him to slip out and get to the woods as he had done earlier in the day. The barn was completely surrounded.

After a few minutes had gone by, Booth called to Baker that Herold wanted to surrender. "Captain, there is a man in here who wants to surrender." Baker told him to come out and to bring his weapon. Booth replied, "He has no arms, they are all mine." Herold was now banging against the door, calling to be let out. Baker opened the door slowly, and as soon as Herold emerged he was hustled off by two guards who bound him securely to a tree near the house. Years later Richard Baynham Garrett, the youngest of Richard Garrett's five children, would describe the scene he witnessed as a young man: "The poor little wretch was dragged away, whining and crying like a child, and securely bound to a tree in the yard. . . . He kept up his whimpering until the Captain had to order him gagged."[9]

Baker continued the pressure on Booth. He gave him two more minutes. Booth answered, "Well Captain, you may prepare a stretcher for me. Throw open your door, draw up your men in a line, and let's have a fair fight."[10] Conger had heard enough. He grabbed a small shock of hay and, lighting it, thrust it into a pile of brush that the men had piled against the rear wall of the barn.[11] The fire spread rapidly, shooting across the dried straw that covered the floor of the barn and lapping up the walls on either side. The fire illuminated the inside of the building. Booth could be clearly seen by peering through the open slats in the side of the barn. He was leaning on one crutch, the butt of the Spencer carbine resting against one hip. In his other hand he held a Colt revolver.

The fire spread rapidly and black smoke rose up the walls and rolled across the ceiling. Booth began to feel the intense heat building inside the barn. At first he looked around as if assessing the situation, somewhat bewildered. He moved toward the door that opened slightly so that his movements could be observed. He was ten feet from the door, a rifle in one hand, revolver in the other. One crutch had fallen at his feet. Suddenly a shot was heard. Booth threw up his hands in a reflex reaction, then fell to the floor of the barn. For several seconds everyone stood frozen, stunned at what had happened. Then Baker rushed into the barn and knelt over the motionless Booth. Conger soon followed, and the two men dragged Booth outside and laid him under a locust tree not far from the door.

The crowd of soldiers fell back to avoid the heat of the raging fire. Conger ordered two men to carry Booth to the house, where he was laid out on the front porch. A small straw mattress had been taken from the house and laid on the porch floor. Conger, Baker, and Doherty knelt around the prostrate body as several of the cavalrymen pressed close to see the infamous murderer of their president. Booth was still alive, although his wound appeared fatal. He was paralyzed from the neck down and felt no pain. In fact, he could feel nothing. The bullet had struck him in the neck and passed through a cervical vertebra, severing part of the spinal cord. Baker thought he heard Booth utter the word "water." He attempted to give him some water by dipping a rag in a cup and placing it in his mouth. It was of little use. Booth then muttered, "Kill me." Baker told him that he didn't want to kill him. Conger gave orders for two of the men to hurry to Port Royal and find a doctor.[12] Every effort must be made to save Booth's life.

The man who shot Booth was Sergeant Boston Corbett. He had fired a single shot through an open slat with his Colt revolver, striking Booth in the side of the neck. He claimed to have been no more than twelve feet from where Booth was standing:[13] "I immediately took steady aim upon him with my revolver and fired—shooting him through the neck and head."[14] Contrary to common belief, it was not against orders. Conger made that clear when he underwent questioning by his superiors the next day: "They had no orders either to fire or not to fire."[15]

Corbett's act would become part of the stuff that conspiracies are made of. It would be repeated over and over that Corbett carried secret orders from Edwin Stanton to make sure Booth could never talk or tell his story. Too many people would be dragged down if Booth had been allowed to live, they whispered. Some would say Conger shot Booth and that Corbett agreed to take the fall. Still others would claim Booth shot himself, committing suicide before he could be dragged back to Washington and exhibited like some crazy animal. All are wrong. Boston Corbett was telling the truth. He did shoot Booth—and with reason, although not everyone can accept his reasoning. He would later testify during the conspiracy trial: "It was not through fear at all that I shot him, but because it was my impression that it was time the man was shot; for I thought he would do harm to our men in trying to fight his way through that den if I did not."[16]

Shortly after dawn Dr. Charles Urquhart arrived from Port Royal. Booth was still alive, although barely. Urquhart carefully examined Booth and then informed the three officers that it was hopeless. Booth could not live much longer. The paralysis was shutting down most of his vital functions. Soon it would shut him down completely. Even though paralysis had stilled his respiratory muscles, Booth's breathing continued—slow and labored—through the use of his diaphragm.[17] As the men stood about watching his lifeless form, Booth opened his eyes. Conger noticed his lips quiver slightly. He was trying to speak. He knelt down, placing his ear close to Booth's lips. The words came haltingly, "Tell . . . my . . . Mother . . . I . . . die . . . for my country." Conger repeated the words, asking Booth if that is what he said. He signaled, "Yes."[18]

It was a few minutes past seven o'clock when Booth died. He died from asphyxia; he was literally out of breath. A Rochester newspaper graphically described the moment: "As he began to die, the sun rose and threw beams into the treetops. It was of a man's height when the struggle of death twitched and flickered in the fading bravo's face. His jaw drew spasmodically and obliquely downward; his eyeballs rolled toward his feet, and began to swell; lividness, like a horrible shadow, fastened upon him, and, with a sort of gurgle and sudden check, he stretched his feet and threw his head back and gave up the ghost."[19]

It was twelve days since the night of April 14 when he had entered the box of Ford's Theatre and ended the life of Abraham Lincoln. Not everyone in the country believed that Lincoln ascended into heaven and Booth into hell. Large numbers believed it was the other way around.[20]

Luther Baker took an old army blanket from behind his saddle and gave it to two of the men on the porch. Booth's body was placed in the blanket and the blanket sewn tight. Wrapped in the makeshift shroud, the body was placed in the back of an old farm wagon that Baker had commandeered from a local Black farmer named Ned Freeman. Freeman had been hired by Baker to take the body in his wagon back up to Belle Plain, where the *John S. Ide* was waiting.

Before the body was placed in the blanket, however, Conger carefully went through all of the pockets. He removed the little memorandum book which Booth used as a diary, a small stickpin with the inscription "Dan Bryant to J.W.B.," a bill of exchange (No. 1492, dated October 27, 1864) drawn on the Ontario Bank of Canada and made out to J. Wilkes Booth for 61 pounds, 12 shillings, and 10 pence. Conger looked at the bank draft and then wrote his initials on the back for future identification purposes. In the little memorandum book were five small photographs of women: four actresses and Booth's alleged fiancée, Lucy Lambert Hale, the daughter of former senator John Parker Hale of New Hampshire.[21] Also in Booth's pocket was the small-boxed compass that Thomas Jones had given to him at the time of the Potomac River crossing. Conger also removed a small file with a cork on one end, a small pipe, and a spur. Along with the personal items were the two Colt revolvers, a Spencer carbine, and Booth's large knife marked "Rio Grande Camp Knife." Conger took the personal items and wrapped them in a piece of paper that he tied with a string.

Conger told Corbett to mount up, and the two men headed back to Port Royal ahead of the rest of the command. From Port Royal they made their way back to Belle Plaine where Conger hailed the steamer *Keyport* to carry him back to Washington. Corbett remained behind at Belle Plaine to await the cavalry. Conger wanted to report directly to Stanton without delay. Herold and the two Garrett brothers would follow under the watchful guard of the cavalrymen.[22]

Soon after Conger and Corbett had left, Baker started out alongside Ned Freeman's old wagon. In the back lay the body of Booth. Doherty and the rest of his command followed later with Davy Herold in tow protesting along the way that he had met Booth by accident and was completely innocent of whatever the soldiers accused him of. They hadn't accused him of anything yet. That would soon follow.

A corporal and his orderly originally accompanied Baker. Shortly after crossing the Rappahannock River, Baker sent the corporal and orderly back to check on the column of cavalrymen. Neither man returned and Baker continued on toward Belle Plaine with his valuable cargo in Ned Freeman's wagon. Baker reached the river three miles above Belle Plaine and, after hiding the body in the bushes under Freeman's care, set out in search of a boat to carry the body out to the steamer. Finding a boat, Luther Baker rowed the body out to the *Ide* anchored offshore.[23]

The *Ide* made the return trip up the Potomac River to the Washington Navy Yard where the ironclad *Montauk* was moored offshore. On the way up the river Lafayette Baker and Everton Conger met the *Ide* and boarded it. Conger had arrived back in Washington and reported to Stanton, giving him all the details about Booth's capture and death. Stanton had then told Baker to proceed at once and meet the *Ide* and then take custody of Booth's body. Stanton was not about to let it fall into anyone else's hands.

Baker commandeered the *C. Vanderbilt*, a mailboat chartered by the War Department, and along with Conger headed down the Potomac. Somewhere between Belle Plaine and Mount Vernon, Baker intercepted the *Ide* and boarded her along with Conger. The *Ide* then proceeded up the river toward the Navy Yard, making a stop at Alexandria on the way. The military had a telegraph station there that was connected to the War Department. Arriving at Alexandria shortly before 11 P.M., Baker sent a telegram to Eckert informing him of Booth's and Herold's capture and asking Eckert to meet him at the Navy Yard.[24]

With Booth's body now in Baker's custody and Stanton assured that it was safely under his care, Baker instructed the captain of the *Ide* to head for the Navy Yard. At 1:45 A.M. the *Ide* pulled alongside the *Montauk* and transferred its infamous cargo. Booth, still wrapped in his shroud, was placed on a carpenter's bench located on deck beneath a canvas awning. Also aboard the *Montauk* were Lewis Powell, George Atzerodt, Michael O'Laughlen, and Edman Spangler. The man who had put them there had joined them.

Just a few hours earlier, as Luther Baker and Ned Freeman had slowly rumbled along the road to Belle Plaine, a military honor guard swung open the large doors of the state capitol building in Albany, New York. Inside the assembly chamber a flag draped coffin rested in front of the speaker's stand. Inside the coffin lay the body of Abraham Lincoln. Over the next twelve hours fifty thousand people would pass the president's body and bow their heads in reverence. In his first inaugural address Lincoln had declared, "This country, with its institutions, belongs to the people who inhabit it."[25] Four years later, Abraham Lincoln would now belong to the country he preserved and the people who inhabited it.

Part Four

The Aftermath

Whether his name shall be hereafter surrounded with honor or shall go down in posterity in infamy, depends upon the man who writes his history.

Galveston Daily News

CHAPTER NINETEEN

To Remove the Stain of Innocent Blood from the Land

> All persons harboring or secreting the said persons . . . or aiding . . . their concealment or escape, will be treated as accomplices in the murder of the President . . . and shall be subject to trial before a military commission, and the punishment of death.
>
> Edwin M. Stanton

Beginning on April 17 and ending with the death of Booth and the capture of Davy Herold on April 26, nine of the ten individuals charged by the government with conspiracy in Lincoln's murder were in custody.[1] Edman Spangler was the first. Following his arrest early on Monday, April 17, he was placed in the Old Capitol Prison located on the corner of A and First Streets, N.E. Arnold and O'Laughlen were next, also imprisoned on April 17. They were put on board the monitor *Saugus* anchored in the Eastern Branch of the Potomac River near the Navy Yard. Numbers four and five were Mary Surratt and Lewis Powell, both arrested on the night of April 17. Mary Surratt was taken to the Carroll Annex of Old Capitol Prison while Powell joined Arnold and O'Laughlen aboard the *Saugus*. Number six was George Atzerodt. Captured on Thursday, April 20, at his cousin's house in Germantown, Maryland, Atzerodt was placed aboard the monitor *Montauk* and later transferred to the *Saugus*. Number seven was Dr. Mudd. Arrested on April 24, Mudd was put in the Carroll Annex of Old Capitol Prison along with Mary Surratt. The last conspirator arrested was Davy Herold, who was captured on April 26, at the Garrett farm. Herold was placed aboard the *Montauk*, where Atzerodt was also being held at the time. The last of the conspirators taken into custody was John Wilkes Booth. His body was placed aboard the *Montauk*, where it remained until April 27 when it was interred at the Arsenal. Only John Surratt was missing. He was still at large, his hiding place unknown to authorities. He was secure among friends in Canada where he would remain for the next several weeks before being spirited off to Europe.

The accused were charged under the conspiracy laws that existed in 1865. Most historians have acknowledged that the defendants were involved in one way or another with Booth's plan to capture Lincoln, but many believe that only Booth, Powell, Atzerodt, and Herold were involved in the conspiracy to assassinate Lincoln. Put another way, there were two separate conspiracies—one to capture, another to kill. Those who subscribe to this theory believe that Mary Surratt, Samuel Mudd, Edman Spangler, Samuel Arnold, and Michael O'Laughlen were convicted of the wrong crime. This conclusion reflects an uninformed knowledge of the conspiracy laws under which the defendants were tried, and this is irrespective of whether the trial was a military trial or a civil trial.

The conspiracy laws in 1865 differed little from present-day conspiracy laws. The present Federal statute describes a general conspiracy as a crime where "two or more persons conspire . . . to commit any offense against the United States, or to defraud the United States, or any agency thereof in any manner or for any purpose."[2] Since conspiracy involves secrecy and concealment, the law lessens the government's burden of proof in proving the essential elements of the conspiracy.[3] There are four elements that must exist to constitute a conspiracy:

1) An agreement between at least two parties,
2) to achieve an illegal goal,
3) a knowledge of the conspiracy and participation in the conspiracy, and
4) at least one conspirator's commission of an overt act in furtherance of the conspiracy.[4]

Most important to the case of the Lincoln conspirators, a person may be a member of an unlawful conspiracy without knowing all of the details of the conspiracy or even all of the other members. If a person understands the unlawful nature of a plan and willingly joins in the plan, even if only on one occasion, it is sufficient to convict the individual for conspiracy even though that person played only a minor role. The law further states that when a felony has been committed in pursuance of a conspiracy that had as its design only a misdemeanor, the misdemeanor becomes merged into the felony.[5] Simply stated, if the intent of the conspiracy is to kidnap and a homicide occurs as a result of the conspiracy, the crime becomes one of homicide, not kidnapping. The aims of the conspiracy may shift or evolve. This last point is especially important when considering the case of the Lincoln conspirators. Booth's original conspiracy to capture shifted to one of murder.

One other aspect of the law needs to be recognized, and that is the concept of "vicarious liability." This concept states that any one person involved in a conspiracy is liable for the actions of another, even though the first person was not directly responsible for the ultimate actions of the other. And finally, a person may only withdraw from a conspiracy by making a meaningful effort to prevent the conspiracy from ultimately taking place. Having a change of heart and simply walking away from a conspiracy is not sufficient in the eyes of the law to absolve a conspirator.

This law clearly applies to those charged and tried as co-conspirators with John Wilkes Booth in the murder of Abraham Lincoln. While some of the conspirators may have thought they were participating only in a plot to kidnap the president and while others believed they had abandoned the plot, they were still involved in the eyes of the law. The eventual murder of Abraham Lincoln could have been prevented if any of the conspirators had gone to the proper authorities and exposed the plot along with the plotters. No one did.

On May 1, President Johnson issued an executive order directing that the persons charged with Abraham Lincoln's murder stand trial before a military commission. Johnson's order rested on Attorney General James Speed's decision that the accused were "enemy belligerents" and not citizens. Their alleged offenses were military in nature and had a military objective: to adversely affect the war effort of the Northern military. It was a decision that appears to have been more influenced by Stanton than by Speed.

Johnson had assumed the presidency on April 15 at 10:00 A.M., two and a half hours after Lincoln had died. Although Johnson was officially in charge of the Federal government, Stanton continued to control much of its operations. The executive order issued by Johnson establishing the commission was drafted in Stanton's hand and was written on War Department letterhead.[6]

There is little in the documentary record that sheds light on what transpired leading to the decision to try the accused before a military commission, but such a decision seems obvious in hindsight. The District of Columbia was still a city whose native civilian population held strong Southern sympathies. The majority of pro-Union men were in the army. Much of the policing activities in the District were carried out by the military since the District was still operating under martial law.[7] Part of the government's case was aimed directly at Jefferson Davis and members of the Confederate government. Because of the climate in the city, Stanton and his colleagues feared jury nullification. It seems reasonable that this possibility was uppermost in Stanton's mind, as well it should have been.

A military trial would insure that the process would remain in loyal hands under government control—and more important, under Stanton's control. A military trial would not significantly alter the process of law, only the control of the proceedings. A common but mistaken perception dominating the popular literature on the trial is that military law and civil law differed significantly in both administration and rules of evidence. The trial closely followed civil law, and both the prosecution and defense attorneys referred to civil precedent in presenting their respective cases. Objections were made and ruled on according to the civil code then in practice. A total of thirty-four objections were made by the prosecution, with all thirty-four sustained, while fifteen objections were raised by the defense and two being sustained.[8] This disparity is cited by some historians as an indication of bias on behalf of the court but may have simply reflected the differing legal skills of the opposing attorneys.

Military trials were not unique in the country's history, but they reached extraordinarily high numbers during the Civil War. Between 1861 and 1865 thirteen thousand persons were tried before five thousand military commissions. Records are incomplete, but enough exist to give a fair picture of this most unusual practice in jurisprudence.[9] The Civil War was unique in American history, and many illegal acts that did not violate civil law were taking place on a daily basis. For example, it was not against civil law to describe in a letter or dispatch what a person saw concerning numbers of troops, their condition, or their disposition. Transporting various goods from a foreign country to certain states was not a civil offense. Nor was using the U.S. postal system to distribute letters and newspapers from one state to another. But these and other similar acts were very much in violation of military law during time of war.

Not everyone within the inner circle of government was in favor of trying the accused before a military commission. Former Attorney General Edward Bates, Secretary of the Navy Gideon Welles, and Secretary of the Treasury Hugh McCulloch expressed opposition to a military trial. Welles wrote in his diary that he felt the accused should be tried by a civil court, but that Stanton insisted that a military court was the proper authority to try the accused. Attorney General James Speed, after showing ambivalence, agreed with Stanton.[10]

Welles's "regret" seems somewhat less than emphatic. Edward Bates felt more strongly on the issue. Bates did not simply "regret" the action; he thought it unconstitutional. But Bates held most of what Stanton did in low regard and even referred to Stanton's actions as dictatorial.[11] In fact, Bates was a frequent behind-the-scenes critic of many of Lincoln's war-related policies. Bates opposed Lincoln's approval admitting West Virginia as the thirty-fifth state in 1863 as unconstitutional even though the Supreme Court had ruled in 1849 that the Congress and the president had the legal authority to decide which government in a state represented the duly constituted government of that state.[12] Bates based his opposition to a military trial on his beliefs that the accused conspirators were civilians, not members of a military organization, and that their alleged crime was not military in nature. Attorney General James Speed believed differently. He issued a formal opinion that explained his support for a military trial.[13] Speed carefully described the various elements that led him to his conclusion. The president was commander in chief of the military; the city of Washington was a war zone ringed by fortifications manned throughout the war by Federal soldiers; martial law existed in the District of Columbia and, though the civilian courts were open and the civilian police were allowed to function in the usual manner, the principal police authority within the city rested with the military. Most important, however, was Speed's characterization of the accused as "enemy belligerents" whose act was not for personal gain or vengeful malice, but was designed to *thwart the military effort* of the government. As enemy belligerents, the accused not only *could* be tried by a military commission under the law of war, but *must* be tried under military law. It was the nature of the accused as well as the nature of the crime that justified their trial by military commission. Speed differed with Bates in that he did not view the accused as civilians. Subsequent critics of the military commission have sided with Bates, believing the accused were civilians with no ties—directly or indirectly—to any clandestine or military effort by the Confederate government. A strong case can be made, however, linking the accused to various clandestine activities on behalf of the Confederacy, supporting Speed's characterization of them as enemy belligerents.[14]

Speed went on to point out that many of the offenses against the laws of war are not crimes under the civil code, and the framers of the Constitution were precise in their language. They empowered the Congress with the authority to define and punish offenses against the laws of war, and did not use the word *crimes* when referring to such offenses as they did when referring to civil law. Breaking a lawful blockade is considered an offense against the laws of war, but not regarded as a crime in civil court. Similarly, to act as a spy is an offense against the law of war, but it is not a civil crime. To violate a flag of truce is an offense against the laws of war that no civil court can consider as a crime. It was this rationale that Speed used in characterizing the accused as "enemy belligerents."

Two of the defense attorneys, Senator Reverdy Johnson (Democrat, Maryland), counsel for Mary Surratt, and Thomas Ewing, counsel for Samuel Mudd and Samuel Arnold, vigorously protested the jurisdiction of the military commission to try their clients while the civilian courts were open and functioning.[15] The commission heard the arguments of both Johnson and Ewing and then met in closed session to consider them. When the commission reconvened it denied the request, ruling it had legal jurisdiction over the trial of the defendants and citing the opinion of the attorney general. The commission's ruling, unlike a ruling in a civil court, could not be appealed to a higher court. It could only be appealed to the president, who had already ruled in favor of the commission's jurisdiction.

The question of legal jurisdiction of the military to try civilians was raised a year later by a citizen of Indiana named Lambdin P. Milligan. Milligan had been arrested and tried before a military commission in Indiana on charges of attempting to disrupt the military operations in that state by violent means. Milligan was found guilty and sentenced to hang. He was able to bring his case before the United States Supreme Court in the fall of 1866. In what has come to be known as a "landmark" decision, the Supreme Court ruled that citizens could not be tried by military tribunal in those jurisdictions where the civilian courts are open and functioning and no military threat was evident. The Court ruled that Indiana was not a war zone, had not been invaded by a hostile force, had not been threatened with invasion by a hostile force, and that martial law cannot exist under such conditions.[16]

But 1865 was not 1866. There was little opposition—and considerable public support—for a military trial of the accused conspirators, although any form of trial would have satisfied a majority of the country. To most Northerners a trial was necessary and those guilty of this terrible crime must be punished. The majority of Northerners agreed with Stanton when he wrote: "The stain of innocent blood must be removed from the land."[17]

During the night of April 29, the six remaining prisoners were transferred to the Old Washington Arsenal, located on a small peninsula where the Potomac and Anacostia Rivers merged before flowing south toward the Chesapeake Bay. The Arsenal was the oldest continuous military base in operation in the United States. In 1836 the first Federal penitentiary was built on its grounds and quickly became a model prison for its time. Shortly after the outbreak of the Civil War, the Arsenal became the main staging area for military supplies. It soon ran out of space for storing the vast supply of munitions that were needed by Union forces. Lincoln closed down the prison and moved all of the prisoners to the Federal penitentiary at Albany, New York. The prison facilities were turned over to the military.

Since the Arsenal was one of the most secure areas in the District of Columbia, Stanton ordered the eight defendants transferred to the old cellblocks. The prisoners now fell within the complete domain of the military and were isolated from any semblance of civilian authority. The militarization was complete.

The government took over the third floor of the penitentiary building, converting it into a trial room. The room measured approximately thirty feet by forty feet with an eleven-foot-high ceiling supported by three wooden columns evenly spaced down the center of the room. Four large windows with iron gratings were along one wall, and two small anterooms adjoined the main room. One of these anterooms was used to hold witnesses, while members of the commission used the other. A prisoners' dock was constructed against the west wall and was at a right angle to the table where the panel of judges or commissioners sat. The dock was four feet wide, elevated off of the floor one foot, and bounded by a railing that separated the prisoners from the rest of the courtroom. The nine judges sat around a large table that faced the witness stand. Select members of the press corps and court reporters occupied another large table adjacent to the witness stand. At the foot of the judges' table was a smaller table around which the prosecution team sat. Members of the defense team sat at two small tables located directly in front of the prisoners' dock. The entire room was freshly whitewashed and outfitted with gas jets for those sessions that ran after dark. During the daylight hours the four windows flooded the room with light, which was enhanced by the newly whitened walls.

The commission convened every day at 10:00 A.M. and continued until finished with that day's work, no matter how late the hour. An important feature of the trial had the verbatim testimony recorded in shorthand by a system known as phonography. The phonographic recordings were transcribed at the end of each session, and copies were provided to the judge advocate and defense counsel before the next day's session. This record of the previous day's testimony was then read in open court to allow the two sides an opportunity to correct the record.[18]

Early in the proceedings a motion was made that the daily reading be dispensed with since each side was presented with an official copy of the preceding day's testimony.[19] Thomas Ewing, defense counsel for Samuel Mudd, agreed, and the other defense counsels offered no objection. Judge Advocate Holt, however, did object. Holt thought it would be a dangerous precedent for them not to read the record in open court "where there are so many lives at stake, . . . and . . . where it is so vastly important . . . that there should be strict accuracy."[20] Accepting Holt's concern, the court agreed to continue following the laborious practice of reading the previous day's testimony at the start of each session. While this added considerably to the length of the proceedings, there would be no misunderstanding as to the accuracy of statements made by witnesses. Either side could object and seek a correction of the record. This is an important point in studying the transcript for historical purposes. While the various nuances of the witnesses reflected in their demeanor, voice inflections, hesitations, and the like cannot be gleaned from the transcript, the researcher can be sure of the accuracy of the transcript as evidenced by its approval by both the defense and the prosecution.

The job of recording the testimony and providing copies to all parties fell on a group of select reporters who took an oath "to record the evidence faithfully and truly."[21] These reporters worked for phonographer Benn Pitman, who was uniquely qualified to oversee the recording process. Pitman was the brother of Isaac Pitman, the Englishman who devised a system of shorthand in 1837 which was adopted worldwide as an accurate and legitimate system of verbatim recordation.[22] Pitman had served the government during the war as a phonographer recording military trials. His most famous trial was the Indiana Treason Trial which eventually wound up before the Supreme Court of the United States (and was known as *ex parte* Milligan). He was hired again by the government to reproduce the daily testimony at the conspiracy trial. As a result of his work he received approval to publish the transcripts he and his recorders produced. The only stipulations placed upon Pitman were that the production of such a publication result in no cost to the government and that it "adhere to strict accuracy."[23]

The Rules of Proceeding specified that a copy of each day's testimony be provided to the judge advocate general and to "the counsel of the prisoners." Pitman also supplied "press copies" to the *Washington Intelligencer* and to commercial telegraphers who transmitted the content of the copies to Philadelphia at the end of each day for publication in the *Philadelphia Daily Inquirer*. Thus, both the *Intelligencer* and the *Inquirer* published verbatim copies of the trial testimony daily. The accounts published in the *Inquirer* were plagued by numerous typographical errors that the Washington newspaper did not experience. This probably resulted from errors in transmission by the telegraphers, who, every evening, wired the large number of transcribed pages to their editor. The *Intelligencer* worked directly from the "press copy" and experienced few transcription errors.

The term "press copy" has caused a certain amount of confusion among some authors, who misunderstand the meaning of "press copy" as used in 1865.[24] While the term in twentieth-century parlance refers to a hard copy passed out to members of the press corps, it had a different meaning in mid-nineteenth-century parlance. The term described the process by which verbatim copies were produced. The transcription of shorthand notes was made with ink, and copies were "lifted" from the original ink transcriptions by laying a piece of tissue paper over the ink transcription, then backing it with a damp cloth, and then applying pressure. In this way, a "copy" was lifted off of the original transcription onto the tissue paper by transferring some of the ink. The use of tissue paper allowed the image to "bleed" through the transparent tissue. In skilled hands, the process was extremely effective.[25]

The trial began on May 10 and lasted until June 29, a total of fifty days. President Johnson's executive order of May 1, establishing the military commission, designated Judge Advocate General Joseph Holt to conduct the trial along with his assistant, Judge Advocate John A. Bingham, and Special Judge Advocate Henry L. Burnett.[26] Responsibility for the prisoners and for carrying out the mandates of the commission was assigned to Major General John C. Hartranft. Sitting in judgment as military commissioners were nine Federal officers whose selection was made by Bingham, but most probably involved Stanton and Holt. The nine officers were Major General David Hunter, Major General Lew Wallace, Brevet Major General August Kautz, Brigadier General Albion Howe, Brigadier General Robert Foster, Brevet Brigadier General Cyrus B. Comstock, Brigadier General Thomas Harris, Brevet Colonel Horace Porter, and Lieutenant Colonel David Clendenin. Within twenty-four hours Comstock and Porter were relieved from serving and replaced by Brevet Brigadier General James Ekin and Brevet Colonel Charles Tompkins.[27]

All nine of the officers were "shooting" officers, having seen combat service during the war. They were a no-nonsense group who obviously felt a strong attachment to the Union and Abraham Lincoln. All of them had shown qualities of leadership in their various capacities during the war. Included among the nine were four graduates of West Point who remained professional soldiers, a former United States marshal, a medical practitioner, an author, and a school teacher. Most important was the fact that none was an attorney or had professional training in the law.

During the trial a total of 366 witnesses gave testimony on a wide range of subjects. The number of witnesses was nearly evenly divided between the prosecution and the defense. Of the 366 witnesses, twenty-nine were Black, all having been slaves at one time. These witnesses were identified in the trial record as "colored" to isolate their testimony from the White witnesses. Of the twenty-nine, eighteen testified for the prosecution and eleven testified for the defense.

Physical descriptions of the accused as reported in the newspapers revealed the prejudice of the times, both positive and negative. Samuel Arnold was described as a young Baltimorean with an "intelligent face, curly brown hair and restless dark eyes." Edman Spangler, on the other hand, had an "unintelligent-looking face . . . swollen by the excessive use of alcohol, a low forehead, brown hair, and anxious-looking eyes." Michael O'Laughlen was a "small, delicate-looking man with pleasing features, uneasy black eyes, bushy black hair, and an imperial, anxious expression shaded by a sad, remorseful look."[28]

George Atzerodt faired worst of all. He was described as a "Teutonic Dugald Dalgettys," a geographic stereotype that long ago escaped the English language. He was short, thickset, round-shouldered, brawny-armed with a stupid expression. He "manifested a stoical indifference to what was going on in the Court." The writer of these observations concluded his description by describing Atzerodt as "crafty, cowardly, and mercenary, his own safety the all-absorbing subject of his thoughts." One can empathize with Atzerodt if his thoughts during the trial tended to focus on his own safety.[29]

Next came Lewis Powell. He was "very tall, with an athletic, gladiatorial frame." He had a "massive robustness of animal manhood in its most stalwart type." He exhibited "neither intellect nor intelligence in his dark gray eyes, low forehead, massive jaws, compressed full lips, small nose, large nostrils, dark hair and beardless face." Most characterizations of Powell have relied on the descriptions given by his defense attorney, William E. Doster, which according to Powell biographer Betty Ownsbey "were melodramatic fiction told in the best Victorian tradition in an attempt to sway the court's sympathy for a good boy gone wrong."[30] Doster described Powell as "rough and illiterate" and attempted to show that he was insane when he attempted to murder Seward. Doster pointed out to the commissioners that Powell "believed in Heaven and General Lee; dresses himself in the clothes of Union dead; stands guard over starving prisoners; . . . has his cup carved out of some

Federal skull."[31] In his closing summation Doster soared into a flight of fancy: "I have formed an estimate of him little short of admiration, for his honesty of purpose, freedom from deception and malice, and courageous resolution to abide by the principles to which he was reared."[32] He ended by quoting Brutus: "This was a man!"[33]

David Herold was "a doltish, insignificant-looking young man, not much over one and twenty years of age, with a slender frame, and irresolute, cowardly appearance." His "Israelite nose" separated his "small, dark hazel eyes" and was located just above his "incipient moustache." The writer of this description was amazed that a villain like Booth would have selected "such a contemptuous-looking fellow" as a co-conspirator.[34]

Mary Surratt and Samuel Mudd were spared all the stereotypical negatives used on the others. Mary, "a belle in her youth," had "rather pleasing features," dark grey eyes and brown hair. Those in the courtroom saw her as "the devoted mother of an attached family, of pious sentiments, and deserving the recommendations so lavishly given of her by her religious advisors." Mary's was the only description that included a lengthy biography of her life, which were sure to "inspire feelings of pity."[35]

Dr. Samuel A. Mudd was the most puzzling of the conspirators. He was "the most inoffensive and decent in appearance of all the prisoners." Described as forty years of age, he was actually thirty-two years old. He was "rather tall, quite thin, with sharp features, a high bald forehead, astute blue eyes, compressed pale lips, and sandy hair, moustache and whiskers."[36] All in all, Dr. Mudd was an aristocrat completely out of place among the other rabble at the bar. But not all of the descriptions of Dr. Mudd were positive. General Thomas Harris, a member of the commission, revealed his own phrenological beliefs when he wrote, "Mudd's expression of countenance was that of a hypocrite. He had the bump of secretiveness largely developed and it would have taken months of acquaintanceship to have removed the unfavorable impression made by first scanning of the man. He had the appearance of a natural born liar and deceiver."[37]

The defense attorneys were a sound and accomplished group of lawyers. The most distinguished was Maryland Senator Reverdy Johnson. At sixty-nine, Johnson had already accumulated a lifetime of honors. He had served in a variety of posts including Maryland's deputy attorney general (1816–17) and United States attorney general (1849–50). Johnson represented the slaveowners in the Dred Scott case and had originally believed in the South's right to secede, only to reverse himself when his own state began to consider it. Second only to Johnson in prestige was Brevet Major General Thomas Ewing Jr., counsel for Samuel Mudd and Samuel Arnold. Ewing had served as chief justice on the Kansas Supreme Court in 1861–62 before resigning to become colonel of the Eleventh Kansas Cavalry. A year later he was promoted to brigadier general and was breveted major general in February 1865.

Frederick Aiken and John W. Clampitt were junior law partners with Reverdy Johnson, and when Johnson withdrew into the background, they assumed control of Mary Surratt's defense. Aiken was a somewhat strange individual. On April 5, 1861, a week before the attack on Fort Sumter, Aiken offered his "intellectual" services to the Confederacy stating that he would rather give his pen than his blood to support the new cause. Apparently rebuffed, he wound up an aide on the staff of Major General Winfield Scott Hancock. John W. Clampitt also served in the Union army, in the Washington Light Infantry. Both Aiken and Clampitt were young attorneys in their late twenties. For both men, Mary Surratt's defense would be the first major case of their careers.[38]

Appointed by the court to act as defense counsel for George Atzerodt and Lewis Powell was William E. Doster. Doster had entered the war with the Fourth Pennsylvania Cavalry and rose to the rank of lieutenant colonel. In March 1865 he was breveted brigadier general for "gallant and meritorious service during the war."[39] Doster had recently served as provost marshal of Washington, a position he filled admirably. In 1862 he had flagged Thomas Nelson Conrad and had him arrested and thrown into Old Capitol Prison. At one time he had come under the evil eye of Lafayette Baker, who had Doster charged with aiding in the smuggling of liquor. Doster quickly countered by proving that the document that he allegedly issued was a forgery. The charges were dismissed. Doster's credentials were impressive. He graduated from Yale University in 1857 and obtained his law degree from Harvard University in 1859. His defense of Atzerodt and Powell was as capable as any lawyer could have provided, and his vigorous objection to the prosecutions attempt to introduce a confession given by Atzerodt to Provost Marshal James McPhail was successful.

The last two attorneys to appear on behalf of the accused were Frederick Stone and Walter S. Cox. Stone was descended from an old Charles County, Maryland, family tracing its lineage back to Thomas Stone, a member of the Continental Congress and signer of the Declaration of Independence. Stone was forty-five years old at the time of the trial and was among the wealthiest residents of Charles County. He was considered the county's leading attorney and in 1870 was a member of the United States Congress. Stone represented Samuel Mudd and Davy Herold. Rounding out the defense attorneys, Cox represented Michael O'Laughlen and Samuel Arnold.

Joseph Holt was Lincoln's judge advocate general. Holt was a Kentucky Democrat who had been a highly successful lawyer in private life. He had served in James Buchanan's cabinet first as postmaster general and later as secretary of war, succeeding John Floyd after the latter resigned his post in December 1860. Although a Kentuckian, Holt became a staunch Unionist and stood by Lincoln and his policies throughout the war. He was a prime mover in calling for a military trial of the accused conspirators and initially tried to keep the trial proceedings secret. Holt, more than anyone else, believed Jefferson Davis and members of his cabinet were directly involved in the assassination.

Holt was considered by most of his peers to be a brilliant lawyer and a serious student of the law. Placed in charge of the prosecution, he felt deficient in his ability to argue the case orally before the commission. Holt agreed to plan the prosecution but let his assistant, John A. Bingham, handle the examination of witnesses and final summation. Like Stanton, Holt has been demonized by many latter-day writers for a seeming disregard for civil liberties. At the time of the trial, however, both Stanton and Holt were held in high regard by the general public and by fellow jurists. Much of the criticism against them is unfounded.

Assistant Judge Advocate General John A. Bingham physically represented the government before the commission. He was born in Pennsylvania in 1815 and moved to Cadiz, Ohio, where he became a lawyer in 1840, serving as district attorney before being elected to the House of Representatives. Defeated in his bid for reelection in 1862, Bingham won reelection in 1864. It was during his second term as a representative from Ohio that Bingham was appointed special judge advocate and assistant to Holt.

Rounding out the prosecution was Henry L. Burnett. Like the nine members sitting on the commission, Burnett was a "shooting" officer. He served as a captain with the Second Ohio Cavalry in Missouri, Kansas, and Kentucky. His outfit took part in the capture of Confederate raider John Hunt Morgan in the summer of 1863. Shortly after Morgan's capture Burnett was appointed a judge advocate in the Bureau of Military Justice where he became involved in prosecuting the Copperheads, who had planned to liberate Confederate prisoners of war held at Camp Douglas in Chicago. His success while serving in the Bureau of Military Justice earned him a brevet appointment of brigadier general of volunteers in March of 1865 and an appointment as a special judge advocate assisting Holt and Bingham.

The commission met for the first time on May 10 at 10:00 A.M. President Johnson's executive order was read, and the defendants were asked if they had any objection to any of the members of the commission. They did not. The defendants next heard the charges and specifications against them for the first time. While each of the accused had specifications tailored to his or her particular case, all were charged with "maliciously, unlawfully, and traitorously . . . conspiring . . . to kill and murder, . . . Abraham Lincoln, . . . Andrew Johnson, . . . William H. Seward, . . . and Ulysses S. Grant, . . . and assaulting, with intent to kill and murder, . . . William H. Seward, . . . and lying in wait with intent . . . to kill and murder the said Andrew Johnson, . . . and the said Ulysses S. Grant." Each pleaded "not guilty."[40] The commission then adjourned to allow the defendants further time to retain counsel and confer with their counsel on the charges and specifications. The defendants' counsel had to be approved by the commission as satisfactory to represent the accused. While some viewed this as sinister, it was more to insure competent counsel since the charges carried the death penalty.

On May 11 the commission met for a second time and approved counsel for Samuel Mudd and Mary Surratt. The remaining six defendants had not yet secured counsel and the commission adjourned until the next day, allowing them time to do so. When the commission met on the twelfth all six defendants submitted counsel for approval. Frederick Stone of Charles County, Maryland, would represent David Herold and Samuel Mudd. Thomas Ewing would represent Samuel Arnold. William E. Doster would represent George Atzerodt, while Walter S. Cox would represent Michael O'Laughlen. William Doster would also represent Lewis Powell, while Thomas Ewing would take on Edman Spangler in addition to Dr. Mudd. At this time Mary Surratt submitted Reverdy Johnson's name as co-counsel along with those of John W. Clampitt and Frederick Aiken to represent her.

Johnson's appointment was immediately challenged by Thomas Harris, who questioned his fitness because of his earlier opposition to requiring voters in Maryland to take a loyalty oath. In November of 1864, the Constitutional Convention of Maryland had passed a new state constitution that was presented to the voters for ratification in a special referendum. The convention also passed a resolution requiring a loyalty oath be taken as a requirement for any citizen to vote. Johnson challenged the requirement, declaring it unconstitutional. In a letter, made public, Johnson told the citizens of Maryland that they were under no obligation to honor such an oath because its enactment was beyond the authority of the convention and was unconstitutional. Johnson eloquently argued his case before the members of the commission, basing his opposition to a loyalty oath on the grounds that the Maryland convention lacked the authority to set standards for voting that went beyond those spelled out in the United States Constitution. Johnson was not opposed to a declaration of loyalty to the Union. He had taken such an oath himself on entering the United States Senate. He objected only to making it a condition to vote that he felt exceeded the constitutional requirements for voting.

After some debate the commission overruled Harris's objection and accepted Johnson as counsel for Mary Surratt. The first victory fell to the defendants. August Kautz appeared to represent the majority of the commission in rejecting Harris's position when he wrote in his diary that Reverdy Johnson "did the other members [of the commission] great injustice if he supposed they united with General Harris in his ill-advised objection."[41]

By the third day counsel for all of the defendants were in place and ready to proceed. At this point Thomas Ewing and Reverdy Johnson rose to challenge the legal jurisdiction of the military commission. They based their arguments on the fact that the civilian courts were open and functioning, and therefore the commission lacked jurisdiction. They argued that the defendants were all civilians and therefore should be tried in civil court and not by the military. Challenging the court's jurisdiction was not unusual. In the several thousand military trials that had been held to date, the court's jurisdiction was challenged in nearly every one of them.[42]

The commission ruled on its own jurisdiction, denying the motion by Ewing and Johnson. It was at this time that Samuel Mudd asked that he be tried separately from the others because his defense would be "greatly prejudiced by a joint trial."[43] Mudd's request was denied. While the commission viewed Mudd as "socially distinct" from his co-defendants, they could see no such legal distinction. He would be tried along with the other seven defendants. With this business concluded, the session was adjourned until the next day, when the actual trial would begin. The prosecution and the defense were complete, witnesses for the prosecution were in tow, and they were ready to begin presenting their case.

Those critics who opposed the military commission on jurisdictional grounds were further bolstered in their criticism when the commission declared that it would try the accused behind closed doors, keeping the proceedings secret. The press objected vigorously to this heavy-handed ploy by the government. Stanton came under the severest criticism, especially by later writers on the subject, but the original decision to hold closed hearings was not Stanton's, it was Holt's. In fact, Stanton favored a public trial. To his way of thinking, a public trial would help expose the Confederate complicity in the murder of the president. Henry Burnett, the man in charge of the trial procedures, wrote to Stanton on May 10, requesting him to make a decision one way or the other: "This evening you expressed the opinion that the charges and specifications should go to the Associated Press with the synopsis of today's proceedings, but at the same time instructed me to consult with Judge Holt in reference to the matter. His opinion is decidedly against any publication of the charges, and in favor only of a very brief synopsis. How shall it be?"

Stanton wrote back to Burnett instructing him to follow the instructions of his superior. On the second day of the trial Holt decided to open up the proceedings to the public. Holt also mandated that the press be given the same transcripts (press copies) that were distributed to the lawyers each morning. Holt never explained his reasoning for this change in tactics, but it seems he suddenly became sensitive to charges of unfairness and realized that Stanton favored a public trial.

The defendants were at a clear disadvantage in being tried by military officers, none of whom had served previously as judges or attorneys. In addition, conviction required only a simple majority instead of a unanimous court. The death sentence required a two-thirds majority. The most serious consequence of trial by military commission lay in the inability of the defendants to appeal the verdict to a higher court. Appeal of a military commission's ruling was only to the president of the United States, although all of that changed in 1866 when the Supreme Court agreed to hear the appeal of Milligan. As a result of the Milligan case, Mudd was able to file an appeal in the United States District Court for the District of Southern Florida in 1868 that eventually ended up in the Supreme Court in 1869. No matter how one compares the military trial with a civil trial, the real difference between the two forms in July of 1865 was the belief by the government that a civil trial would result in jury nullification due to strong Southern sympathies in the civil population of the District of Columbia. Whether real or perceived, it was this fear that motivated the government to seek a military trial, and the accused were definitely at a disadvantage.

Initially, the trial appeared to be two trials in one. The prosecution of Jefferson Davis and his cohorts proceeded as one trial, while the prosecution of Mary Surratt, Samuel Mudd, and the other defendants was viewed as a separate trial.[44] Tried as unindicted co-conspirators along with the eight defendants in court were Jefferson Davis, George N. Sanders, Clement C. Clay, Beverley Tucker, Jacob Thompson, William C. Cleary, George Harper, George Young, "and others unknown." Davis's co-defendants were among the Confederate agents who had operated out of Canada and who the government believed had waged "black flag warfare" against the northeastern states. This included "germ" warfare against New York, Washington, Norfolk, and New Bern. To believe that George Atzerodt or David Herold was an agent of Jefferson Davis seemed almost laughable. That Mary Surratt conspired with any of these ruffians was unthinkable to many. Still, the government saw one great conspiracy made up of many small dots that, when connected, led directly to Richmond.

On May 2, ten days before the actual trial began, President Johnson issued a proclamation offering rewards for the capture of Jefferson Davis and five of his Canadian-based operatives. Johnson's proclamation claimed that evidence in the Bureau of Military Justice clearly showed their complicity in Lincoln's assassination.[45] The claim caused a stir among the general public. A statement coming from the president of the United States was thought to be true or to contain enough truth to warrant trying these men for Lincoln's murder. The public still had strong memories of the raid on St. Albans and the attempt to burn New York City and spread the pestilence of yellow fever throughout the North. These were considered acts of terror and uncivilized. The perpetrators of such acts had little sympathy among the Northern population or the Northern press. While the government claimed it had evidence to show that Davis and his Canadian agents had been behind Lincoln's murder, it did not attempt to put them on trial along with the eight defendants. Thus Davis and his agents became unindicted co-conspirators.

Following his capture on May 10 near Irwinville, Georgia, Jefferson

Davis believed he would be tried by his captors for treason, but also believed they would not be able to convict him on either legal or constitutional grounds. He viewed the charge that he shared complicity in Lincoln's murder with contempt.[46] Davis was also contemptuous of Andrew Johnson. He purportedly said that he "would a thousand times rather have Abraham Lincoln to deal with, as President of the United States, than to have [Andrew Johnson]."[47]

The government's case against the Confederates hinged on the testimony of three witnesses who claimed to have intimate knowledge of their involvement in plotting Lincoln's death. Claiming that the testimony would compromise the witnesses and place them in personal danger, Holt at first convinced the commission to hear their testimony in secret despite protests from the media and public. The attempt was eventually abandoned after parts of the testimony were leaked to the press and appeared in several major newspapers. In an effort to counter wild speculation, the commission decided to release all of the testimony or risk losing the public's support.

The government's three chief witnesses were Richard Montgomery, James B. Merritt, and Sandford Conover. All three witnesses claimed to have been in Canada and to have been taken into the confidence of the Confederate leaders there, particularly Jacob Thompson and George Sanders. Thus, all three had intimate knowledge of the Confederate leaders' alleged relationship with Booth. Of the three witnesses, Conover proved to be the most sensational in linking the Confederacy to Lincoln's death. Conover claimed that he had actually seen Booth together with Thompson and Sanders in Canada and that Thompson had told him that Booth had been authorized by Richmond to kill Lincoln.[48] Merritt reiterated what Conover said, then went further, claiming that Davis had actually authorized the killing in writing.[49] Montgomery confirmed both Conover's and Merritt's testimony that a plot to assassinate Lincoln was in the works and that Thompson only awaited approval from Richmond.[50] The three witnesses claimed to have seen Booth, Powell, and Herold in Canada and that Booth, Surratt, and Atzerodt were among the band of conspirators assigned to murder Lincoln. Conover's testimony placing Booth in the presence of Confederate agents was the link prosecutors had been looking for.[51] But the government's case soon took a dramatic turn for the worse.

No sooner had these men testified than their credibility came under severe attack. As the principal witness against the Confederate leaders, Conover became the focus of these attacks. In Canada he had used the alias James Watson Wallace, while in Washington he testified under the alias Sanford Conover. His real name was Charles A. Dunham. Within days of publication of Conover's testimony by the press, countercharges were appearing in most major newspapers. The essence of the countercharges centered on Thompson and his colleagues' not being in Montreal when Conover claimed he met with them. No sooner had one allegation been exposed as perjurious than another followed. In truth, all three witnesses appeared to have lied.

Because the testimony of Conover and Montgomery and Merritt proved to be perjured, most historians have concluded that the charge of Confederate involvement was without merit. The public, however, had little difficulty with the government's case. Despite the perjury, the public believed there was enough evidence to indict the Confederate government.[52] Holt, however, soon turned his attention to the eight defendants in the dock.

Following his capture, Davis was imprisoned at Fortress Monroe, Virginia. On May 14, Stanton wrote to Major General Henry Halleck that Davis was to remain a prisoner in Fortress Monroe and that "his trial and punishment, if there be any, shall be in Virginia."[53] Sentiment among the press was generally in favor of trying Davis before a military commission. While Stanton and Seward both favored a military trial, Stanton felt that Davis should be tried in a civilian court on the charge of treason first and then tried before a military commission on all of the other charges associated with his alleged complicity in Lincoln's assassination.[54] Neither happened. Davis was released on parole on May 11, 1867, two years and one day after his capture near Irwinsville, Georgia. He was never brought to trial either before a civilian court for treason or before a military tribunal for complicity in Lincoln's murder. The government eventually entered a *nolle prosequi* that closed the case against the Confederate president. Though imprisoned for two years, Davis eventually walked away, becoming a popular hero of "The Lost Cause."

The prisoners in the dock were not as fortunate as Davis. Holt and Bingham pressed the government's case against the unfortunate eight. The guilt of Powell and Herold was a forgone conclusion. Powell's guilt was never disputed. His defense became a plea for his life. He was characterized as simply a rebel soldier carrying out his duty. His actions were no different from those of any rebel soldier with the exception that "he aimed at the head of a department instead of a corps; he struck at the head of a nation instead of at its limbs, . . . he believed he was killing an oppressor."[55]

Herold's defense centered on his inability to commit murder. His attorney pleaded that he was "unfit for deeds of blood and violence; he was cowardly." His only service to Booth was his knowledge of roads; he was a pathfinder and nothing more. Atzerodt, who had been characterized as "crafty, cowardly and mercenary," was simply a boatman. Like Herold, he was either too stupid or too cowardly to participate in murder. His only role was "to furnish the boat to carry the party over the Potomac." He was "the ferryman of the capture." When Booth told Atzerodt "to take charge of the Vice-President, he must have known that the prisoner had not the courage, and therefore did not care particularly whether he accomplished it or not."[56]

The case for Arnold and O'Laughlen was equally simple. Whatever role they may have played was solely as abductors, not accomplices to murder. There was the "Sam" letter that tied Arnold tightly to Booth, and Booth's telegram to O'Laughlen calling him to Washington. Whatever the relationship these two had with Booth and his plot to capture Lincoln, the defense claimed they walked away from both Booth and his crazy scheme. Neither man knew about the murder, nor would they have anything to do with it. But the prosecution didn't buy it. The defense would have to come up with something better than claiming their defendants "walked away" from Booth's conspiracy. Had they "walked" into police headquarters instead of away from Booth, Lincoln would never have been murdered. Thus the concept of "vicarious liability," so common in modern-day jurisprudence, weighed heavily against the accused accomplices.

Edman Spangler was the weakest of the prosecution cases. Well known to Booth, Spangler was an old crony who had the longest association with Booth. It was Spangler whom Booth called to hold his horse that night at the theater. More important, it was Spangler who was accused of slamming the rear door immediately after Booth fled across the stage and out of the theater. Spangler may have been duped by Booth, but he would pay for his being so gullible. The military commission simply could not believe that Booth could have managed his escape from the theater without some sort of help, and the hapless Spangler was it.

The prosecution saved its best efforts for Mary Surratt and Samuel Mudd. The two defendants who garnered the most public sympathy as innocents received the severest attack by the prosecution. While the other six defendants all had direct ties to Booth, Mary Surratt and Dr. Mudd were portrayed as innocent acquaintances by their attorneys. The government had simply made a bad mistake in charging them as co-conspirators. Mary was a simple boardinghouse proprietor who was viewed by many as a victim because of her son John. Dr. Mudd did nothing more than honor his medical oath to care for the injured.

The prosecution painted a different picture. Mary Surratt not only "kept the nest that hatched the rotten egg,"[57] as President Johnson had pointed out, she willingly did Booth's bidding carrying messages to John Lloyd at her tavern where Booth and Herold would reoutfit themselves at the time of their escape. Furthermore, she helped tighten the noose around her own neck by denying she recognized or knew Powell the night of her arrest. The most damaging circumstance for Mary, however, was her son John. The government considered John Surratt a key player in Booth's plot. He was an important link to Richmond.

Samuel Mudd had little more than his good word and a strong defense counsel to fall back on. While his counsel performed well in his defense, his good word did not. The prosecution showed that Mudd had lied repeatedly even when given every opportunity to come clean. Innocent men do not withhold the truth or mislead. Mudd did both and the government easily dismissed his claims of innocence. Thomas Harris had used the shape of Mudd's head to conclude that he was "a natural born liar and deceiver," but the other commissioners had Mudd's own statements to show that he had lied repeatedly. Adamantly maintaining that he had met John Wilkes Booth on only one occasion, the evidence showed that when Booth visited Mudd in the early morning hours of April 15, 1865, it was the fourth time the two men had met. In the end Mudd's status as a physician may have saved him from the gallows, but not life in prison. The nine commissioners voted five to four to hang the doctor. Mudd would be saved by a single vote. Mary Surratt had no such luck to save her.

On June 30 the military commission rendered its decision. All eight defendants were found guilty. Lewis Powell, David Herold, George Atzerodt, and Mary Surratt were sentenced to death by hanging. Samuel Mudd, Samuel Arnold, and Michael O'Laughlen were sentenced to life in prison. Edman Spangler was sentenced to six years. The prison terms were to be served in the penitentiary at Albany, New York, only to be changed later to the military prison at Fort Jefferson located among the Dry Tortugas Islands off the Florida Keys.

Few had expected Mary Surratt to hang. Following the commission's recommendations on sentencing, five of the nine members signed a second recommendation asking President Johnson to grant executive clemency for Mary Surratt in consideration of her sex and age.[58] It was not until July 5, two days before her hanging was scheduled, that Holt carried the commission's findings along with their recommendation of clemency for Mary Surratt to Johnson. Johnson signed the papers approving the sentencing recommendations of the commission but did not sign the clemency plea. When word eventually leaked out that a clemency plea was rejected by Johnson he emphatically denied ever seeing a copy of it and claimed that he was not made aware of it until some time after the hanging. Holt was equally emphatic, claiming he had shown the petition to Johnson who ignored it.

Two years later, in August 1867, Johnson ordered Stanton to send him the clemency papers that Holt insisted he had shown the president. Johnson's personal secretary, Colonel William G. Moore, kept a detailed record of the affair: "He distinctly remembered the great reluctance with which he approved the death warrant of a woman of Mrs. Surratt's age, and that he asked Judge Advocate Genl. Holt, who originally brought to him the papers, many questions, but that nothing whatever was said to him respecting the recommendation of the Commission for clemency in her case."[59] We may never know for sure the true circumstances surrounding the appeal for executive clemency for Mary Surratt. Who was telling the truth was of little use to her at the time.

On the morning of July 6 Generals Hancock and Hartranft began their grim duty of visiting each of the four condemned prisoners and reading them their death warrants. Shortly after the prisoners received official word of their fate, the Arsenal carpenters began work on a gallows. They worked throughout the night until early morning of the seventh, the day of the hanging. During the entire period, their sawing and hammering could be heard by the prisoners as they waited in their cells. July 7 dawned hot and steamy and only grew worse as the sun slowly made its way toward its zenith. Washington's summers were bad enough to warrant giving British officials tropical pay for serving in the city. The weather on the seventh would more than justify their pay.

At 11:00 A.M. the carpenters had finished their grisly work and the large scaffolding stood ready for its grim assignment. Just to the right of the scaffold a squad of soldiers had stacked four wooden gun boxes to hold the bodies of the condemned prisoners. The oppressive heat drove several of the wool-clad soldiers against the brick walls of the buildings in an effort to find some relief in the little bit of shade the wall provided. The burial detail had no such relief. Four narrow slots were dug in the dry earth, four feet deep, seven feet long and three feet wide. What little moisture existed in the freshly turned soil quickly evaporated in the blazing heat.

Shortly after noon the preparations were finished. The graves had been dug, the gun boxes carefully stacked, and the scaffold securely buttressed. The scaffold flooring consisted of two large trap doors, six feet long by four feet wide, held in place by two upright beams. Each beam was attended by a soldier whose sole duty was to keep it secure on its large wooden block. No one except the assigned soldier was to touch the support beams.[60] At the prescribed signal each brace would be struck a sharp blow using a long four-by-four post, knocking it from beneath the traps. With their supporting beams knocked free, the platforms would suddenly drop, swinging on their hinges. The four bodies would fall six feet, only to be snapped short of the ground by the rope fastened about each neck. Properly done, the condemned would have their necks broken and would die instantly as a result of massive spinal cord injury. Improperly done, they would slowly strangle to death dangling at the end of their ropes.

The spectators began to grow restless waiting for the appointed hour. The warrant called for the executions to be completed by two o'clock, and it was now a few minutes past one. Standing in the doorway of the deputy warden's quarters, Major General Winfield Scott Hancock removed a white linen handkerchief from his coat and wiped the perspiration from his face. Hancock had the onerous duty of carrying out the executions. An heroic soldier of considerable capability, this was a duty he loathed carrying out. He had delayed the official proceedings as long as he could in the event President Johnson stayed Mary Surratt's execution. It was now clear to Hancock that such word would not come.

Three hours earlier Hancock had appeared before Judge Andrew Wylie, one of the Justices of the Supreme Court of the District of Columbia, to deliver Johnson's executive order refusing a writ of habeas corpus for Mary Surratt. Mary's lawyers had drafted a writ in hopes of getting Wylie to order her release to civil authorities. Wylie had earlier endorsed the draft and United States Marshal David Gooding had served the papers on Hancock. Hancock appeared in Wylie's chambers at 11:30 A.M. and presented the judge with an executive order from President Johnson suspending the writ of habeas corpus in Mary's case.[61] Wylie was powerless to act. He had no recourse but to acquiesce, allowing the last obstacle to the government's plan to execute Mary Surratt to pass. Hancock returned to the Arsenal grounds where everything was in readiness for the scheduled executions.

Davy Herold was lying on a cot in his cell. He was pale and nervous as he and his seven sisters listened to the ministering words of Reverend Dr. Olds. Lewis Powell sat stoically in his cell, resigned to his fate. George Atzerodt was visited by his mother and common law wife, disbelieving what was about to happen.[62] Fathers Wiget and Walter sat praying with Mary Surratt as she held her daughter Anna in her arms. At half past twelve, all except the religious counselors were escorted from the cellblock.

As the rising sun passed its midday peak, Hancock could delay no longer. Time was slipping toward the inevitable end. There would be a certain cruelty to continue the delay any longer. Hancock emerged from the building indicating to those in the courtyard that the moment had come. Four chairs were carried up the steps and placed on the scaffolding. At two minutes past one o'clock the four condemned prisoners were led from the penitentiary building into the courtyard. Mary Surratt came first supported by Fathers Wiget and Walter. Atzerodt came next followed by Herold. Last to emerge was Lewis Powell accompanied by Reverend Gillette. Leading the procession was General Hartranft and members of his immediate staff. After each of the condemned had been seated in the chairs provided for them, Hartranft read the order of execution. As soon as Hartranft finished, Dr. Gillette made a statement on behalf of Powell thanking Hartranft and his men for the kind manner in which he was treated during his imprisonment.

The prisoners were bound around their arms and legs with strips of white linen. The nooses were adjusted so that the several knots lay snug against the side of the head in order to insure a quick and clean break of the neck. Atzerodt was the only one who spoke aloud: "Good-bye, gentlemen who is before me. May we all meet in the other world."[63] It was twenty-one minutes after one o'clock. Captain Christian Rath, a precise soldier who was officially charged with carrying out the execution, had seen that every detail was ready for the hanging. Making sure everyone save the four condemned had stepped free of the trapdoors, Rath clapped his hands three times. Four soldiers swung the pair of bludgeons forward, striking the upright braces near their base. The crack from their rams resonated throughout the courtyard as the pillars fell away. The eyes of every spectator were transfixed on the wooden trapdoors as they remained suspended in midair. Time seemed frozen. Then with a loud screeching sound the platforms fell from beneath the bodies. The four wretched souls dropped in unison with a snapping thud.[64] Justice had been served.

CHAPTER TWENTY

The Aftermath
Rewriting History

History is not history unless it is the truth.

Abraham Lincoln

Some felt that Mary Surratt's trial was a ruse to force her son to give himself up and save his mother. John Surratt was the one the government really wanted, not his "pious mother."[1] At the time of the trial, John Surratt's whereabouts were not known for sure. Witnesses placed him in Washington in front of Ford's Theatre on the night of April 14, but Surratt claimed he was in Elmira, New York, on his way to Canada at the moment of Lincoln's murder.[2] Learning of Lincoln's assassination on Saturday, April 15, in Elmira, Surratt made his way to Canandaigua, New York, and then to Montreal where he hid out in the home of Confederate agent John Porterfield. From Montreal Surratt was taken across the St. Lawrence River to the small town of St. Liboire where he was hidden in the rectory of the local Catholic priest, Father Charles Boucher.[3]

Surratt stayed in St. Liboire through the entire conspiracy trial and subsequent hanging of his mother on July 7. In August he was taken to Montreal where another priest, Father LaPierre, hid him while making arrangements to take him to Quebec. From Quebec arrangements were made to secure passage aboard the steamer *Peruvian*, which carried Surratt to Liverpool, England. From Liverpool, Surratt eventually made his way to the Vatican in Rome, where he enlisted as a papal Zouave under the alias John Watson.

Surratt was discovered through an ironic twist of fate. Serving as a Zouave at the same time was an old acquaintance of Surratt's, Henri Beaumont de Ste. Marie. Ste. Marie tipped off the United States consul that John Surratt could be found in the Vatican among the Pope's guard. Ste. Marie turned "Watson-Surratt" in to the Vatican authorities in hope of receiving the reward money that had been offered for Surratt's capture. Although the reward had been withdrawn a year earlier, Ste. Marie eventually was awarded fifteen thousand dollars for his tip,[4] which Congress later reduced to ten thousand dollars.[5] Although no extradition treaty existed between the two countries, the Vatican secretary of state, Cardinal Giacomo Antonelli, agreed to have Surratt taken into custody and extradited back to the United States.[6]

Before Surratt could be delivered to the U.S. authorities, he freed himself by breaking loose from his guards and jumping over a cliff, disappearing into a dark ravine below. Having escaped his captors, Surratt made his way to Naples where he boarded a freighter destined for Alexandria, Egypt. Once again the U.S. authorities were tipped off. On arriving in Alexandria, Surratt was met by the American Consul and local police, who arrested him and returned him to the United States, arriving February 19, 1867. Six months later, on June 10, 1867, Surratt was placed on trial in civil court in the District of Columbia charged as an accomplice in the murder of Abraham Lincoln. As in the trial of Mary Surratt, Louis Wiechmann became a principal witness for the prosecution. But unlike Mary's trial, John's ended differently. The jury was unable to reach a unanimous decision and the trial ended with a "hung jury." The government decided to retry Surratt, only this time on a charge of treason rather than murder. On July 17, 1862, Congress had enacted a treason statute that covered certain acts committed during the Civil War. There was no doubt that Surratt had been a Confederate agent and that his alleged role in Lincoln's death fell under this statute. The United States Attorney for the District of Columbia, Edward C. Carrington, actually secured two indictments against Surratt under the treason statute and presented the first indictment to Judge George P. Fisher. Once again the government lost out—Fisher ruled that the government had waited too long to file charges and dismissed the case. The District of Columbia had a two-year limitation on such crimes. Fisher's dismissal was based on the fact that the government listed April 15, 1865, as the date of the alleged offence while its indictment was dated June 18, 1868, three years later. Carrington appealed but the Supreme Court of the District of Columbia upheld Fisher's ruling.[7]

The second indictment under the treason statute was made moot when the grand jury, upon learning of the Court's ruling, decided to officially "ignore" the second treason indictment.[8] Thus, the government had lost out on all three attempts to bring John Surratt to justice. The war was over and animosities had mostly died way. The great majority of people wanted to put the tragedy of the war behind them and get on with life. So too did John Surratt.

A free man, Surratt left Washington behind and made his way to the small town of Rockville, Maryland, located a few miles to the northwest. Here he secured a position teaching at the Rockville Female Academy. In 1870 Surratt decided to capitalize on his Civil War exploits and give a series of public lectures, charging admission of course. Surratt spoke at the Montgomery County Courthouse in Rockville about his role in Booth's attempt to capture Lincoln. The lecture, which Surratt said he was forced to give out of "pecuniary necessity," was carefully crafted, revealing little in the way of names or actions that were not already known. He told of being introduced to John Wilkes Booth, but failed to mention by whom or under what circumstances. He did make one statement that he left hanging. In describing his meeting with Booth, Surratt told his audience that after listening to Booth for several minutes, he interrupted him by saying, "I know who you are and what are your intentions."[9] The question is who told Surratt about Booth and his plans? Having been introduced to Booth by Dr. Samuel Mudd earlier in the day and knowing none of the other conspirators who agreed to join Booth (Arnold and O'Laughlen), it seems logical that it was Samuel Mudd who informed Surratt about Booth's plot to capture Lincoln.

Following his brief stay in Rockville, Surratt made his way to the city of Baltimore. In 1872 he married a local woman by the name of Mary Victorine Hunter, a second cousin of Francis Scott Key.[10] Surratt had found employment with the Old Bay Line, a steamship company that operated on the Chesapeake Bay. By the end of his career in 1915, he had risen to the office of freight auditor and treasurer of the company, an important position.

After his Rockville lecture on December 6, 1870, Surratt spoke in New York at Cooper Union on December 9.[11] After that speech he never spoke publicly again about his role in Booth's conspiracy, nor did any of his children offer any revelations they had heard from their father. To the very end, Surratt remained a good Confederate agent, keeping silent about the people and events associated with his clandestine activities during the war. His arrest and trial in 1867 proved fortunate, for had he been tried in 1865 along with his cohorts he surely would have gone to the gallows. Subsequent writers have felt that the failure to convict Surratt in 1867 was due to his trial before a civil court instead of a military tribunal. His eventual release, however, was more a function of the times than the jurisdiction of trial. By 1867 the country had moved on and the war and Lincoln's murder were in the past. Neither the passion nor the interest continued past the 1865 conspiracy trial. When the grand jury chose to officially "ignore"[12] the final effort to indict John Surratt, it reflected the general feeling throughout the country. Surratt died of pneumonia in 1916 at the age of seventy-two and lies buried in New Cathedral Cemetery in Baltimore.[13]

Not all of the conspirators were as unlucky as Mary Surratt and her three cohorts who were hanged on July 7. Sitting in his prison cell, Samuel Mudd little realized how close he had come to joining Mary and the three men with her on the scaffold. Mudd had been tipped off by one of his jailers on July 6 that he would be spared the gallows. Had he known that a majority of the commission had voted for the death penalty, he would have spent a much more fitful night. Five of the nine commissioners believed Mudd was guilty enough that he should hang along with Mary and her friends. Mudd had escaped the gallows by a single vote. His next stop would be Fort Jefferson in the Florida Keys.

Located seventy miles off of the southern tip of Florida is a group of small islands known as the Dry Tortugas. Situated at one end of the group is Fort Jefferson, the largest masonry fortification built by the United States military. Fort Jefferson was said to be "the safest fort in the world, and the most useless."[14] Useless perhaps, but for the next three years and eleven months it would be home for Samuel Mudd, Samuel Arnold, and Edman Spangler.[15]

Fort Jefferson was an engineering marvel in many ways. Construction of the fort was begun in the winter of 1846 under the direction of Lieutenant Horatio G. Wright, who would eventually command the Sixth Army Corps in the final two years of the Civil War. Construction on the fort continued for nearly three decades until 1875 when the work was stopped, although the fort was not yet finished. The outer walls were forty-five feet high and sat on an underwater foundation fourteen feet in width. Originally designed to accommodate one thousand soldiers, the fort held two thousand military prisoners at the time of Mudd's imprisonment.[16]

Following his conviction Mudd and his fellow prisoners were originally scheduled to be incarcerated in the federal penitentiary in Albany, New York. But Stanton decided that they should remain under military control and ordered their imprisonment shifted to Fort Jefferson. It was during the trip from Washington to Fort Jefferson that Captain George W. Dutton, the officer in charge of the military escort guarding the four conspirators, claimed that Mudd made a surprising admission. According to Dutton, Mudd admitted knowing his guest was John Wilkes Booth and that, on returning from his trip to Bryantown on Saturday, April 15, Mudd admonished Booth for putting his family in jeopardy. He told Booth that he had to leave his house immediately.

Dutton's statement has received only marginal attention from historians. In most accounts written about Samuel Mudd, Dutton's claim is simply reported without any explanation[17] or not mentioned at all.[18] But Dutton's claim had corroboration. In fact, four other individuals made claims that Mudd had admitted that he knew his injured patient was John Wilkes Booth. Most significant among these was Dr. Mudd's own wife, Frances.

In 1901 the famous Lincoln collector and historian Osborn H. Oldroyd set out on a walk to retrace Booth's escape through southern Maryland. Osborn stopped at each of the sites visited by Booth in 1865. One of the stops was the home of Dr. and Mrs. Mudd. Mudd had been dead for eighteen years when Oldroyd visited the farm. According to Oldroyd's biographer, William Burton Benham, Mrs. Mudd made a startling revelation at the time of Oldroyd's visit: "Mrs. Mudd received [Oldroyd] cordially upon learning who he was and the nature of his errand. She told Captain Oldroyd that Dr. Mudd [on his return from Bryantown] upbraided Booth for his rashness and told him that he had inflicted an irreparable injury to the South."[19] This statement by Benham came many years after the incident occurred, which subjects it to the vagaries of memory. But there are two other statements that confirm Mudd's admission that he knew his injured patient was John Wilkes Booth.

Among the military officers on board the USS *Florida* were Brigadier General Levi Axtell Dodd, a member of Major General John Hartranft's staff in charge of the prisoners, and Assistant Paymaster William F. Keeler, who had served aboard the *Monitor* before transferring to the *Florida* in 1864. Both Dodd and Keeler made statements that they too had heard Mudd's admission that he knew Booth at the time of his April visit and knew that he had murdered Lincoln. Dodd's statement, like Dutton's, appeared in articles in the *Washington Star* and the *New York Times*.[20] According to the *Star* article, Dodd had also filed a report with Holt on his return to Washington in which he claimed that Mudd had admitted to knowing it was Booth at his house in April.[21]

While Dodd and Dutton served together at the Arsenal Prison, and may have discussed their claims prior to returning home, a letter written by William Keeler four years later adds further credibility to the story. While living in Chicago in early 1869, Keeler read an article in the local newspaper suggesting that President Johnson was considering granting a pardon to Mudd. Concerned that Johnson was unaware of Mudd's lying about his relationship with Booth, Keeler wrote a letter to his congressman, B.C. Cook, on January 21, 1869, stating, "In conversation with myself, & I think with others on our passage down he [Mudd] admitted what I believe the prosecution failed to prove at his trial—viz—that he knew who Booth was when he set his leg & what crime he was guilty [of]."[22]

So here we have three individuals whose only acquaintance with one another occurred on board the *Florida* transporting Mudd to Fort Jefferson. Dutton and Dodd filed their claims immediately on their return to Washington. Keeler's claim came four years later and was in response to his reading that efforts were being made to gain Mudd a presidential pardon.

There is one more piece to the story of Mudd's admission that he knew his patient was Booth all along. In 1893 Thomas Jones published his memoir about his effort to hide Booth and Herold in the pine thicket and safely send them across the Potomac River to Virginia.[23] Samuel Cox Jr., the adopted son of Samuel Cox, owned a copy of Jones's book and made annotations on several points mentioned by Jones. Among the annotations is one describing a conversation between the younger Cox and Mudd in 1877 when the two men toured Charles County together as candidates for state office.[24] According to the younger Cox, Mudd admitted knowing his visitor was Booth. Mudd also acknowledged there were two meetings between himself and Booth prior to April 15: "He was horrified when told the President had been shot the night before, and, upon asking who had shot him the fellow had answered Booth. He [Mudd] told me his first impulse was to surrender Booth, that he had imposed upon him, had *twice* [emphasis added] forced himself upon him and now a third time, had come with a lie upon his tongue and received medical assistance."[25] Thus Cox Jr. confirms the statements of Dutton, Dodd, and Keeler that Mudd knew his visitor was Booth and that he had killed Lincoln. To believe Mudd's claim of not knowing his injured visitor was John Wilkes Booth would require believing that all four witnesses had lied.

As with most other aspects of Samuel Mudd's story, his imprisonment in Fort Jefferson has been considerably distorted. In 1935 Paramount Pictures released a movie starring Warner Baxter based on Mudd's trial and imprisonment under the gripping title of *The Prisoner of Shark Island.* Fort Jefferson was portrayed as an American "Devil's Island" where prisoners were subjected to inhumane punishment and even thrown in a shark infested moat surrounding the fort. Dr. Mudd was portrayed as an innocent victim whose life was made unendurable because of the false accusations that he had aided John Wilkes Booth in the murder of President Lincoln. If this was not enough to justify his brutal treatment, his attempt to escape the prison two months after his arrival brought even greater punishment to him. The conditions in the prison and the alleged treatments were all exaggerated.

Shortly after his arrival Dr. Mudd was assigned to the post hospital where he could put his medical training to some practical use and enjoy living conditions similar to the other employees in the hospital.[26] From all indications it appeared that Mudd was pleased with his assignment and the opportunity to use his medical skills. Within six weeks Mudd wrote to his wife, "I have had several opportunities to make my escape, but knowing, or believing, it would show guilt, I have resolved to remain peaceable and quiet."[27] "The several opportunities" that Mudd alluded to stemmed from the casual treatment he received from his jailers. The next few weeks, however, would find a change of heart regarding escape. The 161st New York Infantry was replaced by the Eighty-second United States Colored Troops, a replacement that the southern Maryland doctor found especially disturbing. As a former slaveowner and slave capturer, Mudd viewed the new troops as an insult. "To be lorded over by a set of ignorant, prejudiced and irresponsible beings of the unbleached humanity was more than I could submit to," he wrote in a letter to his wife.[28]

Three weeks after Mudd had written his wife that he would not attempt escape, he did just that. Arriving on September 25, 1865, was a supply ship, the *Thomas A. Scott.* Mudd later wrote to his lawyer Thomas Ewing, "I had the advice of many and was promised aid by one of the quartermasters on the boat." The "quartermaster" was a young seaman by the name of Henry Kelly. Precisely who gave Mudd advice and who arranged for Kelly to aid the doctor has never surfaced, but Mudd's escape could not have been planned and carried out by Mudd alone. The effort raises interesting questions that remain unanswered.

Mudd's escape plan was rather simple and showed just how lax his treatment had been. Taking advantage of his ability to move freely about the Fort, Mudd dressed in a clean suit of clothes and simply walked out of the fort and up the gangplank of the *Scott.* Once on deck he was met by Henry Kelly, who took him below and hid him beneath some loosened floorboards in the hold. A routine check of the prisoners back inside the fort soon revealed that Mudd was missing. No ship left the fort without a check of all of the prisoners. A search of the ship was undertaken and Mudd was soon discovered. When challenged by the fort's commandant as to who helped him hide in the hold, Mudd gave up the name of the sailor. Kelly denied any role in Mudd's escape, claiming he was innocent, but Mudd had fingered him as the key man. Kelly was arrested and taken into the fort along with Mudd. In keeping with his character, Mudd criticized the government and all associated with the fort over his treatment following his escape attempt. Others had attempted to flee and upon their capture had had little done to them. In fact, little was done to Mudd. Whatever hardships befell him, his writing privileges were not affected. He was writing home again four days after his capture. In a letter to his brother-in-law, Mudd facetiously described his punishment: "I was placed under a boss, who put me to cleaning old bricks. I worked hard all day, and came very near finishing one brick."[29] In another letter to his brother-in-law dated a week later Mudd wrote: "I am taking my present hardship as a joke. I am not put back in the least. I will soon assume my former position [in the post hospital], or one equally respectable. The only thing connected with my present attitude is the name, and not the reality. I have no labor to perform, yet I am compelled to answer roll-call, and to sleep in the guardhouse at night. This will not last longer than this week."[30]

Mudd's incarceration at Fort Jefferson was hardly cruel. No longer working in the hospital, Mudd was given privileges in the fort's carpenter's shop. On February 20, 1867, Mudd wrote to his wife about his current "occupation": "I occupy my time principally in making little boxes, ornamenting them with different colors and varieties of wood."[31] Mudd had now become a crafter. The restored Samuel A. Mudd house has among its many attractive furnishings several fine articles of cabinetry that were made by Mudd while in prison at Fort Jefferson. These items include an "inlaid center table," a "ladies workbox," and a "number of shells gathered by him while he was a prisoner and arranged in the form of wreaths of flowers."[32] Such items show that Mudd was given full privileges to the prison's carpentry shop along with ample time to use the facilities. That cruelties occurred to certain prisoners appears to be true. An investigation into alleged acts of cruelty took place in 1866, and two officers were subsequently court-martialed for mistreating prisoners.[33] Mudd's treatment, however, stands in contrast to that of other prisoners who were not as fortunate.

Mudd's attempted escape was real enough. It is how it has become portrayed and the consequences of it that have been so mischaracterized. In 1903, Mudd's youngest daughter, Nettie Mudd Monroe, published her biography of her father. Mrs. Monroe explained her father's escape as an effort to reach the safety of the Federal court in Florida for the purpose of seeking protection under a writ of habeas corpus and thereby overturning his wrongful conviction by the justice system.[34] Using Nettie's account of her father's attempted escape, a television documentary titled, *Rewriting History: The Case of Dr. Samuel A. Mudd*, attempted to explain Mudd's escape: "Dr. Mudd's wife tried diligently to have her husband released. But as her efforts appeared fruitless, Dr. Mudd decided that *he must try and get to Key West where he could obtain a Writ of Habeas Corpus* [emphasis added]. On September 25th, 1865, even though he vowed he would not try to escape, Dr. Mudd attempted an escape from Fort Jefferson aboard the U.S. transport, 'Thomas A. Scott.' But before it sailed, he was discovered."[35]

The producers of the documentary only needed to read Mudd's own account of why he attempted to escape to find the real reason. On October 18, 1865, twenty-four days after his attempt, Mudd wrote a letter to his wife in which he explained his actions: "My dear Frank, it is bad enough to be a prisoner in the hands of white men, your equals under the Constitution, but to be lorded over by a set of ignorant, prejudiced and irresponsible beings of the unbleached humanity, was more than I could submit to, when I had every reason to believe my chances of escape almost certain, and would be crowned with success."[36]

Mudd further explained his reason for attempting to escape in a letter to his brother-in-law Jeremiah Dyer as "the humiliation of being guarded by an ignorant, irresponsible & prejudiced negro Soldiery, before an Enlightened People as a justification. We are now guarded entirely by negro soldiers & a few white Officers a skins difference." He then acknowledged, "Could we have had the White Regiment, the 161st N.Y.V. to guard the place *no thought of leaving should have been harbored for a moment*" (emphasis added).[37] Mudd's explanation for his attempted escape from Fort Jefferson was driven by a deep dislike for Black soldiers. His dislike, however, was not limited to Black soldiers, but for Blacks in general. In a letter to his wife dated December 12, 1865, Mudd wrote, "I am sorry to hear of the death of George Garrico and Mr. Bean. Our white population is wonderfully diminishing by death and other causes. The negroes will soon be in the majority, if not already. Should I be released any time shortly, and circumstances permit, I will use all my endeavors to find a more congenial locality."[38] Mudd's suggestion of "White flight" shows that his dislike for Blacks goes beyond having to suffer under "unbleached" soldiery. It was Dr. Mudd's view of Blacks and his dislike for Abraham Lincoln's policies on emancipation that drove him into the waiting arms of John Wilkes Booth.

Mudd's image as an innocent victim whose prosecution was driven by a vengeful government was slow to emerge. It was not until some fifty-five years after his conviction that the public's acceptance of Mudd's guilt began to change. This change was due, in large part, to the efforts of his grandson, Dr. Richard Dyer Mudd, who began a crusade on his grandfather's behalf in the late 1920s shortly after graduating from medical school. Many writers have accepted the sympathetic view put forward by Richard Mudd and other members of the Mudd family.[39]

Most writers accept the erroneous claim that we would never have heard of Dr. Mudd if Booth had not broken his leg in jumping from the box at Ford's Theatre. But a careful reading of the trial testimony of Army Detective Eaton G. Horner clearly shows that Samuel Mudd had been fingered by Samuel Arnold one day before the military authorities first visited Mudd at his home. When Samuel Arnold told Horner on April 17 that Booth carried letters of introduction to Drs. Mudd and Queen, Mudd became a suspect. This information would have sent detectives after Mudd and Queen even if Booth had not broken his leg and had bypassed Mudd's house on his escape route. The fact that Mudd and Booth were linked was also corroborated by statements by George Atzerodt that appeared in the *National Intelligencer:* "Booth told Atzerodt about two weeks before the murder that he had sent provisions and liquor to Dr. Mudd's for the supply of the party on their way to Richmond with the President."[40] If this was not sufficient, Louis Wiechmann linked Samuel Mudd to Booth when he told of the meeting between Booth, Surratt, Mudd, and himself at Booth's hotel room in Washington on December 23, 1864. Irrespective of whether Booth had broken his leg and stopped by Dr. Mudd's during the early morning hours of April 15, the government had considerable cause to pick up Mudd and consider him an intimate of John Wilkes Booth.

If Louis Wiechmann had seriously damaged the defense of Mary Surratt, he proved devastating to Mudd's case. Mudd had claimed to have met Booth on only one occasion and then only by accident. The government believed differently. Wiechmann's revelation of the meeting in Washington in December and how Booth invited the three men to his hotel where a conversation took place was devastating to Mudd's defense.

Mudd's attorney attacked Wiechmann from the start. He challenged the witness, discrediting his account of the meeting by proving that Mudd could not have been in Washington on the day Wiechmann claimed the meeting occurred. Ewing was emphatic in his summation: "There is no reliable evidence that [Dr. Mudd] ever met Booth before the assassination but *once on Sunday and once the following day in November last*" (emphasis added). Mudd had lied to his own lawyer about his meetings with Booth.

Frederick Stone, who along with Thomas Ewing defended Mudd, came to believe that he too had been duped by Mudd. In 1883 shortly after Mudd's death, the journalist George Alfred Townsend wrote a column about the doctor from Charles County. Townsend interviewed Stone and came away with an extraordinary quote: "The court very nearly hanged Dr. Mudd. His prevarications were painful. He had given his whole case away by not trusting even his counsel or neighbors or kinfolk. It was a terrible thing to extricate him from the coils he had woven about himself. He had denied knowing Booth when he knew him well. He was undoubtedly accessory to the abduction plot, though he may have supposed it would never come to anything. He denied knowing Booth when he came to his house when that was preposterous. He had been even intimate with Booth."[41]

On January 30, 1869, Frances Mudd wrote her last letter to her husband at Fort Jefferson. She began by writing, "When I last wrote I was hoping that it would be the last letter I would write to you on that miserable island, but I now feel very, very hopeful that this will be my last."[42] Frances was right. It was her last letter to her husband. On February 8 President Johnson granted Samuel Mudd and the two surviving conspirators imprisoned in Fort Jefferson a full and unconditional pardon. Johnson's pardon specifically referred to Mudd's humanitarian service during a serious yellow fever epidemic that had occurred at Fort Jefferson in the summer of 1867.[43]

In August 1867 the first case of yellow fever appeared among one of the soldiers at the fort. A week later a second case appeared in another soldier from the same company. By the end of the month a third case had occurred. All three involved soldiers of Company K. Within three weeks the epidemic was at its peak, infecting two out of every three persons among the fort's population. The post doctor and all four of the post's nurses were dead within three weeks of the first case. On September 7 Dr. Daniel Whitehurst came from Key West to care for the sick. Mudd and Whitehurst had to handle the 270 patients now infected with the deadly virus.

Yellow fever was among the most widely feared and violent diseases that ravaged the world in the nineteenth century. Historically, it may have first appeared in the Western Hemisphere among members of Columbus's second expedition to the Americas in 1495. It was first described as an epidemic in Mexico in 1648, where it was believed to have been imported from Western Africa on slave ships. During the seventeenth, eighteenth, and nineteenth centuries the disease was prevalent throughout the Caribbean. It steadily spread along the sea lanes of the Atlantic Ocean, eventually reaching South America and Africa. While today we know the biological basis of this disease, the nineteenth-century world did not. They instead believed yellow fever to be spread from one human being to another by physical contact. Yellow fever is a disease that is viral in nature and is only passed between hosts by the mosquito, *Aedes aegypti*, which lives close to human habitations and reproduces in stagnant pools of water, which were abundant throughout Fort Jefferson.[44] The virus is not infectious and is incapable of spreading among individuals without the aid of an intermediary host such as the mosquito. Their misunderstanding of this key fact of how the disease spread led mid-nineteenth-century medical experts to advocate quarantine.

The virus becomes established in the host, where it circulates in the blood stream. It is then transmitted by mosquitoes sucking the blood from infected individuals and moving on to noninfected individuals. The symptoms of the disease can range from mild to horrific. In its mildest form, yellow fever produces symptoms that are grippe-like, including fever, headache, and nausea. In its severest form, the disease produces high fever, frequent vomiting, severe epigastric pain, and jaundice, which gives the infected individual a bronze or yellow complexion. Near the end stage of the disease the patient experiences "black vomit" resulting from chronic bleeding into the stomach, which results in shock and death. There is no cure or specific treatment for yellow fever. Up to fifty percent of patients with the severe form of the disease die, primarily due to the primitive conditions where the disease is most prevalent.

Yellow fever was prevalent throughout the southern United States, and several areas, especially along the Gulf Coast and the Florida Keys, experienced severe epidemics at regular intervals. So severe was one epidemic in 1801 that it became a major factor in convincing Napoleon to sell the Louisiana Territory to the United States the following year. By 1900 as many as ninety epidemics had ravaged urban areas throughout the United States.

Dr. Whitehurst had originally served as post surgeon at Fort Jefferson but left in 1861 because of his wife's strong allegiance to the Confederacy. When word of the post surgeon's death in 1867 reached him in Florida, Whitehurst hurried to the Island, offering his assistance to Mudd, who was now in charge of caring for the sick patients. Both Mudd and Whitehurst worked tirelessly as the epidemic raged on. By September 17 both Arnold and O'Laughlen had contracted the disease. On the twenty-third O'Laughlen died. Arnold recovered. Spangler and Mudd escaped contracting the deadly form of the disease, although Mudd appears to have had a mild attack, experiencing fever and headache. The last case of fever was recorded on November 14. In all, thirty-eight people died out of the 270 or more stricken. Mudd had been sick himself for about nine days in October when the wards were filled with patients. While little could be done to actually treat those sick with yellow fever, Mudd performed a great service caring for them and relieving their pain wherever possible. Believing the disease contagious, he placed himself at great risk in treating the sick for as much as fourteen hours a day.

As a result of his medical services during the epidemic a petition was drawn up requesting clemency and Mudd's immediate release from prison. Every noncommissioned officer in the garrison signed the petition. The two officers, however, along with the new post surgeon, did not sign the petition for reasons that can only be guessed or surmised. While there is no record that the petition ever reached President Johnson, he clearly recognized Mudd's efforts in combating the epidemic as evidenced by the wording of his pardon statement. Johnson cited Mudd's efforts: "Samuel A. Mudd devoted himself to the care and cure of the sick, and interposed his courage and his skill to protect the garrison, otherwise without medical aid, from peril and alarm, and thus, as the officers and men unite in testifying, saved many valuable lives and earned the admiration and the gratitude of all who observed or experienced his generous and faithful service to humanity."[45]

Mudd's pardon was dated February 8, 1869, but the bureaucracy took another four weeks to see to Mudd's release on March 8. He arrived home in Maryland to his wife and four children on March 20, 1869. Mudd had been absent for nearly four years. Nine months and eighteen days after his return his fifth child, Henry, was born. Over the next seven years the Mudds would have four more children, bringing their family to nine children—five boys and four girls.[46]

Tragedy continued to visit Mudd after his freedom. Henry died after just eight months, and the Mudd's would lose another son, Andrew, in 1882 at the age of twenty-four. Henry Lowe Mudd, Mudd's father, passed away in 1877 the year Sam ran for the state legislature. Mudd continued to farm tobacco and supplement his income with his medical practice. In January of 1883, Mudd contracted what was thought to be pneumonia and died on January 10 of that year. He was forty-nine years old. At the time of his death he was survived by his wife, seven children, and one granddaughter, Mary Melita Gardiner. Eventually Dr. Mudd would have thirty-two grandchildren, including Richard Dyer Mudd (1901–) and Louise Mudd Arehart (1917–), two grandchildren who devoted considerable effort to crafting an image of a kindly, country doctor who was persecuted by a vengeful government for following his Hippocratic oath in rendering medical assistance to John Wilkes Booth. Their efforts have met with considerable success.

Samuel Arnold and Edman Spangler survived the yellow fever epidemic and their imprisonment in Fort Jefferson. Three weeks after issuing his pardon to Dr. Mudd, President Johnson issued pardons freeing both Arnold and Spangler. Spangler came out of prison without a home, money, or apparent destination. Befriended by Samuel Mudd during his incarceration, Spangler made his way back to Maryland where he eventually showed up on Mudd's doorstep. Mudd welcomed his prison mate and invited him to stay on, giving him a small piece of land where he might build himself a house.[47] For the next six years Spangler remained a part of the Mudd family using his carpentry skills around the farm.[48] In February of 1875 he succumbed to a respiratory ailment and was buried in an unmarked grave in the old St. Peter's cemetery. In 1983, the Surratt Society and the Samuel A. Mudd Society jointly sponsored a project to mark the grave with a small tombstone that reads, "Edman 'Ned' Spangler Aug. 10, 1825–Feb. 7, 1875 erected by the Surratt Society in conjunction with the Dr. Samuel A. Mudd Society."

Unlike Ned Spangler, Sam Arnold had a family and a home to which he could return. Arnold became something of a recluse and in his own words was a "misanthrope."[49] His dislike for people was a natural reaction to his conviction and imprisonment for four years in Fort Jefferson. Arnold returned to Baltimore where his father operated a bakery and confectionery store out of his residence on Fayette Street. In 1848 Sam's father, George Arnold, had purchased a 118–acre farm in a section of Baltimore known as Hookstown. Today, the 118–acre farm that made up a part of the Baltimore community of Hookstown, is home to the famous Pimlico racetrack. George Arnold eventually deeded the farm where Sam Arnold frequently stayed to his wife's brother, William Bland. Sam appears to have alternated between the two places, at least for a while. In 1894 he was employed as a butcher at Fells Point in Baltimore. By 1902 he was living in Friendship, Maryland, at the home of a close friend, Mrs. Ann Garner. Arnold had written a letter to his mother on July 6, 1865, while imprisoned in the Washington Arsenal in which he described Mrs. Garner as "a second mother."[50] The Garner home in Friendship, located approximately twelve miles south of Annapolis, Maryland, provided a safe haven for the reclusive Arnold.

Sometime during the 1890s Arnold decided to record a memoir of his relationship with Booth and the conspiracy to capture Lincoln. His intention was to have the document published after his death in an effort to sway public opinion in his favor. When word of his manuscript leaked to the press, however, the *Baltimore American* contacted Arnold offering to publish his story. Arnold remained adamant about not allowing his manuscript to be published until after he died. Then something quite strange happened. In 1902, another man by the name of Samuel Arnold died and several newspapers, assuming it was the conspirator, wrote lengthy obituaries that gave the real Arnold an opportunity to see just how he would be portrayed by the press after his real death.[51] Accounts of his role as a conspirator of Booth were unflattering. Unhappy with what he read, Arnold decided to allow the *Baltimore American* to publish his story, believing he would be completely vindicated. The manuscript was published in serial form beginning on December 2, 1902, and running through December 20, 1902. As might be expected, Sam's story was self-serving and filled with righteous indignation toward just about everyone who had been involved in the events of the conspiracy, including Sam's old school chum John Wilkes Booth. Arnold described the capture effort as "purely humane and patriotic in its principals."[52] While attempting to portray the plot against Lincoln in a patriotic light, Arnold justified James Speed's approval of a military trial when he admitted that the conspiracy was "legitimate as an act of war."[53] Indeed, capturing the commander in chief of the enemy force was an act of war. In 1943 an antiquarian book dealer who had purchased the memoir published the original manuscript in a limited edition of 199 copies,[54] and in 1995, a series of newspaper articles covering much of Arnold's memoir was republished by Heritage Books, edited by Michael W. Kauffman.[55]

Whether Arnold was happy with the response to his memoir is not known, but it seems unlikely. By 1902 when the memoir first appeared there was little sympathy for any of those convicted in Lincoln's murder. Four years after publication and while still living in the Garner farmhouse in Friendship, Maryland, Arnold became seriously ill. In June 1906 he moved into the Baltimore home of his sister-in-law, where he died, presumably of tuberculosis, on September 21, 1906, at the age of seventy-two. He lies buried in Green Mount Cemetery in Baltimore where Michael O'Laughlen and John Wilkes Booth are also buried. Arnold was survived by only John Surratt, who would live for another ten years before dying in 1916.

CHAPTER TWENTY-ONE

Life after Death

> Search then the ruling passion: there, alone,
> The wild are constant, and the cunning known;
> The fool consistent, and the false sincere.
>
> *Alexander Pope*

The fire from the burning tobacco barn blazed throughout the early morning hours casting a red glow over the scene unfolding at the Garrett farmhouse. A column of grey smoke rose skyward sending a signal to everyone within a two-mile radius that something was happening. The hidden eyes that had watched Yankee horsemen riding from Port Royal didn't have to guess who was behind the smoke. It was all too common a scene in the war-ravaged countryside. By midmorning the troopers were gone leaving the Garrett barn a blackened pile of smoldering embers. The smoke that rose from the barn would eventually subside, only to be replaced by the smoke of conspiracy rising in its place. The conspiratorialists would soon begin obscuring what had taken place that April morning at the Garrett farm.

On October 24, 1994, a small group of lay historians filed into the large white building that housed the circuit court for the city of Baltimore. They had come in response to a petition that had been filed with the court requesting permission to exhume the body of John Wilkes Booth from its grave in the family plot in Baltimore's Green Mount Cemetery.[1] The petitioners claimed a legal right to do so, stating the "public interest" as their justification. The legal right was based on the fact that among the petitioners were several individuals who bore a collateral relationship to John Wilkes Booth. The justification was based on their belief that the body in the grave was not that of the killer of Abraham Lincoln, but another man's, an innocent victim of a deep and sinister plot.

The principal movers behind the petition were two avocational historians who claimed that it was not Booth who was killed in the Garrett barn. Booth had escaped earlier and made his way to the small town of Enid, Oklahoma Territory, where he died by suicide in 1903 using the name David E. George. It was an old story retold many times in newspaper articles and dime-store paperbacks. Now it would be heard again, this time in a court of law where the shocking claims of conspiracy would be subjected to legal scrutiny. It was a scrutiny long overdue.

A book had been published in 1907 that eclipsed all of the previous sensational claims that John Wilkes Booth was never killed in Richard Garrett's barn.[2] Finis L. Bates, a Tennessee lawyer, published his personal account of having heard the confession of a Texas saloon keeper, John St. Helen, who claimed to be the assassin of Abraham Lincoln. According to Bates, John St. Helen and David E. George were names adopted by Booth. Basing their petition on the book's allegation, the two historians submitted additional "evidence" to support the claim. Their evidence consisted of a resurrection of old tales that had circulated through a half century of newspaper articles.[3]

Prior to their attempt to "dig up" Booth's body, one of the petitioners had convinced the producers of the NBC television series *Unsolved Mysteries* that the story of Booth's escape was true and was worthy of a television production. In 1991 NBC aired the program as part of the *Unsolved Mysteries* show. Flushed with the success of having the story of Booth's alleged escape viewed by millions of people, the two historians made an effort to convince the Circuit Court for the City of Baltimore that the only sure way to settle the mystery of whether the body in the grave was really that of John Wilkes Booth was to dig it up and subject the bones to forensic examination. Unknown to the presiding judge, and many of the courtroom spectators, the body of John Wilkes Booth had been exhumed before, not once but twice, and his remains positively identified on both occasions. But twice was not enough. Only a third time would satisfy the latest advocates of this strange request for resurrection.

The court day arrived and the petitioners submitted seventy pages of "evidence" to support their contention that the body in the grave was not that of Lincoln's killer. The cemetery corporation opposed the petition and requested that the court hold a hearing on the matter. Joining with the officers of the cemetery were several prominent historians whose expertise in the assassination of Lincoln was well established. The strange tale harkened back to the year 1903 and involved a cast of extraordinary characters.

The story begins on January 13, 1903, with the death of David E. George, an obscure drifter, in Enid, Oklahoma Territory. George, who was prone to bouts of alcoholism, had come to Enid only weeks before from El Reno, Texas, located seventy miles south of Enid. Arriving in Enid, George registered at the Grand Avenue Hotel. It appears he was in his early sixties when he died, which would place his date of birth sometime around 1840.[4] There was nothing about his life that would have led anyone to believe that he would be remembered beyond the publication of his obituary, which appeared in the local paper the day following his death. It was at this point that his remarkable saga began.

A local Enid woman named Mrs. E.C. Harper read of George's death in a local obituary column. Recognizing the name, she wondered if it could be the same man she had met three years earlier in El Reno, Texas, who, believing he was about to die, told her he was John Wilkes Booth. Mrs. Harper, a twenty-eight–year-old widow named Jessica Kuhn at the time, first met David George while visiting a close friend who lived in El Reno.[5] According to Mrs. Harper, George was a boarder in the woman's house. On the day of Mrs. Harper's visit, George returned home from work feeling seriously ill. It seems he had taken a heavy dose of a drug that had adversely affected him. He told Mrs. Harper he felt he was going to die. Mrs. Harper became alarmed and sent for a local doctor. While waiting for the doctor to arrive she listened to the dying man's "confession."[6] Now that he was dying he had to tell someone his incredible secret.

Miraculously, George did not die that day in 1900 but recovered fully and lived another three years before finally succumbing to a lethal dose of self-administered strychnine. On reading the obituary, Mrs. Harper sent her husband, the Reverend E.C. Harper, over to the funeral parlor to ask about George. The Reverend Harper told the undertaker that he recognized the corpse as that of the man who had "confessed" to his wife in El Reno that he was John Wilkes Booth, the assassin of Abraham Lincoln. Mrs. Harper, now a resident of Enid, came to the conclusion that the corpse at the funeral home was indeed her David E. George, a.k.a. John Wilkes Booth, of El Reno. The George-Booth story quickly made its way to the editor of the local newspaper, and soon it was sweeping the country.

The story reached Finis L. Bates at his law offices in Memphis, Tennessee. Reading the story of George, Bates was stunned. He claimed that he also had met a man who confessed to being John Wilkes Booth. In 1872, thirty-one years earlier, while practicing law in Granbury, Texas, Bates was asked to listen to the dying confession of a local saloon keeper named John St. Helen. St. Helen told Bates that he had been part of a plot that Vice President Andrew Johnson had engineered to kill Abraham Lincoln. Fortunately for St. Helen he was not in the barn at the time the Sixteenth New York Cavalry arrived. He had escaped earlier. In his place was another man by the name of "Ruddy."

"Ruddy," it turned out, was Franklin Roby, the overseer for Samuel Cox. It was Roby who Samuel Cox had told to hide Booth and Herold in a pine thicket near the boundary of his plantation. It was Roby who then led Thomas Jones to the thicket and showed him where he had hid the two fugitives. All this, of course, was true. But here the truth ended.

According to Bates's story, Ruddy safely piloted Booth and Herold over the Potomac and to Port Royal where the three Confederate soldiers, Ruggles, Bainbridge, and Jett, were waiting for them. At this point, Booth, a.k.a. St. Helen, discovered that he had carelessly left several of his personal items, including his little memorandum book, in William Lucas's wagon. Booth-

St. Helen asked Ruddy to return to Lucas's cabin and retrieve his lost items. Ruddy agreed. In the meantime, Booth, provided with a horse by one of the Confederate soldiers, safely made his escape south. Meanwhile, Ruddy retrieved Booth's lost articles and made his way to the Garrett farm where he stopped for the evening. Unable to find a place to sleep in the crowded farmhouse of Richard Garrett, Ruddy slept in the old farmer's tobacco barn. It proved to be a fatal mistake. During the early morning hours members of the Sixteenth New York Cavalry awakened him, and before he could explain who he was he was shot by Boston Corbett. Meanwhile, Booth was making his escape that carried him to Mexico, then Texas and California before winding up in Enid.

Bates listened intently to the incredible tale of the sick man. But like David E. George, John St. Helen did not die. Bates, unaware of St. Helen's recovery, decided to pursue a claim for part of the reward money set aside for the capture of Booth. In 1900, some twenty-five years after hearing St. Helen-Booth's confession, lawyer Bates petitioned the United States government for the reward money. The government placed Bates's claim in its "crackpot file." Of course, the government believed it knew that John Wilkes Booth had been killed at the Garrett farm, and it had dispensed all of the reward money to the legitimate claimants. As far as the government was concerned the case was closed. Why Bates had waited twenty-five years after hearing St. Helen's confession before acting is not clear. Having lost his claim for the reward money, Bates placed it in his files and forgot all about it. That is, until he read the claim by Mrs. E.C. Harper that John Wilkes Booth had only recently died in Enid under the alias of David E. George. Could David E. George be the same man Bates knew as John St. Helen?

Bates, ever the entrepreneur, hopped aboard the next train out of Memphis and, arriving in Enid, went straightway to the local undertaker, where he asked to see the remains of the man named David E. George. It was the very same man Bates had listened to in 1872 in Granby, Texas, over thirty years before, or so Bates said. David E. George was John St. Helen, and since John St. Helen was John Wilkes Booth, George must be John Wilkes Booth. The man who had confessed to Mrs. Harper was the same man who confessed to Finis Bates. The circle was closed and Bates was ready to go after the government once again for the huge reward offered for Booth's body, dead or alive. What Bates must have realized, but apparently ignored, was that the reward money had been disbursed thirty-five years earlier. No matter, it was worth a try. At the very least, Bates was sitting on an incredible story that he was ready to pursue with vigor.

To make matters even better for Bates, the body of George went unclaimed. For years it was kept in the back room of a furniture store owned by the undertaker who had embalmed him. It became one of the special sights in Enid as people would come to the store and ask to see the body of John

Wilkes Booth.[7] Bates asked the undertaker, who had been appointed administrator of George's estate, if he could take the body. The undertaker agreed and Bates shipped the body back home to Memphis.

Bates was not about to let his crucial piece of evidence be buried in some potter's field. Better it be stored in his house. For the next three years Bates hounded the government, offering to turn over the embalmed remains of the infamous Booth for the reward money. His offer was repeatedly rejected and his claims went nowhere. But Bates was the consummate entrepreneur. If he could not convince the government to make him a wealthy man, he would take his case to the American people and let them make him wealthy.

While Bates waited for the government to answer his claims he continued caring for the body of David E. George, which had become mummified. Bates regularly lathered the corpse with petroleum jelly to keep it from drying and cracking. In between his lawyer duties he began writing a book in which he told his amazing story—or rather the amazing story of David E. George–John St. Helen–John Wilkes Booth. And what a story it was. In 1907 Bates published his evidence in a book titled *The Escape and Suicide of John Wilkes Booth; or, the First True Account of Lincoln's Assassination, and Containing a Complete Confession by Booth, Many Years after the Crime*. At first it created a mild sensation, selling some 75,000 copies,[8] but it soon became discredited by critics who wrote of its numerous flaws and inaccuracies. Bates had failed in his attempt to make his fortune based on a personal relationship with "John Wilkes Booth," but Bates wasn't finished yet. Always the businessman, he still had his "mummy," and George's confession.

Bates next tried to interest Henry Ford in buying his "mummified Booth." Like Bates, Ford was an entrepreneur, although one who made Bates's efforts pale by comparison. Ford had a sharp nose for making a buck.[9] He had purchased from the widow of John T. Ford the rocking chair that Lincoln had sat in the night he was shot. Ford then put the rocker on display in his museum village in Dearborn, Michigan. Bates thought that Ford's exhibit would be greatly enhanced by adding the mummy to the rocker. For a brief moment, Ford also thought the mummy might prove worthy. Ford put one of his investigators on the case and asked him to find out what he could about Bates's mummy. Ford's investigator was Frederick Black, an attorney and editor of Ford's *Dearborn Independent*. Bates lost out again when Black reported back to Ford that the whole story was without foundation and bordered on the silly.

Bates was not through, however. He took the mummy on the road, exhibiting it to thousands of wide-eyed spectators willing to be gulled by his fantastic tale. He showed the mummy at fairs and various circus sideshows until he tired of the travel and finally sold the mummy to a small traveling carnival. The mummy toured the country traveling to nearly as many places and covering as many miles as the authentic John Wilkes Booth had done when he was alive. Although a popular attraction, it never generated the income that Booth had as America's matinee idol. The mummy eventually ran its show-business course and simply disappeared from sight sometime around 1940.

For a while Bates's story of Booth's escape and his mummy faded from the public's attention, but never completely. In 1991 the producers of *Unsolved Mysteries* became interested in the story. They were approached by the two men who later sought to exhume Booth's body. The producers concluded that the John St. Helen-David E. George caper would make for interesting television. But rather than rely on the Bates evidence that had been previously discredited, they introduced new evidence that they claimed had "never been published nor heard before."[10] The core of this evidence centered on the recollections of four individuals who were said to have viewed Booth's body shortly after his death. Two of the four individuals were Union soldiers: Sergeant Wilson D. Kenzie and Lieutenant William C. Allen. The third witness, Basil E. Moxley, was an employee of John T. Ford at his Baltimore Opera House who claimed to have served as a "pallbearer" during the reburial of Booth's body in Baltimore in 1869. The fourth eyewitness was one of Booth's physicians, Dr. John Frederick May. May was called to the *Montauk* by the government to identify Booth's body the same day it arrived back in Washington.

Wilson D. Kenzie has been called "the linchpin of the Booth escape theories" for good reason.[11] A Union soldier who had served the majority of his military service in the First United States Artillery, Kenzie claimed that he was among the soldiers at the Garrett farm and that the man killed there was not John Wilkes Booth. On March 31, 1922, fifty-seven years after Booth's death, Kenzie swore in an affidavit that he rode with the troopers as they closed in on Booth and Herold at the Garrett farm:

> I went in pursuit with them [the Sixteenth New York Cavalry]; and we all brought up at the Garrett barn where Booth was supposed to be; and Corbett's company surrounded the barn. Boston Corbett shot the man through a crack in the barn and killed him instantly. They brought the man out and put him on the porch and covered him with a blanket except his feet. Joe Zisgen had discovered that it wasn't J. Wilkes Booth and then they covered him up so no one could see his face, as I rode up Joe Zisgen called "Here, come here Sargent, this ain't J. Wilkes Booth at all." As he attempted to uncover the corpse, he was stopped by some of the officers, but the face was exposed enough so I could see the color of his hair and side of his face and from the fact that this man had sandy hair and Booth had very dark hair, I knew at

> once it wasn't he. His body was exposed, the lower part of it and he had no injured leg that I could see and he did not have on riding boots, but I think ordinary shoes and I sized him up as being an ordinary Virginia farmer. What I do know and positively state is that it was not the body of John Wilkes Booth.[12]

A few months after his first statement, Kenzie produced a second statement in which he wrote, "This fellow's a red-headed Virginian . . . he was red-headed and red-haired. There was no chance of a mistake . . . one of the three officers of high rank [Conger, Baker, Doherty] seized the blanket and shouted to me: 'Don't repeat that.' . . . My company commander, Lieutenant Norris [Lieutenant Hardman P. Norris, commanding Battery F, First United States Artillery], husband of a niece of Secretary Stanton, warned me also to keep quiet."[13]

These two statements form one of the principal legs supporting the claim that the body in the barn was not that of John Wilkes Booth. Kenzie claimed he was personally acquainted with Booth, having met him while he was stationed in New Orleans during the war and while Booth was appearing on stage in that city. Kenzie tells of his meeting with Booth:

> Our quarters in New Orleans was a very attractive place and visited by a great many people, among them being John Wilkes Booth, who was a frequent caller.
>
> The first time he came there he had a pass and all were required to have passes who came to enter our quarters. He attracted my attention and the second time he called I introduced myself to him and at that introduction he told me he was John Wilkes Booth.
>
> Booth was very fond of good horses and we had a great many in the service and during these meetings and interviews we became very good friends and associates, covering a period of about four months so that my knowledge and acquaintance with him was impressed upon my mind. Afterwards the whole Company knew him.[14]

Booth was in New Orleans in 1864 but only one month, not for four months as Kenzie stated. Booth arrived the first week of March and remained until April 9, when he left for an engagement in Boston.[15] While Kenzie is not specific as to the dates of Booth's visits to Battery F's quarters, he does say that shortly after Booth's visit Battery F was ordered "out on the Red River expedition." This campaign took place in May of 1864, which is consistent with Booth's being in New Orleans in March and April of that year.

In August 1864, Battery F was transferred to Washington, D.C. Its ranks depleted as a result of its engagements in Louisiana, Battery F was consolidated with Battery A after the two units arrived in Washington. The newly consolidated unit went into camp on Arlington Heights, Virginia, across the Potomac River from Washington, where it was located at the time of Lincoln's assassination. Kenzie claims he was at Ford's Theatre on the night of the assassination: "Norris [second lieutenant in command of the company at the time of its transfer to Arlington Heights] left the Company while we were at Arlington Heights about the time of the assassination of President Lincoln, which left the Company in my charge as First Sergeant acting as Quarter-Master Sargent which entitled me to a monthly pass, and gave me the privilege of going anywhere in Washington, night or day, and I frequently went to the theaters."[16]

One such occasion was the night of April 14: "I was looking at my program and did not see Booth when he jumped. I heard the shot and saw Booth standing on the platform and recognized him instantly. I then looked at my program to see if Booth was in the play but did not find him. Then I discovered the commotion on the stage and in Lincoln's box, and then I stood up and saw Booth with his hand raised shouting "Sic semper tyrannis." As Booth turned to move off, I noticed that he was dressed with high riding boots and limping in his right [*sic*] leg."[17]

Ten days later, on the afternoon of April 24, Kenzie claims he joined the members of the Sixteenth New York Cavalry as they set out in search of Booth:

> Everybody had been looking for Booth in a kind of free for all game as there had been a big reward offered. Corbett's Company or the Company with which he was connected, as they came out [from the Lincoln Barracks in Washington, D.C.] I enquired where they were going and they told me they were going out looking for Booth; and I said wait till I get my saddle on my horse and I will go with you. I went in pursuit of them; and we all brought up at the Garrett barn where Booth was supposed to be; and Corbett's company surrounded the barn.
>
> Boston Corbett shot the man, through a crack in the barn, and killed him instantly. They brought the man out and put him on the porch and covered him with a blanket except his feet.[18]

At this point in his story, Kenzie makes his way over to the porch where the dead man was lying under a blanket. Kenzie describes what he saw: "As he [Zisgen] attempted to uncover the corpse, he was stopped by some of the officers, but the face was exposed enough so that I could see the color of his hair and side of his face and from the fact that this man had sandy hair and Booth had very dark hair, I knew at once it wasn't he. His body was exposed, the lower part of it and he had no injured leg that I could see and he did not have on riding boots, but I think ordinary shoes and I sized him up as being an ordinary Virginia farmer. What I do know and positively state is that it was not the body of John Wilkes Booth."[19]

The man referred to in Kenzie's affidavit as Joe Zisgen is important to the story and appears to be the connection between Kenzie and the Sixteenth New York Cavalry. Zisgen had been a member of the First United States Artillery stationed in New Orleans. At the end of his tour with the First U.S. Artillery, Zisgen reenlisted in the Sixteenth New York. According to Kenzie, he and Zisgen had become good friends while serving together in Battery F in New Orleans. It was at this time that the two men got to know Booth when Booth visited their quarters in New Orleans. "Joe Zisgen of our Company knew Booth as well as I did. . . . Joe Zisgen . . . knew Booth in New Orleans."[20]

Zisgen enlisted in the First United States Artillery (Regular Army) in September of 1858 at Albany, New York. In September of 1862 his unit was transferred to New Orleans where Wilson Kenzie was already stationed as a member of the Sixth Michigan Volunteer Infantry. When Kenzie's enlistment in the Sixth Michigan expired in November of 1862 he reenlisted for three years in Battery A of the First United States Artillery where he became friends with Joseph Zisgen, then a member of Battery F. But Kenzie and Zisgen were together in New Orleans only until September 1863, a period of ten months, when Zisgen's enlistment ended. At this point, Zisgen returned to his home in New York state where he enlisted in the Sixteenth New York.

Kenzie began his affidavit by describing his meeting with Booth in the spring of 1864 just before the Red River campaign in May. According to Kenzie's statement, Joe Zisgen was a part of these meetings. Here Kenzie's story begins to unravel. Zisgen was not in New Orleans in the spring of 1864. He was in Vienna, Virginia, serving with the Sixteenth New York Cavalry at the very time Kenzie claims Booth was a frequent visitor to Battery F's quarters. While Kenzie and Booth may have been acquainted, Zisgen was serving in Virginia.

Kenzie's next reference to Zisgen occurs in the early morning hours of April 26 at the Garrett farm. Zisgen was one of the twenty-six troopers of the Sixteenth New York Cavalry who were present at the Garrett farm. While the record does not show a Wilson Kenzie among the capture party, Kenzie maintained he was there. How did a member of the First United States Artillery get to the Garrett farm with the Sixteenth New York?

The First United States Artillery had been transferred to Washington, D.C., in August of 1864 following the Red River campaign, and had been stationed on Arlington Heights overlooking the District of Columbia from the Virginia side of the river. The Sixteenth New York, on the other hand, was stationed in Vienna, Virginia, also south of the Potomac River and not far from the camp of the First United States Artillery. On April 24, however, the Sixteenth New York was in Washington, D.C., and not Vienna, Virginia. It had been transferred to Washington where it had been assigned to march in Lincoln's funeral procession as it made its way from the White House to the Capitol Building. The transfer occurred on Wednesday, April 19.

When Lafayette C. Baker received permission to use the Sixteenth New York Cavalry to pursue Booth into Virginia, it was still located in Washington, not Vienna, Virginia. For Wilson Kenzie to join the Sixteenth New York Cavalry he would have had to be in Washington on a pass. Kenzie claims to have been a first sergeant and acting quartermaster of Company F at the time. Because of his rank and quartermaster position he was free to go into the District as a part of his duties. His service records disagree, however. Kenzie was not commissioned as first sergeant until July 24, 1865, three months after Booth's capture. There is no record of his ever serving as regimental quartermaster at any time during his service. At the time of Booth's capture, Kenzie was a corporal and had been promoted to that rank only one month before. As such, he was not free to go into the District as he claimed, but would need to secure a pass through regular channels.

There is another problem with Kenzie's story. At no time does he mention traveling down the Potomac River by steamer. He appears to be unaware that the Sixteenth New York left Washington aboard the *John S. Ide.* The men of the Sixteenth New York boarded the *Ide* in Washington and started down the river to Belle Plaine located on the Virginia side. Belle Plaine is reachable overland from Arlington Heights and from Vienna. Had Kenzie returned to Arlington Heights, saddled his horse and ridden all night toward Belle Plaine, he could not have reached it as quickly as the *John S. Ide* did.

Kenzie knew that the Sixteenth New York had been previously bivouacked at Vienna, Virginia. In recreating his story he apparently was unaware of their transfer into the District and assumed they left from Vienna, not Washington. If Kenzie believed the Sixteenth New York left camp from Vienna, it would explain his failure to mention traveling several hours by steamer down the Potomac River. Kenzie's story of traveling with the Sixteenth New York cavalry is completely at variance with the facts.

Kenzie was wrong about several important points in his affidavit. Joe Zisgen could not have met Booth in New Orleans. Kenzie was not a sergeant at the time of Lincoln's assassination, nor was he ever company quartermaster. There is no record of his receiving a pass into Washington on April 14, and he could not have traveled with the Sixteenth New York aboard the *John S. Ide.*

Kenzie's service record shows that he was a good soldier who served his unit and his country well. His military exploits, however, are better documented than his extramilitary search for John Wilkes Booth. When Kenzie prepared his affidavit in 1922 he was seventy-eight years old and in the twilight of his life; an old soldier filled with memories of exciting times, some of which he may have shared vicariously through his old comrade, Joseph Zisgen.

Joseph Zisgen never left a statement or reminiscence on the subject. It seems incredible that he kept silent for so many years about such a startling observation as the wrong man's being captured at the Garrett farm. Kenzie and Zisgen can be placed on the list of doubtful eyewitnesses, which brings us to our next eyewitness, Lieutenant William C. Allen

Allen is another of the important eyewitnesses that the proponents of the "Booth escaped" theory use to support their claims. Allen's name first surfaced as a witness to the events at the Garrett farm in 1937, seventy-two years after Booth's death and twenty-nine years after Lieutenant Allen himself had died. Hannah Allen, widow of Lieutenant William C. Allen, attended a Grand Army of the Republic convention in Madison, Wisconsin, in 1937 where she stole the show with her revelations about her late husband's alleged claim. Mrs. Allen regaled reporters covering the convention with her claim that her husband had been present at the Garrett farm on April 26. He had witnessed the capture of Booth and had seen his body after he had died. Hannah claimed her husband confided to her that the dead man on the Garret porch had red hair. Allen knew Booth had "hair like a raven."[21] Allen is the second eyewitness to claim that the dead man had red hair, not black. Just who was William C. Allen and how did he get to the Garrett farm on April 26?

Allen was a member of the 151st New York Volunteer Infantry, having enlisted for three years as a private on August 27, 1862. He was promoted to sergeant on October 22, 1862, and to second lieutenant on February 18, 1865. He ended his service on June 26, 1865, having served thirty-four months. In July 1864, Allen was captured at the battle of Monocacy during Jubal Early's failed raid on Washington, D.C. He was taken to Libby Prison in Richmond where he was exchanged on December 21, 1864, and returned to his regiment at Petersburg, Virginia, on inauguration day, March 4, 1865. The 151st served at Petersburg until that town fell on April 2, and then chased Lee's retreating army to Appomattox Court House. It was present at the surrender of the Army of Northern Virginia on April 9.

Following Lee's surrender, the 151st New York marched seventy miles south to Danville, Virginia, arriving on April 27, the day after Booth died. While the 151st New York was en route to Danville, however, it appears Lieutenant Allen was several hundred miles to the north at his home in LeRoy, New York. On April 20, Allen applied for emergency leave to return home and visit his ailing father who was seriously ill and dying. Leave was granted on April 22, and Allen headed north to New York. There is nothing in the record to indicate that Allen decided to detour from his trip from Danville to New York and join in the search for Booth 175 miles to the northeast.

Unlike the case of Wilson Kenzie where an old soldier appears to have embellished his military career, William Allen made no such claims about himself. All of the claims came from his widow some thirty years after his death. Her claims ran far afield, including the claim that her husband was in the Secret Service and worked for Lafayette C. Baker. She also claimed that her husband "was a living image of Wilkes Booth," so much so that the newspapers of the day, needing a photograph of Booth, used a photograph of her husband "taken only a week before . . . , and printed it through the country captioned as the President's assassin."[22]

Mrs. Allen's story that her husband was present at Garrett's farm and that he later claimed the body was not that of John Wilkes Booth can be dismissed as another assassination fable fabricated by the elderly widow of a veteran who once served his country well. Of the three eyewitnesses who have been attributed with denying the dead man was Booth, two, Joseph Zisgen and William Allen, never left any statement of such a claim, while the third, Wilson Kenzie, made statements that are at variance with all of the known evidence. But the story of Booth's escape does not die easily. Two remaining "witnesses" have also been used by "escape theorists" as offering proof that Booth did not die at the Garrett farm. They are Basil Moxley and Dr. Frederick May.

Basil Moxley was employed as the doorman at John Ford's Opera House in Baltimore. In 1903 Moxley told a Baltimore newspaper reporter that he had been one of the individuals present at the interment of Booth's remains in Green Mount Cemetery in 1869. He told the reporter that the remains had "red or reddish hair." He referred to the burial of Booth in 1869 as a "mock funeral." Moxley's statement appeared thirty-four years after the event.[23] As with the previous witnesses who left statements concerning Booth, how do Moxley's claims hold up?

Following the examination and autopsy of Booth's body on board the *Montauk*, the remains were sewn up in the same army blanket in which it had been placed at the Garrett farm. The body was then placed in a boat and taken ashore. While rumors soon surfaced that the body was weighted and dropped overboard into a remote part of the Potomac River, it was actually taken to the Washington Arsenal. Edwin Stanton testified during Andrew Johnson's impeachment hearing before the House Judiciary Committee in 1867 as to the disposition of the body:

> Q. What was done with the body of Booth?
>
> A. I did not see him interred. I gave directions that he should be interred on the premises of the Ordnance Department; and the officer to whom I gave directions reported that he was so interred.
>
> Q. Did you give directions as to the particular manner in which he should be interred?
>
> A. I gave directions that he should be interred in that place, and that the place should be kept under lock and key.[24]

A wooden box, used to ship rifled muskets, was used as a coffin. The box was tightly sealed and buried beneath the floor of a room in the arsenal that had been used to store ordnance. Both Lafayette Baker and Thomas Eckert were present at the burial and later testified to the event. Eckert was later questioned before the House Judiciary Committee about the location of the grave:

> Q. In what room was the burial to take place?
> A. In a large room in the arsenal building.
> Q. Please describe the room.
> A. . . . [I]t is the largest room in the building, perhaps thirty feet square, and possibly more. . . . It is in the Old Penitentiary Building.[25]

After the body was buried, the brick floor was replaced and the heavy door to the building was locked tightly and the key turned over to Stanton.[26]

In 1867 the War Department decided to tear down the portion of the Arsenal building where Booth's body was buried. Buried along with Booth were the bodies of Mary Surratt, George Atzerodt, Lewis Powell, and David Herold. On October 1, 1867, the five bodies were disinterred and moved to Warehouse No. 1 where they were reburied. Each grave contained a wooden marker with the name of the person in the grave. The graves remained undisturbed for the next sixteen months. In February 1869 Edwin Booth, brother of John Wilkes Booth, wrote to President Andrew Johnson requesting his brother's body: "Your excellency would greatly lessen the crushing weight of grief that is hurrying my mother to the grave by giving immediate orders for the safe delivery of the remains of John Wilkes Booth to Mr. Weaver."[27]

Johnson agreed. On February 15, 1869, five days after receiving Edwin Booth's letter, Johnson responded: "The Honorable Secretary of War will cause to be delivered to Mr. John Weaver, Sexton of Christ Church, Baltimore, the remains of John Wilkes Booth, for the purposes mentioned in the within communication."[28] Within the month Johnson would complete his act of compassion by releasing the remaining four bodies to their respective families and issuing presidential pardons to the three surviving conspirators serving their sentences in Fort Jefferson.

In compliance with Edwin Booth's request, the body was turned over to John H. Weaver, a Baltimore undertaker not far from the Exeter Street house where the Booth family once lived. After Johnson ordered the release of the body, Weaver made arrangements for the Washington undertaking firm of Harvey and Marr to receive the body and hold it until Weaver could arrange to transport it to Baltimore for burial.

At Warehouse No. 1 two soldiers began digging away at the earth that covered the old musket box holding Booth's remains. At six feet they hit a solid object and soon uncovered the makeshift coffin. When the box was lifted from the grave the name Booth could be made out in black letters on the lid of the case.[29] The box was placed in a wagon from Harvey and Marr's establishment and transported twenty blocks to a large shed located in the rear. Ironically, the shed turned out to be the former stable in the rear of Ford's Theatre where Booth occasionally kept his horse.[30] Its entrance was located on Baptist Alley only a few feet from the backstage door where Booth fled after shooting Lincoln.

It was near eight o'clock in the evening when the box was carried inside and placed on a makeshift table. A small, thin man sat in the main establishment quietly waiting word from the undertakers. He was the youngest son of Junius Brutus Booth Sr. and younger brother of John Wilkes. His name was Joseph Adrian Booth, and he had come to Washington from Baltimore to oversee the identification and shipping of his older brother's remains.[31] Joe would handle the details in Washington and in Baltimore.

From Harvey and Marr's shed the body was shipped by train to Baltimore, where it arrived at 9:00 P.M. Among the people waiting at the train station was John T. Ford. Ford had always been and still was a close and loyal friend of the Booth family. His attachment to the Booths was not only financial, but involved his admiration for their outstanding theatrical abilities and for the small fortune they had helped him acquire. Later that night Ford would telegraph Edwin Booth in New York, "Successful and in our possession." The saved telegram contains the penciled words on its reverse, "John's body."[32]

Among those waiting at Weaver's establishment in Baltimore for Booth's body were Mary Ann Booth and Rosalie Booth, Wilkes's mother and sister. Present also was Joe Booth, John T. Ford, Charles B. Bishop, John H. Weaver, and John Ford's brother Harry Clay Ford. They were all friends of the Booths and had known Wilkes intimately. The skull, hair, teeth, and legs were all examined closely. Several weeks before the assassination Booth had visited a Washington dentist who filled one of his teeth.[33] The "plugged" tooth with its peculiar filling, the black curly hair, the broken left leg with its old shoe, and the high riding boot on the right leg were all identified. No one expressed any doubt at all. It was John's body.

Over the next two days the remains were viewed by several other parties who expressed an opinion on the identity of the body. Norval E. Foard (a reporter from the *Baltimore Sun*), John W. McCoy, Thomas W. Hall, Theodore Micheau, Henry Mears, Joseph Lowery, William Pegram, Henry Wagner, and Basil E. Moxley all agreed. It was the body of John Wilkes Booth. None of the viewers expressed any doubt, including Basil Moxley who thirty-four years later would claim it wasn't Booth's corpse.

On Thursday, February 18, the coffin containing the remains was placed in Weaver's receiving vault of Baltimore's Green Mount Cemetery in the northern section of the city. Here it remained until Saturday, June 26, when it was taken from its place among the several coffins stored in the vault and carried to the cemetery plot where the Booth family would rest. The family had selected several of John's former friends from the acting community as pallbearers. Among this special group was Basil Moxley, known by his friends as "Bas."

In 1903, at the time the David E. George story appeared in newspapers across the country, Bas Moxley shocked the theatrical community by stating in an interview that he was present at the funeral of John Wilkes Booth in 1869 and it was not a funeral at all, but rather a "mock funeral." The body Moxley viewed at Weaver's establishment thirty-four years earlier was not the body of John Wilkes Booth; it was of another man, one with red hair. According to Moxley the government had pulled a switch and sent another body to Baltimore in 1869. Moxley didn't stop with his claim that the body was not Booth's; like most fabricators, he couldn't stop talking: "You can search all records in Washington or interview any officials then in office who are now alive and I will wager you will be unable to learn of any reward being paid out for the delivery of John Wilkes Booth's body to the government."[34]

Moxley was wrong about the reward money. It had been paid out, all of it—a total of $105,000—and a search of the records proves it.

Moxley had been one of at least nineteen people who had viewed the corpse in February of 1869. At the time, he agreed with the others who examined the remains that they were those of John Wilkes Booth. He had not challenged the identification at that time or the color of the corpse's hair, nor had he raised any question during the weeks after the burial. Only after the stories about David E. George appeared in the local papers thirty-four years later did Moxley come forward with his revelation.

The day after Moxley's statement appeared in the *Baltimore American*, an interview with *Sun* reporter Norval E. Foard appeared. Foard was one of the six pallbearers along with Moxley in 1869. In the *News American* article Foard said, "if Mr. Moxley saw the remains in the Weaver shop and says the hair was red he is color blind." Joseph T. Lowery, a Baltimore photographer who was also present at the 1869 viewing, stated: "There was not the slightest doubt in my mind that the face of the dead man I looked upon was that of the actor [Booth], whom I had seen many times in life. The features were the same, although considerably sunken. His dark hair, which was remarkably thick and curly, was well preserved."[35]

A total of nineteen people had viewed the body in 1869 and eighteen of them agreed at the time that it was John Wilkes Booth. Whatever Moxley's game, it had little effect in 1903. It was lumped together with Bates's book and Mrs. Harper's revelations as simply an attempt to gain notoriety. Wilson Kenzie, Joseph Zisgen, William Allen, and Basil Moxley form the foundation for the theory that Booth had escaped. These four witnesses provide no credible evidence that can counter the claims of dozens of others that the body in the barn was indeed that of John Wilkes Booth. But there is one other witness that proponents of this theory drag out from time to time, and he is an important witness with substantial credibility. His name is John Frederick May, a Washington, D.C., physician who served as Booth's doctor on at least one important occasion.

In 1863, Booth came to Dr. May seeking medical help. Booth had developed a bothersome lump on his neck on the left-rear side approximately three inches below the base of the skull. Because it was an annoyance as well as a small disfigurement, Booth sought medical advice. May examined the lump and declared it a "fibroid tumor." May told Booth it ought to be removed. Booth agreed and told May to go ahead and remove it. The minor operation resulted in a fine linear incision that May cautioned Booth to protect so that it could heal properly. If properly healed it would leave only a barely noticeable scar. A few days after the removal Booth returned to May. The new scar had been torn open, leaving "a broad, ugly-looking scar, produced by the granulating process."[36] The scar took on a distinctive appearance.

An interesting sidelight to this incident was later revealed by May. Booth asked the doctor to tell anyone who might ask about the operation that he removed a bullet that had lodged in the actor's neck. Booth wanted to pass off the incident as a result of some jealous lover who sought revenge for one of his many sexual escapades. That Booth himself promulgated the story can be seen in the statement of Davy Herold while he was being interrogated following his arrest. His interrogators asked Herold when he first met Booth. His answer included this statement: "It was the night Booth played the 'Marble Heart'—about two years ago, the time when Booth had a ball taken from his neck by some surgeon in Washington."[37]

Just how the authorities learned that Dr. May was the attending physician is not apparent. Perhaps they learned from Herold's statement. In any event, a messenger was sent to Dr. May's residence requesting him to come to the Navy Yard at once to identify a body. Dr. May's young son, William, accompanied him to the Navy Yard. In 1925 William May wrote an account of that day on board the monitor. May said that as a fourteen-year-old boy he had assisted his father in removing the tumor from Booth's neck by holding a basin beneath the wound while his father operated.

Arriving on board the ship, Dr. May and his young son were met by Joseph Barnes, surgeon general. Barnes escorted the two over to the table where Booth's body was laid out under a tarpaulin. Before removing the tarpaulin to reveal the body, Dr. May described the identifying scar to Barnes. William May quoted his father's words to the surgeon general: "If the body lying under that tarpaulin is the body of John Wilkes Booth, you will find a scar on the back of his neck, and let me describe the scar before it is seen by me. It looks more like the scar made by a burn than the cicatrix made by a surgical operation."[38]

Barnes replied, "You have described the scar as well as if you were looking at it." The judge advocate general then questioned May while still on board the monitor:

> Q. Do you recognize the body as that of J. Wilkes Booth from its general appearance, and also from the particular appearance of the scar?
>
> A. I do recognize it, though it is very much altered since I saw Booth. It looks to me much older, and in appearance much more freckled than he was. I do not recollect that he was at all freckled. I have no doubt it is his body. I recognize the features.[39]

In January 1887, May wrote an essay titled, "The Mark of the Scalpel."[40] In it he recounted his experiences, describing Booth's coming to his office and his removing the fibroid tumor, the resulting scar, and his positively identifying the unusual appearance of that scar as a result of its having been torn open.[41] May then gave the proponents of the conspiracy theory more fuel for their smoky fire. He said the corpse had a broken right leg. To May's later chagrin, it was Booth's left leg that was broken, not his right leg. May was a highly skilled clinician. His statement gave credence to those who claim Booth escaped. Forget the scar, the hair, the tooth, the physical appearance. In his place was another man, "much older" whose right leg was broken and whose appearance was "freckled." Dr. May appeared to be describing a man other than John Wilkes Booth. And yet, May was asked point blank, "Do you recognize the body as that of J. Wilkes Booth?" May answered, "I do recognize it, . . . I have no doubt it is his body."[42] May explained the difference in Booth's appearance, writing that he had known Booth "in the vigor of life and health" and was shocked to see him now as a "haggard corpse." The corpse which May examined bore the mark of his scalpel a year and a half earlier.

The conspiratorialists continue to exert surgical skill in carefully carving words and phrases from May's account, making sure to leave behind the Washington surgeon's emphatic conclusions, "I recognize the likeness. I have no doubt that it is the person from whom I took the tumor, and that it is the body of J. Wilkes Booth."[43] If Edwin Stanton and Lafayette Baker had conspired to substitute another body for John Wilkes Booth's, why would they be so inept as to break the wrong leg? It is more reasonable to assume that May erred in writing his report and recorded the right leg instead of the left leg.

The government left little to chance. On the afternoon of April 27, an autopsy was performed on Booth's remains by Surgeon General Barnes at the direction of Stanton. The autopsy report was published in the multivolume *Medical and Surgical History* as "Case—J. W. B.—."[44] Stanton's order calling for an autopsy and identification of the body is contained in a letter that he and Navy Secretary Welles jointly sent to the commandant of the Navy Yard who had asked Stanton what should be done with the body:

> You will permit Surgeon General Barnes and his assistant, accompanied by Judge Advocate Genl Holt, Hon. John A. Bingham, Special Judge Advocate, Major [Thomas] Eckert, Wm. G. Moore, Clerk of the War Department, Col. L. C. Baker, Lieut. [Luther] Baker, Lieut. Col. Conger, Chas. Dawson, J. L. Smith, [Alexander] Gardiner (photographer) + assistant, to go on board the Montauk, and see the body of John Wilkes Booth.
>
> Immediately after the Surgeon General has made his autopsy, you will have the body placed in a strong box, and deliver it to the charge of Col. Baker—the box being carefully sealed.[45]

At the conspirators' trial one month later, Barnes was questioned by the Judge Advocate:

> Q. State whether or not you made an examination of the body of J. Wilkes Booth after his death, when brought to this city.
> A. I did.
> Q. Describe to the Court the scar which is alleged to have been on his neck.
> A. The scar on the left side of the neck was occasioned by an operation performed by Dr. May, of this city, for the removal of a tumor, some months previously to Booth's death.
> Q. What was its peculiar appearance, if it had any peculiar appearance.
> A. It looked like a scar of a burn, instead of an incision; which Dr. May explained from the fact that the wound was torn open on the stage, when nearly healed.[46]

Following May's examination of Booth's body on the *Montauk*, Barnes and Woodward removed two cervical vertebrae and the damaged spinal cord from the neck. The path of the bullet was determined and the vertebrae and spinal cord were wrapped in brown paper and taken by Dr. Woodward to the Army Medical Museum as specimens. Barnes wrote up a report that was submitted to Stanton the same day, April 27, 1865. In his report Barnes stated:

> The left leg and foot were encased in an appliance of splints and bandages, upon the removal of which, a fracture of the fibula

> 3 inches above the ankle joint, accompanied by considerable ecchymosis, was discovered.
>
> The cause of death was a gun shot wound in the neck—the ball entering just behind the sterno-cleido muscle—2-1/2 inches above the clavicle—passing through the bony bridge of fourth and fifth cervical vertebrae—severing the spinal cord and passing out through the body of the sterno-cleido of right side, three inches above the clavicle.
>
> Paralysis of the entire body was immediate, and all the horrors of consciousness of suffering and death must have been present to the assassin during the two hours he lingered.[47]

The last paragraph has less to do with objective medical observation and was probably added by Barnes to indicate to Stanton that Booth did not die easily or without the "horrors of . . . suffering and death." One year later Dr. Janvier Woodward, the surgeon who performed the autopsy aboard the *Montauk*, wrote a letter to Major General G.W. Schofield stating: "the fracture was of the left fibula just above the malleolus."[48] Woodward's is the final word on the question of which bone was broken in which leg.

There is one last physical piece of evidence that relates to Booth that can be used for positive identification—the initials "J. W. B." that appeared as a tattoo on his hand. These initials were located on the back of the left hand in the crotch formed by the thumb and index finger. The most compelling evidence concerning this tattoo can be found in the writings of Booth's older sister Asia. In describing her brother, Asia wrote about Booth's great charm and physical beauty, including his hands. "He had perfectly shaped hands, and across the back of one he had clumsily marked, when a little boy, *his initials in India ink*" (emphasis added).[49]

These initials were known to everyone well acquainted with Booth. There are so many references to them that even the proponents of the "Booth escaped" theory acknowledge their existence. In attempting to explain away the identifying tattoo, the proponents of the "Booth escaped" theory simply state that the corpse examined on the *Montauk* did not have the tattoo. One proponent writes: "If the initials really were on the corpse's hand why didn't the government permit any pictures to be taken of it and why didn't they permit the dozens of Booth's family and friends who were nearby to identify the body? . . . Clearly the body did not have the critical initials."[50]

Alexander Gardner, who had left Matthew Brady to become an independent photographer, was allowed to board the *Montauk* with an assistant, Timothy O'Sullivan, and photograph the body. Gardner returned to his studios accompanied by a military guard who had instructions to confiscate the photographic plate and subsequent print and bring them directly to Stanton.[51] It is not clear why the government should have allowed pictures to be taken or what the photographs would prove that eyewitness testimony would not prove. Presumably Stanton wanted to personally see the corpse of Booth to satisfy himself that Booth had been killed. But photographing the body is one thing, taking a close-up photograph of the initials was another. It would be virtually impossible to photograph the initials so that they would be legible in a photograph and still see the rest of the body including the face. Rather than rely on photographic evidence that is subject to alteration, there are several witnesses who described the initials on Booth's hand and those seen on the corpse.

Sergeants J.M. Peddicord and Joseph H. Hartley had been assigned as guards on the *Montauk* in anticipation of receiving the prisoners arrested for Lincoln's murder. At 1:45 A.M. on April 27, the steamer *John S. Ide* pulled alongside the warship and transferred Booth's body. Hartley, who had relieved Peddicord at midnight, was on duty when the body was brought on board and placed on a carpenter's bench on the deck of the ship. At 6:00 A.M. Hartley awakened Peddicord and led him to the carpenter's bench where he pointed to Booth's body still wrapped in an army blanket. The two men laid open the flap of the blanket revealing the face of a man who had been dead for nearly twelve hours. Several years later Peddicord would read the story in the newspapers that claimed the body on board the *Montauk* was not that of J. Wilkes Booth, but another man. Peddicord knew better and, realizing his special place in history, wrote an article about his experience of April 27, 1865, that was published in the *Roanoke Evening News:*

> One evening I noticed that the officers were looking for something to come up the river, and when I awoke Sergeant Hartley at midnight, I told him of this and turned in until 6 o'clock. In the morning when he called me saying, "Come out here. I have something to show you." I turned out on deck where he was along side a carpenter's bench on which lay the body of a man wrapped about in a soldier's blanket. My order from Hartley was "Take charge of this body and allow no one to touch it without orders from Colonel Baker."
>
> It was the body of the assassin, John Wilkes Booth, which had been brought up the river during the night by the detachment of troops who had captured him. At breakfast when I was relieved by Hartley while I was eating, we unwrapped the face and compared it with a photograph, and I also remember the letters in India ink on the back of his hand in pale straggling characters, "J.W.B.," as a boy would have done it.[52]

In 1926, Sergeant Joseph H. Hartley, Peddicord's comrade who helped guard Booth's body on the *Montauk*, wrote a letter to William Curtis White:

> As you requested the other day, I write the following statement in relation to my personal knowledge of the death of J.W. Booth, whose body was laid out, on the deck of one of the monitors waiting its final disposal. I had some doubt myself as to its being the remains of Booth. He looked so much like a boyhood friend of mine that had his initials picked in India ink on his arm that I was impelled to strip up his sleeve to see whether I was right or not. Instead of "A.W." I found the initials "J.W.B." convincing proof to me of the identity of whose body it was, and I thought no more of the matter until years afterwards when I saw an article in the papers claiming he was still alive. . . . I was a sergeant [*sic*] in the Marines detailed from headquarters with a squad for duty on the monitor, on which the conspirators were temporarily held April 1865.

There seems no doubt that the body on the *Montauk* had the distinctive mark of initials tattooed on the left hand in the base of the "V" formed by the index finger and thumb. The tattoo joins with the other physical evidence supporting the conclusion that the body returned to Washington from the Garrett farm was that of Booth and not someone else.

Among all of the witnesses who left commentary on the identity of the body in the barn there is one eyewitness whose credibility stands out among all others. He is David Herold. Herold accompanied Booth for most of his escape. After his capture, Herold was taken back to Washington and placed aboard the *Montauk* where he was held until transferred to the Washington Arsenal. On Thursday, April 27, detectives questioned Herold. He described what happened on the night of Tuesday, April 25, shortly after the Sixteenth New York Cavalry rode past Garrett's on their way to Bowling Green in search of Willie Jett. Herold tells what happened after the soldiers rode past.

> Garrett says, "I would sooner that you would not stay here all night." I said, "All right. We would sooner not stay here." Booth had told them that he had shot one or two soldiers in Maryland, and asked them to warn him if the Yankees should come so that he could escape. It was then after dark. We didn't know where to go. Garrett says, "I don't want you to stay in the house." Booth asked if he could stay in the barn. Garrett said "Yes." We went down & were locked in the barn. Just before daylight, Booth waked me up, & said that the cavalry had surrounded the barn. I said, "You had better give up." He said, "I will suffer death first." Mr. Garrett then came, and said, "Gentlemen, the cavalry are after you. You are the ones. You had better give yourselves up."[53]

Herold went on to describe the negotiations that took place between Booth and the officers outside the barn. In the course of Herold's account of what happened at the Garrett barn he mentioned Booth by name a total of eight more times. Herold stated unequivocally who the man was who had just been shot in barn: "As I turned round I heard a pistol shot, looked around, and saw one corner of the barn in a light blaze. They jerked the barn door open. *Booth was lying there* [emphasis added]."[54]

Herold's statement could not be clearer or more positive an identification. The man lying on the barn floor was "Booth." Herold had nothing to gain and everything to lose by identifying his companion as Booth. By doing so he placed himself in lethal jeopardy. Herold would have been far better served to insist that the man in the barn was not Booth, that it was anybody other than Booth. By denying that the man in the barn was Booth, Herold could at least claim he did not know his traveling companion was the murderer of the president. But he didn't. He said the man in the barn was "Booth." It doesn't end here.

The dying man was carried to the porch of the Garrett house, where he was laid on a straw mattress. Baker and Conger then took several items from Booth's pockets. Among the items was a memorandum book with notes in it describing the assassination and the escape and a small gold pin that held Booth's undershirt together at the neck. On the back of the pin were engraved the words, "Dan Bryant to JWB."[55] The pin with Booth's initials has never been explained by the escape theorists, presumably because the shallowness of their research left them unaware of its existence. It appears unlikely that someone would go so far as to plant a small identification pin on Booth's undershirt just to mislead the authorities. Finally, there is a bank draft in the amount of 61 pounds, 12 shillings, 10 pence made out to "John Wilkes Booth."[56]

A scar, a "plugged" tooth, tattooed initials, and several personal effects all point to the positive identification of the body in the barn, the corpse on the *Montauk*, and the remains interred in Green Mount Cemetery in Baltimore as those of America's matinee idol turned assassin, John Wilkes Booth. Any conspiracy suggesting it was not Booth's body would have to involve the complicity of literally dozens of people, many of whom had no motive to lie.

The people sitting in the audience fidgeted nervously waiting for the bailiff to announce the momentary appearance of the judge. Several minutes passed before the words sang out over the anxious crowd: "All rise for the Honorable Judge Joseph Kaplan. This Court is now in session." Judge Kaplan entered the courtroom and took his seat behind the bench. The audience sat in complete silence anxiously awaiting the judge's ruling. After what seemed several minutes the judge spoke: "the unreliability of the Petitioners' less than convincing escape/cover-up theory gives rise to the conclusion that there is no compelling reason for an exhumation."[57]

John Wilkes Booth would remain undisturbed in his grave. The court had decided the body in the barn was his. The plaintiffs slumped in disappointment. Was this just another instance of a government cover up? No doubt, conspiracy theorists will now add Judge Joseph Kaplan to their growing list of official deceivers.[58]

CHAPTER TWENTY-TWO

Goodbye, Father Abraham

Rest, noble martyr; rest in peace;
Rest with the true and the brave,
Who, like thee, fell in freedom's cause
The Nation's life to save

Phineas D. Gurley

The president was dead. He had been comatose for the past nine hours giving the impression of being in a deep sleep. The small bedroom of young Willie Clark had held an impressive assemblage of men. In all, fifty-seven individuals are believed to have visited the room during the early morning hours to view the dying president.[1] Not all fifty-seven visited at the same time. The room was too small to accommodate even half or a quarter that number. It is not known for certain who was in the room when Surgeon General Barnes said, "He is gone." As the years passed scores of people claimed to be at Lincoln's side at the moment of his demise. In reality, there were probably no more than twelve.[2] All had anticipated it and wanted to be present when it came. Not everyone made it.

In the front parlor Mary Lincoln lay prostrate on a sofa moaning inconsolably. Reverend Gurley kneeled by the side of the sofa offering a prayer for Mary's sake. When he finished, Robert helped his mother to her feet and, with Gurley's help, escorted her to the front door. Mary, braced by her son, paused at the door. Looking at the theater across the street she exclaimed, "Oh, that dreadful, dreadful house!" Mary and Robert then climbed into the carriage and rode back to the White House.[3]

Back in the Petersen house someone noticed that Lincoln's eyelids were no longer closed but had relaxed in death and opened slightly. It was an unpleasant change to the countenance he had shown while comatose. Someone reached down and smoothed the eyelids shut then placed a silver coin on each eye to keep them from opening again. This simple act of respect for the dead president would become a source of controversy for four otherwise honorable men. Colonel Thomas McCurdy Vincent, a member of Stanton's staff; Maunsell B. Field, assistant secretary of the treasury (New York); Colonel George V. Rutherford; and Dr. Charles Leale, all swore that they had placed the coins on Lincoln's eyes.[4] It seemed a matter of special significance to each man. Such was the greatness of Abraham Lincoln that this simple act held such importance for these distinguished men. Yet, only one was telling the truth.

The president lay in bed for another hour and a half while several members of the cabinet held a meeting called by Stanton moments after Lincoln's death.[5] He ordered that the door to the room where Lincoln's body lay be locked and a guard posted to make sure no one entered without his express permission.[6] The war secretary was in control of the government. It is not known what was discussed during this special meeting, but whatever it was it required an hour of critical time. When the meeting ended, a contingent of soldiers from the Veteran Reserve Corps carefully wrapped the naked body of the president in an American flag and placed him in a plain pine box that General Daniel Rucker had ordered sent to the Petersen house.[7] The *Baltimore Clipper* reported the scene in its Monday morning edition: "The President's body was removed from the private residence opposite Ford's Theatre, . . . at half-past nine o'clock, . . . wrapped in the American flag. It was escorted by a small guard of cavalry, Gen. Augur and other military officers following on foot."[8]

This unusual gesture of wrapping the president's body in an American flag is worth noting. The *Baltimore Clipper*'s claim that the body was removed from the private residence "wrapped in the American flag" is supported by Mary Lincoln's close friend Elizabeth Dixon. Dixon had hurried over to the Petersen house at Robert Lincoln's request to help comfort his mother. She accompanied Mary Lincoln back to the White House and stayed with her for two more hours before returning home. On leaving the White House, Mrs. Dixon started down the stairs from the second floor where she met the military guard coming up the stairs carrying the body of the president. In a letter to her sister, she wrote: "I met the cortege bringing up the remains of the murdered President which were taken into the great State bedroom, wrapped in the American flag."[9]

Leaving the Petersen house, the hearse along with its escort moved north on Tenth Street to G Street where it turned west and headed toward the White House. The escort included General C.C. Augur, General D.H. Rucker, Colonel Louis H. Pelouze, Captain Finley Anderson, Captain D.C. Thomas, Captain J.H. Crowell, and Captain C. Baker.[10] Arriving at the White House, the body was taken to a guest room located in the West Wing on the second floor. Here the body was placed on a table that had been set up just for the autopsy. It was 11:00 A.M.

Present were Surgeon General Barnes; Dr. Robert Stone, the family physician; army surgeons Charles Crane, Charles S. Taft, and William M. Notson; Assistant Quartermaster General Daniel Rucker; Lincoln's close Illinois friend Orville Hickman Browning; and army assistant surgeons Janvier

Woodward and Edward Curtis. Woodward and Curtis would perform the autopsy. Curtis later described the scene:

> Dr. Woodward and I proceeded to open the head and remove the brain down to the track of the ball. The latter had entered a little to the left of the median line at the back of the head, had passed almost directly forward through the center of the brain and lodged. Not finding it readily, we proceeded to remove the entire brain, when, as I was lifting the latter from the cavity of the skull, suddenly the bullet dropped out through my fingers and fell, breaking the solemn silence of the room with its clatter, into an empty basin that was standing beneath. There it lay upon the white china, a little black mass no bigger than the end of my finger— . . . the cause of such mighty changes in the world's history as we may perhaps never realize.[11]

The bullet was a small sphere of soft lead 0.44 inches in diameter. The force of smashing through Lincoln's skull had flattened the bullet into the shape of a small coin. By slicing away successive layers of the brain, the surgeons were able to expose the path the bullet had traversed. A line of coagulated blood left in the bullet's wake marked the track of the ball. While the path of the bullet together with its final resting place were obvious from a careful examination of the brain, four of the doctors disagreed in later reports as to where the bullet had lodged. Woodward and Stone said it lodged on the *left* side, while Barnes and Taft said it was located just behind the *right* eye. One hundred years later the doctors and attendants performing the autopsy on President John F. Kennedy would create confusion by leaving different descriptions of what they saw. To both presidents, the details little mattered.[12]

The autopsy completed, Dr. Charles D. Brown, of the Washington undertaking firm of Brown and Alexander began making the president presentable for viewing. The body was cleaned and embalmed and a fine, white cloth placed over it. Later that afternoon Stanton personally supervised the dressing of the body. He used the Brooks Brothers suit worn by Lincoln at his second inauguration ceremony. The suit Lincoln had worn to the theater would be returned to Mary Lincoln, who would give it to Alphonso Donn, the White House doorman. Donn, a favorite of young Tad Lincoln, had taken the boy to Grover's Theatre on the night of April 14 to see the performance of *Aladdin! Or His Wonderful Lamp*. Tad, twelve years old, learned of his father's assassination from the theater manager who had interrupted the play to announce to the audience that the president had been shot. Grief stricken, the young boy was taken back to the White House by Donn, who watched over him until Mary Lincoln returned.

The Monday morning papers carried a brief announcement concerning the arrangements for the funeral. Assistant Secretary of the Treasury George A. Harrington was entrusted with the overall responsibility for the funeral procedures.[13] Benjamin B. French, Lincoln's commissioner of buildings, was put in charge of the corpse. The funeral service was scheduled to begin at noon on Wednesday, April 19. The East Room of the White House was chosen as the site. After the funeral service a special procession would escort the body to the Capitol where it would lie in state. Major General Christopher Columbus Augur was placed in charge of the military procession that would accompany the body to the Capitol.

Under Harrington's direction an army of carpenters invaded the East Room and began fashioning the "Temple of Death" that would hold the president's coffin. The East Room ran the entire width of the building, a total of eighty feet. It was forty feet deep and its ceilings were twenty-two feet high. It was an impressive hall able to accommodate the six hundred guests who were invited to witness the service. The windows, cornices, mirrors and chandeliers were draped with the finest black cloth.

The catafalque measured sixteen feet along its side by ten feet across its end. At each corner was a seven-foot-tall post that supported a large arched canopy that reached a height of eleven feet. The canopy was so tall that the central chandelier that hung over the catafalque had to be temporarily removed to accommodate it. The entire structure was covered in a variety of fine silks, satins, and velvet of the deepest blacks and purest whites obtainable. Resting in this magnificent temple was the ornate coffin holding the body of the president. The base of the coffin rested four feet off the floor. Bordering all four sides of the central body of the catafalque was a ledge approximately two feet wide and elevated one foot from the floor. Those viewing the body would step up onto the ledge and slowly walk past the casket gazing directly into the face of the dead president.

On Monday evening the president's pallbearers entered the second floor Guest Room where Lincoln's body reposed. They had removed their shoes to muffle the tread of their steps as they walked past the room where the grieving widow lay in a fitful state.[14] Assuming their positions on either side of the large casket, they carefully lifted it by its ornate silver handles and quietly carried it down the stairs into the East Room where it was placed on the waiting catafalque. All the while Mary Lincoln lay in a terrible state of anguish in her bedroom upstairs. She could not bear to face anyone outside of her immediate family and personal servants.

By early morning a line, seven abreast, stretched for over a mile down Pennsylvania Avenue. For the next several hours it continued to grow, the end no closer to the White House than it had been at dawn.[15] At 9:30 A.M. the gates surrounding the White House lawn were thrown open and the great mass of humanity began walking slowly toward the south portico. The large number of soldiers lining the way to enforce order were not needed. The sanctity of the event was enough to ensure the civility of those who came to see their President one last time.

For eight hours the mass of people came and passed the ornate casket on either side. Two people glimpsed the president's face every two seconds, sixty every minute, thirty-six hundred every hour until over twenty-five thousand persons had filed through the room, and still there were thousands waiting when the doors closed.[16] They would have to wait until the following morning when the body would lie in state in the Capitol. From 5:30 P.M. until 7:30 P.M. a special delegation of four hundred people from Lincoln's home state of Illinois were admitted into the White House for a private viewing.[17] Upstairs, Mary Lincoln remained in seclusion unable to greet her husband's old friends.

After the final visitor was ushered out of the East Room at 7:30, Harrington's special crew of carpenters moved back into the great room. They began building a set of raised steps that ran the entire circumference of the room, transforming the great hall into an amphitheater. In this way many more people would be able to witness the funeral ceremonies, which would take place the next day. Working through the night, the crew of carpenters toiled away, finally completing their task just in time for the invited guests to begin taking their places in prearranged sections that Harrington had marked off with white ribbons. The room would hold just over six hundred dignitaries and guests.

Seated before the catafalque at the foot of the coffin was Robert Lincoln along with two of Mary Lincoln's sisters, Mrs. Elizabeth Todd Edwards and Mrs. Clark Smith. Elizabeth was Mary Lincoln's eldest sister, who had become her surrogate mother after the death of their mother in 1825. Also seated with them were two of Mary Lincoln's cousins who had remained faithful to the Union, Dr. Lyman Beecher Todd and General John B. Todd, and Lincoln's two secretaries and close friends, John G. Nicolay and John Hay. At the head of the coffin, sitting all alone, was General Ulysses S. Grant.[18]

Wednesday dawned to the booming of cannonade that continued at fifteen-minute intervals throughout the day. By 10:00 A.M. the city had swelled with thousands of people who began lining the route from the White House to the Capitol. For the next three hours the people would wait in solemn quiet for the entourage to pass. Inside the White House preparations were complete for the funeral service to begin. Shortly after eleven o'clock various groups began arriving at the Treasury Department, which served as a staging area for the many dignitaries. Once again Assistant Secretary Harrington had arranged for an orderly process, ensuring the utmost efficiency and convenience for those who represented the nation and the family's close friends. These included the various officers of the executive and judiciary branches of government, and members of the Senate and House of Representatives, governors of several states, prominent members of the military, the diplomatic corps, foreign representatives, and members of various committees and commissions. Also present were sixty clergymen from all parts of the country, who were given the honor of being the first group to enter the hall where the ceremonies would take place.

At noon President Johnson entered the room accompanied by his cabinet, except for William Seward who was still recovering from his injuries. At ten minutes past twelve the Reverend Phineas D. Gurley approached the catafalque, signaling the beginning of the service. Reverend Thomas Hall, pastor of Epiphany Episcopal Church in Washington, began the formal service by reading from the gospel of St. John, "I am the Resurrection and the Life saith the Lord; he that believeth in me, though he were dead, yet shall he live, and whosoever liveth and believeth in me shall never die."[19]

These words heralded the Episcopal burial service and were meant to comfort the bereaved with the belief that the soul of the deceased would live forever in the Kingdom of Heaven.[20] It mattered not to many of those present that Abraham Lincoln was not a member of any religious denomination and had not been baptized into the Christian faith. The question of Lincoln's religious beliefs was one that had been turned against him time and again by his enemies.[21] Now, all that was past.

Timed to coincide with the service taking place in the White House, churches all across the United States were holding their own services on behalf of the president. Record numbers of people attempted to crowd into houses of worship. Many people had to be turned away. In several instances services had to be moved from church sanctuaries to larger municipal buildings to accommodate the large throngs.[22] It was a remarkable tribute to one man.

Back at the White House the chaplain of the Senate, Edwin H. Gray, closed the religious ceremonies beseeching "the God of Justice" to bring treason to an end and the perpetrators of the horrible crime to final justice.[23] With the obsequies ended, eight members of the Veteran Reserve Corps, all sergeants, walked from the north doorway where they had been waiting.[24] The lid of the casket was gently closed and the eight sergeants took their places, four on a side. Clasping the handles they lifted the coffin to their shoulders and slowly carried it to the magnificent hearse waiting outside the north portico. The official service over, Abraham Lincoln was about to join the people who knew him best, loved him most, and had stood by him through good times and bad.

The coffin was placed on a hearse pulled by six grand white horses. On either side walked a specially chosen contingent of soldiers of the Veteran Reserve Corps whose duty it was to attend the coffin day and night. It would never be out of their sight or out of their reach.[25] As the solemn procession began to move down the avenue toward the Capitol building, cannons increased their rhythmic booming to every sixty seconds.[26] Known as "minute guns," the firing at sixty-second intervals denoted distress according to military tradition.[27] The military units that would form the procession accompanying the hearse had been waiting for several hours. Now each group fell into line at their designated place as the cortege approached the point where they had been stationed. The honor of leading the procession was given to a detachment of the Twenty-second Regiment, United States Colored Troops.[28]

The cortege that made its way to the Capitol was so great that it had to double back on itself as it marched up the avenue. Victor Searcher, in his book *Farewell to Lincoln*, described the procession:

> Five thousand government workers, seventy abreast, stretched from curb to curb, a solid phalanx of marching men. Delegations from nearby cities; workers from the Navy Yard; local railroad employees and transportation people from docks and shipyards and from Alexandria and Baltimore; a fire hose company from Philadelphia of which the late President had been an honorary member; a host of fraternal lodges and societies; church bodies by the dozens; clergymen; school children and teachers; state and city officials; convalescents from military hospitals (the saddest sight in the march; some bandaged, some armless, others hobbling on crutches, all determined to pay their last respects); survivors of the War of 1812; Fenian brotherhoods and German singing societies; Italian, Swiss, French, and Polish clubs; saddle and harness makers; Seth Kinman, eccentric California hunter attired in moccasins and buckskin breeches; Chief Agonagwad of the Winnebago Indians; these and many, many more, evidenced the public urge to venerate the honored dead.[29]

The final leg of the march stretched down Pennsylvania Avenue for a mile and a half. All along the great avenue the buildings were draped in black. Windows were somberly decorated and displayed posters that proclaimed "Memento Mori." The Capitol flew its flags at half-staff. Every window, every housetop, every available spot had been filled two hours before the funeral cortege was scheduled to begin.[30]

Reaching the east side of the Capitol building the honor guard removed the coffin from its platform and carried it up the broad stairway into the rotunda. Inside the building the coffin was set upon a great catafalque draped in black and bordered with silver fringe. Above the dais was the recently completed dome. Early in his administration Lincoln had been advised to suspend work on the dome because its great expense would only add an additional burden to the mounting debt caused by the war. It would be a symbol of government largess during a war of great sacrifice. But Lincoln's vision went beyond the moment. "No," he said. "Let the work go on. It will be a symbol to the people that we intend for the Union to go on." Now the newly painted interior and its eight large murals depicting the nation's stirring history were shrouded out of respect for the republic's savior. "Abraham Lincoln lay in the ark of the Republic."[31]

The next morning, at 8:00 A.M., the large doors were slowly swung open, and the people began to stream into the great hall. Throughout the day and into the night they came in columns of two. Reaching the catafalque the two lines split, each passing alongside the open coffin and merging on the far side. By the thousands they continued to arrive until it was time for Abraham Lincoln to leave.

The Baltimore and Ohio train depot was located three blocks from the Capitol. By exiting from the east side of the building the hearse and its entourage left the grounds and once again passed by tens of thousands of people who had remained along the streets waiting for still another glimpse of the fallen president. Order continued to be the rule of the day. While pickpockets were out in force, there seemed to be few incidents as if even this predatory segment showed a level of respect unprecedented in the capital city's history. The short trip to the depot was conducted in complete silence. No bands or drums were heard. Only the rhythmic cadence of the soldiers' feet broken by the clop of horses' hooves. The hearse was attended at all times by the special sergeants who marched by its side. In front were four companies of the Veteran Reserve Corps. Immediately behind the hearse were General Grant and his staff along with other military dignitaries. These units were followed by government officials led by President Johnson, who rode in a carriage escorted by a military guard.

At the depot a special nine-car train waited, its boiler fired and ready to drive the large pistons that turned the massive wheels of the engine. Immediately in front of the engine was a second locomotive that would run in advance of the funeral train by ten minutes. This "pilot engine" would ensure a clear track for the president's return home. It would precede the funeral train all the way to Springfield. The journey would cover 1,664 miles and require fourteen days, making stops in Baltimore, Harrisburg, Philadelphia, New York City, Albany, Buffalo, Cleveland, Columbus, Indianapolis, Chicago, and finally, Springfield. The route would follow Lincoln's inaugural trip to Washington in February 1861. Only Pittsburgh and Cincinnati would be bypassed, shortening the trip by two hundred miles.[32]

The first six cars were brand new passenger coaches provided by the Baltimore and Ohio Railroad. Next came a baggage car. The eighth was the special presidential coach built in anticipation of carrying a victorious president around the reunited country during the four years of his second term. Now it would carry the body of the president on his first and last trip in the magnificent coach. The last car was the private coach of the officers of the Philadelphia, Wilmington and Baltimore Railroad that had been offered to

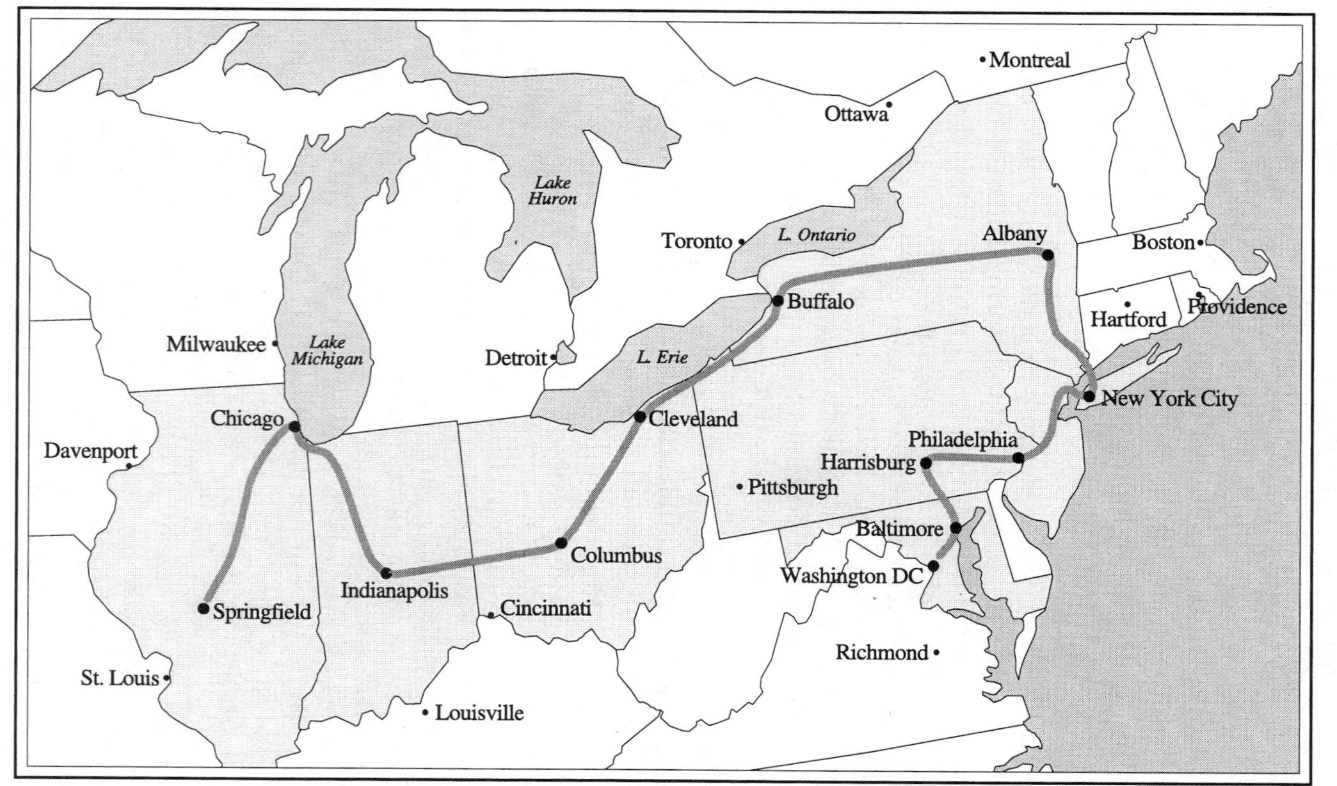

Route of the funeral train from Washington, D.C., to Springfield, Illinois. The train traveled 1,664 miles and made scheduled funeral stops in eleven cities.

the President as his own private car during his first term in office. It would now carry the members of the Lincoln family and the guard of honor.

The special coach carrying the president's body had never been seen by the commander in chief while he was alive. In fact, the public had never seen it. It was completed only two months before Lincoln's death. He had been invited to inspect the car for the first time and take a trial ride on Saturday, April 15.[33] The events of Friday, April 14, caused a delay of six days.

The special car was forty-eight feet in length and eight and one half feet in width. The enclosed part of the car was forty-two feet long by eight feet wide. A corridor, or hallway, extended the entire length of the car along one wall. The car consisted of three compartments: a large stateroom, a drawing room, and a parlor or dining room. The drawing room contained a small washroom. The stateroom was designed as the president's quarters and was located in the center of the car. It was considerably larger than the two end rooms. The stateroom doubled as the president's office and bedroom. It contained four sofas, two of them seven and a half feet long with hinged backs that folded down making a double bed large enough to accommodate the president's six foot, three and three-quarter inch frame. The dining room contained no facilities for storing or preparing food, or for storing linens, dishes, and silverware. A separate car was provided for preparing and serving meals. In a recent study for the City of Alexandria, Virginia, H. Robert Slusser described the interior: "Woodwork in the interior was black walnut and oak. The walls were upholstered from the seat rail to the headlining with rich corded crimson silk that had a tufted pattern. The headlining, also of crimson silk, was gathered in each panel to a rosette in the center. The clerestory above was painted zinc white and decorated with the coat of arms of the states. The curtains were of light green silk."[34]

There were chandeliers of cut glass and wall-to-wall carpeting. Twelve windows ran along each side of the car and the spaces between the windows were decorated with oil paintings. In addition to the four sofas there were several reclining armchairs used in furnishing the car. Certainly a desk must have been provided for Lincoln's use while traveling. Although the United States Military Rail Road made an inventory of all of the car's furnishings when it was completed, the inventory list has never been located.

The exterior of the car was painted a rich chocolate color, which had been rubbed with oil and rottenstone to produce a deep, shiny finish that enhanced the overall appearance of the car. Directly beneath the sixth and seventh windows was a five and a half foot oval panel containing the United States coat of arms. The car was unusual in that it had four trucks of four wheels each, giving the car a total of sixteen wheels for the body to ride on, double the usual number. The use of these unusual trucks have led to the conclusion by some that the car was armor-clad in an attempt to make it bullet proof. The reminiscences of several individuals who worked on the construction of the car seem to refute this idea.[35] The presence of twelve large windows on each side of the car would defeat any purpose of making the car bulletproof or bombproof.

Shortly after Lincoln's death, Mary Lincoln insisted on having her husband taken home to Springfield. New York City, along with Washington, floated proposals to inter the remains in their respective cities but Mary was adamant. Stanton bowed to Mary's wishes and issued orders on April 18 to the officer in charge of the Military Car Shops in Alexandria, Virginia, to prepare a suitable funeral car. Myron H. Lamson, who had worked as the assistant foreman in overseeing the construction of the president's car, requested permission to make a few alterations to the recently completed car so it could be used as the funeral coach. Stanton gave his approval. Lamson prepared a special catafalque that was mounted in the center of the stateroom. The catafalque contained clamps that held the casket secure when on the train and allowed for easy removal at those stops where it was scheduled for public viewing.[36]

In assuming control over transporting the corpse back to Springfield, Stanton appointed a commission of railroad men to make all of the arrangements involving the numerous railroads the train would pass over on its trip. The funeral train would travel over sixteen different rail lines on its 1,600–mile journey to Springfield. Its speed would range from five to twenty miles per hour, the slower speed when passing crowds, the faster speed when running through the rural countryside. The train would take priority over all rail traffic for the twelve days it traveled from Washington to Springfield. Wartime regulations were still in effect and the War Department, under its secretary, declared the trip a "military necessity." This meant, among other things, that the military would decide where and when the train would travel and who would ride along with the casket to Springfield. The major problem was in deciding which cities would be official stops and which cities would be passed by. Every community pleaded with the government to allow it to formally honor the president. The specially appointed commission found it impossible to honor every request since it would have added several days and hundreds of miles to the trip home. Still, most of the communities along the way were determined to honor their fallen president to the maximum effort of their abilities. For many it simply meant standing along the roadbed with heads uncovered as the train passed.

Once the route had been released, memorial arches were constructed over the tracks for the train to pass under while en route. All along the sixteen hundred mile journey thousands upon thousands of citizens turned out and stood or sat in their buggies and wagons waiting for the train. In many instances these people turned out twenty-four hours in advance. In certain remote stretches an entire family would sit by the roadbed waiting for the train to appear. In other instances, the tracks were lined with crowds that often numbered over ten thousand. In many areas women covered the tracks with flowers as a symbol of respect. It was a heartfelt outpouring from the common citizens who understood what Abraham Lincoln had meant to them just as he had understood what the common citizen meant to him. These were the people Lincoln had in mind when he spoke those immortal words, "government of the people, by the people, for the people," and they knew it.

Back in Washington preparations continued. The small casket of Willie Lincoln had been placed aboard the train for the trip to Springfield where he would be interred with his father. Willie had died in the White House in February of 1862, and his body had been placed in the crypt of the prestigious Carroll family in Georgetown's Oak Hill Cemetery. The Lincolns had planned on taking their beloved son home to Springfield when the president's term expired in March 1869. Now he would return at his father's side four years sooner than planned.

Also accompanying his father home was Robert Lincoln. Mary Lincoln and young Tad remained in Washington, Mary too sick to make the trip and little Taddy too young to leave his mother's side. Supreme Court Justice David Davis, Major General David O. Hunter, and Ward Hill Lamon were among Lincoln's closer friends who rode with Robert in the special family car located behind the funeral coach. The War Department was represented by Brigadier General Edward D. Townsend, the navy by Rear Admiral Charles E. Davis. Among the dozens of politicians were several senators, representatives, and four governors including Richard Oglesby of Illinois. Rounding out the contingent were a number of newspaper correspondents who filed detailed reports at each stop along the long journey. There were nine coaches in all, eight carrying passengers and a ninth carrying their baggage.

The train with its passengers sat in the Washington depot as the pilot train slowly pulled out of the terminal to the tolling of church bells. At 8 A.M. sharp, Reverend Gurley offered a final prayer, "O Lord, strengthen us under the pressure of this great national sorrow as only Thou can strengthen the weak. Comfort us, as Thou canst sanctify a people when they are passing through the fiery furnaces of a great trial."[37] A final amen and the signal was given. The train slowly pulled out of the station and began its sorrowful journey. Mingling about the station were several hundred soldiers who, on seeing the engine start to move, spontaneously formed in line and presented arms as the train slowly passed.[38] Through the draped windows the passengers were able to catch a glimpse of a long line of Black faces passing by. They were members of the Eighth United States Colored Artillery that had marched in the funeral procession a few days earlier.[39] As the coach bearing the president's body passed by the last soldier, a voice called out, "Goodbye, Father Abraham."

The first stop was at Camden Yards in Baltimore only thirty-eight miles from Washington by rail. The train arrived at 10:00 A.M. Once again huge crowds lined the way making it impossible to move on any of the sidewalks that surrounded the depot buildings.[40] The casket was removed to the Mercantile Exchange Building in downtown Baltimore. A heavy downpour pelted the people standing along the route to the Exchange. Baltimore was an enigma in many ways. A slave city in a slave state, it harbored the largest population of free Blacks in the country. A city with strong Southern sympathies, it sent as many soldiers into the Union army as made their way south to the Confederate cause. It was home to John Wilkes Booth and would become home to John Surratt. Now its people turned out by the thousands to view the president as he visited their city for the last time.

The procession made its way through the city streets in a wide loop allowing more citizens to see the great hearse carrying the president's body. Ironically, as the procession made its way west along Baltimore Street, it passed within a half block of the old Booth home on Exeter Street. The parade took nearly three hours to complete its course, leaving only a little more than one hour for the public to view the president's body.[41] Fewer than five thousand people made it past the coffin during the short time it was placed on view. At 3:00 P.M. the coffin was closed and returned to its special car for the trip to Harrisburg. Back at the Exchange Building the disappointed crowds began demanding that the city reopen the building for the thousands who were unable to get inside. The protest became so great that the mayor and city council agreed to open the building the next day. Early the next morning thousands of Baltimoreans silently filed past the coffinless catafalque paying their respect to Lincoln's spirit even though his corpse was now miles away.[42]

At 5:30 P.M. the train reached the state line, where it stopped to take on Pennsylvania governor Andrew Curtin and members of his military staff. The train next made an unscheduled stop in the city of York fifty miles to the north of Baltimore. Six young ladies, dressed in black, were granted permission to enter the funeral coach and place a large shield made of red, white, and blue flowers on the coffin. General Townsend had granted the ladies' request but told them that no more than six would be allowed to enter the car and the ceremony must be quick. The ladies complied and, laying their wreath of flowers on the flag-draped casket, quickly departed. Outside the coach a band played a requiem while every bell tower within sound tolled their tribute.[43]

The train arrived in the capital city of Harrisburg at 8:30 P.M., and the coffin was taken to the House of Representatives in the capitol building amidst a heavy downpour and the booming of minute guns.[44] At 9:00 P.M. the doors were opened to the public and the long solemn procession of people once again filed by the coffin in homage. For the next three hours they came, three thousand an hour: men, women, children. At midnight the doors were closed and the undertakers moved in to "refresh" the president by touching up the black splotches that had started to appear on his face and neck. At 7:00 A.M. the doors were opened once again and the public continued to file through. The long lines had stood throughout the night waiting until morning. Few were willing to give up their place in line. At 11:15 A.M. the coffin was placed back on the hearse and the great procession began wending its way to its refuge on the special train. Newspapers reported thousands of people lined the streets along the route.[45] No one had anticipated the size or fervor of the crowds. The local officials were taken completely by surprise.

From Harrisburg the train headed back east to Philadelphia. It had traveled only a third of the way when it reached the city of Lancaster. The crowds around the depot of this small town were estimated at 40,000.[46] As the train approached the city it passed through a small tunnel. Standing near the entrance to the tunnel was a lone figure hunched over with both hands wrapped around the silver head of a wooden cane. The man stood motionless as the train approached and one by one the coaches slowly rolled by. As the funeral car passed the old man raised his hat a few inches off of his head where he held it suspended for no more than two seconds. The car passed and the old man lowered his hat, turned, and walked down the tracks leading away from town.[47] The man was Thaddeus Stevens, an unrelenting abolitionist and radical Republican who saw little good in whatever Lincoln did. His policies were too little, too slow, and too soft. Stevens had pushed Lincoln to emancipate the slaves, and when Lincoln did, he pushed him to give the newly freed slaves the vote, as if it was within Lincoln's power to do so. Now the old man would turn his wrath against a new president. The old one was no longer a problem.

At 4:30 P.M. the train pulled into the Broad Street Station in Philadelphia where again a hearse carried the coffin past tens of thousands of spectators. Philadelphia broke tradition with Baltimore and Washington by using five coal black horses instead of the traditional four white ones. The hearse arrived at Independence Hall at 7:00 P.M. Viewing that evening was by invitation only, with special passes being issued to the select few. Samuel C. Stuart, a police officer from the Fourth District, was one of the lucky ones. Standing on the steps of the Old Court House, where he was on duty, he was approached by a man named John Butler who handed him one of the special passes. As soon as Stuart's tour ended he hurried over to Independence Hall where he used his pass to get inside. He convinced the doorman to let him keep the pass as a precious memento of the solemn occasion.[48]

All through the night the lines continued to form. By dawn's first light they stretched over three miles extending "from the Delaware to the Schuylkill Rivers."[49] At 5:00 A.M. city officials decided to open the doors and let the people begin their passage. Estimates reached 300,000. Someone had cut one of the restraining ropes that were used to keep the line of people orderly. As hundreds pushed their way forward toward the entrance to the building the police quickly formed a long cordon and tried to push the people back. For a brief period bedlam broke out, people shoving and pushing. Eventually the situation was brought under control and the orderly process continued without any further trouble. At 1:00 A.M. the doors were swung shut and the casket placed back on the grand hearse and returned to the Broad Street Station.

Monday morning, April 24 dawned clear. At 4:00 A.M. the train left Philadelphia and headed for New York, eighty-six miles away. The stopover had taken thirty-three hours and had seen the largest gathering of people to date. At Morrisville, opposite the city of Trenton, the governor of New Jersey and his retinue boarded the train. Stopping briefly in Trenton for a half hour, the train then continued on to Newark and then Jersey City arriving at 10 A.M. From here the coffin was ferried across the Hudson River to New York. In New York a new engine with seven new cars would be supplied. Only the special funeral coach would be ferried across the river to join the new train.

As in each of the previous cities designated for ceremonies, tens of thousands of people lined the streets wherever the entourage was scheduled to pass. Along the way were various choruses and glee clubs that broke into song as the hearse passed. At Jersey City it was the Liederkrantz Society, in New York City it was a German Chorus.[50] The *New York Times* described the city crowds as "immense" and "almost soundless, but intensely interested and deeply sympathetic."[51] All of the sidewalks, windows, roofs, lampposts, and trees were filled to capacity with onlookers. Space was at a premium. Several entrepreneurs made available the windows of their office buildings for a rental fee. The owner of 627 Broadway offered three large windows, noting that the room was carpeted and provided with easy chairs giving "every accommodation for viewing the funeral procession of our beloved President."[52] Another enterprising merchant had misjudged the demand for mourning memorabilia. J.R. Hawley ran an ad in the *New York Times* apologizing for being unable to meet the unprecedented demand for "mourning badges and rosettes." Hawley was able to round up alternate material and started to fill orders on a first-come basis, cash only. Badges without pin or crepe were twenty-five cents, rosettes, and pins with likenesses were forty cents each. He sold out a second time.[53]

The hearse arrived at the city hall. Over its main doorway a banner carried the simple words "A Nation Mourns."[54] The coffin was taken inside and placed on a specially constructed dais. Dr. Brown, the official traveling embalmer took over, once again refreshing the president's appearance. When Brown finished his work Mrs. Charles E. Strong, accompanied by Major General Ambrose E. Burnside, entered carrying a special arrangement of flowers on behalf of the city. The arrangement consisted of a large shield made of scarlet azaleas and double nasturtiums. On the shield was a large cross made of pure white japonica and orange blossoms. Also placed on the casket were white flowers arranged in the letters "A.L."[55]

At this point, a seemingly strange event occurred. Jeremiah Gurney Jr., a New York photographer, had been granted permission to photograph the body and surrounding scene. Gurney was given exclusive use of the hall for thirty minutes.[56] He set up his camera at a spot several feet above the dais where the coffin rested. Gurney had intended to make a commercial venture of his unique picture but when word reached Stanton in Washington he erupted angrily, ordering all of the plates destroyed and the officers on duty at the time of the incident relieved. Brigadier General Edward D. Townsend, in charge of the arrangements, telegraphed Stanton that he was the one in charge at the time the picture was taken and therefore responsible. He asked whom he should appoint in his place when relieved. Stanton backed down, telegraphing Townsend to remain in charge until the remains were "finally interred."[57]

Despite appeals from Lincoln's guards in New York to preserve the pictures, Stanton refused. General Dix had sent a print of one of Gurney's pictures to Stanton to convince him that the photographs were not objectionable. Stanton was adamant. The plates were apparently destroyed while the lone print made its way into the war secretary's files, where it remained for twenty-two years. Stanton's son Lewis discovered the print and sent it to John Nicolay who, along with John Hay, was writing a ten-volume biography of Lincoln. Nicolay decided not to use the photograph and placed it in his own papers, which eventually made their way into the collections of the Illinois State Historical Society. The picture remained unknown to the world until 1952 when a fifteen-year-old high school student named Ronald Rietveld who was researching the Nicolay papers discovered the photograph.[58] It remains one of the most haunting photographs associated with Abraham Lincoln.

At 1:00 P.M. the doors were opened to the public. New York held her place as the number one city in the nation. Over 500,000 people were waiting in line, eclipsing the record set in Philadelphia only hours before. The *New York Times* described Lincoln's appearance for its readers: "The color is leaden, almost brown; the forehead recedes sharp and clearly marked; the eyes deep sunk and close held upon the socket; the cheek bones, always high, are unusually prominent; the cheeks hollowed and deep pitted, the unnaturally thin lips shut tight and firm as if glued together, and the small chin, covered with slight beard, seemed pointed and sharp."[59] The description, while unflattering, was accurate.

The New York viewing continued for twenty-five hours with only a small part of the enormous crowd able to view the body. Still, the people waited in line in hopes of seeing the coffin. At 2:00 P.M. the casket was carried on a grand hearse in a long procession that wound its way through the streets of New York to the Hudson River Railroad Depot. Numerous stereographs of the procession attest to the extent of the tribute.

Another interesting incident occurred during the New York stopover. The city council issued an order forbidding Negroes to march in the procession.[60] This ruling caused a great deal of outrage among the five thousand Blacks that had made extensive preparations in anticipation of marching. Surely they, as much as anyone else, had reason to honor their fallen president. Word reached Stanton of the prohibition, and he sent a telegram to the city council and officials in charge of the body stating: "that no discrimination respecting color should be exercised in admitting persons to the funeral procession tomorrow."[61] The telegram pointed out that in the nation's capital, a Black regiment formed part of the president's escort. The committee scrambled to explain its action by pointing out that the request by the Black organizations to march in the procession had not met the Thursday (April 20) deadline for applications. The request was submitted on Friday, April 21.[62] While the late filing was true, the *Albany Times* questioned the committee's explanation, asking, "does anybody believe that the application of any organization of white men would have been refused even if made so late as Monday?"[63] The city relented, but the damage had been done. Many of the Black marchers had left the city assuming they would not be allowed in the procession. By the time word reached the disbanded units, only three hundred individuals could be reached in time. Police Superintendent John Kennedy, who favored allowing Blacks to march, thought it best to assign a police escort for the Black units that remained.

One of the more intriguing episodes occurred during the procession to the Hudson River Railroad Depot where the president's body would leave for the state capital at Albany. As the hearse moved along Broadway a large Saint Bernard dog by the name of Bruno bolted into the street as the hearse passed by and took a place beneath the carriage, where it remained for the rest of the trip to the docks. The *New York Times* marveled at what faithful instinct caused the dog to follow the president as he made his way out of the city.[64]

From New York City the entourage made its way to the state capital of Albany. On the way the train made a half-hour stop in the town of Poughkeepsie where a young soldier glimpsed a view of the special car and its contents. He wrote to his brother back home:

> President Lincolns remains passed through here last Tuesday. It stopped here half an hour. The train consisted of nine cars. They were all trimmed beautifully in mourning and other appropriate emblems for the occasion. I saw the coffin but it was not allowed to be opened. I can not describe the coffin to you. It was trimmed beautifully and splendid wreaths of flowers ornamented it. It was a solemn sight to see the train and to hear the bells toll and the fare well salute fired in memory of the departed dead. It was estimated that there was as many as 25,000 persons at the depot when the train came in. The corpse was carried in the same

> car that he went to Washington in four years ago last March. It was the nicest car That I ever saw.[65]

Arriving in Albany at 11:00 P.M. the casket was taken to the state house where it was opened for public viewing through the night and early morning hours. The crowds of people coming into Albany from the surrounding countryside by train were so great that the Northern Railroad had to resort to using freight cars to carry all of the people demanding passage to the capital.[66] It was Tuesday, April 25, and the president was only a quarter of the way home. He had been dead for ten days and his killer was still loose. Four hundred miles to the south, John Wilkes Booth was told that he and his friend would have to sleep in the Garrett tobacco barn. During the early morning hours of April 26, while thousands of Albany citizens filed past the coffin of their president, John Wilkes Booth would meet his end at the hands of New York cavalrymen.

Wednesday morning dawned overcast for the Lincoln entourage. At noon another grand procession took place carrying the casket from the state house back to the depot. At 4 P.M. precisely, the locomotive *E.H. Jones* chugged out of the station and headed for Buffalo. For the next three hundred miles the funeral train would cut across the widest part of New York State, all the way from the Hudson River to Lake Erie. Along the way it would pass through a half dozen major towns and cities and be seen by over a million people. Heavy rains accompanied the entire trip. Yet at every major population center the people arrived by the hundreds of thousands. The long ribbon of track that ran west seemed to be a magnet pulling vast numbers of people from the surrounding countryside. From small villages and rural farms the people came to catch a glimpse of the great train and pay their respect to the man who had become their martyred president. Bonfires and torches formed a ribbon of orange and yellow light that stretched across the rolling farmland of central New York. Along the way women stood by the tracks and held out bouquets of wildflowers as the funeral coach slowly rolled past, then cast them onto the tracks when it had passed them by. A reporter for the *New York Times* traveling aboard the train wrote that every crossroad along the way was filled with men and women in country wagons. A party of thirty young women lined a clearing bowing their heads in rehearsed unison as the train slowly ambled past. At Johnsville the train stopped briefly for lunch. Twenty-two women uniformly dressed in black skirts and white waists with black scarves carefully tied about their left arm waited on the passengers, providing them with refreshments. In return for their kindness the ladies were allowed to walk through the funeral car and see the coffin.[67]

The train continued on, passing through Schenectady, Little Falls, Herkimer, Utica, Syracuse, Rochester, and Batavia. At Batavia the train switched engines and former President Millard Fillmore climbed aboard to ride the final leg into Buffalo. Like Andrew Johnson, Fillmore acceded to the presidency as a result of the president's untimely death. Zachary Taylor had served seventeen months before he succumbed to what doctors in that day called "cholera morbus."[68]

At 7:00 A.M. the train pulled into Buffalo. Rather than devote precious hours to a time-consuming procession through the city, Buffalo decided to use the time to let the public view the president. The casket was taken to St. James Hall where it was placed on a special catafalque. For the next eleven hours the people passed by the flower-covered casket paying their respect. A reporter for the *Rochester Daily Union and Advertiser* wrote to his readers back home that the body looked more like a mummy than a corpse. "Still," he wrote, "the expression of the face was beautiful—a calm, mild, yet determined look, and just a trace of good humor about the mouth. We have never seen a corpse which had more the look of a sleeper than this."[69]

At ten minutes past ten o'clock on the evening of April 27, the train departed Buffalo for Cleveland, 183 miles away. At 1:00 A.M. the train made a brief stop in Westfield, New York, to take on wood and water. Although not part of the schedule, five young women were permitted to board the funeral car and place a special floral arrangement on the coffin. The modest tribute was allowed out of deference to young Grace Bedell who, four and a half years earlier, had written to Lincoln the candidate urging him to grow a beard because his face was so thin.[70] Grace had lived in Westfield at the time of Lincoln's inaugural trip in February of 1861. Lincoln had greeted the little girl with a hug and a kiss and said, "You see Grace, I have grown these whiskers just for you."[71] Grace, now sixteen years old, was not among the five young ladies to enter the funeral coach and place flowers on the president's casket. She had moved with her family to Albion, New York, some ninety miles to the northeast of Westfield.

From Westfield the train headed southwest to Cleveland. Again a heavy downpour accompanied the trip. The heavens seemed to be pouring all of their grief onto the funeral procession. All through the rain-soaked night the way along the tracks was illuminated by lanterns held aloft by villagers and farmers who stood for hours waiting for the train to pass.[72] Arriving in Cleveland at 7:00 P.M., the casket was carried once again by a magnificent hearse to Cleveland's Public Park, where it was placed on a catafalque under a large pagoda-shaped tent. It was Friday, April 28, exactly one week since the president had begun his long journey home.

Cleveland was allotted fifteen hours to honor the president. The outdoor arrangements greatly facilitated the handling of the large crowd that gathered in the city's Monument Square. One hundred fifty thousand people comfortably passed the open coffin. At midnight it was off again, this time to the capital city of Columbus.

The train reached Columbus at 7:30 A.M. The casket was taken to the capitol building escorted by the Eighty-eighth Ohio Volunteer Infantry.[73] It was the hardest service the Eighty-eighth had performed since being designated the Governor's Guard at the time of its formation in 1862. During its three years of service it had never left the state of Ohio.

Twelve hours later the train was on its way to Indianapolis. Scioto, Hilliards, Pleasant Valley, Unionville, Milford, Woodstock, Vagenburgh, and Urbana—it was the same everywhere. Bonfires lighted the tracks allowing the thousands of spectators to see the funeral car as it slipped past in the night. Within a few minutes it was all over. Hours of waiting were met with a momentary glimpse, but those that witnessed it would never forget it. At Urbana there was music from an instrumental band and a touching hymn by a choir that stood on the station platform. When the train stopped briefly to take on water, several women were permitted to enter the funeral car and place a floral cross on the casket.[74] Shortly after midnight the train crossed the border into Indiana.

The train arrived in Indianapolis at 7:00 A.M. in a heavy downpour. It was now Sunday, April 30. The papers described the hearse in detail. It was fourteen feet long, five feet wide, and thirteen feet high and covered in black velvet. It was curtained in black with silver fringe. Twelve white plumes sat atop the roof, and the sides of the car were studded with large silver stars. Eight white horses covered with black blankets, each topped with a black plume, pulled the car through the streets.[75] The committee in charge of events had decided that all of the children from each of the Sunday schools throughout the city would have the honor of walking past the open casket first.[76] The heavy rains forced the city to curtail their plans for an outdoor ceremony.

The train left Indianapolis at midnight on the thirtieth. At 1:40 A.M. it passed through the small village of Lebanon where a hundred Chinese lanterns were suspended above the tracks. Bonfires continued to illuminate the tracks all across the prairie. Bells in every hamlet and village tolled continuously while small bands stood on station platforms and played dirges.[77] It was the same scene repeated at each place where people congregated. Within a few hours the train had crossed over the border onto the prairie land of Illinois. Abraham Lincoln was home at long last.

At eleven o'clock on the morning of May 1 the train slowly made its way into downtown Chicago. Chicago was unique among all of the cities that hosted Lincoln's remains in that it had decided it would not have any formal ceremonies: no speeches, prayers, or eulogies. It would pay a silent respect to its neighbor and let the people have their time. For the rest of the day and all of the next, people from miles around poured into the great city. The New York area had turned out just over a million and a half people, but Chicago, while unable to match New York's aggregate, turned out a much higher percentage of Illinoisians. This was Lincoln's home. In front of one house the owner erected a bust of Lincoln "supported by black velvet and studded with thirty-six golden stars, with the motto: 'We loved him much, but now we love him more.'"[78]

At 8:00 P.M. Lincoln ended his stay in the city of broad shoulders. The casket was carried from the Cook County Court House and placed on a hearse drawn by eight large black horses. At 9:30 P.M. the train began the final leg of its fourteen-day odyssey. The small engine with its long tail of cars headed out across the black prairie toward Springfield. Lincoln would soon be home and with the people he knew best: "To this place and to the kindness of these people I owe everything," he had said four years earlier on bidding his neighbors goodbye.[79]

At forty minutes past eight o'clock on the morning of May 3, the funeral train pulled into the Chicago and Alton Depot in Springfield, Illinois. After fourteen days and sixteen hundred miles the train arrived only forty minutes behind schedule. As it approached the capital city of Illinois it passed beneath several specially erected banners strung across the tracks: "Come Home," and "There is Rest for Thee in Heaven," and "Home Is the Martyr." Lincoln had returned to the friends and neighbors he had bid farewell just four years before. Somehow his words at the time of his leaving on February 11, 1861, now seemed strangely poignant, "I now leave, not knowing when or whether ever, I may return." He ended his goodbye by bidding all "an affectionate farewell."[80]

As the train slowly made its way toward the station the tracks were lined with neighbors, their hats removed and their hands carefully placed on their hearts. The prairie town had swelled with thousands of visitors who came from all over the region to pay their respects to the fallen president. The local hotels soon filled, leaving hundreds without accommodations. Still they came. Trains arrived at their respective depots disgorging passengers from Chicago, St. Louis, Indianapolis, and all parts of the country. Ten state governors arrived with their delegations. The cities of Chicago, Cincinnati, Cleveland, Indianapolis, Louisville, Milwaukee, and St. Louis sent large delegations. From Washington, D.C., came senators, congressmen, government officials, and dignitaries. Clergymen, politicians, lawyers, doctors, university and college students and faculties, fraternal societies, firemen, policemen, soldiers, and veterans representing their respective organizations and groups. The assemblage was overwhelming. The city of 12,000 swelled until it overflowed its capacity to handle the enormous influx.

The committee on arrangements published notices in the local newspapers that called on the residents to "throw open their homes and exercise the most liberal hospitality to strangers." Farmers were asked to bring to town "good dry straw" and food to share with the multitude of visitors.[81] In keeping with the spirit of Lincoln, the citizens responded to the committee's appeal by opening their houses to people they had never met before. The local Masons set up a large kitchen and dining area where they provided free meals to their visiting brothers. No one was asked if he was a Mason, however, and the women cheerfully fed anyone who showed up hungry. It seemed as if Lincoln's ideal of brotherhood had been finally reached in one great moment of sharing. The man who had waged war had now brought peace and brotherhood in its wake, if only for a brief few days.

Battery K of the Missouri First Regiment of Light Artillery had served in Tennessee all of 1863 and in Arkansas all of 1864 and 1865. Forts Henry and Donelson, Shiloh, Corinth, Helena, and Little Rock were names displayed upon its regimental colors. Now it was given the distinction of firing its guns in honor of its wartime commander in chief who, like them, was a veteran of the greatest war ever waged in the history of conflict. Every ten minutes, beginning at sunrise and continuing until sunset, the guns of Battery K boomed. At the end of the day they concluded by firing a thirty-six-gun salute, one for each of the states now comprising the reunited United States of America. Mississippi, Alabama, Virginia, and even South Carolina along with all their sister states had salutes fired on their behalf.[82] To the men of Battery K, the Union was whole once again thanks to Father Abraham.

A group of local dignitaries designated the "Committee on the Order of Procession" was formed to determine just who would march and where their place would be. It was an immensely important task as every group sought a place of special honor. In charge of the Order of Procession was Lincoln's old Springfield acquaintance and political adversary, Major General John A. McClernand. McClernand had proven to be a mixed blessing to Lincoln. A Democrat who generally sided with Lincoln's opponents, McClernand also brought large numbers of Illinois's young Democrats into Lincoln's army. Major General Joe Hooker was named marshal in chief. The committee divided the funeral procession into eight segments called divisions. Each division was headed by a designated marshal who was accompanied by special aides made up of various dignitaries, both military and civilian.[83]

Leading the First Division and serving as marshal was Colonel C.M. Prevost of the Sixteenth Regiment of the Veteran Reserve Corps. Six military aides followed by several military units accompanied Prevost. The 146th Illinois Volunteer Infantry led the military escort. Following the 146th Illinois were several other military units. The Twenty-fourth Michigan Volunteer Infantry was one such unit. Entering the war in 1862, the regiment quickly made up for lost time serving in the battles of Fredericksburg, Chancellorsville, Gettysburg, Wilderness, Spotsylvania, Cold Harbor, and Petersburg. At Gettysburg it had sustained a sixty-four percent casualty rate, losing 316 men out of 496 engaged. Along with the Twenty-fourth Michigan were the 146th Illinois, Company E of the Twenty-third Regiment of the Veteran Reserve Corps, the Forty-sixth Wisconsin, and a battalion of the Fourteenth Iowa. All were veterans of some of the war's bloodiest battles.

The Second Division followed with more officers and military units.

Not formally scheduled but spontaneously falling in among the uniformed troops in this division were large numbers of disabled veterans who wanted to show their respect. No one protested the unscheduled appearance. These battle-hardened soldiers were "Lincoln's men," and they were determined to march up for their fallen commander.

The Third Division consisted of the "Officiating Clergy" who were followed by the "Surgeons and Physicians of the Deceased." Next came the "Guard of Honor" followed by the magnificent hearse pulled by six black horses. The hearse and horses had been loaned to Springfield by the city of St. Louis. Cost for its transportation had been donated by the railroads. On either side of the hearse walked the honorary pallbearers. Immediately behind the hearse walked Old Bob, Lincoln's horse. He was draped in a large black blanket trimmed in silver fringe specially prepared for him. The Reverend Henry Brown, a Black minister who had done odd jobs for the Lincoln family and had become one of their many friends, led the horse in the procession.[84] Old Bob needed special care since his fame was spreading rapidly. If left unprotected, souvenir hunters would have trimmed all the available hair from the poor horse, leaving him practically denuded. Missing from the procession was Fido, the family dog. Fido was every bit a Lincoln. A common mixed breed that wagged his tail constantly, he was everyman's dog. An instant hit following Lincoln's election, Fido was taken to the studios of photographer F.W. Ingmire where the enterprising photographer took several images of the dog that he offered for sale.[85]

Following Old Bob was a carriage carrying Robert Lincoln and Mary Lincoln's cousin, Elizabeth Todd Grimsley. Elizabeth Grimsley was the daughter of John Todd and was Mary's favorite relative. She attended Lincoln's inaugural ball in 1861 and stayed on in the White House for six months following Lincoln's inauguration. Like so many others, Cousin Lizzie tried to get Lincoln to appoint her to a government job. She had Lincoln's Springfield friends, including Lincoln's old law partner and mentor John T. Stuart, write to him asking that he appoint her postmistress. In a letter to Stuart, Lincoln asked, "Will it do for me to go on and justify the declaration that . . . I have divided out all the offices among our relatives?" Later she asked for a Naval Academy appointment for her son John. Johnny received the appointment, she did not. Now she was riding with Robert in place of Mary.

Strangely missing from family and friends was the woman who had meant the most to Lincoln and who showed him every kindness at a time when his world had turned so very dark. Sarah Bush Johnston Lincoln was absent from her stepson's funeral. Now in her seventy-eighth year, "Aunt Sairy" learned from her son-in-law Dennis Hanks that her boy was dead. Five months later William Herndon, Lincoln's law partner, would visit the old woman at her home at Goosenest Prairie eight miles south of Charleston, Illinois. Herndon made notes of his visit and conversation with Sarah Lincoln about her son: "I did not want Abe to run for Pres[i]d[en]t—did not want him Elected—was afraid Somehow or other—felt in my heart that Something would happen to him and when he came down to See me after he was Elected Pres[i]d[en]t I still felt that Something told me that Something would befall Abe and that I should see him no more."[86] Years later Dennis Hanks would tell his listeners that when he told "Aunt Sairy" that he had bad news about her stepson, she said before he could tell her, "I knowed they'd kill him. I ben awaitin fur it"[87]

Sarah Lincoln was too infirm to make the trip, and Lincoln's favorite cousin, John Hanks, had come in her place. John would have been at the funeral in his own right. Lincoln considered him a close and good friend. He was the best of a bad lot of the Hanks clan. Cousin John had sailed down the Mississippi with Lincoln in 1830 and was credited with carrying an old fence rail into the 1860 Republican convention in Chicago. John would claim it was a rail split by his cousin Abe. It would give rise to the sobriquet "The Rail Splitter Candidate." John would take his place among those walking behind the hearse, but none among the tens of thousands of mourners would know who he was or why he was in the procession.

Back in Washington Mary Lincoln was too distraught to leave her bed. For five weeks she would remain within her room, refusing to see any visitors who came to express their condolences.[88] For the next three weeks her only effort would be to insist on her husband's burial site at Oak Ridge Cemetery in Springfield. She sent a telegram to Robert telling him that Oak Ridge would be his father's final resting place.[89] Despite the efforts to build a tomb in the center of town, Mary Lincoln won out. Her husband would be laid to rest in the place of her choosing but without her presence.

Following the family came the government officials and dignitaries. First the Federal, then foreign ministers, then state and territories, then the District of Columbia. The Springfield city fathers made up the Fifth Division. The Sixth Division was made up of the Christian Commission, "other kindred commissions," delegations from universities and colleges, followed by clergy, lawyers, physicians, and members of the press. The Seventh Division contained Freemasons, Odd Fellows, other fraternal organizations as well as firemen. The last Division consisted of "Citizens at Large and Colored Persons." All of the organizations were instructed to march eight abreast and keep their groups in close alignment. No carriages or vehicles were allowed except for the funeral hearse and transportation for family members.[90]

To identify the various marshals who were placed in charge of the several divisions, special color sashes and scarves were issued. The grand marshal wore a red, white, and blue sash. Aides to the grand marshal wore red, white, and blue scarves, while marshals wore red scarves and their aides wore blue scarves. Marshals of each individual section within a division wore white scarves "draped with a black rosette on the right shoulder, and tied with crepe on the left side."[91] All in all, there was little room for error and none would occur. Literally thousands of people marched with precision, maintaining the dignity and decorum required of the solemn event.

The procession formed along Washington Street facing the state capitol building. When it was ready to leave for the cemetery it proceeded east along Washington two blocks to Eighth Street where it turned south for two blocks to Monroe and then turned west marching four blocks to Fourth Street. At Fourth Street it turned north and followed the road all the way to the cemetery entrance. It was, in effect, a large U-turn that passed within two blocks of the Lincoln's home at Eighth and Jackson before heading north to the cemetery.

On reaching the cemetery, the procession made its way along a narrow road that led between two ridges separated by a small brook. Built into one of the hillsides was a large receiving vault whose facade resembled a Greek temple. Two large vault doors opened into the receiving crypt. The president's casket was placed inside the vault on a large marble slab. To its left sat a smaller casket containing the remains of young Willie Lincoln who had accompanied his father on the long trip from Washington.[92] The hillside immediately behind the vault was covered with spectators whose elevated position gave them a perfect view of the ceremony below.

The ceremony opened with a prayer followed by a hymn and several scriptural readings. The choir sang and then Reverend A.C. Hubbard read Lincoln's second inaugural address. The people listened intently to the speech that had captured the nation only eight weeks before: "the judgments of the Lord, are true and righteous altogether." Could this tragic death really be a judgment of the Lord? Was it the nation's final payment for the sins it had brought upon itself? All across the land preachers were drawing the analogy—as Christ gave his blood to save the world, so Lincoln gave his blood to save the nation.

Bishop Matthew Simpson, America's Methodist leader, delivered the funeral oration. He told of the millions of people who turned out across the countryside to honor their fallen leader. "Three weeks have passed and the nation has scarcely breathed easily yet," he said. "More eyes have looked upon the procession for sixteen hundred miles by night and by day . . . than ever before watched. . . . We ask why." The answer, Simpson said, "is to be found in the man himself."[93] No person so identified "with the heart of the people—understanding their feelings or was more connected with them" than Abraham Lincoln—and the people knew it.[94] Simpson finished and Reverend Phineas Gurley offered yet another prayer. A Springfield choir sang a special hymn that Gurley had written shortly after the service in the White House:

Rest, noble martyr; rest in peace;
Rest with the true and Brave,
Who, like thee, fell in Freedom's cause
The Nation's life to save.

Over one million Americans viewed the remains of Abraham Lincoln as he lay in state in various cities along the long road to Springfield. More than seven million people gathered along the city streets and country fields to pay their respect to the funeral train as it slowly made its way across the country. One in every four Americans had come to see their president or watch his funeral train pass by. All through the day and long dark night people stood for hours, some for days, to watch the lonesome train pass. Small fires cast their glow across the tear-stained faces of America. It was over. The world had never seen anything like it before, nor was it likely ever to see anything like it again. Abraham Lincoln had come home as he had predicted after one of his prescient dreams—home at last.

Back in Washington, a government clerk working for the Department of the Interior returned to his boardinghouse after a long day of tedious paperwork. Exhausted, he could not sleep. The deep sorrow that welled inside him compelled him to write. It was what he did best. Sitting at a small table near the center of his room he dipped his pen into an inkwell and tearfully began to inscribe the words that fell from his wounded heart. He wrote of a captain and his ship that had passed through a terrible storm before safely reaching port:

O Captain! My Captain! rise up and hear the bells;
Rise up—for you the flag is flung—for you the bugle trills,
For you bouquets and ribbon'd wreaths—for you the
  shores a-crowding,
For you they call, the swaying mass, their eager faces turning;
    Hear Captain! dear father!
    This arm beneath your head!
    It is some dream that on the deck,
      You've fallen cold and dead.

My Captain does not answer, his lips are pale and still,
My father does not feel my arm, he has no pulse nor will,
The ship is anchor'd safe and sound, its voyage closed and done,
From fearful trip the victor ship comes in with object won;
    Exult O shores, and ring O bells!
    But I with mournful tread,
    Walk the deck my Captain lies,
      Fallen cold and dead.[95]

It seemed to Walt Whitman as if the ancient Biblical prophecy had come true. The sun had turned to darkness, and the moon to blood.

NOTES

Abbreviations

NARA	National Archives Record Administration
OR	U.S. War Department, *The War of the Rebellion: A Compilation of the Official Records of the Union and Confederate Armies.* 128 vols. Washington, D.C.: Government Printing Office, 1880–1901.
RG	Record Group

Introduction

1. Williams reports the figure in personal communication concerning the Lincoln bibliography that he is currently compiling with the assistance of Brown University.

2. The other three persons are Jesus Christ, William Shakespeare, and Napoleon.

3. The three books are Thomas R. Turner, *Beware the People Weeping* (Baton Rouge: Louisiana State University Press, 1982); William Hanchett, *The Lincoln Murder Conspiracies* (Urbana and Chicago: University of Illinois Press, 1983); and Thomas R. Turner, *The Assassination of Abraham Lincoln* (Malabar, Fla.: Krieger Publishing Company, 1999).

4. Hanchett, *Lincoln Murder Conspiracies*, p. 3.

5. William Hanchett, "Perspectives on Lincoln's Assassination," in George S. Bryan, *The Great American Myth* (Chicago: Americana House, 1990), p. ix.

6. Among these books are Otto Eisenschiml, *Why Was Lincoln Murdered?* (Boston: Little, Brown, 1937); Eisenschiml, *In the Shadow of Lincoln's Death* (New York: Wilfred Funk, 1940); Theodore Roscoe, *The Web of Conspiracy* (Englewood Cliffs, N.J.: Prentice-Hall, 1959); David Balsiger and Charles E. Sellier Jr., *The Lincoln Conspiracy* (Los Angeles: Schick Sunn Classic Books, 1977); and Robert Lockwood Mills, *It Didn't Happen the Way You Think* (Bowie, Md:. Heritage Books, 1994).

7. Perhaps the best book written on the Lincoln assassination is George S. Bryan, *The Great American Myth* (New York: Carrick and Evans, 1940), which was reprinted in 1990. Bryan, nevertheless, relied heavily on secondary sources failing to take advantage of the large primary record then available.

8. John Y. Simon, remarks at the Fifth Annual Ford's Theatre Symposium, "Lincoln's Assassination: Old Assumptions, New Insights," Washington, D.C., August 3, 1998.

9. Eisenschiml, *Why Was Lincoln Murdered?*

10. Honorable Steny Hoyer, "The Samuel A. Mudd Relief Act of 1997," quoted in Edward Steers Jr., "His Name Is Still Mudd" (Gettysburg, Pa.: Thomas Publications, 1997), pp. 134–37.

11. William A. Tidwell, James O. Hall, and David W. Gaddy, *Come Retribution: The Confederate Secret Service and the Assassination of Abraham Lincoln* (Jackson: University of Mississippi Press, 1989), p. xiii.

12. Jefferson Davis, *The Rise and Fall of the Confederate Government*, 2 vols. (New York: Da Capo Press, 1990), 2:426.

13. "Black flag" was presumably a reference to the pirate black flag that bore a skull and crossbones and signified a "no-holds barred" type of warfare. Thus no one was excluded nor was any action excluded in achieving a successful end, including murder. The term "black flag warfare" appeared in the *Philadelphia Age*, a daily newspaper, on March 11, 1864, in reference to Colonel Ulric Dahlgren's raid and the papers found on his body. In denouncing Dahlgren's alleged plan to sack Richmond and kill Jefferson Davis, the *Age* referred to the action as "black flag warfare," condemning the Lincoln administration and its supporters. See Joseph George Jr., "Black Flag Warfare," *Pennsylvania Magazine of History and Biography*, July 1991, p. 314.

14. Statement of George A. Atzerodt. Joan L. Chaconas, "Unpublished Atzerodt Confession Revealed Here for the First Time," *Surratt Courier* 13, no. 10 (October 1988): 1–3.

15. Tidwell, Hall, and Gaddy, *Come Retribution*, pp. 416–21.

16. For one such opinion see Mark E. Neely Jr., "Come Retribution, A Review," *American Historical Review* 95, no. 3 (June 1990): 913–14.

17. In Bryan, *Great American Myth*, p. 7.

1. The Apotheosis

1. The weapon used by Booth was a cap and ball pocket pistol manufactured in Philadelphia by Henry Deringer. The word "derringer" has come to mean other makes of small, one-shot pistols of similar design.

2. Henry S. Safford to O.H. Oldroyd, June 25, 1903, Ford's Theatre, Washington, D.C.

3. Howard K. Beale, ed., *Diary of Gideon Welles*, 3 vols. (New York: W.W. Norton and Company, 1960), 2:283–86. Hereafter referred to as Beale, ed., *Welles Diary*.

4. The laws of succession in April of 1865, should the president and vice president be killed or incapacitated, called for the president pro tempore of the Senate to serve as acting president. Senator Lafayette S. Foster of Connecticut held this position.

5. Charles A. Leale, *Lincoln's Last Hours: Address Delivered before the Commandery of the State of New York Military Order of the Loyal Legion of the United States* (New York: privately printed, 1909).

6. Emerson Reck, *A. Lincoln: His Last 24 Hours* (Columbia: University of South Carolina Press, 1994), p. 157.

7. John G. Nicolay and John Hay, *Abraham Lincoln: A History*, 10 vols. (New York: Century Publishing Company, 1890), 10:302.

8. David B. Chesebrough, *"No Sorrow like Our Sorrow": Northern Protestant Ministers and the Assassination of Abraham Lincoln* (Kent, Ohio: Kent State University Press, 1994), p. 1.

9. Ibid., pp. 36–37.

10. Ibid., p. 39.

2. You Are in Danger

1. Emma LeConte, quoted in Carolyn L. Harrell, *When the Bells Tolled for Lincoln: Southern Reaction to the Assassination* (Macon, Ga.: Mercer University Press, 1997), p. 59.

2. *Texas Republican*, April 28, 1865.

3. *Galveston Daily News*, April 27, 1865. For an excellent essay on the reaction in Texas to Lincoln's death see John M. Barr, "The Tyrannicide's Reception: Responses in Texas to Lincoln's Assassination," *Lincoln Herald* 91, no. 2 (summer 1989): 54–63.

4. Joshua Allen to "Mother," January 26, 1861, Illinois Historical Preservation Agency, Springfield, Il. Joshua Allen's politics led him into the subversive organization known as the Knights of the Golden Circle, where he supported the secession of southern Illinois into the Confederacy. His activities resulted in his arrest and imprisonment in the Old Capitol Prison in Washington, D.C. He was later elected to the Thirty-seventh and the Thirty-eighth U.S. Congress filling the seat of his former law partner Major General John A. Logan, who joined the Union army. Allen was defeated for reelection in 1864 by Logan, who denounced him as a traitor.

5. Harold Holzer, *Dear Mr. Lincoln: Letters to the President* (Reading, Mass.: Addison-Wesley, 1993), p. 340.

6. Ibid., p. 342.

7. Ibid., p. 336.

8. Elizabeth Keckley, *Behind the Scenes; or, Thirty Years a Slave, and Four Years in the White House* (1968; reprint, New York: Oxford University Press, 1988), p. 120.

9. Tidwell, Hall, and Gaddy, *Come Retribution*, pp. 227–33.

10. Norma B. Cuthbert, ed., *Lincoln and the Baltimore Plot, 1861* (San Marino, Calif.: Huntington Library, 1949).

11. David C. Mearns, ed., *The Lincoln Papers*, 2 vols. (New York: Doubleday, 1948), 2:442.

12. Ibid., 2:443.

13. Cuthbert, ed., *Lincoln and the Baltimore Plot*, p. xv.

14. Ibid., p. 84.

15. *Baltimore Sun*, February 25, 1865, p. 1, col. 2.

16. *Baltimore American*, February 26, 1865, p. 1, col. 4.

17. *New York Times*, February 25, 1861, p. 1, col. 1.

18. Elihu B. Washburne, "Abraham Lincoln in Illinois," *North American Review* 141 (1885): 456–57.

19. Benson J. Lossing, *A History of the Civil War, 1861–1865, and the Causes that Led Up to the Great Conflict* (New York: War Memorial Association, 1912), p. 109.

20. Rufus Rockwell Wilson, *Lincoln in Caricature* (New York: Horizon Press, 1953), p. 109.

21. Ward Hill Lamon, *Recollections of Abraham Lincoln, 1847-1865*, ed. Dorothy Lamon Teillard (Chicago: A.C. McClung, 1895), p. 33.

22. Ibid., p. 274.

23. Carl Sandburg, *Abraham Lincoln: The War Years*, 4 vols. (New York: Charles Scribner's Sons, 1944), 2:211.

24. Roy P. Basler, ed., *The Collected Works of Abraham Lincoln*, 9 vols. (New Brunswick, N.J.: Rutgers University Press, 1953), 5:484–85.

25. Margaret Leech, *Reveille in Washington* (New York: Harper and Brothers, 1941), p. 303.

26. Robert W. McBride, "Lincoln's Body Guard," *Indiana Historical Society Publications* 5, no. 1 (1911): 21.

27. James O. Hall, "The Mystery of Lincoln's Guard," *Surratt Society News* 7, no. 5 (May 1982): 4–6.

28. Ibid.

29. Archer H. Shaw, *The Lincoln Encyclopedia* (New York: Macmillan, 1950), p. 18.

30. Lamon, *Recollections*, p. 270.

31. Ibid., p. 267.

32. Ibid., p. 268.

33. Ibid., p. 272.

34. Walker Taylor was one of four brothers who fought in the Civil War: two served in the Union army and two served in the Confederate army.

35. Henry T. Louthan, "A Proposed Abduction of Lincoln," *Confederate Veteran*, June 1908, p. 157.

36. Ibid., p. 158.

37. Tidwell, Hall, and Gaddy, *Come Retribution*, pp. 235–36, 281–86.

38. Shaw, *Lincoln Encyclopedia*, p. 17.

39. John Rhodenhamel and Louise Taper, eds., *"Right or Wrong, God Judge Me": The Writings of John Wilkes Booth* (Chicago: University of Illinois Press, 1997), p. 83.

40. Rhodenhamel and Taper, eds., *Right or Wrong*, p. 78.

41. Ibid.

3. All the World's a Stage

1. For a discussion of this view see Rick G. Mundy, "Theatrical Pariah: John Wilkes Booth and the Literature of the Theatre," Ph.D. diss., University of Kansas, 1999, p. 2.

2. Stanley Kimmel, *The Mad Booths of Maryland* (Indianapolis: Bobbs-Merrill Company, 1940), p. 59.

3. Ibid., p. 45.

4. Apocryphal stories of Booth's having married and fathered children can be found in Izola Forrester, *This One Mad Act* (Boston: Hale, Cushman and Flint, 1939), and Theodore J. Nottingham, *The Curse of Cain: The Untold Story of John Wilkes Booth* (Nicholasville, Ky.: Appaloosa Press, 1997).

5. Although Junius Brutus Booth came to admire John Wilkes, he does not appear to have named his son for him. The name can be found among the Booth ancestors who predate the English republican.

6. Kimmel, *Mad Booths*, p. 17.

7. Mundy, "Theatrical Pariah," p. 5. Gene Smith, *American Gothic: The Story of America's Legendary Theatrical Family—Junius, Edwin, and John Wilkes Booth* (New York: Simon and Schuster, 1992), p. 25.

8. Kimmel, *Mad Booths*, p. 21.

9. Ibid., p. 32.

10. The property was leased to him for 1,000 years at a total cost of $733 by Richard W. Hall, the owner of the property. Booth paid Hall ground rent of one cent per year. The property consisted of approximately 180 acres. See Kimmel, *Mad Booths*, p. 37, and n. 12.

11. Kimmel, *Mad Booths*, pp. 63–64.

12. Four of the ten children of Junius and Mary Ann died in infancy: Frederick, Elizabeth, and Mary Ann in 1833 and Henry Byron in 1836.

13. Terry Alford, ed., *John Wilkes Booth: A Sister's Memoir by Asia Booth Clarke*, (Jackson: University Press of Mississippi, 1996), p. 10. Hereafter referred to as Alford, ed., *A Sister's Memoir.*

14. Photographic copies of the baptismal record in the author's files. The original register is maintained at St. Timothy's Hall in Catonsville, Maryland.

15. Rhodenhamel and Taper, eds., *Right or Wrong*, p. 54.

16. While there is no evidence to prove Booth had attended the rally, his writing indicates he was fully aware of the speeches given there. He could also have read them in the Philadelphia papers the next day.

17. Rhodenhamel and Taper, eds., *Right or Wrong*, p. 58.

18. Ibid., p. 62.

19. For contemporary arguments for and against the Christian defense of slavery see Albert Taylor Bledsoe, *Liberty and Slavery* (1856; reprint, Wiggins, Miss.: Crown Rights Book Company, 1989), and Albert Barnes, *An Inquiry into the Scriptural Views of Slavery* (Philadelphia: Perkins and Purves, 1846).

20. Rhodenhamel and Taper, eds., *Right or Wrong*, p. 57.

21. Ibid., p. 64.

22. Ibid., p. 62.

23. Thomas P. Slaughter, *Bloody Dawn* (New York: Oxford University Press, 1991).

24. The complete trial transcript is available in James J. Robbins, ed., *Report of the Trial of Castner Hanway for Treason in the Resistance of the Execution of the Fugitive Slave Law of September, 1850* (1852; reprint, Westport, Conn.: Negro Universities Press, 1970).

25. Today, in the little village of Christiana a large granite obelisk stands on the front lawn of a private home. On the side facing north are the words: "Castner Hanway. He suffered for freedom." On the side facing south are the words: "Killed: Edward Gorsuch. He died for law." It reflects the community's reconciliation to both sides.

26. John Deery, quoted in Richard J.S. Gutman and Kellie O. Gutman, *John Wilkes Booth Himself* (Dover, Del.: Hired Hand Press, 1979), p. 13.

27. Francis Wilson, quoted in Gutman and Gutman, *John Wilkes Booth Himself*, p. 13.

28. Kimmel, *Mad Booths* , p. 153.

29. Asia Booth Clarke, *The Unlocked Book: A Memoir of John Wilkes Booth by His Sister* (New York: G.P. Putnam's Sons, 1938).

30. Alford, ed., *A Sister's Memoir*, p. 9.

31. Ibid., p. 45. These marks became important in the identification of Booth's body at the time of his death.

32. Ibid., p. 48.

33. Mundy, "Theatrical Pariah," p. 17.

34. Rhodenhamel and Taper, eds., *Right or Wrong*, p. 46 n. 6. Mary Ann Booth in writing to her eldest son, Junius Jr., on October 3, 1858, states that John Wilkes is earning $11 a week.

35. Alford, ed., *A Sister's Memoir*, pp. 48–49.

36. Ibid., p. 88.

37. Ibid.

38. Rhodenhamel and Taper, eds., *Right or Wrong*, p. 69.

39. John Wilkes Booth, letter, "To Whom It May Concern," 1864. Quoted in Turner, *Assassination of Abraham Lincoln*, p. 85.

40. Kimmel, *Mad Booths*, pp. 180–81. See also Mundy, "Theatrical Pariah," pp. 83–84.

41. Rhodenhamel and Taper, eds., *Right or Wrong*, p. 94.

42. Ibid., p. 96.

43. Ibid., pp. 93–96, 97 n. 5. See also Arthur F. Loux, *John Wilkes Booth, Day by Day* (privately published, 1990), p. 369. Copy in Surratt Museum Library, Clinton, Maryland.

44. Ibid., p. 57.

45. David E. Long, "'I Say We Can Control That Election': Confederate Policy towards the 1864 U.S. Presidential Election." *Lincoln Herald* 99, no. 3 (fall 1997): 111.

46. Ibid.

47. Charles B. Dew, *Apostles of Disunion: Southern Secession Commissioners and the Causes of the Civil War* (Charlottesville, Va.: Univ. Press of Virginia, 2001), p. 54.

48. Ibid., p. 89.

4. The Black Flag Is Raised

1. Basler, ed., *Collected Works*, 5:144–46.

2. For an excellent treatise on the importance of Kentucky to Lincoln and the Union see Lowell H. Harrison, *Lincoln of Kentucky* (Lexington: University of Press of Kentucky, 2000).

3. Basler, ed., *Collected Works*, 4:532.

4. Ibid., 5:317–18.

5. Ibid., 5:324–25.

6. Ibid., 5:319.

7. Ibid., 5:153.

8. Ibid., 5:434.

9. The United States Navy was already integrated. Estimates place the number of Black sailors serving between 1861 and 1865 at 18,000. See Joseph P. Reidy, "Black Civil War Sailors Project Nearing Completion of Phase I," *Columbiad* 3, no. 2 (summer 1999): 17–20. In September of 1861, five months into the war, Flag Officer Silas Stringham was instructed to use wherever needed Blacks who had escaped to the Federal blockading squadron. By December 1862 Blacks were accepted as enlistees in the navy to serve alongside Whites. In contrast to the army, the navy gave Blacks pay equal to that of White sailors. Blacks enlisted as landsmen and were allowed to advance to the rank of seaman. At least eight Black sailors were awarded the

Congressional Medal of Honor. See William A. Gladstone, *Men of Color* (Gettysburg, Pa.: Thomas Publications, 1993), pp. 148–49; and Donald L. Canney, *Lincoln's Navy* (Annapolis: Naval Institute Press, 1998), pp. 138–39.

10. Dunbar Rowland, ed., *Jefferson Davis, Constitutionalist: His Letters, Papers and Speeches* (Jackson: University of Mississippi Press, 1923), 5:409–11.

11. Ibid.

12. Rowland, ed., *Jefferson Davis*, 5:409.

13. Prior to the formation of the United States Colored Troops (USCT) five regiments of Black soldiers had existed as state militia in Federal service: The First South Carolina; the First, Second, and Third Louisiana Native Guard; and the First Kansas Colored Infantry. These five regiments were amalgamated into the USCT. Gladstone, *Men of Color*, p. 1.

14. Ted Alexander, "Retreat from Gettysburg: Ten Days in July," *North and South* 2, no. 6 (June 1999): 13.

15. U.S. Congress, House, *Report on the Assassination of Abraham Lincoln*, 39th Cong., 1st sess., July 1866 (Washington, D.C.: Government Printing Office, 1866), p. 2. This report is commonly referred to as "The Boutwell Report."

16. Ibid.

17. Basler, ed., *Collected Works*, 6:357.

18. U.S. Congress, House, *Report on the Treatment of Prisoners of War by the Rebel Authorities*, 40th Cong., 3d sess., December 1868 (Washington, D.C.: Government Printing Office, 1869), p. 862. See also William H. Townsend, *Lincoln and the Bluegrass* (Lexington: University of Kentucky Press, 1955), pp. 317–18.

19. George, "Black Flag Warfare," pp. 292–93.

20. Basler, ed., *Collected Works*, 6:203.

21. George, "Black Flag Warfare," p. 301.

22. John W. White to Horace Greeley, February 9, 1864, quoted in George, "Black Flag Warfare," pp. 303–4.

23. Ibid., p. 301.

24. Ibid.

25. James O. Hall, "The Dahlgren Papers: A Yankee Plot to Kill President Jefferson Davis," *Civil War Times Illustrated*, November 1983, p. 33.

26. Hall, "The Dahlgren Papers," p. 33.

27. Lee, under a flag of truce, sent Meade photographic copies of the papers found on Dahlgren's body along with an inquiry whether the action was authorized by the United States government or by Dahlgren's superior officers. See George, "Black Flag Warfare," pp. 309–10.

28. OR, ser. 1, vol. 33, p. 180.

29. *Richmond Whig*, March 7, 1864, p. 2, quoted in George, "Black Flag Warfare," p. 317.

30. The authenticity of the Dahlgren papers has been established beyond any reasonable doubt. See Hall, "The Dahlgren Papers"; and Stephen W. Sears, "The Dahlgren Papers Revisited," *Columbiad* 3 (summer 1999): 63–87.

31. The one million dollars came from a special fund appropriated by the Confederate Congress (February 15, 1864) designated "Secret Service." A request dated April 25, 1864, issued to Secretary of War Judah P. Benjamin with the notation "Thompson," was signed by Jefferson Davis. One dollar in gold was equal to 2.2 dollars

in greenbacks, the equivalent of approximately 23 million dollars in current dollars. See William A. Tidwell, *April '65: Confederate Covert Action in the American Civil War* (Kent, Ohio: Kent State University Press, 1995), p. 129.

32. Wilfrid Bovy, "Confederate Agents in Canada during the American Civil War," *Canadian Historical Review* 2 (11 March 1921): p. 47. See also Albert Hemingway, "Neutral Border Violated," *America's Civil War* (May 1988): p. 43.

33. *New York Times*, May 30, 1865.

34. Hyams's verbatim testimony appears in Ben: Perley Poore, *The Conspiracy Trial for the Murder of the President*, 4 vols. (1865; reprint New York: Arno Press, 1972), 2:409–19.

35. Roscoe, *The Web of Conspiracy*, and Tidwell, Hall, and Gaddy, *Come Retribution*, are the only modern treatises on Lincoln's assassination that mention Luke Blackburn in connection with a germ warfare.

36. Nancy Disher Baird, *Luke Pryor Blackburn: Physician, Governor, Reformer* (Lexington, Kentucky: University Press of Kentucky, 1979), 34.

37. OR, ser. 4, vol. 3, p. 1117, and OR, ser. 4, vol. 2, p. 889.

38. *New York Weekly Tribune*, May 23, 1865.

39. *New York Times*, May 26, 1865.

40. Ibid.

41. *Montreal Gazette*, May 27, 1865.

42. Article quoted in the *Bermuda Royal Gazette*, June 13, 1865.

43. Stewart also produced a geography textbook titled, *A Geography for Beginners* (Richmond: J.W. Randolph, 1864).

44. Judah P. Benjamin to J.A. Seddon, October 25, 1864, NARA, RG 109, M-437, reel 121, frames 669–70.

45. Judah P. Benjamin to Jacob Thompson, Richmond, November 29, 1864, in the William N. Pendleton Papers, 1466, Southern Historical Collection, University of North Carolina Library, Chapel Hill.

46. Twenty thousand dollars in 1864 had the purchasing power of $210,000 in current dollars.

47. Kensey Johns Stewart to Jefferson Davis, December 12, 1864, NARA, RG 109, chap. 7, vol. 24, pp. 64–65. Historian James O. Hall discovered this letter.

48. Jefferson Davis, of course, did not see all of the letters addressed to him. However, in light of his having dispatched Stewart to Canada as a possible successor to Thompson, it is inconceivable that he was not shown Stewart's letter concerning Blackburn's plot to spread contagion among civilian populations.

49. Thomas Nelson Conrad, *A Confederate Spy* (New York: J.S. Ogilvie, 1892), p. 56.

50. Conrad had lived in Washington for "five or more years" and was thoroughly familiar "with the entrances and exits" of the city. See Thomas Nelson Conrad, *The Rebel Scout* (Washington, D.C.: National Publishing Company, 1904), pp. 118–19.

51. Conrad, *Rebel Scout*, pp. 22–23.

52. Conrad, *Confederate Spy*, p. 72.

53. Conrad, *Rebel Scout*, pp. 94–95.

54. Ibid., p. 119.

55. Tidwell, Hall, and Gaddy, *Come Retribution*, p. 283.

56. Conrad, *Rebel Scout*, p. 31.

57. Percy E. Martin, "John 'Bull' Frizzell," in *In Pursuit of . . . Continuing Research in the Field of the Lincoln Assassination*, ed. Laurie Verge (Clinton, Md.: Surratt Society, 1990), p. 91.

58. Conrad, *Rebel Scout*, p. 33.

59. Booth began recruiting cohorts for his capture plan during the first week of August 1864 approximately the same time that Conrad began putting together his plan.

60. The troop of cavalry were members of the Union Light Guard (Ohio) that had been assigned to guard Lincoln in September 1863 when he traveled by carriage or on horseback.

61. Conrad, *Rebel Scout*, p. 124.

62. Ibid., pp. 127–28.

63. Ibid., p. 128.

64. Tidwell, Hall, and Gaddy, *Come Retribution*, p. 286.

65. Ibid., p. 323, and Tidwell, *April '65*, p. 18.

66. The alleged plot by Harney to blow up the White House has been pieced together from several independent sources and described in Tidwell, Hall, and Gaddy, *Come Retribution*, pp. 418–21.

67. Tidwell, Hall, and Gaddy, *Come Retribution*, p. 261.

5. The South Wants Justice

1. Basler, ed., *Collected Works*, 8:514.

2. Cordial Crane to Edwin M. Stanton, July 26, 1865, NARA, M-599, reel 3, frame 0153.

3. Tidwell, Hall, and Gaddy, *Come Retribution*, p. 263.

4. Ibid.

5. Ibid.

6. Rhodenhamel and Taper, eds., *Right or Wrong*, pp. 106–17.

7. Ibid., p. 116.

8. Samuel Bland Arnold, *Memoirs of a Lincoln Conspirator*, ed. Michael W. Kauffman (Bowie, Md.: Heritage Books, 1995), pp. 133–37.

9. Ibid., p. 134.

10. Asia Booth Clarke to Jean Anderson Sherwood, August 15, 1864, Peale Museum, Baltimore, Maryland.

11. Diary of Junius Brutus Booth Jr., Folger Shakespeare Library, Washington, D.C.

12. Arnold, *Memoirs*, p. 22.

13. Ibid.

14. Quoted in Ernest C. Miller, *John Wilkes Booth in the Pennsylvania Oil Region*, (Meadville, Pa.: Crawford County Historical Society, 1987), p. 35.

15. Diary of Junius Brutus Booth Jr., August 28, 1864. See also Loux, *Day by Day*, pp. 401–2; and Clarke, *The Unlocked Book*, pp. 118–19.

16. Arnold, *Memoirs*, p. 42.

17. Arnold, *Memoirs*, p. 43.

18. *Port Tobacco Times and Charles County Advertiser*, November 22, 1860, p. 2, col. 4. Hereafter referred to as *Port Tobacco Times*.

19. *Port Tobacco Times*, December 27, 1861, p. 2, col. 2.

20. Thomas A. Jones, *J. Wilkes Booth* (Chicago: Laird and Lee, 1893), p. 13.

21. Jones was again arrested in Charles County, Maryland, on April 23, 1865, suspected of aiding Booth, and was imprisoned in the Old Capitol on April 25. The Federal authorities could not quite pin down Jones's role, and he was released on parole, May 29. Old Capitol Prison records, supplied by James O. Hall in private communication.

22. Mark E. Neely Jr. *The Fate of Liberty* (Chicago: Oxford University Press, 1991).

23. U.S. War Department, *The War of the Rebellion: A Compilation of the Official Records of the Union and Confederate Armies*, ser. 2, 128 vols. (Washington, D.C.: Government Printing Office, 1880–1901), 2:868.

24. Mark E. Neely Jr., "Some New Light on Thomas A. Jones and a Mysterious Man Named Mudd," *Lincoln Lore*, no. 1721 (July 1981): 4.

25. Sylvester Mudd was the brother of Dr. George D. Mudd of Bryantown. Sylvester lived on the original Mudd family homestead located a short distance from Samuel Mudd's farm. See Richard D. Mudd. *The Mudd Family of the United States*, 2 vols. (Saganaw, Mich.: published by the author, 1951), 1:423.

26. Roberta J. Wearmouth, *Abstracts from the "Port Tobacco News and Charles County Advertiser,"* vol. 2, 1855–1869 (Bowie, Md.: Heritage Books, 1991), p. 110.

27. Mudd, *Mudd Family*, 1:525–26.

28. Neely, *Fate of Liberty*.

29. Union Provost Marshal's File of Papers Relating to Two or More Civilians, NARA, RG 109, M-416, file 6083.

30. Henry Simms was a slave owned by Henry Lowe Mudd, Samuel Mudd's father, and Richard Washington was a slave owned by Samuel Mudd.

31. Elvey Eagleon (Elzey Eglent), John Henry Eagleon (Eglent), and John Sylvester Egleon (Eglent).

32. Samuel Cox was a member of the Confederate underground in Charles County operating a "mail line" that ran from Richmond to Washington. At the time Booth and Herold were making their escape from the military authorities, the two fugitives were directed to a hiding place in a pine thicket by Samuel Cox. Cox turned the pair over to Thomas A. Jones instructing Jones to get them over the river and into Virginia as soon as possible.

33. Union Provost Marshal's File of Papers Relating to Two or More Civilians, NARA, RG 109, M-416, file 6083.

34. Ibid.

35. Ibid.

6. The Key Connection

1. Alford, ed., *A Sister's Memoir*, p. 84.

2. Ibid.

3. Tidwell, Hall, and Gaddy, *Come Retribution*, p. 331. The U.S. Senate failed to confirm Sander's appointment as consul.

4. Testimony of Hosea B. Carter, in Poore, *Conspiracy Trial*, 2:405–9.

5. Tidwell, Hall, and Gaddy, *Come Retribution*, p. 180.

6. Ibid., pp. 178–79.

7. OR, ser. 1, vol. 35, pt. 2, p. 254.

8. According to the testimony of detective Eaton G. Horner, Samuel Arnold stated that Booth had "letters of introduction to Dr. Mudd and Dr. Queen." See Poore, *Conspiracy Trial*, 1:430.

9. Tidwell, Hall, and Gaddy, *Come Retribution*, p. 335.

10. Statement of account for John Wilkes Booth with Jay Cooke and Company, November 16–March 16, Abraham Lincoln Papers, Chicago Historical Society.

11. Civil twilight began at 5:04 A.M. on the morning of April 15, 1865, or approximately one hour after Booth arrived at Dr. Mudd's house. U.S. Naval Observatory, Astronomical Applications Department, "Sun and Moon Data for One Day," April 15, 1865, Waldorf, Maryland, <http://mach.usno.navy.mil/cgi-bin/aa_pap>. Had Booth continued on instead of stopping at Mudd's house, he could not have gone farther than Bryantown before twilight occurred. Traveling during daylight hours was out of the question since crossing the river would have been obvious to anyone searching the river.

12. Testimony of John C. Thompson, in Poore, *Conspiracy Trial*, 2:269.

13. Jack D. Brown et al., eds., *Charles County Maryland: A History* (Hackensack, N.J.: Custombook, 1976), p. 109.

14. Samuel Alexander Mudd married Sarah Frances Dyer November 26, 1857. Father Peter B. Lenaghan performed the service. In all, nine Mudd children were baptized at St. Peters Church, four prior to 1865, and five after 1865. The earliest was baptized November 7, 1858, and the last February 3, 1878.

15. Statement of Samuel A. Mudd, NARA, M-599, reel 5, frames 0212–0239. Hereafter referred to as Mudd Wells statement.

16. Ibid.

17. Poore, *Conspiracy Trial*, 1:30–32.

18. Rhodenhamel and Taper, eds., *Right or Wrong*, p. 123.

19. Testimony of Thomas Gardiner, in Poore, *Conspiracy Trial*, 1:363.

20. Poore, *Conspiracy Trial*, 3:433.

21. Ibid., p. 435.

22. Edward Steers Jr., *His Name Is Still Mudd* (Gettysburg, Pa.: Thomas Publications, 1997).

23. *Washington Star*, August 3, 1865, p. 1, col. 1.

24. Benn Pitman, *The Assassination of President Lincoln and the Trial of the Conspirators* (Cincinnati: Moore, Wilstach and Baldwin, 1865), p. 326.

25. Affidavit of Samuel A. Mudd, in Clara E. Laughlin, *The Death of Lincoln* (New York: Doubleday, Page, 1909), pp. 215–20.

26. James O. Hall, "You Have Mail . . . ," *Surratt Courier* 25, no. 7 (July 2000): 8–9.

27. The Harbin interview by George Alfred Townsend occurred in 1885 and appeared in the *Cincinnati Enquirer*, April 18, 1892.

28. On reaching the Virginia shore on Sunday, April 23, Booth and Herold made their way to the home of Elizabeth Quesenberry, a member of the Confederate Underground. Quesenberry sent word to Harbin to come at once and take charge of the two fugitives. Harbin arrived and soon passed Booth and Herold to William

Bryant, one of Harbin's men. Harbin instructed Bryant to take the two men to their next destination, the home of Dr. Richard Stuart known as Cleydael.

29. Poore, *Conspiracy Trial,* 1:362.

30. Poore, *Conspiracy Trial,* 1:363.

31. Osborn H. Oldroyd, *The Assassination of Abraham Lincoln* (Washington, D.C.: O.H. Oldroyd, 1901), p. 259.

32. Alfred Isacsson, "Some Points Concerning John Harrison Surratt, Jr.," *Surratt Courier* 20, no. 8 (August 1995): 8–9.

33. James O. Hall, *The Surratt Family and John Wilkes Booth* (Clinton, Md.: Surratt Society, 1984), p. 9.

34. David W. Gaddy, "The Surratt Tavern—A Confederate 'Safe House'?" in *In Pursuit of . . .,* ed. Verge, p. 129.

35. Hall, *Surratt Family,* p. 9.

36. *Baltimore American,* July 10, 1865, col. 3.

37. Betty J. Ownsbey, *Alias "Paine"* (Jefferson, N.C.: McFarland and Company, 1993).

38. Tidwell, Hall, and Gaddy, *Come Retribution,* p. 340.

39. Ownsbey, *Alias "Paine,"* p. 17.

40. Tidwell, Hall, and Gaddy, *Come Retribution,* p. 339.

41. The spelling changed from Payne to Paine.

42. Richard Smoot, *The Unwritten History of the Assassination of Abraham Lincoln* (Clinton, Mass.: W.J. Coulter, 1908), pp. 7–8. The only extant copy of this small pamphlet is in the Rare Book Room of the Library of Congress.

43. *Trial of John H. Surratt,* 2 vols. (Washington, D.C.: Government Printing Office, 1867), 1:273.

44. Ownsbey, *Alias "Paine,"* p. 39.

45. *Trial of John H. Surratt,* 1:275.

46. Testimony of Louis J. Wiechmann, in Poore, *Conspiracy Trial,* 1:73–74. See also testimony of Honora Fitzpatrick, in Poore, *Conspiracy Trial,* 2:89–91.

47. Louis J. Wiechmann, *A True History of the Assassination of Abraham Lincoln and of the Conspiracy of 1865,* ed. Floyd E. Risvold (New York: Alfred E. Knopf, 1975), p. 432.

7. A Shift in Plans

1. Terry Alford, remarks at the Fifth Annual Ford's Theatre Symposium, "Lincoln's Assassination: Old Assumptions, New Insights," Washington, D.C., August 3, 1998.

2. Frequently confused by many writers as taking place at Soldiers' Home. For an accurate account of this episode see William Hanchett, "The Ambush on the Seventh Street Road," in *In Pursuit of . . .,* ed. Verge, pp. 151–63.

3. Chaconas, "Unpublished Atzerodt Confession."

4. Arnold, *Memoirs,* p. 149. See also *Trial of John H. Surratt,* 1:510.

5. Benning's Bridge was located four and a half miles to the southeast of the Seventh Street (Campbell) Hospital. Once across the bridge it is another ten miles south to Surrattsville. Riding hard, Booth and his cohorts could reach the bridge in thirty minutes and be in Surrattsville in two hours' time.

6. John H. Surratt, "The Rockville Lecture," reproduced in Wiechmann, *True History*, pp. 428–41.

7. Kimmel, *Mad Booths*, pp. 204–5.

8. "An Address by President Lincoln," *Philadelphia Inquirer*, March 18, 1865, p. 1, col. 1.

9. Salmon P. Chase, secretary of the treasury (1861–64), later chief justice of the Supreme Court (1864–73).

10. Wiechmann, *True History*, p. 432.

11. Arnold, *Memoirs*, p. 150.

12. Wiechmann, *True History*, pp. 432–33.

13. Arnold, *Memoirs*, p. 150.

14. George J. Olszewski, *Historic Structures Report: Restoration of Ford's Theatre* (Washington, D.C.: Government Printing Office, 1963), p. 121.

15. On March 23, Booth sent a telegram to Louis Wiechmann from New York City. Rhodenhamel and Taper, eds., *Right or Wrong*, p. 142.

16. Rhodenhamel and Taper, eds., *Right or Wrong*, p. 143.

17. Ibid.

18. Chaconas, "Unpublished Atzerodt Confession," p. 3.

19. Atzerodt's brother John also worked for McPhail but had been in Charles County searching for Booth. It was John Atzerodt who sent word to McPhail that brother George had ties to Montgomery County, Maryland, where his cousin owned a farm. It was at this farm that Atzerodt was taken into custody in the early morning hours of April 20.

20. On May 1, 1865, while in custody, George Atzerodt gave a seven-page statement to Maryland provost marshal James L. McPhail that was taken down by McPhail's assistant, John L. Smith. This statement disappeared only to resurface in 1977 when Joan L. Chaconas, a past president of the Surratt Society of Clinton, Maryland, and of the Lincoln Group of the District of Columbia, uncovered the statement among the personal papers of Captain William E. Doster, the court-appointed defense attorney for Atzerodt. A photocopy of the statement was obtained by Chaconas and subsequently published in the *Surratt Courier* (13, no. 10), the newsletter of the Surratt Society located in Clinton, Maryland. The original statement was purchased by Floyd E. Risvold.

21. Chaconas, "Unpublished Atzerodt Confession," p. 3.

22. Watson was arrested in Baltimore on March 18, 1864, suspected of blockade running. He was eventually released after taking the oath of allegiance and made his way to New York City. Tidwell, Gaddy, and Hall, *Come Retribution*, p. 415.

23. Ownsbey, *Alias "Paine,"* pp. 65–66.

24. Chaconas, "Unpublished Atzerodt Confession," p. 4.

25. The circumstances and persons believed involved in this plot were first discussed in Tidwell, Hall, and Gaddy, *Come Retribution*, pp. 418–21.

26. Harney appears on one payroll for "Engineer Service—Preparation of Torpedoes" for the period April–June 1864.

27. Mike Wright, "The Infernal Machine," *Invention and Technology* 15, no. 1 (summer 1999): 44–50.

28. Report of Zedekiah McDaniel, in Poore, *Conspiracy Trial*, 3:517–20.

29. Tidwell, Hall, and Gaddy, *Come Retribution*, p. 163.

30. Poore, *Conspiracy Trial*, 3:520.

31. Old Capitol Prison morning report, April 13, 1865, NARA, RG 393.

32. Rains was in command of the Torpedo Bureau.

33. Otto Eisenschiml, ed., *Vermont General: The Unusual War Experiences of Edward Hastings Ripley (1862–1865)* (New York: Devin-Adair Company, 1960), pp. 306–7. Ripley did not reveal the full name of Snyder.

34. Tidwell, Hall, and Gaddy, *Come Retribution*, p. 420.

35. Keckley, *Behind the Scenes*, p. 177.

36. Basler, ed., *Collected Works*, 8:404.

37. Testimony of Thomas T. Eckert on May 30, 1867, Judiciary Committee, House of Representatives, *Impeachment Investigation*, 39th Cong., 2d sess., and 40th Cong., 1st sess. (Washington, D.C.: Government Printing Office, 1867), 674. Hereafter referred to as *Impeachment Investigation.*

8. A Day of Jubilation

1. Basler, ed., *Collected Works*, 8:410.

2. Ibid., 8:410 n. 1.

3. Don E. Fehrenbacher and Virginia Fehrenbacher, eds., *Recollected Words of Abraham Lincoln* (Stanford: Stanford University Press, 1996), p. 86.

4. Van Alen had written to Lincoln on at least seven prior occasions on various political matters. He appears to have been sufficiently acquainted with Lincoln and his wife to invite them to stay at his home when visiting in New York. See Reck, *A. Lincoln*, p. 10.

5. Basler, ed., *Collected Works*, 8:413.

6. Nicolay and Hay, eds., *Complete Works*, 8:94.

7. Basler, ed., *Collected Works*, 8:223.

8. Ibid., 8:223 n. 1.

9. Fehrenbacher and Fehrenbacher, eds., *Recollected Words*, p. 114.

10. Johnston surrendered to Sherman on April 26. One month later, on May 26, Kirby Smith surrendered what remained of his forces to Major General E.R.S. Canby. On May 29 President Johnson granted amnesty and pardon to all persons who directly or indirectly participated in the rebellion. All property rights were restored except for slaves. On April 2, 1866, Johnson issued his proclamation declaring the insurrection officially closed. See E.B. Long and Barbara Long, *The Civil War, Day by Day: An Almanac, 1861–1865* (New York: Doubleday, 1971), pp. 682–96.

11. Frederick Seward was representing his father who was still in bed recovering from a serious carriage accident.

12. Fehrenbacher and Fehrenbacher, eds., *Recollected Words*, p. 398.

13. Fehrenbacher and Fehrenbacher, eds., *Recollected Words*, pp. 397–98.

14. *New York Times*, May 7, 1865, p. 1, col. 4.

15. William C. Davis, *Jefferson Davis: The Man and His Hour* (New York: Harper Collins, 1991), p. 655.

16. Beale, ed., *Welles Diary*, 2:282–83.

17. Julia Dent Grant, *The Personal Memoirs of Julia Dent Grant*, ed. John Y. Simon (New York: G.P. Putnam's Sons, 1975), p. 155.

18. Ulysses S. Grant, *Personal Memoirs of U.S. Grant*, ed. E.B. Long (Cleveland: World Publishing Company, 1952), p. 565.

19. Donald C. Pfanz, *The Petersburg Campaign: Abraham Lincoln at City Point, March 20–April 9, 1865* (Lynchburg, Va.: H.E. Howard, 1989), p. 15.

20. Ver Lynn Sprague, "Mary Lincoln—Accessory to Murder," *Lincoln Herald* 81, no. 4 (winter 1979): 238–42.

21. Ibid., p. 240.

22. Julia Grant, *Personal Memoirs*, ed. Simon, p. 146. The officer was Adam Badeau, one of two staff officers to escort Mary Lincoln and Julia Grant. Badeau describes the incident in *Grant in Peace from Appomattox to Mount McGregor: A Personal Memoir* (New York: C.L. Webster, 1887), pp. 352–60.

23. Sprague, "Accessory to Murder," p. 238. Otto Eisenschiml, *Why Was Lincoln Murdered?* Roscoe, *The Web of Conspiracy*.

24. Roscoe, *The Web of Conspiracy*, p. 20.

25. John Sleeper Clarke was a popular comic actor who married Asia Booth, John Wilkes Booth's older sister, on April 28, 1859.

26. *Washington Evening Star*, February 11, 1865, p. 2, col. 4.

27. Reck, *A. Lincoln*, pp. 42–43. The "oath of Dec. 8, 1863" was the result of an amnesty proclamation signed by the president on December 8, 1863. The proclamation granted a pardon to all persons previously engaged in the rebellion who now wished to "resume their allegiance to the United States" and who signed the oath of allegiance. Basler, ed., *Collected Works*, 7:53–56.

28. Basler, ed., *Collected Works*, 8:412.

29. Francis F. Browne, *The Everyday Life of Abraham Lincoln*, (Hartford: Park Publishing Company, 1886), p. 704.

30. Basler, ed., *Collected Works*, 6:506.

31. Fehrenbacher and Fehrenbacher, eds., *Recollected Words*, p. 112.

32. Thomas P. Lowry, *Don't Shoot That Boy* (Mason City, Iowa: Savas Publishing Company, 1999), p. 3.

33. Ibid., p. 216.

34. Ibid., p. 122.

35. Gideon Welles, "Lincoln and Johnson," *Galaxy*, April 1872, p. 56.

36. Browne, *Everyday Life*, p. 704.

37. At 4:40 A.M. on the morning of April 15, Stanton ordered Assistant Secretary of War Charles A. Dana to wire the United States marshal in Portland, Maine, to arrest Jacob Thompson immediately. Thompson did not come and was not arrested. See Turner, *Beware the People Weeping*, p. 125.

38. Reck, *A. Lincoln*, p. 47.

39. C. Percy Powell, ed., *Lincoln, Day by Day: A Chronology, 1809–1865*, 3 vols. (Washington, D.C.: Lincoln Sesquicentennial Commission, 1960), vol 3.

40. Lincoln had a deep fascination with all things mechanical, especially weaponry. He was mechanically inclined and is the only president to have received a patent. See *Report of the Commissioner of Patents, for the Year 1849*, pt. 1, *Arts and Manufactures* (Washington, D.C.: Office of Printers to House of Reps., 1850), p. 262. Lincoln's patent was for an "improved method of lifting vessels over shoals." Although a patent was issued, it was never licensed or used.

41. Several instances appear in Powell, ed., *Day by Day*, vol. 3.

42. Quoted in Reck, *A. Lincoln*, p. 49.

43. Justin G. Turner and Linda Levitt Turner, eds., *Mary Todd Lincoln: Her Life and Letters* (New York: Fromm International Publishing Corporation, 1987): pp. 284–85.

44. In 1860, Isham Haynie campaigned on behalf of Democratic candidate for president Stephen A. Douglas. During the first two years of the war he served in the western theater. He was present at Fort Henry and Fort Donelson and wound up commanding the First Brigade, Third Division, of McPherson's Seventeenth Corps stationed in Memphis, Tennessee. Haynie resigned in March of 1863 after the Senate failed to approve his appointment as brigadier general of volunteers. Ezra J. Warner, *Generals in Blue* (Baton Rouge: Louisiana State University Press, 1964), pp. 222–23.

45. There is disagreement as to which book Lincoln actually read from, the other choice being *The Nasby Papers* by Petroleum V. Nasby (David Ross Locke). According to Governor Oglesby, "Lincoln got to reading some humorous book—I think it was by 'John Phoenix.'" Katherine Helm, *The True Story of Mary, Wife of Lincoln* (New York: Harper and Brothers Publishers, 1928), p. 256. John Phoenix was the pen name of George W. Derby, member of the Army Corps of Topographical Engineers. His satirical book was titled, *Phoenixiana; or, Sketches and Burlesques* (D. Appleton and Company, 1856). See "The Last Book Lincoln Read," *Lincoln Lore*, no. 1704 (February 1980): 11–12.

46. Helm, *Wife of Lincoln*, p. 256.

47. Reck, *A. Lincoln*, p. 56.

48. William H. Crook, *Through Five Administrations*, ed. Margarita Spalding (New York: Harper and Brothers, 1907).

49. Crook, *Five Administrations*, p. 66.

50. Reck, *A. Lincoln*, p. 55.

51. Crook, *Five Administrations*, pp. 74–75.

52. Turner and Turner, eds., *Letters*, p. 285.

53. William Hanchett, "Persistent Myths of the Lincoln Assassination," *Lincoln Herald* 99, no. 4 (winter 1997): 175.

54. Ibid., p. 176.

55. Crook's quotation of Lincoln's statement that there were those who wanted to take his life is even featured on the dust jacket of a recent book: Richard Bak, *The Day Lincoln Was Shot* (Dallas: Taylor Publishing Company, 1998).

56. Reck, *A. Lincoln*, p. 54.

57. Ibid., p. 57.

58. A search of the playbills, tickets, and newspapers for the April 14, 1865, evening performance failed to discover the scheduled time for the play that evening. Times for a matinee (3:00 P.M.) and evening performance (8:00 P.M.) for Saturday, October 1, 1864, are listed in: Olszewski, *Restoration of Ford's Theatre*, p. 117.

59. Basler, ed., *Collected Works*, 8:413.

60. Smith Stimmel, "Experiences As a Member of President Lincoln's Bodyguard, 1863–1865," *North Dakota Historical Quarterly* 1, no. 2 (January 1927): 32.

61. Testimony of Henry R. Rathbone, in Poore, *Conspiracy Trial*, 1:195.

9. Decision

1. Benjamin P. Thomas, *Lincoln's New Salem* (Springfield: Abraham Lincoln Association, 1934), p. 48.

2. Wolfgang Mieder, *The Proverbial Lincoln* (New York: Peter Lang, 2000), p. 1.

3. Powell, *Day by Day*, 3:173.

4. Abraham Lincoln to James W. Hackett, August 17, 1863, Basler, ed., *Collected Works*, 6:392.

5. Ibid.

6. For a listing of ten of these occasions see Olszewski, *Restoration of Ford's Theatre*, p. 105. In addition to these, Lincoln also attended performances on December 14, 15, 17, 1863, and February 10, 1865.

7. Ibid.

8. *Washington Evening Star*, February 11, 1865, p. 2, col. 6.

9. Eisenschiml, *Why Was Lincoln Murdered?* pp. 11–21; Roscoe, *The Web of Conspiracy*, pp. 23–25; Mills, *It Didn't Happen the Way You Think*, pp. 1–10.

10. Olszewski, *Restoration of Ford's Theatre*, p. 7.

11. Ibid., pp. 107–22.

12. This performance was one of three that Booth agreed to appear in after quitting the theater on May 28, 1864. All three were benefit performances for actor friends. One was in New York, and two were in Washington. *The Apostate* was a benefit for John McCullough.

13. Rhodenhamel and Taper, eds., *Right or Wrong*, p. 144.

14. Wiechmann, *True History*.

15. Poore, *Conspiracy Trial*, 2:548.

16. Poore, *Conspiracy Trial*, 3:33.

17. Oldroyd, *The Assassination of Abraham Lincoln*, p. 14.

18. Olszewski, *Restoration of Ford's Theatre*, pp. 54–55, and Poore, *Conspiracy Trial*, 2:548–52.

19. Poore, *Conspiracy Trial*, 1:175.

20. Ibid., 2:538–39.

21. Pitman, *Assassination*, p. 113.

22. Poore, *Conspiracy Trial*, 1:118.

23. Chaconas, "Unpublished Atzerodt Confession."

24. Poore, *Conspiracy Trail*, 1:241.

25. Ibid.

26. Eisenschiml, *Why Was Lincoln Murdered?* pp. 391–92.

27. Testimony of John Matthews, *Impeachment Investigation*, pp. 782–88. Matthews did not testify at the conspiracy trial in 1865.

28. Rhodenhamel and Taper, eds., *Right or Wrong*, pp. 151–53.

29. Ibid. See pp. 124–27 and 147–50 for the full text of both letters.

30. Ibid., p. 153

31. Horace Porter, *Campaigning with Grant* (New York: Century, 1907), pp. 498–99.

32. U.S. Grant, *Personal Memoirs*, ed. Long, pp. 155–56.

33. Statement of George A. Atzerodt, April 25, 1865, while on board the

Montauk, in Laurie Verge, ed., *From War Department Files* (Clinton: Surratt Society, 1980), p. 68.

34. Ibid., p. 69.

10. *Sic Semper Tyrannis*

"Thus always to tyrants." The motto of Virginia through 1865.

1. Olszewski, *Restoration of Ford's Theatre*, p. 53.
2. Testimony of Joseph Burroughs, in Poore, *Conspiracy Trial*, 1:230.
3. Testimony of Peter Taltavull, in Poore, *Conspiracy Trial*, 1:179–80.
4. Timothy S. Good, *We Saw Lincoln Shot* (Jackson: University Press of Mississippi, 1995), p. 73.
5. Poore, *Conspiracy Trial*, 1:187–89.
6. Good, *We Saw Lincoln Shot*, pp. 80–81.
7. Poore, *Conspiracy Trial*, 1:194–95.
8. Frank Ford to Walter J. Olszewski, April 13, 1962, quoted in Olszewski, *Restoration of Ford's Theatre*, p. 62.

11. The Wound Is Mortal

1. Leale, *Lincoln's Last Hours*, p. 2.
2. Ibid.
3. Ibid., p. 3.
4. Ibid.
5. Ibid.
6. Ibid., p. 4.
7. Clara Harris to Mary Washington, April 25, 1865, private collection, xerographic copy in the Surratt House and Museum Library, Clinton, Maryland.
8. Leale, *Lincoln's Last Hours*, p. 4.
9. Reck, *A. Lincoln*, p. 119.
10. Ibid., pp. 120–21.
11. Reck, *A. Lincoln*, pp. 122–23. See also Leale, *Lincoln's Last Hours*, p. 7.
12. Reck, *A. Lincoln*, p. 123.
13. Poore, *Conspiracy Trial*, 1:179.
14. Leale, *Lincoln's Last Hours*, p. 7.
15. Ibid.
16. *Sunday Times-Telegraph* (Pittsburgh), February 12, 1928, and *New York Tribune*, February 8, 1931.
17. Reck, *A. Lincoln*, p. 126.
18. Mose Sandford to John Beatty, Esq., April 17, 1865, private collection, xerographic copy in Surratt House and Museum Library, Clinton, Maryland.
19. George J. Olszewski, "House Where Lincoln Died: Furnishing Study," April 15, 1967 (Washington, D.C.: National Park Service, U.S. Department of the Interior, 1967).
20. Eighth Census of the United States,1860 (District of Columbia), NARA, RG 29, M-653, reel 102.
21. Reck, *A. Lincoln*, p. 131.

22. A sinapism is a paste of ground mustard seed. The paste is applied directly on the skin and covered with a cloth. Its action is to stimulate blood circulation through its irritating effect on the skin.

23. Elizabeth L. Dixon to "My dear Louisa," reproduced in *Surratt Society News* 7, no. 3 (March 1982): 3–4.

24. Ibid., p. 4.

25. Taking into account all of the statements describing the events that unfolded in the Petersen house, a total of fourteen physicians appeared at Lincoln's bedside during the night: Drs. Charles A. Leale, Charles S. Taft, C.D. Gatch, Albert F.A. King, Ezra W. Abbott, C.H. Lieberman, J.C. Hall, S.T. Ford, J.F. May, William B. Notson, Robert King Stone, and Army Surgeon General Joseph K. Barnes, Assistant Surgeon General Charles H. Crane, and Surgeon D. Willard Bliss. See Olszewski, *Restoration of Ford's Theatre.*

26. Benjamin P. Thomas and Harold M. Hyman, *Stanton: The Life and Times of Lincoln's Secretary of War* (New York: Alfred A. Knopf, 1962), p. 396.

27. Ibid.

28. Beale, ed., *Welles Diary,* 2:286.

29. Patricia Carley Johnson, "I Have Supped Full on Horrors: The Diary of Fanny Seward," *American Heritage,* Oct. 1959, pp. 64–101.

30. Major Thomas T. Eckert, assistant superintendent of the military telegraph.

31. Thomas and Hyman, *Stanton,* p. 397. Eckert had been notified at his home on Thirteenth Street by one of his telegraphers, Thomas A. Laird, who was at the theater with a second telegrapher, George C. Maynard. David Homer Bates, *Lincoln in the Telegraph Office* (1907; reprint, Lincoln, Nebraska: University of Nebraska Press, 1995), p. 371.

32. Beale, ed., *Welles Diary,* 2:287.

33. Ibid. Welles fixes the time of his and Stanton's arrival in his diary at a little past eleven. This is an important notation, for at this hour John Wilkes Booth was certainly across the Navy Yard Bridge and even past Forts Baker and Wagner. These last outposts were in contact with General C.C. Augur's headquarters by military telegraph, but it was too late to seal off the environs of the city and trap Booth and Herold as so many conspiracy theorists claim.

34. The succession law of 1792 determined presidential succession at the time of Lincoln's death. This law specified that should the president and vice president be unable to function, the president of the Senate pro tempore would succeed as acting president followed by the Speaker of the House. There was no provision for the secretary of war in the succession act. Seward, as secretary of state, was charged with the responsibility of calling upon each of the states to choose electors to elect a new president. With Seward dead, it is not clear what process would follow short of the appointment and confirmation of a new secretary of state by the Senate. See Michael Maione and James O. Hall, "Why Seward?" *Lincoln Herald* 100, no. 1 (spring 1998): 29–34.

35. Howard K. Beale, ed., *The Diary of Edward Bates, 1859–1866,* vol. 4 of the *Annual Report of the American Historical Association,* 1930 (Washington, D.C.: Government Printing Office, 1933), p. 473.

36. Reck, *A. Lincoln,* p. 142.

37. Maxwell Whiteman, introduction to *While Lincoln Lay Dying* (Philadelphia: Union League of Philadelphia, 1968), p. 3.

38. Ibid., p. 4.

39. Ibid., p. 5.

40. Eisenschiml, *Why Was Lincoln Murdered?* p. 78.

41. Arthur F. Loux, "The Mystery of the Telegraph Interruption," *Lincoln Herald* 81, no. 4 (winter 1979): 234–37.

42. Charles Hamilton sold the first telegram at auction. A photograph of the telegram appears in the Charles Hamilton Auction Catalogue 22, October 25, 1967. The telegram is now in private hands; a photographic copy is in the author's files. The telegram to General Grant is discussed in an article by James O. Hall, "The First War Department Telegram about Lincoln's Assassination," *Surratt Courier* 22, no. 1 (January 1997): 5–6.

43. Ibid.

44. Whitman, *While Lincoln Lay Dying*, p. 6.

45. Reck, *A. Lincoln*, p. 141.

46. Ibid.

47. Poore, *Conspiracy Trial*, 1:329.

48. Poore, *Conspiracy Trial*, 1:328.

49. The testimony of Silas T. Cobb can be found in Poore, *Conspiracy Trial*, 1:251–55. The testimony of John Fletcher can be found in Poore, *Conspiracy Trial*, 1:326–41.

50. Metropolitan Police Headquarters for the District of Columbia was located at 488 Tenth Street. Ford's Theatre was located at 511 Tenth Street.

51. Tidwell, Hall, and Gaddy, *Come Retribution*, p. 438.

52. Testimony of John Lee, in Poore, *Conspiracy Trial*, 1:62. See also Michael Henry to James O'Beirne, July 20, 1865, collection of Scott Balthasar, copy in author's files.

53. These items were introduced as exhibits at the conspiracy trial. See NARA, M-599, reel 15, frame 0057.

54. The Kirkwood House register was introduced as exhibit 24 at the conspiracy trial. See NARA, M-599, RG 153, reel 15, frame 0299.

55. David D. Dana to "Hon. Joseph Holt, Judge Advocate General," October 3, 1865, NARA, RG 94, M-619, reel 458, frames 0466–0472.

56. Statement of David D. Dana, AGO Reward File, NARA, RG 94, M-619, reel 458, frames 0466–0472.

57. Charles Sabin Taft, "Abraham Lincoln's Last Hours," *Century Magazine* (Feb. 1895), p. 35.

58. Reck, *A. Lincoln*, p. 157.

59. Ibid.

60. Ibid.

61. Ibid., p. 159.

62. Frank E. Edgington, *A History of the New York Avenue Presbyterian Church* (Washington, D.C.: Published by the New York Avenue Presbyterian Church, 1961), p. 252.

12. Surrattsville

1. The Eastern Branch is now known as the Anacostia River.

2. Joan L. Chaconas, "Crossing the Navy Yard Bridge," *Surratt Courier* 21, no. 9 (1996): 5–7.

3. Testimony of Silas T. Cobb, in Poore, *Conspiracy Trial*, 1:251–55. Moonrise

for the Washington, D.C., area occurred at 10:10 P.M. on the night of April 14 and reached its transit at 3:17 A.M. In addition, the phase of the moon was waning with 89 percent illumination. With a clear sky, Booth and Herald would have considerable moonlight to guide them on their escape. U.S. Naval Observatory, Astronomical Applications Department, "Sun and Moon Data for One Day," April 14, 1865, Washington, D.C., <http://mach.usno.navy.mil/cgi-bin/aa_pap>.

4. Poore, *Conspiracy Trial*, 1:252–53.

5. Fort Baker was in telegraphic communication with General Augur's headquarters but did not receive notice of the assassination until well after Booth and Herold had passed between the two forts into southern Maryland. See NARA, RG 393, pt. 2, vol. 186.

6. Statement of David E. Herold, NARA, RG 153, M-599, reel 4, frames 0442–0485.

7. Testimony of John M. Lloyd, in Poore, *Conspiracy Trial*, 1:116.

8. Gaddy, "Surratt Tavern," p. 234.

9. Hall, *Surratt Family*.

10. Wiechmann, *True History*, p. 433.

11. Ibid., p. 14.

12. Testimony of William Norton and John C. Thompson, in *Trial of John H. Surratt*, 1:510–17.

13. The unusual name T.B. was taken from the initials of a prominent landowner in the area, Thomas Brooke. It was little more than a crossroad and a tavern.

14. Testimony of Louis J. Wiechmann, in Poore, *Conspiracy Trial*, 1:85–86.

15. Testimony of John M. Lloyd, in Poore, *Conspiracy Trial*, 1:122.

16. Testimony of John Nothey, in Poore, *Conspiracy Trial*, 2:250. Statements of Mary E. Surratt, NARA, M-599, reel 6, frames 0233–0257, 0170–0200.

17. Testimony of George Calvert, in Poore, *Conspiracy Trial*, 2:222–23.

18. Wiechmann, *True History*, p. 164.

19. Ibid., p. 165.

20. Testimony of Louis J. Wiechmann, in Poore, *Conspiracy Trial*, 1:86.

21. Poore, *Conspiracy Trial*, 2:250.

22. Testimony of John Lloyd, in Poore, *Conspiracy Trial*, 1:118.

23. Ibid., p. 122.

24. Ibid.

25. Ibid., p. 126.

26. Ibid., p. 119.

27. Chaconas, "Unpublished Atzerodt Confession."

28. Ibid., p. 138.

29. *Trial of John H. Surratt*, 1:288.

30. Chevalier would eventually license the unique feature, and it would begin appearing on better quality glasses several years later.

31. Poore, *Conspiracy Trial*, 1:118.

32. Ibid.

33. Ibid.

34. Poore, *Conspiracy Trial*, 1:119.

35. Ibid.

36. Ibid.

13. Dr. Mudd

1. Mudd, *Mudd Family*, 1:409.

2. *University of Maryland Fiftieth Annular Circular of the School of Medicine*, session 1857–1858 (matriculates, 1856) (Baltimore: Sherwood and Co., 1857), p. 14.

3. Testimony of John F. Hardy, in Poore, *Conspiracy Trial*, 3:432.

4. Testimony of George D. Mudd, in Poore, *Conspiracy Trial*, 2:391.

5. Ibid.

6. Statement of Alexander Lovett, NARA, RG 94, M-619, reel 456, frames 0488–0490.

7. Joshua Lloyd, a detective on O'Beirne's staff, was unrelated to John Lloyd.

8. Cottingham heard from detective Joshua Lloyd that Lloyd knew both John Surratt and David Herold, and he thought they might be found in the Surrattsville area.

9. George Cottingham to James R. O'Beirne, May 1, 1865, NARA, M-619, reel 458, frames 0390–0398.

10. Testimony of Alexander D. Lovett, in Poore, *Conspiracy Trial*, 1:271. In his report to Major O'Beirne dated April 29, 1865, Lovett mistakenly said that he first visited Mudd's house on Wednesday, April 19. Lovett's testimony during the trial along with that of the other detectives and George D. Mudd place the date as Tuesday, April 18, 1865. See Poore, *Conspiracy Trial*, 1:258–81, 2:392.

11. Testimony of George Mudd, in Poore, *Conspiracy Trial*, 2:392.

12. Nettie Mudd, *The Life of Dr. Samuel A. Mudd* (1906; reprint, LaPlata, Md.: Dick Wildes Printing, 1975), p. 32.

13. Statement of Samuel A. Mudd, NARA, M-599, reel 5, frames 0212–0225. Hereafter referred to as Mudd Wells statement.

14. Ibid.

15. Statement of Samuel A. Mudd, NARA, RG 153, M-599, reel 5, frames 0226–0239. Hereafter referred to as Mudd voluntary statement.

16. Statement of Alexander D. Lovett, in Poore, *Conspiracy Trial*, 1:268.

17. Ibid., p. 263.

18. Ibid., p. 268.

19. Ibid.

20. Testimony of John F. Hardy, in Poore, *Conspiracy Trial*, 3:432.

21. Mudd voluntary statement.

22. Poore, *Conspiracy Trial*, 3:432.

23. Mudd's claim of arriving home around 5:00 P.M. is at variance with the testimony of John F. Hardy who stated that Mudd arrived at Hardy's house "very near sundown . . . the sun was not fifteen minutes high that Saturday evening." Sunset for the Waldorf, Maryland, area on Saturday, April 15, 1865, was at 6:44 P.M. with twilight ending at 7:12 P.M. See U.S. Naval Observatory, Astronomical Applications Department, "Sun and Moon Data for One Day," Saturday, April 15, 1865, for Waldorf, Maryland, <http://mach.usno.navy.mil/cgi-bin/aa-pap>.

24. Poore, *Conspiracy Trial*, 3:436.

25. Tidwell, Hall, and Gaddy, *Come Retribution*, p. 446.

26. Samuel Cox owned thirty-seven slaves. See Eighth Census of the United States, 1860, Slave Schedules (Maryland), NARA, RG 29, M-653, reel 484.

27. In many later writings Cox is referred to as "Colonel Cox," a misnomer. He was known by his neighbors as Captain Cox.

28. *Port Tobacco Times*, 20 June 1861.

29. George E. Stevens, letter to "Mr. Editor," 10 January 1862, reproduced in Donald Yacovone, ed., *A Voice of Thunder: A Black Soldier's Civil War* (Urbana, Ill.: Univ. of Illinois Press, 1998), 162–65. Stevens, the son of a prominent Black Philadelphia merchant and staunch abolitionist, became the cook and personal servant of Benjamin Tilghman, an officer in the 26th Pennsylvania Infantry attached to the First Brigade, Hooker's Division, stationed in Charles County in the fall and winter of 1861–1862. Stevens supplied the *Weekly Anglo-African* newspaper of New York with highly literate and detailed observations while with the 26th Pennsylvania in Charles County. Stevens would later enlist in the famous 54th Massachusetts at the time of its formation. Stevens' writing is published by Donald Yacovone in *A Voice of Thunder*. I am indebted to Jane Singer of Venice, California for bringing the Scroggins incident to my attention. Singer is currently working on a book about Confederate clandestine operations in the North.

30. No record has been found of whether Cox was charged in any way with the murder of Jack Scroggins. Cox continued to work as a Confederate agent throughout the war and survived the war as one of Charles County's leading citizens. Maryland law forbade masters from administering more than ten lashes for any one offence, although a master could bring a slave before a Justice of the Peace and receive permission to administer up to thirty-nine lashes in special cases. In no instance could a master whip a slave to death. See Jeffrey R. Brackett, *The Negro in Maryland. A Study of the Institution of Slavery* (1889; reprint; Baltimore: Johns Hopkins Univ. Press, 1969), 115. By the time of the Civil War the homocide of a slave was placed on the same level as the homicide of a white in virtually every Southern state. See Thomas D. Morris, *Southern Slavery and the Law, 1619–1860* (Chapel Hill, N.C.: Univ. of North Carolina Press, 1996), 172.

31. Edward Steers Jr., "Dr. Mudd's Sense of Timing: The Trip into Bryantown," *Surratt Courier* 24, no. 9 (September 1999): 4–8.

32. Mudd Wells statement.

33. Mudd, *Life of Dr. Samuel A. Mudd*, p. 33.

34. Statement of Colonel Henry H. Wells, NARA, RG 94, M-619, reel 458, frame 0205.

35. Testimony of Alexander Lovett, in Poore, *Conspiracy Trial*, 1:260.

36. Contrary to what some authors have written, the name Booth was not part of the inscription nor was the word "Booth" scratched out. The entire inscription simply read "J. Wilkes."

37. Mudd voluntary statement.

38. Mudd Wells statement.

39. Eisenschiml, *Why Was Lincoln Murdered?* p. 267.

40. Ibid., p. 265.

41. A detailed analysis of the evidence showing that the photograph introduced at the trial and distributed to the various military groups was a photograph of John Wilkes Booth can be found in Edward Steers Jr., "Otto Eisenschiml, Samuel Mudd, and the 'Switched' Photograph," *Lincoln Herald* 100, no. 4 (winter 1998): 167–80.

42. Mudd Wells statement. See also Poore, *Conspiracy Trial*, 1:216.
43. Ibid.

14. Here in Despair

1. Statement of Electus Thomas, NARA, RG 153, M-599, reel 6, frames 0376–0379.
2. Herold statement.
3. Statement of Ausy [Oswell] Swann, NARA, RG 153, M-599, reel 6, frame 0227.
4. Ibid.
5. Ibid.
6. Poore, *Conspiracy Trial*, 2:300.
7. At least 132 local Charles County men went south to serve in the Confederate military. See Daniel D. Hartzler, *Marylanders in the Confederacy* (Westminster, Md.: Family Line Publications, 1986).
8. On June 20, 1861, one hundred Federal troops landed at Chapel Point and made their way to Cox's house three and half miles inland. They searched the house and grounds for weapons but finding none, returned to Washington. *Port Tobacco Times*, June 20, 1861.
9. Cox had owned thirty-seven slaves in 1860. See Eighth Census of the United States, Slave Schedules (Maryland), NARA, RG 29, M-653, reel 484.
10. Statement of Ausy [Oswell] Swann, NARA, M-599, reel 6, frame 0227.
11. Endorsement of William Norris, chief of the Signal Bureau (Confederate States of America), "Thomas A. Jones Application for Membership in the Society of the Army and Navy of the Confederate States in the State of Maryland," C.S.A. Maryland Records, Maryland Historical Society, Baltimore, Maryland.
12. Jones, *J. Wilkes Booth*.
13. Ibid., pp. 40, 43.
14. Ibid., p. 65.
15. Ibid., p. 67.
16. Ibid., p. 73.
17. Ibid., p. 74.
18. Ibid., p. 77.
19. Ibid., p. 78.
20. Booth shaved off his moustache at the Mudd house. See Mudd Wells statement, frame 0218. Also, William Rollins when shown a photograph of Booth remarked that it was the same man he saw cross the Rappahannock River on April 24, "except that his moustache was off." See statement of William Rollins, NARA, M-599, reel 6, frame 0079.
21. Jones, *J. Wilkes Booth*, pp. 81–82.
22. *Baltimore Clipper*, morning edition, April 15, 1865.
23. Turner, *Assassination of Abraham Lincoln*, p. 119.
24. William Shakespeare, *King Lear*, 3.2.57–60.
25. Turner, *Assassination of Abraham Lincoln*, p. 120.
26. Oscar A. Kinchen, *Confederate Operations in Canada and the North* (North Quincy, Mass.: Christopher Publishing House, 1970), pp. 208–9.

27. *Baltimore Clipper*, April 21, 1865, p. 1, col. 1.

28. Ibid., p. 1, col. 2.

29. Jones, *J. Wilkes Booth*, p. 93.

30. Jones writes in his memoir that he put Booth and Herold on the river on "Friday." This would be Friday, April 21. See Jones, *J. Wilkes Booth*, p. 98. Tidwell, Hall, and Gaddy, in *Come Retribution*, also place the date of the river crossing on April 21 (p. 454). Booth, however, gives the date of his river crossing as Thursday, April 20. Booth prepared a handwritten calendar in the memorandum book that he carried with him and used as a diary. The calendar runs from Monday, April 17, through Sunday, June 18. Booth has crossed out each day beginning with April 17 and ending with April 25, the day before his death. The block for Thursday, April 20, is marked with the notation "on Poto**." The block for Friday, April 21, is marked with the notation "Swamp," presumably referring to the mouth of the Nanjemoy River where Booth and Herold spent the day after failing in their first attempt to cross the river. The block for Saturday, April 22, is marked with the notation "Poto***." The author accepts Booth's notations as the authority in describing his movements.

31. Moonrise was at 2:02 A.M. The phase of the moon was a waning crescent with 31 percent illumination.

32. Jones, *J. Wilkes Booth*, pp. 106–7.

33. Ibid., pp. 109–10.

34. Ibid., p. 110.

15. The Roundup

1. In his unpublished confession, Atzerodt stated that during a meeting at the Herndon House on Friday evening, April 14, Booth had said he was going to kill the president and that Wood (Lewis Powell) was going to murder the secretary of state.

2. *Baltimore American and Commercial Advertiser*, July 10, 1865, p. 1, col. 6.

3. Testimony of James Kelleher, in Poore, *Conspiracy Trial*, 1:507–8.

4. Poore, *Conspiracy Trial*, 1:395. See also 1:396.

5. Testimony of Washington Briscoe, in Poore, *Conspiracy Trial*, 1:402.

6. Testimony of John Greenawalt, in Poore, *Conspiracy Trial*, 1:341–52.

7. Edward Steers Jr. and James O. Hall, *The Escape and Capture of George Atzerodt* (Clinton, Md.: Surratt Society, 1980). *Washington Daily National Intelligencer*, July 10, 1865, p. 1, col. 4 (hereafter referred to as the *Washington Intelligencer*). See also Laurie Verge, ed., "George Andrew Atzerodt," *Surratt Courier* 6, no. 11 (1981), 5–6.

8. Testimony of Hartman Richter, in Poore, *Conspiracy Trial*, 2:515.

9. Testimony of John Caldwell, in Poore, *Conspiracy Trial*, 2:148–49.

10. Statement of Lucinda Metz, NARA, RG 153, M-599, reel 3, frames 0579–0580.

11. Records of the Judge Advocate General's Office (Army), Court-Martial Case File, NARA, RG 153, MM 2513. The author is indebted to Dr. Thomas P. Lowry for providing a copy of this file.

12. Ibid.

13. Ibid.

14. Statement of William Gaither, NARA, RG 153, M-599, reel 3, frames 0548–0553.

15. Ibid.

16. Statement of Robert Kinder, NARA, M-599, reel 4, frames 0161–0162.

17. Testimony of Hezekiah Metz, in Poore, *Conspiracy Trial,* 1:353.

18. Among those at dinner who testified at the conspiracy trial were Hezekiah Metz and the brothers James and Somerset Leamon. See Poore, *Conspiracy Trial,* 1:353–57, 2:501–6.

19. Testimony of Somerset Lamon [Leamon], in Poore, *Conspiracy Trial,* 2:502.

20. Testimony of Hartman Richter, in Poore, *Conspiracy Trial,* 2:516.

21. Statement of James W. Purdom, NARA, RG 153, M-599, reel 2, frames 0227–0229.

22. Statement of Frank O'Daniel, NARA, RG 94, M-619, reel 455, frames 0835–0838.

23. Statement of George G. Lindsley, NARA, RG 153, M-599, reel 2, frames 0233–0234.

24. Statement of Solomon Townsend, NARA, RG 94, M-619, reel 455, frames 0565–0566.

25. Statement of Zachariah W. Gemmill, NARA, RG 153, M-599, reel 2, frames 1014–10019.

26. Benjamin B. Hough to Edward D. Townsend, December 20, 1865, NARA, M-619, reel 458, frames 0162–0170.

27. Testimony of John W. Wharton, in Poore, *Conspiracy Trial,* 3:340.

28. Percy E. Martin, "The Hookstown Connection," *Surratt Courier* 5, no. 7 (July 1980), pp. 5–6.

29. Memorial of James L. McPhail, Voltaire Randall, and Eaton Horner, in John B. Horner, *Lincoln's Songbird* (Gettysburg, Pa.: Horner Enterprises, 1991), pp. 37–48.

30. Poore, *Conspiracy Trial,* 2:99.

31. Percy E. Martin, "Surprising Speed in the Identification of Two Baltimore Conspirators," in *In Pursuit of. . .,* ed. Verge, p. 167.

32. *Baltimore Clipper,* April 19, 1865, p. 1, col. 5.

33. See testimony of Eaton G. Horner, in Poore, *Conspiracy Trial,* 1:423–35.

34. Poore, *Conspiracy Trial,* 1:435.

35. *Baltimore American,* Monday, July 10, 1865, p. 1, col. 3

36. Statement of Samuel Bland Arnold, RG 94, M-619, reel 458, frames 0305–0312; and *Baltimore American,* "Statement of Arnold on His Arrest," January 19, 1869, p. 1, col. 1. The Dr. Garland mentioned in the note has not been identified.

37. Arnold, *Memoirs,* p. 9.

38. Poore, *Conspiracy Trial,* 3:382.

39. The statement appeared in an *Evening Star* article titled, "Tragic Memories." McDevitt thought he received the tip from the actor John McCullough but McCullough has since been shown to have been in Canada at the time and not in Washington. McDevitt received a tip from someone, but the person's identity remains unknown at present. *Washington Evening Star,* April 14, 1894. The article also appeared in the *Indianapolis News,* April 14, 1894.

40. A.C. Richards to Louis J. Wiechmann, April 29, 1898, reproduced in Wiechmann, *True History,* p. 177.

41. Poore, *Conspiracy Trial,* 1:87.

42. Ibid., 3:386.

43. Wiechmann, *True History*, p. 178.

44. Testimony of W.H. Smith, in Poore, *Conspiracy Trial*, 2:14.

45. *Baltimore Clipper*, April 20, 1865, p. 1, col. 5.

46. *Trial of John H. Surratt*, 1:162.

47. Tidwell, Hall, and Gaddy, *Come Retribution*, p. 430.

48. Testimony of W.H. Smith, in Poore, *Conspiracy Trial*, 2:15.

49. Hancock's broadside, dated April 24, 1865, is found in Letters Received, Secretary of War, NARA, RG 107, file 5160 (no. 1882).

16. Virginia at Last!

1. Tidwell, Hall, and Gaddy, *Come Retribution*, p. 457.

2. Ibid., p. 456.

3. Verge, ed., *War Department Files*, p. 2.

4. The farm was owned by Peregrine Davis but was farmed by his son-in-law John J. Hughes. Herold reveals in his statement that he knew both Davis and Hughes and hunted the property. See Herold statement, in Verge, ed., *War Department Files*, pp. 1–21. See also Tidwell, Gaddy, and Hall, *Come Retribution*, pp. 454–57.

5. James O. Hall, personal communication.

6. Verge, ed., *War Department Files*, p. 11.

7. Jones, *J. Wilkes Booth*, pp. 109–10.

8. Statement of Elizabeth Quesenberry, NARA, RG 153, M-599, reel 5, frames 0557–0559. Hereafter referred to as Quesenberry statement.

9. Statement of William Bryant, NARA, RG 153, M-599, reel 4, frames 0095–0097.

10. Quesenberry statement.

11. Statement of Richard Stuart, NARA, RG 153, M-599, reel 6, frames 0205–211. Hereafter referred to as Stuart statement.

12. Stuart had a full house on April 24. In addition to himself and his wife, Julia Calvert Stuart, were nine other family members including two Confederate officers: Captain S. Tuberville Stuart (son-in-law) and Major Robert W. Hunter (future son-in-law).

13. Stuart statement, frame 0205–0206.

14. Ibid., frame 0207.

15. Ibid., frame 0209.

16. Ibid., frames 0207–0208.

17. Statement of William Lucas, NARA, RG 153, M-599, reel 5, frames 0144–0147.

18. Ibid., frame 0146.

19. Ibid.

20. Statement of William Lucas, NARA, M-599, reel 5, frames 0144–0147.

21. Edward Steers Jr., *The Escape and Capture of John Wilkes Booth* (Gettysburg, Pa.: Thomas Publications, 1983), p. 51.

22. Booth actually wrote two notes to Stuart. The first enclosed five dollars in payment for the food Stuart gave Booth and Herold. Booth had second thoughts and, returning the note to his memorandum book, wrote a second one reducing the

amount to two dollars and fifty cents. The first note was recovered with the memorandum book while the second note was recovered from Stuart. The two notes supported Stuart's contention that he did not help Booth in any substantive way except to give him food.

23. According to William Rollins, it was closer to noon when the wagon drove up to the dock. See statement of William Rollins, NARA, M-599, reel 6, frame 0079.

24. Tidwell, Hall, and Gaddy, *Come Retribution*, p. 464.

25. Tidwell, *April '65*, p. 190.

26. Statement of William Rollins, NARA, RG 153, M-599, reel 6, frame 0079.

27. Statement of Willie Jett, NARA, RG 153, M-599, reel 4, frames 0086–0099. Hereafter referred to as statement of Jett.

28. Tidwell, Gaddy, and Hall, *Come Retribution*, p. 461.

29. Testimony of Willie Jett, in Poore, *Conspiracy Trial*, 1:308–12.

30. Statement of Jett.

31. Tidwell, Gaddy, and Hall, *Come Retribution*, p. 465.

32. Ibid.

33. Tidwell, Gaddy, and Hall, *Come Retribution*, p. 467.

34. Sunset occurred at 6:54 P.M. on April 24, 1865, and twilight ended at 7:22 P.M. See Astronomical Charts, U.S. Naval Observatory.

35. Statement of Jett.

17. The Cavalry Arrives

1. See statement of Luther B. Baker, NARA, RG 94, M-619, reel 455, frames 0665–0686.

2. Statement of Jett.

3. Richard Baynham Garrett, "A Chapter of Unwritten History," ed. Betsy Fleet, *The Virginia Magazine* 71, no. 4 (October 1963): 392.

4. Ibid., p. 393.

5. OR, ser. 1, vol. 46, pt. 3, p. 937.

6. Statement of James Owens. See Tidwell, Hall, and Gaddy, *Come Retribution*, p. 468.

7. OR, series 1, vol. 46, pt. 1, p. 1317.

8. Lafayette C. Baker, *History of the United States Secret Service* (Philadelphia: published by L.C. Baker, 1867). Hereafter referred to as Baker, *Secret Service*.

9. Baker, *Secret Service*, p. 198.

10. Ibid.

11. Charles H. Crane to Thomas A. McParlin (Medical Department, Army of the Potomac), April 22, 1865. Private collection.

12. Gutman and Gutman, *John Wilkes Booth Himself*, p. 31.

13. Doherty was still a lieutenant at the time referred to by Schneider and did not receive his commission appointing him captain until after the incident at Garrett's farm.

14. NARA, RG 94, M-619, reel 456, frame 0286.

15. Edward Steers Jr., "Otto Eisenschiml, Samuel Mudd and the 'Switched' Photograph" *Lincoln Herald* 100, no. 4 (winter 1998): pp. 167–80; and James O. Hall, "Dr. Mudd and Booth's Photograph," *Surratt Courier* 23, no. 8 (1998): 3–9.

16. Statement of Luther B. Baker, NARA, RG 94, M-619, reel 455, frames 0665–0686. Hereafter referred to as statement of Luther B. Baker.

17. This statement by Rollins is additional proof that the photograph he was shown by Baker was of a man with a moustache.

18. Statement of William Rollins, NARA, RG 94, M-619, reel 457, frames 0550–0561.

19. Report of Edward P. Doherty, OR, ser. 1, vol. 46, pt. 1, p. 317–22. Hereafter referred to as Report of Edward P. Doherty.

20. Statement of Luther B. Baker.

21. According to Lucinda Holloway, Mrs. Garrett's sister and a boarder at the Garrett house, Booth had asked Jack Garrett to take him to Guinea Station, not Orange County Court House, which Garrett agreed to do the next day. See Lucinda Holloway, "The Capture and Death of John Wilkes Booth," in Francis Wilson, *John Wilkes Booth* (New York: Houghton Mifflin, 1929), pp. 209–17.

22. Statement of John M. Garrett, NARA, RG 94, M-619, reel 457, frames 0500–0525.

23. Report of Lieutenant Edward P. Doherty.

24. Statement of Luther B. Baker.

25. Report of Edward P. Doherty.

26. Ibid. See also statement of Luther B. Baker.

18. Tell Mother I Die for My Country

1. Statement of Sergeant Andrew Wendell, Company E, Sixteenth New York Cavalry, NARA, RG 94, M-619, reel 456, frames 0248–0257.

2. The new moon occurred on April 25 at 9:13 A.M. On the early morning of April 26 it was a waxing crescent with only 2 percent illumination.

3. Statement of Boston Corbett, NARA, RG 94, M-619, reel 456, frames 0253–0262.

4. Testimony of Luther B. Baker, in *Trial of John H. Surratt*, 1:318.

5. Statement of Luther B. Baker.

6. Statement of Boston Corbett.

7. Ibid.

8. Statement of Luther B. Baker.

9. Betsy Fleet, ed., "A Chapter of Unwritten History. Richard Baynham Garrett's Account of the Flight and Death of John Wilkes Booth," *Virginia Magazine of History and Biography* 71, no. 4 (October 1963), 387–407.

10. Statement of Luther B. Baker.

11. Statement of Everton J. Conger, NARA, RG 94, M-619, reel 455, frames 0691–0703. Hereafter referred to as statement of Everton J. Conger.

12. Ibid.

13. A.M. Gone to "Dear Mary," May 15, 1865, copy in author's collection. The letter reads in part, "I was in Washington & Georgetown again to day. Had a long talk with the *Sergeant* who shot Booth the Assassin . . . fired only one shot, at the distance of about twelve feet."

14. Statement of Boston Corbett.

15. Statement of Everton J. Conger.

16. Testimony of Sergeant Boston Corbett, in Poore, *Conspiracy Trial*, 1:326.

17. Autopsy report of Janvier Woodward, *The Medical and Surgical History of the War of the Rebellion (1861–1865)*, 4 vols. (Washington, D.C.: Government Printing Office, 1875), vol. 4, p. 452.

18. Statement of Everton J. Conger. Baker claimed in his statement that he was the one who listened to Booth's admission. See statement of Luther B. Baker.

19. *Rochester Daily Union and Advertiser*, May 1, 1865, p. 2, col. 3.

20. For an excellent review of those who looked on Lincoln's death as a good thing see John M. Barr, "The Tyrannicide's Reception: Responses in Texas to Lincoln's Assassination," *Lincoln Herald* 91, no. 2 (summer 1989): 58–64.

21. John Parker Hale was an ardent abolitionist. According to Asia, Booth sent Lucy a valentine on February 14, 1865. See Rhodenhamel and Taper, eds., *Right or Wrong*, p. 135 n. 4. See also p. 139 n. 1 for the poem.

22. Fleet, "Unwritten History," p. 400.

23. Statement of Luther B. Baker.

24. Telegrams Collected by the Office of the Secretary of War (unbound) 1860–1870, NARA, RG 107, reel 337, frame 1581.

25. Basler, ed., *Collected Works*, 4:269.

19. To Remove the Stain of Innocent Blood from the Land

1. John H. Surratt Jr. was in Canada where friends were hiding him from the U.S. and Canadian authorities. He would remain at large until November 26, 1866, when he was arrested at Alexandria, Egypt, and returned to the United States on February 19, 1867, to stand trial in a civil court.

2. Robert R. Arreola, Angela R. Brown, Isabella Ord, and Norman Minnear, "Federal Criminal Conspiracy," *American Criminal Law Review* (winter 1997): 617–44.

3. Ibid., p. 618.

4. Ibid., pp. 619–20.

5. United States Criminal Code, chap. 18, sec. 371.

6. The original of this document is in a private collection. A xerographic copy is in the author's files. The original draft is on War Department stationery, which has been crossed out and "Executive Chamber" written in its place. The entire document is in the handwriting of Stanton. A xerographic copy of the order is reproduced in Edward Steers Jr., "To Remove the Stain of Innocent Blood From the Land," *Lincolnian* 1, no. 2 (November–December 1982): 4–5.

7. Martial law came into existence in the District of Columbia as a result of Lincoln's proclamation of September 24, 1862 (see Basler, ed., *Collected Works*, 5:436). Martial law was still in effect at the time of Lincoln's assassination and the trial of the conspirators, and was not revoked by President Johnson until after the trial and execution had taken place.

8. Joseph George Jr., "Military Trials of Civilians under the Habeas Corpus Act of 1863," *Lincoln Herald* 98, no. 4 (winter 1996): 134.

9. Neely, *Fate of Liberty*.

10. Beale, ed., *Welles Diary*, 2:303.

11. Beale, ed., *Diary of Edward Bates*, 4:141.

12. Edward Steers Jr., "Montani Semper Liberi: The Making of West Vir-

ginia," *North and South* 3, no. 2, (1999): 18–33 . See also *Luther v. Borden*, 17 Howard 1, 45–46 (1849).

13. James Speed, *Opinion of the Constitutional Power of the Military to Try and Execute the Assassins of the President* (Washington, D.C.: Government Printing Office, 1865).

14. Ibid., pp. 15–16.

15. Pitman, *Assassination*, pp. 251–67.

16. *Ex parte Milligan*, 4 Wall, 2, 18 L. Ed. 281.

17. War Department circular dated "Washington April 20, 1865." See also Fleet, "Unwritten History," p. 399.

18. Pitman, *Assassination*, p. 21.

19. Poore, *Conspiracy Trial*, 1:223.

20. Ibid., p. 224.

21. Pitman, *Assassination*, p. 22.

22. In 1860, Ben Pitman published a manual of his brother's phonographic method: Benn Pitman, *The Manual of Phonography* (Cincinnati: Phonographic Institute, 1860).

23. Pitman, *Assassination*, p. iii.

24. An example is found in Vaughan Shelton, *Mask for Treason* (Harrisburg, Pa.: Stackpole, 1965). Shelton assumed the words "press copy," meant that Pitman had set up a flatbed press and supplied printed copies of each day's testimony to the newspapers ("press"). Shelton apparently was unaware of the process of "lifting" copies from an inked page by blotting a damp sheet of tissue paper over the original.

25. John Calder Brennan, "The Three Versions of the Testimony in the 1865 Conspiracy Trial," *Surratt Courier* 8, no. 3 (March 1983): 3–6.

26. Burnett was the judge advocate who successfully prosecuted Lambdin P. Milligan a year earlier in Indiana.

27. Porter and Comstock were replaced on May 10. Both officers were members of Grant's staff and removed for that reason. It was thought inappropriate for them to serve since Grant had been a target of Booth's assassination plot. See Turner, *Assassination of Abraham Lincoln*, p. 151.

28. Poore, *Conspiracy Trial*, 1:12.

29. Ibid.

30. Ownsbey, *Alias "Paine,"* p. 2.

31. Ibid., pp. 181–200.

32. Ibid., p. 199.

33. Ibid., p. 200.

34. Poore, *Conspiracy Trial*, 1:13.

35. Ibid.

36. Ibid., p. 12.

37. Thomas M. Harris, *The Assassination of Lincoln: A History of the Great Conspiracy* (Boston: American Citizen Company, 1892), p. 80.

38. Elizabeth Steger Trindal, *Mary Surratt: An American Tragedy* (Gretna, La.: Pelican Publishing Company, 1996), pp. 147–51.

39. Roger D. Hunt and Jack R. Brown, *Brevet Brigadier Generals in Blue* (Gaithersburg, Md.: Olde Soldier Books, 1990), p. 169.

40. Pitman, *Assassination*, pp. 18–21.

41. Quoted in Turner, *Beware the People Weeping*, p. 150.
42. Turner, *Beware the People Weeping*, p. 149.
43. Pitman, *Assassination*, p. 23.
44. Turner, *Beware the People Weeping*, pp. 48–49.
45. Poore, *Conspiracy Trial*, 1:7.
46. Davis, *Jefferson Davis*, p. 641.
47. Ibid.
48. Testimony of Sanford Conover, in Poore, *Conspiracy Trial*, 3:115–43.
49. Testimony of James B. Merritt, in Poore, *Conspiracy Trial*, 3:95–115.
50. Testimony of Richard Montgomery, in Poore, *Conspiracy Trial*, 3:83–94.
51. Booth was in Canada and most probably met with George Sanders in Montreal in October of 1864. See Tidwell, Hall, and Gaddy, *Come Retribution*, p. 333.
52. Turner, *Beware the People Weeping*, pp. 214–15.
53. OR, ser. I, vol. 49, pt. II, p. 759.
54. Turner, *Beware the People Weeping*, p. 132.
55. Doster argument, in Pitman, *Assassination*, p. 310.
56. Doster summation, in Pitman, *Assassination*, p. 305.
57. Wiechmann, *True History*, p. 301.
58. The five members were David O. Hunter, August V. Kautz, Robert S. Foster, James E.A. Ekin, and Charles H. Tompkins. Not signing the recommendation were Lew Wallace, Thomas M. Harris, David R. Clendenin, and Albion P. Howe.
59. Quoted in James O. Hall, "The Mercy Recommendation for Mrs. Surratt: The Holt-Johnson Controversy," *Surratt Courier* 15, no. 8 (August 1990): 4–5.
60. *Washington Intelligencer*, July 8, 1865.
61. Wiechmann, *True History*, pp. 280–81.
62. *Washington Intelligencer*, July 8, 1865.
63. Ibid.
64. Ibid.

20. The Aftermath: Rewriting History

1. During Mary Surratt's trial her defense attorneys put five Catholic priests on the witness stand who testified to her deep piety.
2. Wiechmann, *True History*, pp. 428–40.
3. Alfred Isacsson, "John Surratt: The Assassination, Flight, Capture and Trial," *Surratt Courier* 18, no. 7 (1993): 4–7.
4. Mark Wilson Seymour, ed., *The Pursuit and Arrest of John H. Surratt: Despatches from the Official Record of the Assassination of Abraham Lincoln* (Austin, Tex.: Civil War Library, 2000), p. 90.
5. U.S. Congress, House, *H.B. Sainte-Marie: Letters from the Secretary of War ad Interim Relative to a Claim of Sainte-Marie for Compensation Furnished in the Surratt Case*, 40th Cong., 2d sess., 1867, p. 24.
6. Isaccson, "John Surratt," p. 7.
7. James E.T. Lange and Katherine DeWitt Jr., "The Three Indictments of John Harrison Surratt, Jr.," *Surratt Courier* 17, no. 1 (1992): 6.
8. Ibid.
9. Wiechmann, *True History*, p. 428.

10. Isacsson, "John Surratt," p. 7. John and Mary were married in Alexandria, Virginia.

11. See *Washington Evening Star*, December 16, 1870.

12. In learning of the Supreme Court of the District of Columbia's ruling upholding Judge Fisher's dismissal of the first treason indictment, the grand jury ruled "ignoramus" on the second treason indictment which means in legal parlance, "we ignore." See Lange and DeWitt, "Three Indictments," p. 7.

13. Isacsson, "John Surratt," p. 7.

14. Oldroyd, *The Assassination of Abraham Lincoln*, p. 150.

15. Michael O'Laughlen died of yellow fever on September 23, 1867, while imprisoned. Samuel A. Mudd to Frances Mudd, 23 September 1867, in Mudd, *Life of Dr. Samuel A. Mudd*, p. 267.

16. Rodney Bethel, *A Slumbering Giant of the Past* (Hialeah, Fla.: W.L. Litho, 1979).

17. Samuel Carter III, The *Riddle of Dr. Mudd* (New York: G.P. Putnam's Sons, 1974), p. 236–37; Hal Higdon, *The Union vs. Dr. Mudd* (Chicago: Follett Publishing Company, 1964), p. 133; Elden C. Weckesser, *His Name Was Mudd* (Jefferson, N.C.: McFarland and Company, 1991), p. 143.

18. Bryan, *The Great American Myth*; Eisenschiml, *Why Was Lincoln Murdered?*; Roy Z. Chamlee Jr., *Lincoln's Assassins* (Jefferson, N.C.: McFarland and Company, 1990).

19. William Burton Benham, *Life of Osborn H. Oldroyd: Founder and Collector of Lincoln Mementos* (Washington, D.C.: privately published by W.B. Benham, 1927), pp. 26–27.

20. *Washington Star*, August 3, 1865, p. 2, col. 4. Also in *New York Times*, August 4, 1865, p. 1, col. 1.

21. A search of the National Archives failed to produce General Dodd's official report filed with Holt.

22. William F. Keeler to Congressman B.C. Cook, January 21, 1869, copy in author's files.

23. Jones, *J. Wilkes Booth*.

24. An advertisement appears in the *Port Tobacco Times* listing "Dr. Samuel A. Mudd" and "Samuel Cox, Jr." as candidates for "delegate" on the "Democratic and Conservative" ticket. See *Port Tobacco Times*, November 2, 1877, p. 1, col. 1. Cox was elected, while Mudd was defeated.

25. Quoted in Steers, *His Name Is Still Mudd*, p. 54.

26. Mudd, *Life of Dr. Samuel A. Mudd*, p. 115.

27. Ibid., p. 119.

28. Ibid., pp. 131–32.

29. Ibid., p. 124.

30. Ibid., p. 129.

31. Ibid., p. 225.

32. *The Committee for the Restoration of the Dr. Samuel A. Mudd House, Inc. Newsletter* 1, no. 8 (September 1980), 2.

33. See NARA, RG 94, M-619, reel 451, for the documents associated with the investigation.

34. Mudd, *Life of Dr. Samuel A. Mudd*, pp. 120–21.

35. *Rewriting History: The Case of Dr. Samuel A. Mudd*, written and directed by Paul Davis, produced by Dennis Fedoruk, Light Vision Films, Atlanta, Georgia, 1995.

36. Mudd, *Life of Dr. Samuel A. Mudd*, p. 131–32.

37. Samuel A. Mudd, letter to Jeremiah Dyer, 21 October 1865, in Mudd, Nettie, *The Life of Dr. Samuel A. Mudd* (1906; reprint, Marietta, Ga.: Continental Book Company, 1955), 350–51.

38. Ibid., p. 144.

39. Examples include Hal Higdon, *The Union vs. Dr. Mudd* (Chicago: Follett Publishing Company, 1964); Samuel Carter III, The *Riddle of Dr. Mudd* (New York: G.P. Putnam's Sons, 1974); Elden C. Weckesser, *His Name Was Mudd* (Jefferson, N.C.: McFarland and Company, 1991); John E. McHale Jr., *Dr. Samuel A. Mudd and the Lincoln Assassination* (Parsippany, N.J.: Dillon Press, 1995).

40. *Washington Intelligencer*, 8 July 1865, col. 6, p. 1.

41. Statement by Frederick Stone in Higdon, *The Union vs. Dr. Mudd*, p. 208.

42. Mudd, *Life of Dr. Samuel A. Mudd*, p. 317.

43. Steers, *His Name Is Still Mudd*, pp. 116–17.

44. Yellow fever is caused by a small, ribonucleic acid (RNA) virus and is one of a class of hemorrhagic viruses that cause severe gastrointestinal bleeding resulting in shock and death.

45. Steers, *His Name Is Still Mudd*, pp. 116–17.

46. Richard D. Mudd, *Dr. Samuel Alexander Mudd and His Descendants* (Saginaw, Mich.: privately printed by Richard D. Mudd, 1979).

47. According to Nettie Mudd, Dr. Mudd's youngest daughter, Spangler received five acres but never built his house on the property. See Mudd, *Life of Dr. Samuel A. Mudd*, p. 322.

48. There is some confusion in the literature as to the exact whereabouts of Spangler between the time of his release in March of 1869 and his death in February 1875. Most authors rely on Nettie Mudd's statement that Spangler died eighteen months after arriving at the Mudd farm (see Mudd, *Life of Dr. Samuel A.* Mudd, p. 322). This would mean that Spangler did not arrive until the summer of 1873 leaving a little over four years unaccounted for. It seems certain that Spangler made his way to the Mudd farm soon after his release arriving in the spring of 1869 and staying for approximately six years, not eighteen months. Nettie Mudd was not born until three years after Spangler's death and did not write her book until thirty-one years after his death. Had Spangler lived and worked elsewhere for the period between April 1869 and February 1875 some record of his existence would have been discovered.

49. Arnold, *Memoirs*, p. 39.

50. Percy E. Martin, "Samuel Bland Arnold Revisited," in *In Pursuit Of*. . . , ed. Verge, p. 34.

51. Arnold, *Memoirs*, p. xiv.

52. Ibid., p. 43.

53. Ibid.

54. Samuel Bland Arnold, *Defence and Prison Experiences of a Lincoln Conspirator* (Hattiesburg, Miss.: Book Farm, 1943).

55. Arnold, *Memoirs*.

21. Life after Death

1. Circuit Court for the City of Baltimore, case no. 94297044/CE187741, October 24, 1994.

2. Finis L. Bates, *Escape and Suicide of John Wilkes Booth, Assassin of President Lincoln* (Memphis: Pilcher Printing Company, 1907).

3. The evidence is summarized in two articles that appear in a publication of the Surratt Society titled, *The Body in the Barn*, ed. Laurie Verge (Clinton, Md.: Surratt Society, 1993), pp. 3–10.

4. John Wilkes Booth was born on May 10, 1838.

5. James O. Hall, "The Case of David E. George," *Surratt Courier* 17, no. 3 (March 1992): 3–5.

6. William G. Shepherd, "Shattering the Myth of John Wilkes Booth's Escape," *Harper's Magazine*, November 1924, pp. 702–19.

7. Ibid., p. 718.

8. Bryan, *The Great American Myth*, p. 333.

9. In addition to his success with automobiles, Ford turned his daily piles of scrap wood, left over from constructing Ford bodies, into a bonanza. Ford converted the scrap into charcoal that he bagged and marketed under the name of his favorite Uncle, "Kingsford." The charcoal briquettes were highly popular, and could only be purchased at Ford dealerships. Today "Kingsford" charcoal can be purchased through a number of outlets and is the leading charcoal sold on the open market.

10. This "new" evidence is discussed in Nathaniel Orlowek, "Why We Believe Booth Died in 1903," in *The Body in the Barn*, ed. Verge, pp. 3–6.

11. Steven G. Miller, "Wilson D. Kenzie, the Linchpin of the Booth Escape Theories," in *The Body in the Barn*, ed. Verge, p. 25.

12. Affidavit of Wilson D. Kenzie, March 13, 1922, Beloit, Wisconsin, David Rankin Barbee Papers, Georgetown University Library, Georgetown, District of Columbia. Hereafter referred to as Kenzie affidavit.

13. Orlowek, "Why We Believe," p. 3.

14. Kenzie affidavit, 1.

15. Rhodenhamel and Taper, eds., *Right or Wrong*, pp. 102–5.

16. Kenzie affidavit, pp. 2–3.

17. Ibid., p. 3.

18. Ibid.

19. Ibid.

20. Ibid., p. 1.

21. Rufus Woods, *The Weirdest Story in American History: The Escape of John Wilkes Booth* (Wenachee, Wash.: privately printed, 1944).

22. Steven G. Miller, "Did Lieut. William C. Allen Witness the Shooting of John Wilkes Booth," in *The Body in the Barn*, ed. Verge, p. 38.

23. Moxley's statement appeared in the *Baltimore American*, June 3–6, 1903.

24. U.S. Congress, House, *Testimony of Edwin M. Stanton before the Judiciary Committee of the House*, 40th Cong., 1st sess., 1867.

25. Bryan, *The Great American Myth*, p. 294.

26. Ibid.

27. Ibid., p. 306.

28. Ibid., p. 307.

29. Ibid., p. 308.

30. *Washington Evening Star*, February 16, 1869.

31. Bryan, *The Great American Myth*, pp. 308–9.

32. Bryan, *The Great American Myth*, p. 309. The original of the telegram is in the Edwin Booth artifacts located in the Players Club in New York.

33. Ibid., p. 280.

34. Interview of Basil Moxley in the *Baltimore American*, June 6, 1903, p. 6.

35. Quoted in Bryan, *The Great American Myth*, p. 313.

36. John Frederick May, *The Mark of the Scalpel* (Washington, D.C.: Columbia Historical Society, 1910).

37. Verge, ed., *War Department Files*, p. 2. Booth played in *The Marble Heart* at Ford's Theatre on Wednesday, November 11, 1863. This may be the time Herold is referring to although Booth also played at Grover's Theatre in Washington.

38. William May to Captain Dudley Knox, May 18, 1925, printed in James F. Epperson, ed., "The Positive Identification of the Body of John Wilkes Booth," *Civil War Naval Chronology* (Washington, D.C.: Government Printing Office, 1971).

39. Statement of John Frederick May, NARA, RG 153, M-599, reel 4, frames 361–365. Hereafter referred to as May statement.

40. May, *Mark of the Scalpel.*

41. According to May, the incision had been torn open by Booth's co-star Charlotte Cushman during a theatrical performance. Miss Cushman had thrown her arms around Booth's neck and hugged him so vigorously during the play that she tore the incision open. As a result when the wound healed it left a large, circular mark whose new tissue gave the appearance of a "burn" scar. A search of the various theatrical records for 1863 has failed to turn up any performance in which Booth and Cushman performed together. Cushman was living in Europe at the time of the alleged incident. Personal communication, Terry Alford, November 8, 2000.

42. May statement.

43. Ibid.

44. *The Medical and Surgical History of the War of the Rebellion (1861–1865)*, 4 vols. (Washington, D.C.: Government Printing Office, 1875), vol. 4, p. 452.

45. Leonard F. Guttridge, "Identification and Autopsy of John Wilkes Booth: Reexamining the Evidence," *Navy Medicine*, January–February 1993, 20.

46. Poore, *Conspiracy Trial*, 2:60.

47. "The Booth Autposy," in *The Body in the Barn*, ed. Verge, pp. 67–68.

48. Janvier Woodward to General G.W. Schofield, letter book, 1865, p. 212, Laboratory and Museum, Surgeon General's Office, NARA, RG 94, July 19, 1866.

49. Alford, ed., *A Sister's Memoir*, p. 45.

50. Orlowek, "Why We Believe," p. 4.

51. D. Mark Katz, *Witness to an Era: The Life and Photography of Alexander Gardner* (New York: Viking Penguin, 1991), pp.161–62.

52. James O. Hall, "The Body on the Monitor," in *The Body in The Barn*, ed. Verge, p. 70.

53. Herold statement, in Verge, ed., *War Department Files*, p. 14.

54. Ibid., p. 15.

55. *Trial of John H. Surratt*, 1:309.

56. Statement of Luther B. Baker, NARA, M-619, reel 455, frame 0689. See also Testimony of Everton J. Conger, in Poore, *Conspiracy Trial* 1:319. This draft was subsequently identified at the conspiracy trial by a Canadian banker, Robert Anson Campbell, as the one he handed personally to Booth the preceding year. See testimony of Robert Anson Campbell, in Poore, *Conspiracy Trial,* 2:87–88.

57. Circuit Court for Baltimore City, case no. 94297044/CE187741, May 26, 1995.

58. The decision of Judge Kaplan was appealed to the Maryland Court of Appeals. On June 4, 1996, Judge C.J. Wilner ruled for the court, upholding the decision of Judge Kaplan. Court of Appeals of Maryland, September term 1995, no. 1531.

22. Goodbye, Father Abraham

1. For a listing of fifty-five persons whose presence can be documented see George J. Olszewski, "House Where Lincoln Died: Furnishing Study," Division of History, Office of Archeology and Historic Preservation, National Park Service, U.S. Department of Interior, April 15, 1967, pp. 24–26. In addition to the fifty-five listed by Olszewski, Drs. Robert K. Stone and William Notson are known to have visited, bringing the total to fifty-seven.

2. As best can be determined the twelve were Joseph Barnes, Charles Leale, Robert Stone, William Notson, Edwin Stanton, Gideon Welles, Maunsell Fields, Phineas Gurley, Charles Sumner, Robert Lincoln, James Tanner, and Major Almon F. Rockwell.

3. Maunsell B. Field, *Memories of Many Men and of Some Women* (New York: Harper and Brothers, 1875), p. 326.

4. There is no evidence to place Vincent or Rutherford in the room at the instant of death although they were in the house, presumably in the parlor where Stanton had held his investigation.

5. Beale, ed., *Welles Diary,* 2:288. Present were Stanton, Welles, Usher, Dennison, and Speed. Absent were McCullough and Seward.

6. Field, *Memories,* p. 326.

7. Mose Sandford to John Beatty, April 17, 1865, private collection, xerographic copy in Surratt House and Museum Library, Clinton, Maryland. Sandford writes: "General Rucker came immediately to our Shop and had a Common pine box made to bring him from 10th St to the White House in."

8. *Baltimore Clipper,* April 15, 1865, Saturday afternoon, p. 1, col. 1.

9. Dixon letter, 4.

10. *Baltimore Clipper,* April 15, 1865, Saturday afternoon, p. 1, col. 1.

11. Edward Curtis, quoted in Dorothy Merserve Kunhardt and Philip B. Kunhardt Jr., *Twenty Days* (New York: Harper and Row, Publishers, 1965), p. 95.

12. For a detailed account of the autopsy findings for Lincoln and Kennedy see John K. Lattimer, *Kennedy and Lincoln: Medical and Ballistic Comparisons of Their Assassinations,* (New York: Harcourt Brace Jovanovich, 1980).

13. *Albany Times and Courier,* April 20, 1865, p. 2, col. 4.

14. Kunhardt and Kunhardt, *Twenty Days,* p. 120.

15. Ibid.

16. Merrill D. Peterson, *Lincoln in American Memory* (New York: Oxford University Press, 1994), p. 14.

17. Kunhardt and Kunhardt, *Twenty Days*, p. 122.
18. Ibid., p. 125.
19. John 11:25–26.
20. The Lincolns were married by an Episcopal priest according to the Episcopal "Book of Common Prayer." Although Mary Todd was a Presbyterian, she agreed to the Episcopal service out of deference to her benefactors, the Edwardses, in whose home the marriage took place. Wayne C. Temple, *Abraham Lincoln: From Skeptic to Prophet* (Mahomet, Ill.: Mayhaven Publishing, 1995), pp. 28–32.
21. Edward Steers Jr., "Was Mistah Abe Babsized?" *Lincoln Herald* 101, no. 4 (winter 1999): 164–73; Steers, "A Question of Faith," *North and South* 2 no. 7 (1999): 30–35.
22. Chesebrough, *"No Sorrow like Our Sorrow,"* p. xiv.
23. Temple, *From Skeptic to Prophet*, p. 330.
24. There were a total of twelve soldiers assigned to accompany the coffin. See Temple, *From Skeptic to Prophet*, p. 335.
25. For complete listing of the three company-grade officers and twenty-five enlisted men (all sergeants) from the Veteran Reserve Corps who served as Lincoln's honor guard, see Temple, *From Skeptic to Prophet*, p. 365.
26. Kunhardt and Kunhardt, *Twenty Days*, p. 131.
27. H.L. Scott, *Military Dictionary Comprising Technical Definitions; Information on Raising and Keeping Troops; Actual Service, Including Makeshifts and Improved Materiel; and Law, Government, Regulation, and Administration Relating to Land Forces* (1864; reprint, Yuma, Ariz.: Fort Yuma Press, 1984), p. 424.
28. *Albany Times and Courier*, April 20, 1865, p. 3, col. 1.
29. Victor Searcher, *The Farewell to Lincoln* (New York: Abingdon Press, 1965), pp. 79–80. Hereafter referred to as Searcher, *Farewell.*
30. *Albany Times and Courier*, April 20, 1865, p .2, col. 4.
31. Searcher, *Farewell*, p. 85.
32. Wayne Wesolowski and Mary Cay Wesolowski, *The Lincoln Train Is Coming . . .* (Lisle: Illinois Benedictine College, 1995), pp. 5–8.
33. H. Robert Slusser, *Mr. Lincoln's Railroad Car*, Alexandria Archeology Publications, Number 76 (Alexandria: Office of Historic Alexandria, 1996), p. 10. There is no record indicating that Lincoln had accepted the invitation to inspect the car.
34. Slusser, *Mr. Lincoln's Railroad Car*, p. 9.
35. R. Gerald McMurtry, ed., "The Lincoln Funeral Car," *Lincoln Lore*, no. 1431 (May 1957), pp. 1–4.
36. Slusser, *Mr. Lincoln's Railroad Car*, p. 11.
37. Searcher, *Farewell*, p. 90.
38. *New York Times*, April 22, 1865, p. 1, col. 2.
39. Searcher, *Farewell*, p. 93.
40. *New York Times*, April 22, 1865, p. 1, col. 3.
41. Ibid.
42. Searcher, *Farewell*, p. 100.
43. *New York Times*, April 22, 1865, p. 1, col. 4.
44. Ibid.
45. *New York Times*, April 23, 1865, p. 1, col. 6.
46. Ibid.

47. Richard Nelson Current, *Old Thad Stevens: A Story of Ambition* (Madison: University of Wisconsin Press, 1942), p. 208.

48. The pass is in the collection of the author.

49. *New York Times*, April 24, 1865, p. 8, col. 1.

50. Kunhardt and Kunhardt, *Twenty Days*, p. 158.

51. *New York Times*, April 25, 1865, p. 1, col. 3.

52. Ibid.

53. *New York Times*, April 24, 1865, p. 8, col. 6.

54. *New York Times*, April 25, 1865, p. 1, col. 3.

55. Ibid., p. 1, col. 5.

56. Ibid., p. 1, col. 6.

57. Philip B. Kunhardt Jr., Philip B. Kunhardt III, and Peter W. Kunhardt, *Lincoln* (New York: Alfred A. Knopf, 1992), p. 375.

58. Ronald Rietveld, professor of history at the California State University, Fullerton, was granted permission to examine the John George Nicolay papers in the Illinois State Historical Society Library where he discovered the remarkable print of Lincoln in death.

59. *New York Times*, April 25, 1865, p. 1, col. 6.

60. Kunhardt and Kunhardt, *Twenty Days*, p. 153.

61. *New York Times*, April 27, 1865, p. 3, col. 2.

62. *Albany Times and Courier*, April 27, 1865, p. 2, col. 5.

63. Ibid.

64. *New York Times*, April 26, 1865, p. 1, col. 6.

65. Morrison Alexander to Robert Alexander, April 29, 1865, author's collection. The special car used to carry the body back to Springfield was not the car Lincoln used on his inaugural journey to Washington.

66. *Albany Times and Courier*, April 27, 1865, p. 3, col. 1.

67. *New York Times*, April 28, 1865, p. 8, col. 1.

68. Cholera morbus was a popular term during the civil war for acute gastroenteritis that was always accompanied by diarrhea, cramps, and vomiting. It often proved fatal.

69. *Rochester Daily Union and Advertiser*, April 28, 1865, p. 2, col. 2.

70. Edward Steers Jr., "A Puttin' on (H)airs," *Lincoln Herald* 91, no. 3 (1989): 86–90.

71. Basler, ed., *Collected Works*, 4:129–30. Grace Bedell's letter is reproduced along with Lincoln's reply.

72. *New York Times*, April 29, 1865, p. 1, col. 5.

73. *Rochester Daily Union and Advertiser*, May 1, 1865, p. 4, col. 1.

74. *New York Times*, May 1, 1865, p. 5, col. 2.

75. Ibid., p. 1, col. 2.

76. Ibid., p. 5, col. 3.

77. Ibid., May 2, 1865, p. 1, col. 2.

78. Ibid., p. 1, col. 3.

79. Basler, ed., *Collected Works*, 4:190.

80. Ibid.

81. Searcher, *Farewell*, p. 241.

82. *New York Times*, May 5, 1865, p. 1, col. 1.

83. A detailed list of the divisions and their composition occurs in a special broadside printed at the time and distributed to the participants. The broadside is titled, "Obsequies of President Lincoln. Order of Funeral Procession." Collection of the author.

84. *New York Times*, May 5, 1865, p. 1, col. 1.

85. Fido, like his master, met a cruel death by assassination. One day while approaching a drunken stranger in his usual friendly style, Fido was knifed to death by the man.

86. Sarah Bush Johnston interview by William H. Herndon in Douglas L. Wilson and Rodney O. Davis, eds., *Herndon's Informants* (Urbana: University of Illinois Press, 1998), p. 108.

87. Kunhardt and Kunhardt, *Twenty Days*, p. 87.

88. Keckley, *Behind the Scenes*, p. 201.

89. *New York Times*, May 3, 1865, p. 5, col. 3.

90. "Obsequies of President Lincoln. Order of Funeral Procession."

91. Ibid.

92. It would be the first of several interments for Lincoln.

93. *Rochester Daily Union and Advertiser*, May 5, 1865, p. 4, col. 2.

94. *New York Times*, May 5, 1865, p. 1, col, 3.

95. Walt Whitman, *Leaves of Grass*, ed. Jerome Loving (New York: Oxford University Press, 1990), pp. 262–63.

BIBLIOGRAPHY

Alford, Terry, ed. *John Wilkes Booth: A Sister's Memoir by Asia Booth Clarke.* Jackson: University Press of Mississippi, 1996.

Anderson, John Q., ed. *Brockenburn: The Journal of Kate Stone, 1861–1868.* Baton Rouge: Louisiana State University Press, 1955.

Arnold, Samuel Bland. *Defense and Prison Experiences of a Lincoln Conspirator.* Hattiesburg, Miss.: Book Farm, 1940.

———. *Memoirs of a Lincoln Conspirator.* Ed. Michael W. Kauffman. Bowie, Md.: Heritage Books, 1995.

Ashmun, George. "Recollections of a Peculiar Service." *Magazine of History* 3, no. 4 (April 1906): 248–54.

Badeau, Adam. *Grant in Peace from Appomattox to Mount McGregor: A Personal Memoir.* New York: C.L. Webster, 1887.

Baird, Nancy Disher. *Luke Pryor Blackburn: Physician, Governor, Reformer.* Lexington: University Press of Kentucky, 1979.

Bak, Richard. *The Day Lincoln Was Shot.* Dallas: Taylor Publishing Company, 1998.

Baker, Lafayette C. *History of the United States Secret Service.* Philadelphia: published by L.C. Baker, 1867.

Balsiger, David, and Charles E. Sellier Jr. *The Lincoln Conspiracy.* Los Angeles: Schick Sunn Classic Books, 1977.

Barbee, David Rankin. Papers. Georgetown University, Georgetown, District of Columbia.

Barnes, Albert. *An Inquiry into the Scriptural Views of Slavery.* Philadelphia: Perkins and Purves, 1846.

Basler, Roy P., ed. *The Collected Works of Abraham Lincoln.* 9 vols. New Brunswick, N.J.: Rutgers University Press, 1953.

Bates, David Homer. *Lincoln in the Telegraph Office.* New York: Century, 1907.

Bates, Finis L. *Escape and Suicide of John Wilkes Booth, Assassin of President Lincoln.* Memphis: Pilcher Printing Company, 1907.

Beale, Howard K., ed., *The Diary of Edward Bates, 1859–1866*, vol. 4 of the *Annual Report of the American Historical Association*, 1930. Washington, D.C.: Government Printing Office, 1933.

———. *Diary of Gideon Welles.* 3 vols. New York: W.W. Norton, 1960).

Benham, William Burton. *Life of Osborn H. Oldroyd: Founder and Collector of Lincoln Mementos.* Washington, D.C.: privately published by W.B. Benham, 1927.

Bledsoe, Albert Taylor. *Liberty and Slavery.* 1856. Reprint, Wiggins, Miss.: Crown Rights Book Company, 1989.

Bethel, Rodney. *A Slumbering Giant of the Past.* Hialeah, Fla.: W.L. Litho, 1979.

Borchers, Raymond. "President Lincoln's Car." *Lincoln Herald* 86, no. 4 (winter 1984), pp. 212–16.

Borreson, Ralph. *When Lincoln Died.* New York: Appleton-Century, 1965.

Brackett, Jeffrey R. *The Negro in Maryland.* 1889. Reprint, New York: Negro University Press, 1969.

Brennan, John C. "General Bradley T. Johnson's Plan to Abduct President Lincoln." *Chronicles of St. Mary's* 22 (November–December 1974), pp. 1–3.

Brown, Jack D., et al., eds. *Charles County Maryland: A History.* Hackensack, N.J.: Custombook, 1976.

Browne, Francis F. *The Everyday Life of Abraham Lincoln.* Hartford: Park Publishing Company, 1886.

Bryan, George S. *The Great American Myth.* New York: Carrick and Evans, 1940. Reprint, Chicago: Americana House, 1990.

Burlingame, Michael, and John R. Turner Ettlinger, eds. *Inside Lincoln's White House: The Complete Civil War Diaries of John Hay.* Carbondale: Southern Illinois University Press, 1965.

Cain, Marvin R. *Lincoln's Attorney General: Edward Bates of Missouri.* Columbia: University of Missouri Press, 1965.

Campbell, Helen. *The Case for Mrs. Surratt.* New York: G.P. Putnam's Sons, 1943.

Canney, Donald L. *Lincoln's Navy.* Annapolis: Naval Institute Press, 1998.

Carter, Samuel, III. *The Riddle of Dr. Mudd.* New York: G.P. Putnam's Sons, 1974.

Chamlee, Roy Z., Jr. *Lincoln's Assassins: A Complete Account of Their Capture, Trial, and Punishment.* Jefferson, N.C.: McFarland and Company, 1990.

Chesebrough, David B. *"No Sorrow like Our Sorrow": Northern Protestant Ministers and the Assassination of Abraham Lincoln.* Kent, Ohio: Kent State University Press, 1994.

Clarke, Asia Booth. *The Unlocked Book: A Memoir of John Wilkes Booth by His Sister.* New York: G.P. Putnam's Sons, 1938.

Conrad, Thomas Nelson. *A Confederate Spy.* New York: J.S. Ogilvie, 1892 .

———. *The Rebel Scout.* Washington, D.C.: National Publishing Company, 1904.

Crook, William H. *Through Five Administrations.* Ed. Margarita Spalding. New York: Harper and Brothers, 1907.

Current, Richard N., ed. *The Encyclopedia of the Confederacy.* New York: Macmillan, 1993.

Cuthbert, Norma B. *Lincoln and the Baltimore Plot, 1861.* San Marino, Calif.: Huntington Library, 1949.

Davis, Jefferson. *The Rise and Fall of the Confederate Government.* 2 vols. New York: Da Capo Press, 1990.

Davis, William C. *Jefferson Davis: The Man and His Hour.* New York: Harper Collins, 1991.

Derby, George W. *Phoenixiana; or, Sketches and Burlesques.* New York: D. Appleton and Company, 1856.

Dillon, David C., ed. *The Lincoln Assassination: From the Pages of the "Surratt Courier" (1986–1999).* Clinton, Md.: Surratt Society, 2000.

Doster, William E. *Lincoln and Episodes of the Civil War.* New York: G.P. Putnam's Sons, 1915.

Edgington, Frank E. *A History of the New York Avenue Presbyterian Church.* Washington, D.C.: published by the New York Avenue Presbyterian Church, 1961.

Eisenschiml, Otto. *In the Shadow of Lincoln's Death.* New York: Wilfred Funk, 1940.

———. *Why Was Lincoln Murdered?* Boston: Little, Brown, 1937.

———, ed. *Vermont General: The Unusual War Experiences of Edward Hastings Ripley (1862–1865)*. New York: Devin-Adair Company, 1960.

Epperson, James F. "The Positive Identification of the Body of John Wilkes Booth." *Civil War Naval Chronology*. Washington, D.C.: Government Printing Office, 1971.

Fehrenbacher, Don E., and Virginia Fehrenbacher, eds. *Recollected Words of Abraham Lincoln*. Stanford: Stanford University Press, 1996.

Field, Maunsell B. *Memories of Many Men and of Some Women*. New York: Harper and Brothers, 1875.

Furtwangler, Albert. *Assassin on Stage: Brutus, Hamlet, and the Death of Lincoln*. Urbana: University of Illinois Press, 1991.

George, Joseph, Jr. "Black Flag Warfare." *Pennsylvania Magazine of History and Biography* (July 1991).

Gladstone, William A. *Men of Color*. Gettysburg, Pa.: Thomas Publications, 1993.

Goldsborough, William W. *The Maryland Line in the Confederate Army*. 1869. Reprint, Gaithersburg, Md.: Butternut Press, 1983.

Good, Timothy S. *We Saw Lincoln Shot*. Jackson: University Press of Mississippi, 1995.

Grant, Julia Dent. *The Personal Memoirs of Julia Dent Grant*. Ed. John Y. Simon. New York: G.P. Putnam's Sons, 1975.

Grant, Ulysses S. *Personal Memoirs of U.S. Grant*. Ed. E.B. Long. Cleveland: World Publishing Company, 1952.

Gutman, Richard J.S., and Kellie O. Gutman. *John Wilkes Booth Himself*. Dover, Del.: Hired Hand Press, 1979.

Hall, James O. *The Surratt Family and John Wilkes Booth*. Clinton, Md.: Surratt Society, 1984.

———. "The Dahlgren Papers: A Yankee Plot to Kill President Jefferson Davis." *Civil War Times Illustrated*, November 1983.

Hanchett, William. *The Lincoln Murder Conspiracies*. Urbana and Chicago: University of Illinois Press, 1983.

Harrell, Carolyn L. *When the Bells Tolled for Lincoln*. Macon, Ga.: Mercer University Press, 1997.

Harris, Thomas M. *The Assassination of Lincoln: A History of the Great Conspiracy*. Boston: American Citizen Company, 1892.

Harrison, Lowell H. *Lincoln of Kentucky*. Lexington: University Press of Kentucky, 2000.

Hartzler, Daniel D. *Marylanders in the Confederacy*. Westminster, Md.: Family Line Publications, 1986.

Headley, John W. *Confederate Operations in Canada and New York*. New York: Neale Publishing Company, 1906.

Helm, Katherine. *The True Story of Mary, Wife of Lincoln*. New York: Harper and Brothers Publishers, 1928.

Herndon, William H., and Jesse W. Weik. *Abraham Lincoln: The True Story of a Great Life*. 2 vols. New York: D. Appleton and Company, 1906.

Hertz, Emanuel. *The Hidden Lincoln*. New York: Viking Press, 1938.

Higdon, Hal. *The Union vs. Dr. Mudd*. Chicago: Follett Publishing Company, 1964.

Holzer, Harold. *Dear Mr. Lincoln: Letters to the President*. Reading, Mass.: Addison-Wesley, 1993.

Horner, John B. *Lincoln's Songbird*. Gettysburg: Horner Enterprises, 1991.

Hunt, Roger D., and Jack R. Brown. *Brevet Brigadier Generals in Blue.* Gaithersburg, Md.: Olde Soldier Books, 1990.

Hynd, Alan. *Arrival: 12:30: The Baltimore Plot against Lincoln.* Camden, N.J.: Thomas Nelson, 1967.

Investigation and Trial Papers Relating to the Assassination of Abraham Lincoln (LAS file). Microcopy 599. National Archives Records Administration, Washington, D.C.

Johnson, Patricia Carley. "I Have Supped Full on Horrors: The Diary of Fanny Seward." *American Heritage* 10, no. 6 (Oct. 1959), pp. 64–65, 96–101.

Jones, Thomas A. *J. Wilkes Booth.* Chicago: Laird and Lee, 1893.

Jones, John Paul, ed. *Dr. Mudd and the Lincoln Assassination: The Case Reopened.* Conshohocken, Pa.: Combined Books, 1995.

Katz, D. Mark. *Witness to an Era: The Life and Photography of Alexander Gardner.* New York: Viking Penguin, 1991.

Keckley, Elizabeth. *Behind the Scenes; or, Thirty Years a Slave, and Four Years in the White House.* 1968. Reprint, New York: Oxford University Press, 1988.

Kimmel, Stanley. *The Mad Booths of Maryland.* Indianapolis: Bobbs-Merrill, 1940.

Kinchen, Oscar A. *Confederate Operations in Canada and the North.* North Quincy, Mass.: The Christopher Publishing House, 1970.

Klapthor, Margaret Bowen, and Paul Dennis Brown. *The History of Charles County, Maryland.* LaPlata, Md.: Charles County Tercentenary, 1995.

Kunhardt, Dorothy Merserve, and Philip B. Kunhardt Jr. *Twenty Days.* New York: Harper and Row, 1965.

Lamon, Ward Hill. *The Life of Abraham Lincoln.* 1872. Reprint, Lincoln: University of Nebraska Press, 1999.

———. *Recollections of Abraham Lincoln, 1847–1865.* Ed. Dorothy Lamon Tiellard. Chicago: A.C. McClung, 1895.

Lattimer, John K. *Kennedy and Lincoln: Medical and Ballistic Comparisons of Their Assassinations.* New York: Harcourt Brace Jovanowich, 1980.

Laughlin, Clara E. *The Death of Lincoln.* New York: Doubleday, Page, 1909.

Leale, Charles A. *Lincoln's Last Hours: Address Delivered before the Commandery of the State of New York Military Order of the Loyal Legion of the United States.* New York: privately printed, 1909.

Lee, Jean B. *The Price of Nationhood.* New York: W.W. Norton, 1994.

Leech, Margaret. *Reveille in Washington, 1860-1865.* New York: Harper and Brothers, 1941.

Letters Received by the Office of the Adjutant General (Main Series) 1861–1870. Microcopy 619. National Archives Records Administration, Washington, D.C.

Lincoln Obsequies File. Rare Book Room, Library of Congress, Washington, D.C.

Long, David E. "'I Say We Can Control That Election': Confederate Policy towards the 1864 Presidential Election." *Lincoln Herald* 99, no. 3 (fall 1997).

Long, E.B., and Barbara Long. *The Civil War, Day by Day, 1861–1865.* Garden City, N.Y.: Doubleday, 1971.

Lowry, Thomas P. *Don't Shoot That Boy.* Mason City, Iowa: Savas Publishing Company, 1999.

Macrone, Michael. *Brush Up Your Shakespeare!* New York: Harper and Row, 1976.

Maione, Michael, and James O. Hall. "Why Seward?" *Lincoln Herald* 100, no. 1 (spring 1998).

Mahoney, Ella V. *Sketches of Tudor Hall and the Booth Family.* Bel Air, Md.: privately printed by the author, 1925.

McHale, John E., Jr. *Dr. Samuel A. Mudd and the Lincoln Assassination.* Parsippany, N.J.: Dillon Press, 1995.

McMurtry, R. Gerald, ed. "The Lincoln Funeral Car." *Lincoln Lore,* no. 1431 (May 1957), pp. 1–4.

Mearns, David C., ed. *The Lincoln Papers.* 2 vols. New York: Doubleday, 1948.

The Medical and Surgical History of the War of the Rebellion (1861–1865). Washington, D.C.: Government Printing Office, 1870.

Mencken, August. *By the Neck.* New York: Hastings House Publishers, 1942.

Mieder, Wolfgang. *The Proverbial Lincoln.* New York: Peter Lang, 2000.

Miers, Earl S., ed., *Lincoln, Day by Day: A Chronology: 1809–1865.* 3 vols. Washington, D.C.: Lincoln Sesquicentennial Commission, 1960.

Miller, Ernest C. *John Wilkes Booth in the Pennsylvania Oil Region.* Meadville, Pa.: Crawford County Historical Society, 1987.

Mills, Robert Lockwood. *It Didn't Happen the Way You Think.* (Bowie, Md.: Heritage Books, 1994).

Moore, Guy W. *The Case of Mary Surratt.* Norman: University of Oklahoma Press, 1954.

Mudd, Nettie. *The Life of Dr. Samuel A. Mudd.* 1906. Reprint, LaPlata, Md.: Dick Wildes. Printing, 1975.

Mudd, Richard D. *Dr. Samuel Alexander Mudd and His Descendants.* Saginaw, Mich.: privately printed by Richard D. Mudd, 1979.

———. *The Mudd Family of the United States.* 2 vols. Saganaw, Mich.: Privately printed by Richard D. Mudd, 1951.

Neely, Mark E. *The Abraham Lincoln Encyclopedia.* New York: McGraw-Hill, 1982.

———. *The Fate of Liberty.* Chicago: Oxford University Press, 1991.

Newman, Ralph G. *"In This Sad World of Ours, Sorrow Comes to All": A Timetable for the Lincoln Train.* Springfield, Ill.: Civil War Centennial Commission, Illinois, 1965.

Nicolay, John G., and John Hay. *Abraham Lincoln: A History* . 10 vols. New York: Century Publishing Company, 1890.

———, eds. *Complete Works of Abraham Lincoln.* Harrogate, Tenn.: Lincoln Memorial University, 1894.

Oldroyd, Osborn H. *The Assassination of Abraham Lincoln.* 1901. Reprint, Bowie, Md.: Heritage Books, 1990.

Olszewski, George J. *Historic Structures Report: Restoration of Ford's Theatre.* Washington, D.C.: Government Printing Office, 1963.

Ownsbey, Betty J. *Alias "Paine."* Jefferson, N.C.: McFarland and Company, 1993.

Papers Relating to Suspects in the Lincoln Assassination, Records of the Provost Marshal's Office. Record Group 110. National Archives Records Administration, Washington, D.C.

Peterson, Merrill D. *Lincoln in American Memory.* New York: Oxford University Press, 1994.

Peterson, T.B. *The Trial of the Alleged Assassins and Conspirators at Washington City, D.C., in May and June, 1865.* Philadelphia: T.B. Peterson and Bros, 1865.

Pfanz, Donald C. *The Petersburg Campaign: Abraham Lincoln at City Point, March 20–April 9, 1865.* Lynchburg, Va.: H.E. Howard, 1989.

Pinkerton, Allan. *History and Evidence of the Passage of Abraham Lincoln from Harrisburg, Pa., to Washington, D.C.* Chicago: Republican Press, 1868.

Pitman, Benn. *The Assassination of President Lincoln and the Trial of the Conspirators.* Cincinnati: Moore, Wilstach and Baldwin, 1865.

———. *The Manual of Phonography.* Cincinnati: Phonographic Institute, 1860.

Poore, Ben: Perley. *The Conspiracy Trial for the Murder of the President.* 4 vols. 1865. Reprint, New York: Arno Press, 1972.

Porter, Horace. *Campaigning with Grant.* New York: Century, 1907.

Pratt, Fletcher. *Stanton, Lincoln's Secretary of War.* New York: W.W. Norton, 1953.

Reck, Emerson. *A. Lincoln: His Last 24 Hours.* Columbia: University of South Carolina Press, 1994.

Records of the Judge Advocate General's Office (Army). Record Group 153. Court-Martial Case File, MM 2513. National Archives Records Administration, Washington, D.C.

Report of the Commissioner of Patents, for the Year 1849, part 1, *Arts and Manufacturers.* Washington, D.C.: Office of Printers to House of Representatives, 1850.

Rhodenhamel, John, and Louise Taper, eds. *"Right or Wrong, God Judge Me": The Writings of John Wilkes Booth.* Chicago: University of Illinois Press, 1997.

Robbins, James J., ed. *Report of the Trial of Castner Hanway for Treason in the Resistance of the Execution of the Fugitive Slave Law of September, 1850.* 1852. Reprint, Westport, Conn.: Negro Universities Press, 1970.

Roscoe, Theodore. *The Web of Conspiracy.* Englewood Cliffs, N.J.: Prentice-Hall, 1959.

Rowland, Dunbar, ed. *Jefferson Davis, Constitutionalist: His Letters, Papers and Speeches.* Jackson: University of Mississippi Press, 1923.

Sandburg, Carl. *Abraham Lincoln: The War Years.* 4 vols. New York: Charles Scribner's Sons, 1944.

Schultz, Duane. *The Dahlgren Affair.* New York: W.W. Norton, 1998.

Searcher, Victor. *The Farewell to Lincoln.* New York: Abingdon Press, 1965.

Sears, Stephen W. "The Dahlgren Papers Revisited." *Columbiad* 3 (summer 1999).

Seward, Fanny. "I Have Supped Full on Horrors." Ed. Patricia Carley Johnson. *American Heritage* 10, no. 6 (Oct. 1959), 61–65, 96–101.

Shaw, Archer H. *The Lincoln Encyclopedia.* New York: Macmillan, 1950.

Sheads, Scott Sumpter, and Daniel Carroll Toomey. *Baltimore during the Civil War.* Linthicum, Md.: Toomey Press, 1997.

Shelton, Vaughan. *Mask for Treason.* Harrisburg, Pa.: Stackpole, 1965.

Shepherd, William G. "Shattering the Myth of John Wilkes Booth's Escape." *Harper's Magazine*, November 1924, pp. 702–19.

Slaughter, Thomas P. *Bloody Dawn.* New York: Oxford University Press, 1991.

Smith, Gene. *American Gothic: The Story of America's Legendary Theatrical Family—Junius, Edwin, and John Wilkes Booth.* New York: Simon and Schuster, 1992.

Smoot, Richard. *The Unwritten History of the Assassination of Abraham Lincoln.* Clinton, Mass.: W.J. Coulter, 1908.

Speed, James. *Opinion of the Constitutional Power of the Military to Try and Execute the Assassins of the President.* Washington, D.C.: Government Printing Office, 1865.

Steers, Edward, Jr. "Dr. Mudd and the 'Colored' Witnesses." *Civil War History* 46, no. 4 (Dec. 2000), pp. 324–36.

———. "Freedom Began Here." *North and South* 1, no. 4 (April 1998), pp. 34–43.

———. *His Name Is Still Mudd.* Gettysburg, Pa.: Thomas Publications, 1997.

———. "Risking the Wrath of God." *North and South* 3, no. 7 (Sept. 2000), pp. 59–70.

Steers, Edward, Jr., and James O. Hall. *The Escape and Capture of George Atzerodt.* Clinton, Md.: Surratt Society, 1980.

Stimmel, Smith. "Experiences As a Member of President Lincoln's Body Guard." *North Dakota Historical Quarterly* 1, no. 2 (January 1927): 7–32.

Stoddard, William O. *Inside the White House in War Times.* New York: Charles R. Webster, 1890.

Taft, Charles Sabin. "Abraham Lincoln's Last Hours." *Century Magazine* (Feb. 1895).

Temple, Wayne C. *Abraham Lincoln: From Skeptic to Prophet.* Mahomet, Ill.: Mayhaven Publishing, 1995.

Thomas, Benjamin P. *Lincoln's New Salem.* Springfield, Ill.: Abraham Lincoln Association, 1934.

Thomas, Benjamin P., and Harold M. Hyman. *Stanton: The Life and Times of Lincoln's Secretary of War*. New York: Alfred A. Knopf, 1962.

Tidwell, William A. *April '65. Confederate Covert Action in the American Civil War.* Kent, Ohio: Kent State University Press, 1995.

Tidwell, William A., James O. Hall, and David W. Gaddy. *Come Retribution: The Confederate Secret Service and the Assassination of Abraham Lincoln.* Jackson: University of Mississippi Press, 1989.

Toomey, Daniel Carroll. *The Civil War in Maryland.* Linthicum, Md.: Toomey Press, 1983.

Townsend, George Alfred. *The Life, Crime and Capture of John Wilkes Booth.* New York: Dick and Fitzgerald, 1865.

Townsend, William H. *Lincoln and the Bluegrass.* Lexington: University of Kentucky Press, 1955.

Trial of John H. Surratt in the Criminal Court for the District of Columbia. 2 vols. Washington, D.C.: Government Printing Office, 1868.

Trindal, Elizabeth Steger. *Mary Surratt: An American Tragedy.* Gretna, La.: Pelican Publishing Company, 1996.

Turner, Justin G., and Linda Levitt Turner, eds. *Mary Todd Lincoln: Her Life and Letters.* New York: Fromm International Publishing Corporation, 1987.

Turner, Thomas R. *The Assassination of Abraham Lincoln.* Malabar, Fla.: Krieger Publishing Company, 1999.

———. *Beware the People Weeping.* Baton Rouge: Louisiana State University Press, 1982.

Union Provost Marshal's File of Papers Relating to Two or More Civilians. Record Group 109. National Archives Records Administration, Washington, D.C.

U.S. Bureau of the Census. Eighth Census, Population (Maryland), 1860. Microcopy 653, reel 473. National Archives Records Administration, Washington, D.C.

———. Eighth Census, *Slave Index* (Maryland), 1860. Microcopy 653, reel 484. National Archives Records Administration, Washington, D.C.

U.S. Congress, House. *Report on the Assassination of Abraham Lincoln.* 39th Cong., 1st sess., July 1866. Washington, D.C.: Government Printing Office, 1866.

U.S. Congress, *H.B. Sainte Marie: Letters from the Secretary of War Ad Interim Relative to a Claim of Sainte Marie for Compensation Furnished in the Surratt Case.* 40th Cong., 2d sess.

U.S. Naval Observatory. Astronomical Applications Department. Washington, D.C. <http://mach.usno.navy.mil/cgi-bin/aa_pap>.

U.S. War Department. *The War of the Rebellion: A Compilation of the Official Records of the Union and Confederate Armies.* 128 vols. Washington, D.C.: Government Printing Office, 1890–1901.

U.S. Navy Department. *Official Records of the Union and Confederate Navies in the War of the Rebellion.* 30 vols. Washington, D.C.: Government Printing Office, 1894–1914.

University of Maryland Fiftieth Annular Circular of the School of Medicine. Session 1857–1858. Baltimore: Sherwood and Company, 1857.

Verge, Laurie, ed. *The Body in the Barn.* Clinton, Md.: Surratt Society, 1993.

———. *In Pursuit Of, . . . Continuing Research in the Field of the Lincoln Assassination.* Clinton, Md.: Surratt Society, 1990.

Warner, Ezra J. *Generals in Blue.* Baton Rouge: Louisiana State University Press, 1964.

———. *Generals in Gray.* Baton Rouge: Louisiana State University Press, 1959.

Washburne, Elihu B. "Abraham Lincoln in Illinois." *North American Review* 141 (1885): 456–57.

Wearmouth, John M., and Roberta J. Wearmouth. *Thomas A. Jones: Chief Agent of the Confederate Secret Service in Maryland.* Port Tobacco, Md.: Stones Throw Publishing, 2000.

Wearmouth, Roberta J. *Abstracts from the "Port Tobacco News and Charles County Advertiser,"* vol. 2, 1855–69. Bowie, Md.: Heritage Books, 1991.

Weckesser, Elden C. *His Name Was Mudd.* Jefferson, N.C.: McFarland and Company, 1991.

Wesolowski, Wayne, and Mary Cay Wesolowski. *The Lincoln Train Is Coming. . . .* Lisle: Illinois Benedictine College, 1995.

Wiechmann, Louis J. *A True History of the Assassination of Abraham Lincoln and of the Conspiracy of 1865.* Ed. Floyd E. Risvold. New York: Alfred E. Knopf, 1975.

Wills, Mary Alice. *The Confederate Blockade of Washington, D.C., 1861–1862.* Shippensburg, Pa.: Burd Street Press, 1998.

Wilson, Francis. *John Wilkes Booth.* New York: Houghton Mifflin, 1929.

Wilson, Douglas L., and Rodney O. Davis, eds., *Herndon's Informants.* Urbana: University of Illinois Press, 1998.

Wilson, Rufus Rockwell. *Lincoln in Caricature.* New York: Horizon Press, 1953.

Whiteman, Maxwell. *While Lincoln Lay Dying.* Philadelphia: The Union League of Philadelphia, 1968.

Wright, Mike. "The Infernal Machine." *Invention and Technology* 15, no 1 (summer 1999).

INDEX